Joan Littlewood's Theatre

Joan Littlewood was one of the most visionary and influential theatre directors of the twentieth century. Drawing on extensive archival research and detailed performance histories, and paying close attention to wider political and cultural forces, this innovative study presents a fresh examination of Littlewood's treatment of the politics of war, Renaissance plays, marginalised communities and popular culture in productions such as *Oh What a Lovely War*, *A Taste of Honey* and *Richard II*. The book breaks new ground with a sustained examination of Littlewood's para-theatrical activity that centred on her ambitious plans for the Fun Palace – a multifaceted cultural centre – and her numerous playground projects for young people. Alert to critical thinking on ethics, citizenship, cultural politics, class and space, *Joan Littlewood's Theatre* will deepen and extend knowledge and understanding of the innovative theatrical, cultural and community-based practices generated by Littlewood throughout her career.

NADINE HOLDSWORTH is an Associate Professor in the School of Theatre, Performance and Cultural Policy Studies at the University of Warwick. Her research focuses on British political theatre since the 1930s and theatre's relationship to the nation and globalisation. She is the author of *Theatre & Nation* (2010) and *Joan Littlewood* (2006), and co-editor, with Mary Luckhurst, of *A Concise Companion to Contemporary British and Irish Drama* (2007).

CAMBRIDGE STUDIES IN MODERN THEATRE

Volumes for Cambridge Studies in Modern Theatre explore the political, social and cultural functions of theatre while also paying careful attention to detailed performance analysis. The focus of the series is on political approaches to the modern theatre with attention also being paid to theatres of earlier periods and their influence on contemporary drama. Topics in the series are chosen to investigate this relationship and include both playwrights (their aims and intentions set against the effects of their work) and process (with emphasis on rehearsal and production methods, the political structure within theatre companies and their choice of audiences or performance venues). Further topics will include devised theatre, agitprop, community theatre, para-theatre and performance art. In all cases the series will be alive to the special cultural and political factors operating in the theatres examined.

Books published

Maria DiCenzo, *The Politics of Alternative Theatre in Britain, 1968–1990: The Case of 7:84 (Scotland)*
Jo Riley, *Chinese Theatre and the Actor in Performance*
Jonathan Kalb, *The Theatre of Heiner Müller*
Richard Boon and Jane Plastow, eds., *Theatre Matters: Performance and Culture on the World Stage*
Claude Schumacher, ed., *Staging the Holocaust: The Shoah in Drama and Performance*
Philip Roberts, *The Royal Court Theatre and the Modern Stage*

Nicholas Grene, *The Politics of Irish Drama: Plays in Context from Boucicault to Friel*
Anatoly Smeliansky, *The Russian Theatre after Stalin*
Clive Barker and Maggie B. Gale, eds., *British Theatre between the Wars, 1918–1939*
Michael Patterson, *Strategies of Political Theatre: Post-war British Playwrights*
Elaine Aston, *Feminist Views on the English Stage: Women Playwrights, 1990–2000*
Gabriele Griffin, *Contemporary Black and Asian Women Playwrights in Britain*
Loren Kruger, *Post-imperial Brecht: Politics and Performance, East and South*
David Barnett, *Rainer Werner Fassbinder and the German Theatre*
Mary Luckhurst, *Dramaturgy: A Revolution in Theatre*
Scott Boltwood, *Brian Friel, Ireland, and The North*
Gerwin Strobl, *The Swastika and the Stage: German Theatre and Society, 1933–1945*
Gene A. Plunka, *Holocaust Drama: The Theater of Atrocity*
Nadine Holdsworth, *Joan Littlewood's Theatre*

Joan Littlewood's Theatre

Nadine Holdsworth

CAMBRIDGE
UNIVERSITY PRESS

CAMBRIDGE
UNIVERSITY PRESS

University Printing House, Cambridge CB2 8BS, United Kingdom

Cambridge University Press is part of the University of Cambridge.

It furthers the University's mission by disseminating knowledge in the pursuit of education, learning and research at the highest international levels of excellence.

www.cambridge.org
Information on this title: www.cambridge.org/9781107532045

First published 2011
First paperback edition 2015

A catalogue record for this publication is available from the British Library

Library of Congress Cataloguing in Publication data
Holdsworth, Nadine.
Joan Littlewood's theatre / Nadine Holdsworth.
p. cm. – (Cambridge studies in modern theatre)
Includes bibliographical references.
ISBN 978-0-521-11960-3 (hardback)
1. Littlewood, Joan – Criticism and interpretation. I. Title.
PN2598.L577H655 2011
792.02′33092–dc22

2010037663

ISBN 978-0-521-11960-3 Hardback
ISBN 978-1-107-53204-5 Paperback

Contents

Illustrations

Acknowledgements

The process of writing this book has been a long one and along the way I have been helped by numerous organisations and individuals who deserve my thanks. At the top of my list sits Murray Melvin, actor and archivist, at the Theatre Royal Stratford East. I would like to thank him, and his accomplice, Mary Ling, for the care and dedication they have shown in creating the theatre's archive and for granting me unrestricted access to the archive and permission to quote from manuscripts and to reproduce many of the photographs contained in this volume. More than this, I thank them for their help, hospitality, conversation and wonderful sense of fun whenever I visited the beautiful Theatre Royal. Thanks also to the staff and archivists at the Harry Ransom Humanities Research Center at the University of Texas at Austin for granting access to and permission to reproduce photos and to quote from the Michael Barker Collection relating to Joan Littlewood and Theatre Workshop. I would particularly like to thank Katherine Feo for her efficient response to my queries and requests. I'm grateful to Peggy Seeger for allowing me access to the Ewan MacColl and Peggy Seeger Archive held at Ruskin College, Oxford, and to Valerie Moyes who arranged my visit there. I would also like to thank staff at the British Library manuscripts department for their help during my visits to read material held in the Lord Chamberlain's Collection. Thanks to Jeff Vickers, Carole Hopkin and the Dudley Studio Collection for granting permission to reproduce photographs and Karen Fisher for her work getting me copies of photos from the Theatre Royal collection.

Acknowledgements

Several people kindly gave up their time to offer constructive feedback on chapters of this manuscript and I am extremely grateful to Colin Chambers, Jim Davis, Maria Delgado, June Favre, Helen Nicholson, Janelle Reinelt, Juliet Rufford and Liz Schafer in this regard – the book has been improved by their input. Shelley Ayliffe, Ben Fowler and David Coates were efficient and helpful research assistants. In various ways the following people have also helped in the process of developing, researching and writing this book: Richard Boon, Maggie Gale, Ben Harker, Laura Jukes, Katie Klassen, Derek Paget, Liese Perrin, Peter Rankin and Barbara Wheeler-Early. I would also like to thank Vicki Cooper and Rebecca Taylor at Cambridge University Press for their advice, patience and support in getting this book to publication and David Bradby for his advice and help in getting the book published for his series. I also owe a huge debt of thanks to Richard Perkins who helped me more than he will know in tracking down last-minute references in his usual calm and wise way. The late Clive Barker did a great deal to ease my path as a researcher and I will always be grateful to him and sorry that he will not get to see the final result.

Research visits for this book were funded by the Arts and Humanities Research Council (AHRC) through the Small Grant in the Creative and Performing Arts Scheme and the book was completed with assistance from the AHRC's Research Leave Scheme. I am most grateful to the AHRC for its support of this project. I have also received support from the University of Warwick's Humanities Research Fund and the Research Development Fund to help my attendance at conferences and to enable the inclusion of illustrations. Thanks also to the University of Warwick for granting me study leave and to my colleagues in the School of Theatre, Performance and Cultural Policy Studies for their support and general brilliance.

This book could not have been completed without the unwavering support of my family, especially Geoff Willcocks, who has learnt when to steer clear and when to offer tea – this is a difficult line to tread and I truly appreciate him for treading it with love and care over many years. For providing endless distractions and reasons to be doing anything other than writing I thank my son Corin – you have kept me sane and I dedicate this book to you.

1 A peculiar history: life, love and theatre

Joan Littlewood's autobiography *Joan's Book*, published in 1994, draws attention to many of the problems of trying to map a life, even when conducted by the person who lived it. Defiantly long, rambling and picaresque in its recollection of events, Littlewood's typically idiosyncratic decision to present her life through anecdote and 'recorded' conversation highlights the impossibility of autobiography to be anything other than a narrativised account of the bits that the author deems important. Documenting conversations that occurred decades before, and some before Littlewood was born, *Joan's Book* is testament to the failings and creativity of autobiography. In fact, Littlewood playfully acknowledges this partial quality in her subtitle, 'Joan Littlewood's peculiar history as she tells it'. In Littlewood's case, she marshals *Joan's Book* to do several things. It is a reconstitution of her life as a theatrical plot with lines attributed to goodies, baddies, main parts and bit parts according to her memory or her unerring sense of the theatrical in terms of the cut and thrust of human interaction. She uses it as a platform to slate her enemies and to extol the virtues of others, and at times it reads like an extended love letter to her artistic collaborator and partner Gerry Raffles whose role Littlewood embellishes wherever feasible. There is both a delightful and frustrating disregard for detail or accuracy, but this does not suggest that *Joan's Book* is not truthful or authentic. It is true to the moment of writing and the person writing it; in a sense this is all that writing can ever be.

This introduction does not seek to provide a comprehensive account of Littlewood's life, but instead it draws attention to some of the key events, influences, relationships and approaches to theatre that galvanised her and contributed to the body of work focused on in the rest of the book. It draws on many documents – early notebooks, interviews, biographies, articles and testimonies from collaborators and friends – to piece together a collage of opinion and conjecture about Littlewood and how her theatre moved and shifted in relation to changing times.

But first it is important to get a sense of the woman who became one of the pre-eminent international theatre figures of the mid-twentieth century, a woman who shook up the theatrical establishment and made a lasting impression on how theatre was made and what it represented. Walking through Stratford in east London, where Littlewood was artistic director of the Theatre Royal for many years, her impact and that of her company, Theatre Workshop, is embedded in the local cultural and street scene. Inside the Theatre Royal photographs of Littlewood and her productions adorn the walls, and the room where she worked and slept for many years houses the theatre's archive, including her small writing desk and the eclectic library of books on everything from economics to world literature that she amassed over the years. The street outside the Theatre Royal has been renamed Gerry Raffles Square and Littlewood's image is prominent in a millennium plaque on Great Eastern Road. There are also plans to commission a statue of Littlewood that will be situated outside the Theatre Royal.

It is somewhat ironic that Littlewood should be so associated with a particular locality because she demonstrated a marked geographical restlessness during her life. After being brought up in Stockwell in south London, she spent a summer in Paris with her art teacher, moved to Manchester, went back to London with plans to move to Moscow and then, albeit with intermittent temporary relocations to the Lake District and Middlesbrough, she returned to Manchester, a city where she instinctively felt at home. In 1952, Theatre Workshop, the company she co-founded with Ewan MacColl, made the decision to lease the Theatre Royal in Stratford, within the London Borough of Newham where she based herself until the untimely death of Raffles in 1974, after which she moved to France. She also embarked on long periods of work and travel in Germany, Tunisia, Senegal and Nigeria, and toured work to France, Czechoslovakia, Sweden, Russia and the United States.

Admiring the twinkle in her eye and her ability to appeal to the senses with 'language that bypassed logic, making only emotional sense', Kenneth Tynan reflected that a few centuries ago 'such a woman might easily have been burned as a witch'.[1] As a person, Littlewood provoked both intense loyalty and fierce animosity. She was bright, funny, well read and charmingly irreverent, but could be brutal and obscene, and referred to her infamous tongue-lashings as a 'good murder'.[2] Provocative and temperamentally inclined to take an anti-establishment stance, she was full of contradictions: a fierce supporter of collective working and autocratic; gentle in approach and abrasive in manner; socially responsible and anarchic; impressively well read and distrustful of academia. She was aware of her abilities and deeply resented the lack of support and recognition she received from the British arts establishment. In a letter sent to Ewan MacColl in the 1980s she lamented, 'for all you hear of us, any of us – we might never have existed', yet she could be wilfully self-effacing and blocked many attempts to investigate her work while she was alive.[3] As *Joan's Book* indicates, she had a fondness for self-mythologising, hyperbole and theatrics and this could be both entertaining and infuriating for those who knew her, as truth eroded in the murky waters of a good anecdote or pithy phrase.

As a woman, she cuts an interesting figure. Unmarried for most of her life, childless, domestically inept, chain-smoking and with a conversational style peppered with expletives – flat-footed actors were referred to as 'turds on blankets' – Littlewood failed to conform to the dominant roles assigned to women in the mid-twentieth century. She had no interest in her physical appearance beyond a penchant for hiding her high forehead with a trademark woolly hat or cap. She never wore make-up and her limited wardrobe defied any overt representation of femininity. With a curious antipathy towards material possessions, from an early age she was a free spirit who relished her autonomy and ability to live, work and travel as an independent woman.

After meeting, falling in love with and moving in with Ewan MacColl, she came under increasing pressure to marry. She refused several of MacColl's proposals and aborted their baby, describing the event as a 'brutalised, sordid business but not as bad as being trapped in

Coburg Street', before she finally relented and married MacColl at Pendleton Town Hall on 15 September 1935.[4] It was a low-key affair designed to appease MacColl's mother and to avoid bringing the Communist Party into disrepute.[5] But their 'fertile creative and intellectual partnership soon outgrew the constraints of bourgeois monogamy'.[6] MacColl was a notorious seducer of women and Littlewood fell in love with Raffles, nine years her junior. Littlewood abhorred the loss of independence for women signalled by marriage and particularly disliked the implications of giving up her surname. In fact, she refused to use her married name and was incandescent when, after she had separated from MacColl, she had to use her married name to secure a passport to tour to Sweden. Whilst in Sweden she wrote indignantly about the treatment of women there, recording that 'men treat the women like servants'.[7]

Yet it would be inaccurate to refer to Littlewood as a feminist. When asked if her life had been 'harder, better, worse, or different for [her] being a woman director in the theatre', Littlewood replied, 'I don't believe in that stuff ... I'm not a feminist.'[8] She was not interested in the collective position of women in society, neither did she seek out female friendship and, despite some evidence to the contrary, claimed, 'You'd have to leave our theatre if you'd had a baby'; of her own childlessness, she explained, 'I couldn't. I couldn't have managed.'[9] Littlewood's work was paramount, although she pursued familial-style relationships, often framing her role as a matriarchal figure whereby 'my actors were my children'.[10]

Keen to deflect attention away from her status as a woman working in a hostile patriarchal environment, she did acknowledge that 'it was difficult as a working-class person'.[11] Her background and early experiences ignited an intuitive alignment to a staunch politics of the left. When asked if she still considered herself a 'left-wing idealist' in an interview conducted in the final year of her life, she replied indignantly, 'I'm not a left-wing idealist! ... I've always been a communist.'[12] Yet, typically, Littlewood had a tempestuous relationship with the Communist Party as a political institution. She hated dogmatism and was often frustrated by the Communist Party's inflexibility on the relationship between art and activism and, like many on the political left, the revelations around Stalin's regime rocked her to the core. Nonetheless, Littlewood's politics were a driving force behind her theatrical endeavours and cultural activism and grew from her experience growing up and making theatre in the tumultuous years between the 1920s and the 1970s.

Born 6 October 1914 in the shadow of the outbreak of the First World War to a young unmarried mother, Littlewood was raised in her grandparents' house in Stockwell in south London, where a warm, loving environment made up for her bad-tempered mother. Choosing to supplement their income by taking in lodgers, her grandparents' house was full of people, intricate relationships and the usual family antagonisms. Academically and creatively gifted, Littlewood grew up an outsider in the environments she inhabited: the illegitimate child of the family, a non-believing scholarship girl at a Catholic convent school and a working-class scholarship girl at the Royal Academy of Dramatic Arts (RADA) amongst the affluent British debutantes and Americans who dominated the place. She found RADA utterly devoid of purpose, intellectual stimulation and engagement with her background or the experiences of many during this period.

Whilst many people prospered from rising standards of living and the growth of affluent suburbia in Britain of the 1920s and 1930s, many others suffered a period of extreme physical, social and economic deprivation. Unemployment rose rapidly when a worldwide economic recession took hold. To survive, people faced the indignity of the means test and, as the widespread housing crisis deepened, poor living conditions and malnutrition ensured the spread of tuberculosis and the rise of rickets and anaemia, causing many premature deaths. One of the slogans of the day, 'poverty in the midst of plenty', captured the contradictions of the era and the anger felt against the moral bankruptcy of capitalism that allowed for the prosperity of some at the expense of many.

The extreme circumstances of this period prompted many people to register their voice and opposition to the times in which they lived. Many people, from different backgrounds and professions, became aware of the class divisions prevalent in Britain and decided to align themselves with the working class to fight for the causes of socialism and social justice. Many people showed their discontent by withdrawing their labour in the 1926 General Strike or through participation in large-scale demonstrations such as the Hunger Marches that took place across Britain organised by the National Unemployed Workers' Movement. These events, coupled with a growing awareness of her relatively deprived circumstances, sharply defined Littlewood's loyalties.

Despondent about the vacuous work she encountered at RADA and excited by the potential of a socially committed art, Littlewood left. A self-possessed, nomadic figure, after ditching RADA she travelled to Paris for the second time. She initially went with her school art teacher who was keen to foster her potential as an artist. Her second visit secured an enduring relationship with the city. Returning from Paris, Littlewood set off for the working-class, industrial heartland of Manchester, targeted so she could contact Archie Harding, a BBC producer who awarded her first prize in a verse-speaking competition at RADA. Through Harding, she secured irregular radio work reading poetry, acting and presenting pioneering regional radio documentaries.

Working with the producer D. G. Bridson, who was part of a growing movement dedicated to representing 'ordinary' working people on the radio, she produced several programmes on the north's major industries that spliced narrative, soundscape, song and 'actuality' recordings of workers and machinery, including *Cotton*, set in Oldham, and *Coal*, based on their time as embedded researchers in a mining village in County Durham. She followed this collaboration up with her own *Classic Soil*, broadcast in the North Region on 6 July 1939. This feature read present-day Manchester through Engels's *The Condition of the Working Class in England* (1844). It cut contemporary working-class voices with extracts from Engels's text to highlight the poignancy of Engels's revolutionary thinking for the contemporary moment.[13] However, during this period, people faced intense scrutiny and persecution for communist sympathies and Littlewood was temporarily blacklisted by the BBC and placed under surveillance by the security services.

Theatre of Action and Theatre Union

Littlewood's life was turned upside down when Harding introduced her to MacColl. He described the intense impact of their meeting: 'we were drunk with ideas, lightheaded with talk . . . each of us jubilant at having discovered an ally'.[14] Together they devoted their energies to 'create a theatre which would be more dynamic, truthful and adventurous than anything the bourgeois theatre could produce'.[15] MacColl was already heavily involved in the international Workers' Theatre Movement (WTM), which had been growing in international reach and prominence since 1926. He formed Theatre of Action in 1934 following work with groups such as the Clarion Players and the Red Megaphones in Manchester and made connections with other radical theatre groups in the United States, the Soviet Union and Germany as a way of sharing scripts and ideas and forging a sense of an international community harnessing theatre on behalf of the revolutionary cause.

Alongside her radio work, Littlewood secured employment as an assistant stage manager at the Manchester Repertory Theatre in Rusholme, where its drab middlebrow comedies quickly earned Littlewood's dismissal of it as a 'lousy piss kitchen'[16] – although she stayed long enough to work with one of her heroes, the exiled German expressionist playwright Ernst Toller, on a production of his *Draw the Fires* in 1935.[17] She joined Theatre of Action during rehearsals for a variety show that included *Newsboy* (1934), songs by Brecht and Hanns Eisler, an antiwar sketch and a recitation of *The Fire Sermon*, a poem by Sol Funaroff. Littlewood, by now in a relationship with MacColl, joined him to run Theatre of Action as 'a benevolent dictatorship with the benevolence omitted wherever artistically necessary'.[18] Their experimental creative impulse aligned with an ideological commitment to service the working class and their political struggle, to advocate peace in the face of war and to serve the promotion of communism. In a lecture outlining their position, Littlewood explained:

> Our work has been created by the class struggle – and in times like these we are called on more than ever before to reflect the life of the people – to give voice to their tragedy – to teach them too and help them to understand the things going on around them. We must never let this work flag. As the circumstances become more difficult our work must become more intense and our understanding must deepen – both our political understanding and our understanding of theatre.[19]

The political climate evidently became much more complicated following the rise of fascism across Europe, when a class-versus-class reading of the world needed to be supplemented with a broad alliance of 'popular front' politics. MacColl and Littlewood agreed that the changing political climate required a more sophisticated, discursive analysis than the short, sharp shock of agitprop that had dominated the WTM; they determined to place themselves at the vanguard by excavating major political works of the past by Aristophanes and Lope de Vega and by forging a vibrant theatre aesthetic combining international developments emanating from practitioners such as Vsevolod Meyerhold and Erwin Piscator and the films of Sergei Eisenstein and Vsevolod Pudovkin that could capture and speak to these changing times.

Derek Paget has written persuasively about the influence of Léon Moussinac's seminal book *The New Movement in the Theatre* (1931) on Littlewood and MacColl. Neither of them could be accused of small-island parochialism; and just as their interests embraced international politics, they were keen to be conversant with and to learn from the best theatre developments from across the globe. Unashamedly championing modernity and a new aesthetic imagination ushered in by cinema and radio, through vivid descriptions and extensive illustrations, Moussinac's book captures the dynamism of the new theatrical age by documenting the experimental European theatre aesthetic pioneered by directors such as Piscator, Meyerhold, Adolphe Appia and Edward Gordon Craig in the beginning of the twentieth century. He documents work that combined a revolutionary agenda with an assured theatricality, multiple performance strategies, different approaches to the actor as performer and a confident embrace of all the possibilities opened up by new technologies.

From studying and admiring these revolutionary practitioners, Littlewood and MacColl appreciated how the construction of a theatre event, the placing of materials and information, elemental sets, multilevel staging and the clever compression of time and space could influence both its theatrical and political impact. So from their earliest work they employed styles and techniques such as expressionism, constructivism and montage, which placed them firmly in opposition to the dominant literary naturalism that dominated the British stage.

As such, Paget argues that Littlewood and MacColl's theatre companies provided the 'Trojan Horse' through which these practices began to infiltrate postwar British theatre.[20]

In 1936 they formed a new interdisciplinary company called Theatre Union, a loose alliance of actors, designers and technicians who participated in their production of *The Miracle at Verdun*. As a company, they worked hard and played hard. Wild parties, walking on the moors and sexual intrigue accompanied a rigorous programme of reading, conversations about art and politics, and rehearsals. Ever confident of their ability to create significant theatre, Littlewood and MacColl issued an ambitious manifesto:

> The Theatre must face up to the problems of its time: it cannot ignore the poverty and human suffering which increases every day. It cannot, with sincerity, close its eyes to the disasters of its time. Means Test suicides, wars, fascism and the million sordid accidents reported in the daily press. If the theatre of to-day would reach the heights achieved four thousand years ago in Greece and four hundred years ago in Elizabethan England it must face up to such problems. To those who say that such affairs are not the concern of the theatre or that the theatre should confine itself to treading in the paths of 'beauty' and 'dignity', we would say "Read Shakespeare, Marlowe, Webster, Sophocles, Aeschylus, Aristophanes, Calderon, Moliere, Lope de Vega, Schiller and the rest." The Theatre Union says that in facing up to the problems of our time and by intensifying our efforts to get at the essence of reality, we are also attempting to solve our own theatrical problems both technical and ideological. By doing this we are ensuring the future of the theatre, a future which will not be born in the genteel atmosphere of retirement and seclusion, but rather in the clash and turmoil of the battles between the oppressors and the oppressed.[21]

True to their manifesto, Theatre Union's productions tackled the problems of the day head-on, but without sacrificing aesthetic experimentation, beauty or theatrical pleasure. It announced its arrival with a production of Lope de Vega's *Fuente Ovejuna* (1612–14) framed to support the Republican cause in the Spanish Civil War; this was followed by MacColl's adaptation of the satirical antiwar play *The Good Soldier Schweik* in May 1939 and *Last Edition*, an extensively researched, large-scale antiwar living newspaper project, appeared in March 1940. Each production brought a new integration and layering of space, narrative, image, sound, stylised movement, song and choreography.

Regarded as a political irritant, Theatre Union faced state intervention in their activities when the police targeted their young recruits, warning them and their parents that association with Littlewood and MacColl was potentially damaging to their futures. These difficulties culminated during a second run of *Last Edition*, when the police arrested and prosecuted Littlewood and MacColl for contravening the 1843 Theatre Act by giving an unlicensed performance. These events, coupled with the sapping of Theatre Union's personnel for the war effort, curtailed Theatre Union's public activities, but not before a strong nucleus formed to take their work further after the war.

Theatre Workshop: origins and relationships

Despite living in war-torn cities full of bombed-out buildings and the realities of rationing, the immediate postwar period was a time of hope as people moved beyond a constant state of fear and deprivation. The collective cultural consensus moved to the left during the war and there was a widespread feeling that there should be no return to the social misery and political unrest of the 1930s. Littlewood hoped to capitalise on this widespread political realignment that saw Labour achieve a landslide victory in the 1945 general election and prompted various attempts to tackle social problems through the introduction of the welfare state. Promoting the benefits of a rich cultural life for effective civic life, she dreamed of a 'people's theatre' that would revolutionise British theatre and bridge 'the gulf between creative art and the lives of ordinary people'.[22] As such, she stressed the importance of reaching a wide audience and determined to tour 'to places where the people have been starved of good theatre'.[23]

In the immediate postwar period, Littlewood's optimism had solid foundations. The wartime thirst for experiences of music, art, dance and theatre, escapist or otherwise, prompted the formation of the Entertainments National Service Association (ENSA) in 1939 and the Council for the Encouragement of Music and the Arts (CEMA) in 1940. After the war, cultural activity in theatres, galleries and concert halls burgeoned, supported by the newly established Arts Council that came into being on 9 August 1946 to replace CEMA and ENSA. No longer were West End impresarios, such as Hugh 'Binkie' Beaumont, to keep a stranglehold on Britain's theatrical diet as state subsidy opened the door for new building programmes and the opportunity for producers to take more risks.

In this context, the Theatre Union stalwarts who reformed as Theatre Workshop after the war – Littlewood, MacColl and Raffles, together with Rosalie Williams and Howard Goorney – were confident that a secure future lay ahead. Fuelled with youthful exuberance, determined self-belief and a dogged faith in their ability to create socially committed and theatrically innovative productions, the next eight years involved a tangled web of personal relationships and a perilous hand-to-mouth existence touring the north of England, Scotland and Wales, playing often ill-conceived, one-night stands and short bookings in out-of-season theatres, schools and community halls and one infamous stint at Billy Butlin's holiday camp in Filey. These dates occurred amidst more lucrative, intellectually stimulating and creatively energising tours of West Germany in 1947, followed by Czechoslovakia and Sweden in 1948 and Norway in 1950, where they received a rapturous reception.

Despite significant hardship, over this eight-year period the company embarked on a fertile vein of creative activity driven by MacColl's writing and their shared passion for European classics and contemporary plays. The company secured widespread critical praise for their energy, originality and theatrical imagination in shows including a double bill of MacColl's ballad opera *Johnny Noble* (1945), which employed an intricate recorded score, a cappella singing, dance and naturalistic sequences; with Molière's *The Flying Doctor* (1649–50), which drew on the grotesque comedy and caricature of the Marx Brothers and commedia dell'arte; the British premiere of Federico García Lorca's erotic tale of sexual desire *The Love of Don Perlimplin and Belisa in the Garden* (1931); and *Operation Olive Branch*, MacColl's free adaptation of Aristophanes' *Lysistrata*. Assessing the importance of Theatre Workshop's experimentation, theatrical flair and political impetus during this period, Morris Linden, chair of the Friends of Theatre Workshop Group based in Scotland, explained how they had the potential to reinvigorate a British theatre stifled by commercialism, overreliance on the star system and lack of originality with work created by 'a producer of genius' that was 'fresh, delightful and stimulating'.[24]

The company survived by pooling resources such as Raffles's compensation from an industrial accident and Goorney's army gratuities. Company members also learnt to multitask. So each member engaged in a wide range of activities from acting to set construction and costume making. Despite these demands, minimal wages and the prospect of living communally in short-term digs with no security, Littlewood and MacColl continued to attract new recruits with their vision of a socially committed 'people's theatre', and they were soon joined by key personnel including David Scase, John Bury, Harry H. Corbett and the Laban-trained dancer and choreographer Jean Newlove. Harry Greene, who joined the company in 1950, explained the willingness of individuals to sign up for self-imposed hardship:

> We were happy to be alive, to be able to make sacrifices for an ideal. We were not so concerned with demanding our material rights, but were more concerned with human rights. In those days we didn't expect subsidy as a right, we were all dedicated and willing to work for every penny to plough back into the company for the benefit of all.[25]

The new name, Theatre Workshop, signalled Littlewood's increasing emphasis on the processes inherent in making theatre. In the early years of Theatre Union and Theatre Workshop this meant committing to a regular study and training regime encompassing impassioned lectures on theatre history, theatre and communism and theories of acting, and physical training encompassing relaxation, voice and movement exercises. Littlewood believed that good theatre was not just a happy accident, but born from effort and endeavour. In an early radio programme transmitted on the North of England Home Service on 5 August 1947, Littlewood described the creative process in the following terms:

> The artist's progress is no luxury tour. There is no smooth autobahn along which one rides to one's objective. The path, if you can call it that, is a rough one always mounting upwards, disappearing now and then in morasses and swamps, a perilous path twisting through barren places, littered with the bones of dead enterprise.[26]

Marking herself apart from the dominant British theatrical tradition that presumed an actor's training ceased after graduation from drama school, Littlewood insisted that everybody worked at a level that expanded their skills set, knowledge and ability to create committed, visually arresting, multitextured work. She also believed passionately in the ensemble, the 'composite mind' engaged in a co-operative sharing of ideas, skills and creativity.

Through training, Littlewood worked to increase physical awareness, dexterity and control by adapting Rudolph Laban's ideas on the interrelationship between time, space and energy to physical characterisation, rhythm and spatial dynamics. A great admirer of Laban, this aspect of the company's training took on heightened significance after she persuaded Jean Newlove, who had been Laban's assistant, to join the company in 1948. According to MacColl, 'Under her tutelage, the dormant capabilities of the actors in the group underwent a complete transformation.'[27]

Littlewood also incorporated ideas drawn from Meyerhold's quasi-scientific conception of biomechanics to encourage economical movement as well as physical clarity and expressiveness and drew on Émile Jaques-Dalcroze's work on eurhythmics to control and manipulate shifts in rhythm individually and collectively. She hoped to release and hone the creative imagination by drawing on Stanislavsky's influential text *An Actor Prepares*, first published in Britain in 1937, and regularly employed exercises such as the 'magic if' and given circumstances, the circle of attention and work with units and objectives.[28] This formal training was, unusually, supplemented with games and improvisation 'to develop initiative, excite curiosity, exercise the imagination', with a view to encouraging her ensemble to be inventive, to trust their instincts and to develop the capacity to be *real* and responsive in performance.[29] Despite their dedication, enthusiastic critical reception and amazing stores of resourcefulness such as rescuing and restoring lighting equipment found discarded amidst the debris of a plane crash, the company failed to secure funding or a permanent base to support its work.

During the war Littlewood had worked tirelessly to find a way to fund their work; when the company reunited she convinced John Trevelyan, director of education in Westmorland, to install the ensemble in Kendal, where they would support themselves by running training classes and weekend workshops and facilitating local amateur groups. This proposal fell through, but the group pursued a similar arrangement when they relocated from Kendal to Ormesby Hall near Middlesbrough in May 1946 after Colonel and Mrs Pennyman, fancying themselves cultural patrons, invited them to stay having seen their risqué production *Don Perlimplin*. Residing in Ormesby Hall's east wing, complete with kitchen, bedrooms, workshop, stables and courtyard, until April 1947, the company found a relative period of stability living and making work in these grand surroundings.

The company also found tireless backing from the Labour politician Tom Driberg, who tried to rally political support for the company when they made rare incursions into London, as when they played the Park Theatre in Hanwell where he joined several Labour politicians including Nye Bevan, Ian Mikardo and Alf Robens, who extended an invitation for lunch at the House of Commons. Driberg also offered practical support such as originating the tour to Czechoslovakia in 1948 and allowing the company to prepare for the 1952 Edinburgh Festival by sleeping in tents and rehearsing *The Travellers* in a barn in his grounds when they were not bringing in crops to fund their activities.

Particularly well received in the Labour heartland of Scotland, the company seriously considered a permanent base in Glasgow. But their plan to locate in Scotland went the way of numerous prior plans to secure a permanent residency at the Library Theatre, Manchester; to convert a disused church and school into a theatre in central

Manchester; and to convert the dilapidated David Lewis Theatre in Liverpool. The plans for this last venture are indicative of the scope and scale of the company's ambition at this time. Citing Laban as the movement specialist and Nelson Illingworth, Metropolitan Opera Company of New York teacher and founder of Labour Stage in London, as voice coach, Raffles proposed a theatre centre dedicated to monthly productions, to training actors, to adult education, to providing a creative hub for local artists, to international exchange and to cultural regeneration in the region.[30]

Unfortunately, nothing permanent ever materialised and by 1952, following eight years of touring at home and abroad, Theatre Workshop reached crisis point. Exhausted by poverty, poor living conditions and the inability to secure a permanent home, the company voted to relocate to the Theatre Royal, a dilapidated Victorian theatre in the London Borough of Newham in the East End of London, a decision that was at odds with their commitment to the regions and the north of England, but one that was inevitable given their dire circumstances. Founding figure and primary dramatist MacColl refused to make the move. Professionally, he argued that a London setting and reliance on critical acclaim would undermine the ideological basis of the company's work. Personally, he was moving towards a full-time career as a member of the British folk revival and the move to Stratford East coincided with the moment when this side of his creative life was gathering momentum.

The immediate postwar period was characterised by a tangled web of interpersonal relationships and growing personal animosities that probably also contributed to MacColl's decision. MacColl, following relationships with Littlewood and Williams, pursued numerous affairs with young women who passed through the company for workshops, training programmes and productions – a state of affairs that caused Colonel Pennyman to request that MacColl be asked to leave Ormesby Hall, at which point Littlewood evacuated the whole company, arguing in a letter to Raffles that she was fed up with the colonel's 'disgusting interference' in their personal lives.[31] Interference that ranged from concerns over the amount of heating the company used to the sexual preferences and relations of company members.

Despite the fact that their marriage broke down, they divorced in 1948 and they were both embroiled in new long-term partnerships – Littlewood with Raffles and MacColl with Newlove – Littlewood and MacColl had forged an enduring creative partnership and she provided him unwavering personal support during this time. When MacColl was arrested and imprisoned for desertion on 16 December 1946, Littlewood worked tirelessly for his release by petitioning artists including Hugh MacDiarmid and George Bernard Shaw to speak on his behalf and by raising funds to facilitate the commission of a psychiatric report that would support her case that he was temperamentally unsuitable for active service.

Of the court-martial, scheduled for 17 February 1947, Littlewood wrote to Goorney, 'They have the power to break him and me through him,' and in a marked demonstration of loyalty, Littlewood stayed at home to fight MacColl's corner rather than go with Theatre Workshop on a two-month tour of occupied West Germany under the auspices of the Combined Services Entertainment Unit.[32] During this time Littlewood wrote many letters to Raffles expressing her deep regret at their separation. Embedded in these love letters in which she admits that a 'moment in a Manchester Street becomes a breath of you, painful to me because you are not there', she also reveals telling moments of self-doubt about her unfinished education and lack of knowledge.[33] In one moving passage she writes, 'It is terrifying and overwhelming my own mediocrity, my own life hangs about me like a stinking gas from whose fumes I cannot escape – I will change or I will finish it – to hell with it all.'[34] Equally, she charts her despair and disgust at the apathy she detects in her fellow human beings who 'pass on the street like ghosts and grind their chains into their own bodies and minds'.[35] Yet, at the same time, this despair seems to galvanise her and she determines to work tirelessly for MacColl's release, seeing his role as pivotal to the success of Theatre Workshop's ambitions to be a revolutionary cultural force.

But Raffles and MacColl's relationship had grown increasingly acrimonious and, according to Goorney, 'It was a war that never stopped.'[36] With the same political convictions, in every other respect MacColl and Raffles were polar opposites – the intense, often surly, MacColl, who had a working-class chip on his shoulder and refused to ingratiate himself with anybody, versus the upper-middle-class grammar school boy from an affluent family with an enduring sense of *joie de vivre*. Raffles resented MacColl's continuing prominence in Littlewood's life, was deeply distrustful of his capacity for self-interest and accused MacColl of holding Littlewood back with political dogma and a lack of theatrical flair. In this assessment Raffles exhibited the ruthless commercial instincts that would keep Theatre Workshop going for many years at the Theatre Royal, as well as the fierce devotion to Littlewood that characterised their tempestuous relationship.

The Theatre Royal Stratford East

Moving to the barely habitable Theatre Royal marked a new stage in Littlewood's career as she embraced the opportunity to forge and promote her own creative vision beyond the dominant presence of MacColl's playwriting and his strict political orthodoxy. Although she remained resolutely committed to a politics of the left, her period at the Theatre Royal was marked by an increasing theatrical flamboyance and assurance. In the first of her two decades at the theatre, Littlewood developed an international reputation for her theatrical inventiveness in fresh interpretations of classics, in productions that combined energetic new writing with popular theatrics and in groundbreaking representations of working-class life, and developed her collaborative improvisatory theatrical processes. Her work with Theatre Workshop at the Theatre Royal was hailed as a breath of fresh air for a stagnant, stuffy British theatre more attuned to tame middlebrow comedies and Shakespearean star vehicles than vigorous European-inspired productions.

After their opening production of *Twelfth Night* on 2 February 1953, Littlewood developed an ambitious programme devoted to classics such as Molière's *The Imaginary Invalid* (1673); the best of contemporary European and American drama, including plays by George Bernard Shaw, Eugene O'Neill and Sean O'Casey; and works by novelists such as Charles Dickens and Mark Twain adapted for the stage. The company received immediate support from the local paper, the *Stratford Express*, which praised Theatre Workshop's commitment, willingness to experiment, tenacity and theatrical vitality in the face of physical exhaustion, financial struggle and a lacklustre reception. The local population cautiously embraced the newly arrived exotic creative figures and made efforts to ensure they remained fed with cheap food and handouts from the market and sustenance from the Café L'Ange, but this support did not equate to getting people through the door of the theatre.

The wider political and cultural mood was very different from the postwar optimism that shrouded the formation of Theatre Workshop. Unfortunately, this euphoric mood had waned and postwar disillusionment set in as people lived with economic instability heightened by America's withdrawal of aid, a slow physical restructuring and continuing rationing. Equally, the dissolution of empire, Britain's unease about its place in the world order as America gained increasing prominence and the crushing presence of the Cold War did little to boost national confidence.

Labour won the 1950 general election with a reduced majority and subsequently lost the 1951 election to the Conservatives, which briefly put Winston Churchill back in power. His reappointment symbolised the feeling that the country was creeping backwards and there began a period of consensus politics whereby it was hard to distinguish left from right and the next general elections of 1955 and 1959 were both won by the Conservatives. However, the period also saw challenges to consensus politics emerge from a generation who benefited from the progressive policies that inaugurated the welfare state, but who resented the failure of the Labour, and subsequent, governments to enact significant changes to the status quo. Social theorists, novelists, filmmakers and playwrights began to re-evaluate and represent issues of class, metropolitan dominance over the regions and popular culture as a way of challenging the terms of the debate.

In its politics, its theatrical representations of working-class life and language and its location on the margins of the metropolitan cultural centre of London, Theatre Workshop was explicitly connected to this climate of opposition to the postwar consensus. Theatre Workshop hoped to embed themselves within their working-class community, to realise their long-held ambition for a 'people's theatre', and set about trying to make connections with local organisations to promote their work.[37] So, on 24 April 1953, the local paper printed a letter from Raffles inviting local drama societies to use the theatre as a headquarters or source of advice in exchange for their help reaching a potential local audience. He also targeted local Communist Party branches, trade unionists and industrial workers in the hope of attracting a larger working-class audience, although, he later admitted, 'We kept making drives towards trade unionists and ended up among the aristocrats.'[38] However, the company's commitment to a non-hierarchical organisation remained in other ways, such as the inclusion of the theatre's bar staff, maintenance workers and cleaners in credits for shows.

With no money, the company lived and worked in the cold, damp Theatre Royal, taking it in turns to light the temperamental boiler an hour before shows so the audience would not freeze and to slowly overhaul the dilapidated building. In the early years, the company was a fairly stable ensemble with Littlewood as director, Raffles as manager and a core of actors dedicated to the Theatre Workshop approach, including Goorney, Joby Blanshard, Avis Bunnage and Harry H. Corbett. John Bury, who went on to be head of design at the National Theatre, had also joined the company in the Ormesby Hall days. He took responsibility for lighting and stage design and contributed enormously to the company's reputation for creating highly effective sparse, elemental sets. Keen, with Littlewood, to animate every horizontal and vertical axis, his austere networks of levels, ramps, scaffolding, stairs and textured surfaces also provided ideal vehicles for bold, atmospheric, cinematic side lighting used to create the effect of pools, shafts and shadows, as opposed to the painted backdrops and representational settings seen in the West End. The fact that the company knew and trusted Littlewood's methods made up for the fact that there was less and less time for research and training as the company worked tirelessly to produce fortnightly productions.

Littlewood began to attract widespread attention with her experimental productions of plays by Renaissance dramatists. A production of Ben Jonson's *The Alchemist* in 1953 was followed up by *Richard II* and two neglected classics: John Marston's *The Dutch Courtesan* (1605), and *Arden of Faversham* (1592) by an unknown

Renaissance playwright, in 1954. Littlewood chose this latter production, joined by a modern-dress version of Ben Jonson's *Volpone* (1606), when the company were invited to represent Britain at the Théâtre des Nations festival in Paris in 1955, alongside the Peking Opera, the Berliner Ensemble and the Abbey Theatre, Dublin. Regardless of the fact that the company arrived with no subsidy or official support, their performances were acclaimed for their fresh approach, energy and originality. In these productions, Littlewood stripped back the usual reverential treatment of classics to reveal topical political resonances through her deployment of staging and modern dress and willingness to cut and resituate scenes. Justifying her 1957 modern-dress *Macbeth*, which cast Macbeth as a dictator facing a firing squad for his crimes against humanity, Littlewood explained,

> The poetry of Shakespeare's day was a muscular, active, forward-moving poetry, in that it was like the people to whom it belonged. If Shakespeare has any significance today, a production of his work must not be regarded as a historical reconstruction, but as an instrument still sharp enough to provoke thought, to extend man's awareness of his problems, and to strengthen his belief in his kind.[39]

Her success at the Théâtre des Nations festival, followed immediately by the decision of Brecht, encouraged by Oscar Lewenstein, to grant her the rights to direct and play the title role in *Mother Courage* (1939) in 1955, the first professional production of a Brecht play in Britain prior to the groundbreaking visit of the Berliner Ensemble to the country in 1956, put Theatre Workshop firmly on the theatrical map, but this was just a precursor of things to come.

Popular theatricality

Where others might have exploited this critical success with an extended programme of classic productions, Littlewood typically bucked expectations by forging a new vein of work nurturing emerging writers. The theatrical climate irrevocably altered following the premiere of John Osborne's *Look Back in Anger* on 8 May 1956 at the Royal Court theatre in central London, which critics welcomed as the voice of a new generation ushering in a more politically urgent and socially conscious theatre, but as usual Littlewood pushed the envelope when Brendan Behan's *The Quare Fellow* opened two weeks later on 24 May 1956. Set in a prison and addressing the topical issue of capital punishment, Littlewood's production broke new ground in combining probing social commentary with a vibrant popular-theatre-inspired theatricality that made the Royal Court's output seem stuffy and leaden.

However, it was not so much the production as the process that arrived at it that ignited Littlewood's creative impulse. With Behan's approval, during rehearsals Littlewood cut and reshaped his text to find the best way to theatricalise the tragic and comic elements of this hermetically sealed environment, the robust demotic speech, popular song, gallows humour and wry look at the darker recesses of humanity. She was feeling her way towards a style of theatre that combined social authenticity, political commentary and overt theatricality and made her one of the most famous and influential directors of her generation.

The style of theatre was not the only thing to alter for Theatre Workshop in the mid-1950s. Raffles and Littlewood were sharing an elegant house in Blackheath bought for them by Raffles's father, and in 1955 he provided the money for Raffles to buy the theatre, a change that marked a significant shift in the company's organisational structure and decision-making. Whilst the company still nominally operated as a co-operative, the triumvirate of Raffles, who held the purse strings; Littlewood, who dominated artistic policy; and Bury, who drove the aesthetic with Littlewood, were a powerful force. The situation was compounded when key members of the ensemble, including Corbett and Blanshard, left for more lucrative careers elsewhere.

As Littlewood developed a more upfront, rumbustious theatrical aesthetic she looked for new actors such as Roy Kinnear and Barbara Windsor to join the company who could cope with the energetic style she was cultivating. Many were 'discovered' by Littlewood in unusual circumstances: Stephen Lewis, who went on write *Sparrers Can't Sing*, which Littlewood produced in 1960 and turned into a film in 1963, recalled being spotted by Littlewood when he was messing about and joking as a builder's labourer.[40] Similarly, Victor Spinetti, who was working as a compere at a strip club, was taken on after a 'non-audition'.[41] Many gave up more lucrative jobs in the creative industries to work with Littlewood because of her reputation. But, as Goorney highlights, this signalled a radical shift in the creative ethos of the company, as 'the emphasis was now on learning from Joan rather than on learning together as previously'.[42] As the years passed, the cult of 'Joan' ensued, as her role, rather than the collective ensemble, became the central artistic focus, a change that proved devastating for Littlewood's working practice.

The theatre text had never been sacred to Littlewood and she began to focus her attention on inexperienced playwrights who demonstrated, through their capacity for capturing the vitality of demotic speech, an ability to represent the theatricality of working-class life and experience in extreme or closed environments. Whether working with full scripts or fragments of ideas, Littlewood used improvisation to flesh out the details of dialogue, relationships, atmosphere and stage business in a number of successful productions, including *You Won't Always Be on Top* (1957), *A Taste of Honey* (1958) and *The Hostage* (1958). In fact, she would experiment and improvise right up to the last moments of rehearsal before sculpting material to establish key stage pictures, spatial relations, group formations, interactions, rhythms and textures.

> Even then, Littlewood refused to court closure, fixity and the nightly resurrection of slickly packaged corpses. Any sign of complacency, cosiness, milking an easy laugh or 'bloody acting' was denounced in coruscating notes on dressing room walls, derided in an acerbic turn of phrase and rooted out in ongoing rehearsals.[43]

Anything that received rapturous applause would be deliberately dismantled as that particular piece of performance business had reached its apotheosis and would forever be stale or a pale imitation. She was also renowned for stirring things up in the middle of a run if she thought a production had got stale. For instance, Miriam Karlin recalls a time when she worked on *Fings Ain't Wot They Used T'Be* (1959) and Littlewood sent her a note claiming that 'your [*sic*] so bleeding marvellous and you're being fucked by that arsehole, Glynn. Tonight I want you to come on wearing something different and from a different place.'[44] Little did Karlin know that Littlewood had sent an identical note to Glynn Edwards castigating Karlin. As Karlin recalls, 'It worked and she knew it, because we were once again really listening and relating to each other.'[45]

It would be inaccurate to suggest that all actors and playwrights approved of or enjoyed Littlewood's methods. Many actors fell by the wayside, toppled by Littlewood's unusual demands and ferocious work ethic. Frank Norman, who wrote *Fings*, the first production in a new strand of East End musicals created with the composer Lionel Bart, admitted,

> The journey from page to stage was fraught with hazards for the unwary playwright. Powerless to do anything about it, short of call the whole thing off, a forlorn author would sit hunched in the stalls and gaze up at a stage littered with discarded pages as Littlewood tore his play to bits with her bare hands, cut out the heart, gave it the kiss of life and tossed it to the assembled company of improvisers. With the raw material of adlibs she would then proceed to remodel the flesh in her own image.[46]

Regardless of the odd dissenting voice, with their deft combination of sharp social observation, an ability to capture the political zeitgeist and flamboyant music-hall-style theatricality, these productions captured the public's imagination and catapulted Littlewood into stardom. Attended by royalty and stars of the stage and screen such as Judy Garland, Kirk Douglas and Marlene Dietrich, her productions garnered more and more critical attention and acclaim. For example, *The Hostage* received many accolades when it represented Britain, supported by the British Council, at the Théâtre des Nations in April 1959, and *Fings* won the *Evening Standard* award for the best musical of 1960. These productions also sparked the interest of impresarios keen to capitalise on a successful product from a wayward genius who had a habit of courting controversy, and hence very helpful publicity, due to the youth or colourful backgrounds of her writers; and Theatre Workshop's fast-paced, increasingly irreverent productions began moving into the West End on a regular basis.

The West End, the Arts Council and the Lord Chamberlain

Reliance on the West End was complete anathema to Littlewood, who declared, 'Anybody at all who goes into that dusty museum, with a few racketeers, conning people into watching a boring repetition, is either doing straightforward whoring, because they need the dough, or has got a very pretty ego.'[47] Littlewood and Theatre Workshop were reduced to 'whoring' without significant support from the Arts Council as they suffered the same hand-to-mouth existence that plagued their work on the northern touring circuit. In fact, the constant financial battles to stay afloat grew rather than receded with their critical acclaim at home and abroad.

Ultimately, the constant pressure of underfunding, the loss of her ensemble to extended West End runs and accusations that the Theatre Royal had become a try-out venue for the West End led Littlewood to withdraw from British theatre in 1961. Interviewed by Malcolm Muggeridge on Granada television's *Appointment With* (1960–1) in 1961, Littlewood referred to 'the old ladies who run the Arts Council, sipping their tea and deciding what's good for people' as responsible for her retreat from theatre-making.[48] After spending a year and a half estranged from Raffles whilst travelling, trying to get a film of Wole Soyinka's *The Lion and the Jewel* (1959) off the ground, hanging around London drinking heavily and writing the screenplay for and filming *Sparrers Can't Sing*, she returned to the theatre and Raffles in 1963.

She returned to create the politically charged and theatrically inventive *Oh What a Lovely War*, a satirical dissection of the capitalist imperatives, power-brokering, class relations and devastating human consequences of the Great War, a 'War to End All Wars', reinterpreted in the long shadow of the Second World War and the widespread fallout of the Cold War. For many, this production sits at the pinnacle of Littlewood's career and the point when all the elements she had experimented with during her career coalesced in glorious harmony.[49] But, even with the success of *Oh What a Lovely War*, which won the *Evening Standard* drama award, shared the Théâtre des Nations prize with Peter Brook's production of *King Lear* and was turned into a film by Sir Richard Attenborough in 1969, she still could not convince the Arts Council to support her and a slow fizzling out of activities ensued.

Famously declaring of the Arts Council, 'they'd have pissed on my grave',[50] Littlewood's relationship with the national funding body was fractious at best, mutually uncomprehending at worst. Michael Billington has written about 'the indifference, often bordering on rank hostility, of the Arts Council to the company's work', and has argued that the Arts Council's suspicion of Theatre Workshop stands as 'the blackest mark on its post-war record'.[51] The suspicion Billington detects was levelled at Littlewood and Theatre Workshop's blatant left-wing sympathies, their decision to situate themselves in an unfashionable working-class area in the East End, their commitment to theatrical experimentation and Littlewood herself, who refused to ingratiate herself with any potential patrons. These qualities made Littlewood and Theatre Workshop incompatible with the ethos and prevailing cultural conservatism of the Arts Council and several members of the company have referred to the stifling cultural hegemony that blighted their existence.[52]

The Arts Council was not the only body to reject Theatre Workshop; the company also tried without success to attract the support of trade unions, government agencies and local councils, but despite small pockets of money being released, nothing substantial ever materialised. As such, the company became caught in an endless cycle of funding applications, rejections or minimal support, periods of disbandment and creative compromises, which in the early days meant turning their hands to accessible adaptations of Shakespeare to tour to schools and later meant taking advantage of the profits to be made from West End transfers that could be fed back into new work. Lack of official financial support was a constant source of irritation and prompted items such as the note in the programme for the 1967 production of *Macbird* which states, 'This season of Theatre Workshop at the Theatre Royal owes nothing in the way of support, co-operation or even sympathy to the Arts Council of Great Britain, nor to Newham Council.'[53]

Littlewood's approach not only had a detrimental impact on her relationship with the Arts Council, it also placed her at odds with the Lord Chamberlain's censorship. As I have written elsewhere, Littlewood's 'insistence on improvisation as a creative method and the treatment of performance as an organic phenomenon which evolves and shifts also disrupted the insistence on predetermined output, "standards", and the definitive final product necessary for the Lord Chamberlain's approval'.[54] The Lord Chamberlain privileged the dominant authority of text and of set scripted dialogue, whereas Littlewood was determined to promote the live moment of exchange, inspiration and improvisation in generating plays and in the relationship forged with an audience. These qualities led the Lord Chamberlain's office to denounce 'the astonishingly casual and unbusinesslike manner of the theatre' and to accuse Raffles of 'insolence' for advertising productions prior to scrutiny.[55]

This thorny relationship reached a head in 1957, when the Lord Chamberlain's office launched a prosecution against the production of Henry Chapman's *You Won't Always Be on Top*, a play depicting a day in the life of a building site, which breached the terms of the Lord Chamberlain's licence by including unauthorised material. Seeking advice from the Director of Public Prosecution, the Assistant Comptroller noted that 'the changes are of such magnitude as to constitute what is tantamount to a new play, and represent a flagrant disregard of his [the Lord Chamberlain's] authority'.[56] In a typically provocative response to concerns raised, Littlewood admitted that

> the play varies every night. The actors, really living their parts, genuinely improvise, introducing their own new gags and fragments of dialogue: if a gag 'takes' it probably stays in. The other night one character unexpectedly walked off, saying 'Well, I'm going to have a slash.'[57]

One incident, which particularly troubled the censor, arose when Richard Harris, playing Mick, imitated Sir Winston Churchill whilst pretending to open a public lavatory. The imitation of a living person was enough to get the company in trouble but Harris upped the stakes by pouring water from a watering can as if to imitate urination. A high-profile case ensued with people including Kenneth Tynan, George Devine and Lord Harewood setting up a defence fund to support the company. The absurdity of the subsequent prosecution, which included accusations regarding a suggestively positioned ladder, resulted in nominal fines for Littlewood, Raffles, Chapman, Harris and Bury and was instrumental in hastening the abolition of stage censorship in 1968 by highlighting the arcane elitism of the Lord Chamberlain's office – but not before Theatre Workshop clashed a few more times with the Lord Chamberlain's state-sanctioned process of surveillance and intervention steeped in prejudices and anxieties around class, sexuality and politics.

By the early 1960s, Littlewood had become increasingly frustrated with the restrictions of building-based theatre, and after *Oh What a Lovely War* Littlewood directed fewer than twenty shows at the Theatre Royal between 1964 and 1973 and several of these were revivals or adaptations of earlier work. She flirted with the possibility of a screen career and during the late 1960s, like many others, she became fascinated with India and produced a film treatment for *Lall, You Are a Clown* with Santi Chowdhury, and a proposal for a television series called *Max in India*. The former, based in Rajasthan, features a wild, fast-paced psychedelic narrative akin to the early films of Ken Russell or the Beatles' *Magical Mystery Tour* (1967); the latter features six episodes based on James Bond-style adventures in cities across India.[58]

Mainly, she directed her energies towards localised projects that emphasised cultural democracy and the animation of community-based activity and values. In particular, she worked tirelessly to raise awareness of, interest in and financial support for her plans for a Fun Palace, a large-scale community arts complex dedicated to education, entertainment, technological experimentation and social enrichment, which she developed with the iconoclastic architect Cedric Price, who captured her imagination and affection.

Way before its time, the Fun Palace never secured sufficient public support or institutional backing, which was a source of deep, bitter disappointment for Littlewood. Without her Fun Palace, she channelled her energy into local projects with young people, developing adventure playgrounds, temporary gardens, parades, interactive funfairs using the latest technologies and Easter fairs, all in the immediate vicinity of the Theatre Royal. Taking over abandoned spaces or spaces awaiting development in collaboration with people including

Carole Christensen, Gaye Brown, Barbara Wheeler-Early and Martin Goodrich, who went on to found the award-winning Free Form Arts Trust, these transformative initiatives championed the characteristics Petra Kuppers and Gwen Robertson identify as central to community and environmental arts, which 'foreground concepts such as democratic or collaborative practices, everyday life, the local and the private as spaces of agency, engagement with dominant stereotypes, the merging of educative and creative aims, and the respect for multiple voices'.[59] But this pioneering work was about to come to an abrupt end.

After Gerry

In many ways, it is as if the clock stopped for Littlewood after the shocking early death of Raffles in 1975 at the age of fifty-one. Her autobiography ceases on the Christmas before his death, despite the fact that she lived for a further thirty years. She was devastated by Raffles's death and determined to extricate herself from the theatre that she rightly or wrongly held responsible for weakening his health. She established an advisory council to discuss artistic proposals for the theatre beyond her involvement in it and handed over to a new generation headed by Maxwell Shaw, a long-standing Theatre Workshop actor. She arranged for the theatre to be gifted to the London Borough of Newham in 1975 through the Fun Palace Trust and moved to France for the remainder of her life. She never directed another theatre production.

She lived in Vienne, a small town south of Lyon, close to the River Rhône where Raffles, who was diabetic, had died after he had found himself without insulin on a solo French boating holiday. Here she lived a solitary existence, filling her days reading and writing. She also established a long-term friendship with baron Philippe de Rothschild, the exceptionally wealthy cultural patron, translator and poet best known as a highly successful wine grower. Intrigued by his privileged life and colourful stories of scandal and seduction, she edited and published his autobiography in 1984 based on their many long conversations about his life and work.[60] A regular visitor to Château Mouton Rothschild, after her friend's death in 1988 she moved to Paris where she lived as Joan Petitbois and completed her autobiography, *Joan's Book*, which she published in 1994.

She returned to Britain sporadically to visit friends such as Peter Rankin and Victor Spinetti, to support their work or to attend specific functions or conferences. When she did return she was shocked by the apathy and lack of human connection she detected in Britain. In one extended article called 'Home Fires Burning', written for the *Guardian* in 1985, in which she documented a return to her birthplace, Stockwell, she captures her distaste at dilapidated buildings, plastic debris, broken paving slabs and a boarded-up cenotaph.[61] Littlewood spent much of her life fighting the poverty, social injustice and social exclusion she witnessed in Thatcher's Britain in the early 1980s, and her sense of simmering rage is palpable as she documents men and women reduced to 'zombies', youth loitering with menaces on street corners and a young, heavily pregnant woman struggling onto a bus with a pram, young child and no signs of assistance. It is a rage at society's failure to care for and nurture all its citizens that directly or indirectly galvanised all of Littlewood's theatre and community-based practices that provide the focus for the rest of this book.

Methodology and structure

Throughout the process of writing this book, I have been primarily working with the residues of performance history that remain long after the performance event has vanished. The shift from theatre history to theatre historiography has put the process of writing theatre history under the spotlight and highlights its reliance on a flawed process of reinterpretation, narrativising, anecdotal evidence, surmising, summarising, conjecture and representation. These characteristics are as evident in the research processes underpinning this book as in any other. In writing this book I have been exhuming performance remains and collaging shards of evidence to create a picture (partial and reliant on my brushstrokes) of Littlewood's collaborative creative process, the productions she worked on, her political convictions, her social concerns, her ethical dilemmas and how all this sat in relation to the institutional frames she was working within and the lens through which her work was being viewed.

Much of my research has been conducted in archives, principally the archives at the Theatre Royal Stratford East, the Lord Chamberlain's Collection of the British Library and the Harry Ransom Humanities

Research Centre at the University of Texas in Austin. In *The Archaeology of Knowledge*, first published in England in 1972, Michel Foucault drew attention to the relation between knowledge and power and how the archive is embedded in systems of discursivity, which establishes the terms of debate – defined as much by what is not present as by what is. Scrutiny of the politics of the archive and its ramifications reached new heights following the influential publication of Jacques Derrida's *Archive Fever* in 1995, in which he explores the impulses that bring an archive into being, its institutionalisation, its authority and how the location of the archive influences how history and memory is constructed through the process of archivisation.

It is important to call attention to how these theoretical reflections on the archive have currency for *actual* archival research. The historian Carolyn Steedman reminds us, 'Nothing starts in the archive, nothing, ever at all, though things certainly end up there. You find nothing in the archive but stories caught half way through: the middle of things; discontinuities.'[62] This is, of course, true – all archives are flawed, partial and subject to the particular politics of the institutions that hold them. But, let me confess from the start, I have found the archival process seductive. There is something extremely pleasurable in handling and deciphering documents from the past, the scraps of paper, notebooks, photographs, letters, programmes, production notebooks and scripts that bear witness to a historical process. It can be an extremely intimate encounter, perhaps made more so by our increasingly virtual and technologically driven research environment.

However, the archival process is also about the gaps, the silences and the absences that overwhelm it. As a researcher I am responsible for making the archival materials speak. But this is not a neutral activity. I have been helped along the way by the physical and ideological locations of the archives I have used. For instance, the Lord Chamberlain's Collection highlights how theatre practice was controlled, restricted, framed and distorted by state-sanctioned structures of thought and the specific priorities and anxieties of individual readers. This archive also promotes an acute awareness of the absent presence of performance and, as such, draws attention to how Littlewood used the performative as a form of subversion and dissent from the dominant authority of the text. The Ewan MacColl archive, held at Ruskin College in Oxford, named after the great Victorian socialist campaigner and writer who railed against capitalist self-interest and influenced trade unionists, political activists and conservationists, is steeped in the history of the Labour movement, the Workers' Education Association and a radical left-wing agenda. Through the frame of MacColl and the prism of Ruskin College's social and political manoeuvrings, this archive and its institutional context illuminated questions around cultural democracy, accessibility and the arts as political critique that drive many of the discussions in this book.

The Theatre Royal Stratford East archive is perhaps most interesting for the knowledge created outside the formal structure of the archive. Housed in the theatre itself, entering it means entering the highly mythologised space of Littlewood's creative imaginings. And, despite the theatre's reinvention as a leading new writing venue focused on the local diasporic community, the archive is a shrine to Littlewood. Her pictures and production photos hang on the walls, her old desk carries a 'do not touch' sign and her library of books is housed along one wall of the room. The archive's chief archivist, heartbeat and gate-keeper is Murray Melvin, who worked with Littlewood on many seminal productions: he was her Geoff in *A Taste of Honey* and one of her pierrots in *Oh What a Lovely War*. Melvin functions as an embodied archive, activated through memory, imagination and story-telling, who functions in terms of Rebecca Schneider's assertion that historical performance can endure and be enacted outside the formal, ordered construction of 'archival logic'.[63] So, alongside the 'archival logic' of programmes, production photos and scripts chronologically systemised in the Theatre Royal archive, I also encountered a resolutely human dimension that drew attention to many of Littlewood's key characteristics as a human being: her passion, her spirit, her foul mouth, her temper, her warmth, her intellect, her distrust of authority, her creative ingenuity and her love of language.

This archival focus has been supplemented by a concern to situate Littlewood and her theatres within particular historical moments. This involved delving into the sociopolitical history and wider cultural forces of the periods concerned but also an attempt to understand how and why her work was received then in as much as I am obviously informed by the politics of my own time and position in the world. This preoccupation has promoted a significant use of national newspaper reviews to uncover dominant discourses around Littlewood's output at the time it was staged. Given Littlewood's political commitment to decentralisation and localism, I have been keen to deploy local newspaper reports, principally from the *Stratford Express*, to unlock voices that illuminate her relationship with the local population she was keen to serve as a cultural agent.

The chapters in this book reflect two principal preoccupations. First, I uncover the primary focus for Littlewood's political work and socially campaigning agendas by adopting a thematic as opposed to a chronological approach, a perspective that facilitates valuable connections and comparisons across Littlewood's career. I have also been keen to recuperate two aspects of Littlewood's career that have not received sufficient critical attention. As mentioned earlier, from the early 1960s Littlewood became increasingly dissatisfied by the constraints of formal theatre and began focusing her energies on paratheatrical activity that centred on her plans for a Fun Palace, a multifaceted cultural centre, and her numerous playground, community garden and drama projects for young people. These vital aspects of her career receive sustained attention in the final two chapters of this book.

War was the first significant theme to emerge in Littlewood's work and throughout the mid-twentieth century she staged a substantial body of work dedicated to exploring the forces of capitalism, nationalism and imperialism that drive war from the earliest Theatre of Action days to her production of the seminal *Oh What a Lovely War*. Situating this body of work within a broad framework of antiwar activism, in Chapter 2 I investigate Littlewood's theatrical treatment of one of the most pressing concerns of the twentieth century – the rationalisation, machinery and humanitarian consequences of war. I argue that through her theatre work she focused on the pursuit of ethical acts of theatrical witnessing and remembrance to explore the relation between individual trauma, collective loss, survival and hope for the future. I also draw attention to the transnational perspective adopted by Littlewood whereby her broad humanitarian agenda moves between the local and the national, the national and the international in its concerns.

When Littlewood's productions of Renaissance plays by Shakespeare and Ben Jonson are discussed in theatre scholarship it tends to be in terms of a progressive feminist historiography – part of a process of recovery and a reading of her productions as counter to dominant masculinist traditions or as productions that, according to Elizabeth Schafer, 'offered a distinctly alternative vision of the Renaissance classics from that available in the mainstream theatre of the time'.[64] Through a detailed consideration of key production and performance histories, Chapter 3 examines the multiple factors underpinning Littlewood's formidable critical reputation for producing sparse, iconoclastic and transgressive productions of classic plays such as *Richard II*, *Edward II* and *Macbeth*. I am interested in how Littlewood contributed to a reappraisal of the cultural authority of Shakespeare through her irreverent approach to rehearsing, interpreting and staging his works. I am also keen to look afresh at the ways that Littlewood theatrically mediated these plays in order to engage in multilayered debates with the national and European politics of the day around issues such as gender politics, homosexuality, the rise of fascism and popular culture.

A significant core running through Littlewood's theatrical output was her belief that the life-blood of a nation's culture is rooted in the working class. Philip Hedley has referred to Littlewood's theatre as 'working-class rebellion', and after her death several obituaries marked out her depictions of working-class life and the working-class voice as one of her key attributes as a director.[65] Chapter 4 examines Littlewood's stubborn commitment to representing working-class life and communities at a historical juncture when the working class faced accusations of rapidly approaching extinction. I am interested in the geographical, political and cultural shifts that occurred in these representations and in what these reveal about the penetration of contemporaneous debates on working-class identification, culture and cultural expression. Above all, I argue that her productions, whether set and situated in the north of England or the East End of London, engaged with a 'social imaginary' of working-class life and culture in a way that invested this life and experience with credibility as a vital form of situated knowledge.

Chapter 5 focuses on some of Littlewood's most enduringly popular productions, including *The Quare Fellow, The Hostage, A Taste of Honey* and *Fings Ain't Wot They Used T'Be,* that captured the critics' and the theatre-going public's theatrical imagination at the Theatre Royal and in the West End. It extends many of the areas opened up in the previous chapter, but it points to an increasing preoccupation with representations of alternative social structures that remodel conceptions of the traditional working-class family and community by representing those at the margins of society: prisoners, single mothers and sex workers, for instance. The chapter's primary focus, however, is on Littlewood's increasing adoption of theatrical tropes drawn from popular entertainment and I explore the tensions and creative frissons that emerge between the authentic documentation of facets of working-class life combined with or set against a lively theatricality. On the one hand, I argue that this body of work exhibited an implicit faith in the exuberance of heightened theatricality to critique regimes that sought to contain, restrict and undervalue working-class life and experience. On the other hand, I draw attention to a problematic tendency that emerged in Littlewood's practice to romanticise and exoticise aspects of criminality and social deviancy.

Alert to critical thinking on areas such as space, cultural democracy and citizenship, Chapters 6 and 7 offer a detailed appraisal of Littlewood's paratheatrical output. Focusing on the origins, inspiration and socially campaigning agenda at the heart of the Fun Palace, Chapter 6 draws on the documents and designs generated to promote it, to situate this project at the vanguard of artistic, cultural and technological experimentation in 1960s Britain. It assesses the role Littlewood hoped to play in reconceptualising the relationship between education, entertainment and everyday life and charts the reasons that contributed to this project's failure to be fully realised. Chapter 7 focuses on projects materialising in the immediate vicinity of the Theatre Royal that emphasised creative encounters, active citizenship and the animation of community-based activity and spaces for young people. It explores Littlewood's work generating adventure playgrounds, community gardens, educational workshops and drama activities that remodelled her vision of a popular people's theatre for a younger generation.

2 The war game: politics, ethics and representation

Campaigns against war and arms proliferation have been a prominent part of the political, social and cultural landscape throughout the twentieth century and into the twenty-first. From the conscientious objectors of the First World War to the mass spectacle of global antiwar protests in February 2003, individuals and groups have enacted their resistance to Thomas Hobbes's pessimistic assumption that war is a natural human state.[1] Like many other theatre practitioners of her generation Littlewood used theatre as a vehicle to articulate her political and moral abhorrence at the war machine and the numerous traumas it generates.[2] Throughout the mid-twentieth century, she staged a substantial body of work dedicated to exploring the forces of capitalism, nationalism and imperialism that drive war.

For Littlewood, war was not just a distant horror, but had profound ramifications in her personal life. She lost close friends and creative collaborators, Bob Goodman and Alec Armstrong, in the Spanish Civil War. During the Second World War, she lost yet more friends and was acutely aware when hundreds were killed in her adopted home of Manchester after the Luftwaffe bombed the city. In London, an unexploded bomb forced her mother out of her house and Littlewood evacuated her grandparents to MacColl's parents' house in Cheshire, where her grandmother died estranged from everything familiar to her. She also took responsibility for running the campaign to release MacColl after the authorities arrested and imprisoned him for desertion in December 1946.[3] This event also coincided with Theatre Workshop's two-month tour of occupied West Germany in early 1947. Unable to go on tour due to MacColl's impeding court-martial, Littlewood received numerous letters from her lover Raffles and other colleagues, that captured their traumatic encounters with the concentration camps, poverty and devastation in war-torn Germany. All of these events informed Littlewood's instinctive antiwar stance.

From the 1930s, when she participated in antiwar rallies, to the early 1960s, when she produced a shambolic rally for CND at the Royal Albert Hall, and beyond, Littlewood remained steadfast in her belief that the brutality of war betrayed civilisation.[4] Like many of her generation, including MacColl, her pacifism was ideologically rooted in her socialist principles. Throughout history, socialists have found an affinity with the peace movement as the majority of wars connect to the problems of economic injustice and imperial desire for domination of peoples, territories and ideologies that most socialists seek to oppose, but this neat correlation was complicated by the rise of fascism in Europe.

Whereas the First World War could be characterised as an imperialist war, the military struggle against fascism was a different story. Hence socialists who counted themselves pacifists faced a difficult moral and ideological dilemma following the political repression that instigated the Spanish Civil War and the brutal genocide of the Second World War. Pacifists were forced to look hard at their principles and to make difficult decisions that did not sit easy for many. For instance, the writer and philosopher Aldous Huxley, a pacifist and conscientious objector during the First World War, adopted a neutral position during the Spanish Civil War that rankled many on the left, whereas the notorious antiwar campaigner and philosopher Bertrand Russell's pacifism wavered in response to Germany's rampage through Europe during the Second World War. And many others were seduced by the 'just-war' philosophy that argues it is morally permissible in exceptional circumstances to use proportionate force in the protection and preservation of values. John Stuart Mill pithily encapsulated the relativism of this position in his statement, 'War is an ugly thing, but not the ugliest of things.'[5]

For many, including artists and intellectuals such as W. H. Auden, George Orwell and Stephen Spender, the struggle in Spain offered a possible first step to building a new egalitarian world by settling the major ideological conflict of the age between the forces of repression and democracy.[6] Thousands took up arms with the International Brigade, with many drawn from a tradition of left, trade union and communist politics to fight the fascist movements gaining ground throughout Europe, including Britain, where Sir Oswald Mosley formed the British Union of Fascists in 1932. For Littlewood, as for many others, war against the fascists *was* the morally right course of action given the wider ramifications of their ascendancy, and the ideological struggle at the heart of the Spanish Civil War appeared in many productions produced by her in the 1930s and early 1940s. But her position was complicated by the considerable contradictions in the Communist Party's attitude to Spain and Germany in the run-up to the Second World War, and Littlewood, together with MacColl, often found herself caught in the crossfire between their anti-fascism and their desire to hold fast to the party line on key issues during this period.

Despite recognising the need for a 'just-war' approach that responded to the particular ethical dimensions of each given circumstance, Littlewood retained an antiwar impulse throughout her life and she was determined to put her theatre work at the service of the antiwar cause. From Littlewood's perspective, the creativity involved in making theatre provided a potent antidote to forces of destruction evident in war; indeed, the first edition of a Theatre Union newsletter entitled *Bulletin* invited people to get involved with the group as a form of embodied protest against the nihilist impulse of war:

> At a time like the present when the governments of the world are obsessed by a wanton and self-destroying materialism which finds its final expression in warfare, the preservation of the spiritual values of creative art becomes not merely of primary importance but a vital necessity.[7]

This connects with Lewis Hyde's philosophical analysis of the gift of creativity. Creative exchange relies on the donation of time, skill and effort and an emphasis on generating, making, dialogue and sharing that becomes an expression of bondedness, a recognition and commitment to a communion with others and the positive qualities of social interaction. As Hyde argues,

> The creative spirit moves in a body or ego larger than that of any single person. Works of art are drawn from, and their bestowal nourishes, those parts of our being that are not entirely personal, parts that derive from nature, from the group and the race, from history and tradition.[8]

In *Joan's Book* Littlewood writes, 'The inborn violence, murderous feelings, the hate and aggression which are part of us, even our petty feelings, can be transformed by creativity'.[9] So, for Littlewood, the creative act had the potential to be resistant in the relations it opened up with others, as well as in the imaginative territory it opens up for its audience.

Public declarations/antiwar spectacles

According to Paul Fussell, 'the drift of modern history domesticates the fantastic and normalizes the unspeakable. And the catastrophe that begins it is the Great War.'[10] The end of the First World War saw a massive humanitarian reaction against war that set the conditions for the peace movement to flourish, which, according to Martin Ceadel, 'thrives best on a symbiosis of pessimism and optimism'.[11] Pessimism was inevitable given the horrific scale of slaughter carried out during the First World War. Optimism arose as people expected that the international community would rally to ensure that atrocity on this scale never happened again. Economic difficulties and slow progress towards the disarmament proposed by the Treaty of Versailles did nothing to alleviate pessimism in the ensuing years. Nonetheless, the establishment of the League of Nations in 1920, the formation of the No More War Movement in 1921 by Conscientious Objectors of the First World War, the 1928 Kellogg–Briand Pact renouncing war as an instrument of national policy and preparations for a World Disarmament Conference in 1932 pointed towards a more hopeful future. Similarly, the famous 1933 Oxford Union debate that carried the motion 'This House refuses to fight for King and Country', the League of Nations Peace Ballot of 1934–5 and the presence of an International Peace Pavilion at the Paris Exhibition in 1937 pointed not only to an overwhelming antiwar sentiment, but to the public performativity of antiwar protest.

Littlewood's first collaboration with MacColl, *John Bullion: A Ballet with Words* (1934) carried a strong antiwar message.[12] It owed much to a production of *Slickers* (1934), which Littlewood and MacColl watched when they attended a Workers' Theatre Movement (WTM) conference in London during 1934.[13] In *Agit-Prop to Theatre Workshop* (1986), MacColl admitted that the antiwar agenda of *Slickers* and its critique of the ethical vacuum at the heart of capitalist profit-seeking excited them, but that they were appalled by the sub-West End-style production and acting. Whilst he cites *Slickers* as a source for *John Bullion*, MacColl fails to identify the extent of their borrowing. He recalls that they 'reduced the number of characters, then cut out all of them and introduced new ones in their place'.[14] In fact, all the characters in *John Bullion* – Sir Weldon Birthright, Mr Fortune, Lord Winmore, Reverend Pye, Mr Deafen'em and Miss Banks – originate in *Slickers*.

The emblematic character names in *Slickers* indicate an agitprop-style production, but it was actually a rather conventional piece set in the office of an assured, sexually predatory, financial trader and local chairman of the Conservative Association, Sir Weldon Birthright. He encounters representatives of the aristocracy, the press, the church and financial centres on numerous telephones as they seek to profit from the lead-up to war by buying and selling shares in the arms manufacturer Slickers. Distributing the sketch through the WTM association, the producer John Hanmer explained that it is 'essential that the underlying ideas of the play be kept well in the foreground – profits from armaments – war and the stock exchange – mass action against war'.[15] The preoccupation with arms manufacture chimed with an ethical concern at the heart of the pacifist movement during this period. Huxley began his *An Encyclopaedia of Pacifism* (1937) with these words:

> The desire of arms manufacturers to make profits is a standing menace to world peace. It is in their interest to work for policies which are likely to produce dangerous international situations and to work against disarmament and the establishment of world peace, which would spoil their trade.[16]

Littlewood and MacColl strengthened this topical theme by replacing the euphemistic company name Slickers with Vickers, one of the leading British arms manufacturers.

In their theatrical adaptation, Littlewood and MacColl 'slashed and burned Hammer's [*sic*] forty-five minute play in to a frenetic fifteen minutes of dazzling lighting, roaring music, stylised acting, robotic dancing and disorientating sound effects'.[17] Instead of the representational office space and naturalistic dialogue of *Slickers*, Littlewood designed a constructivist setting of three bare platforms on different levels on which figures delivered catchphrases and speeches and executed stylised dance sequences. Whereas *Slickers* has a linear structure and a simple cause-and-effect narrative, *John Bullion* bombards the audience with resonant images and a disjunctive soundscape. Mannequins in swimsuits wearing gas masks appeared alongside recordings of children singing the pastoral hymn 'All things bright and beautiful' before being drowned out by sounds of warfare.

Miss Bank, Birthright's secretary from *Slickers*, becomes three women chained to high stools, wearing black underwear over their white-painted bodies. The masochistic imagery draws attention to the power relations at the heart of the dubious sexual politics only implied by *Slickers*, as these women are passive, objectified and subject to the gaze and advances of three lascivious businessmen. As the businessmen acquire more shares and profit, the typists mechanically record figures on a large blackboard, an image further politicised with the entrance of three disabled ex-servicemen. The embodied presence of loss evoked by the silent, maimed victims taints the disturbing representation of the fetishistic desire for profit. These discordant images contribute to a quality of aesthetic disturbance in which ethical questions arise through theatrical juxtaposition.

Expressionist influences were most apparent in the portrayal of Sir Weldon Birthright, who was 'made-up to look like a grotesque clown and had a stomach padded to Falstaffian proportions covered by a waistcoat fashioned from a union jack'[18] – a visual image that captured Birthright's avarice masked with a symbol of nationalist zeal. The way that war profiteers concealed their motives behind nationalist sentiment had come under scrutiny in the pacifist movement, with

Huxley calling nationalism 'the most powerful of contemporary religions'.[19] He argued, 'Pacifists should make it their business to understand the nature of this evil religion and, having understood it, to steel their minds against the emotional appeals and lying suggestions which are increasingly being made in its name.'[20]

Slickers and *John Bullion* promote a classic utopian international socialist position in which the workers of the world unite to unseat national divisions correspondent with capitalism and war. In *John Bullion*, Littlewood and MacColl modified *Slickers'* ending of an international workers' revolution bursting the capitalist warmongering bubble by employing a mutograph (an early version of the tickertape of *Lovely War*) that announced the advent of peace demonstrations and workers' strikes, intercut with headlines from gossip columns and share prices.

The jagged and disjointed quality of the prose ebbed as the rousing sound of the Internationale drowned out the chaos to create a unified vision of international socialist resistance as the singing 'flowers into several different languages'.[21] Despite its brevity, the piece introduced the themes of power, anti-imperialism, capitalist profiteering, aggressive nationalism and human loss that resurface in many later works produced by Littlewood. Unfortunately, the form, however theatrically exciting, radically departed from the Communist Party's support for Soviet socialist realism and Littlewood and MacColl faced accusations of pursuing individualistic artistry over politics. An accusation they vehemently denied.

In Britain, a significant development in the peace movement occurred when Dick Sheppard founded the Peace Pledge Union (PPU) in 1934.[22] The PPU emerged as an inclusive organisation that united Christians, atheists, socialists and agnostics in a common cause. Alongside regular meetings, rallies and the launch of *Peace News*, the PPU promoted cultural events and in 1936 joined with the Quaker movement in Manchester to invite Littlewood and MacColl to produce Hans Chlumberg's *Miracle at Verdun* (1930). Dedicated to 'The Dead of the Great War', the play had been a popular choice for European practitioners wishing to question the validity of war. The left-wing producer André van Gyseghem staged the British premiere at the

Embassy Theatre, London, on 21 September 1932; the production subsequently transferred to the Comedy Theatre on 25 October 1932 and another production by the People's Theatre followed in 1935. Littlewood and MacColl produced their version in July 1937.

Taking its name from one of the fiercest and most costly battles of the First World War, *Miracle at Verdun* begins in a military cemetery in the Argonne Forest containing a common grave with German and French soldiers. In this play, dead First World War soldiers rise from their graves to measure the extent of their sacrifice against the greed and warmongering of the present. A premise which echoes Siegfried Sassoon's call in 'On Passing the New Menin Gate' (1927–8) that 'Well might the Dead who struggled in the slime / Rise and deride this sepulchre of crime'.[23]

One of the most interesting aspects of Chlumberg's play is its setting in the future – August 1939 – twenty-five years after the outbreak of the First World War and in Chlumberg's imagining a period that would have been characterised by commemorative events. Portentously, this means that Chlumberg's attack on the futility of war is set a month before the outbreak of the Second World War, which gives it a chilling impact. There is little evidence for how Littlewood and MacColl tackled their production, but Ben Harker hits the nail on the head when he accuses this overly wordy naturalistic play of being 'too linear to leave elbow room for Littlewood's unruly inspiration'.[24] It did, however, introduce a new scale to Theatre Union's work – *Miracle at Verdun* involved over fifty actors – and allowed them to embody performative protest against war as a mass spectacle, a quality further developed in their production of Lope de Vega's (1562–1635) *Fuente Ovejuna* (*The Sheep Well*), which brought together a large cast drawn from a number of societies including the Rochdale Curtain and Altrincham Garrick Players, as well as Theatre Union. Once again, the possibilities inherent in collaboration, creative exchange and performance enabled a strategic form of ethical intervention at a moment of devastating ideological crisis: the Spanish Civil War. However, rather than positioning themselves as antiwar, in this instance Littlewood and MacColl wanted to put their theatre work at the service of the Republican cause in Spain – a war worth fighting.

Joining W.H. Auden, who donated the proceeds of his poem 'Spain' to Spanish Medical Aid, Littlewood and MacColl planned to produce the British premiere of *Fuente Ovejuna* as a political fundraiser. According to a correspondent in the *Manchester Guardian*, plans for the production kept falling through, but it was finally realised as part of a campaign to fund the Manchester Foodship for Spain and performed at the Lesser Free Trade Hall in Manchester from 21 to 25 February 1939.[25] Federico García Lorca, whom General Franco's followers murdered in 1936, produced a version of the play with La Barraca in 1933, which used a 1930s setting to heighten its political resonance. Given their interest in Lorca's work, it is possible that this production inspired Littlewood and MacColl.[26] In their programme note they declared, 'It was obviously necessary, in the present political situation, that a cultural expression should be found in the theatre of the forces fighting for the defence of democracy and progress and the preservation of peace.'[27]

Set in 1476, *Fuente Ovejuna* deals with a turning point in Spanish history when the Catholic monarchs, Ferdinand of Aragon and Isabella of Castile and León, came to power, overturning centuries of Muslim rule and ushering in the Spanish Golden Age. By de Vega's lifetime, Spain was a major European power, but the cost of sustaining its empire was having a deleterious impact at home, as high taxation and inflation crippled local industry. Lope de Vega provided a commentary on this situation and on general abuse of power by basing his play on two real-life historical incidents: the first was the seizure of Ciudad Real by Portuguese claimants and its recapture by military force; the second was a local rebellion against the tyrannical grand commander of Fuente Ovejuna in Córdoba that saw the commander, Fernán Gómez de Guzmán, murdered and mutilated. Historical records show that when the monarchy sent investigators to elicit information through interrogation and torture, the locals assumed communal responsibility by confirming only that Fuente Ovejuna was guilty.

In *Fuente Ovejuna*, the narrative revolves around the rapacious commander's pursuit of Laurencia, a spirited and intelligent daughter of a local magistrate, who spurns his advances. After the commander abducts and rapes Laurencia on her wedding day, she passionately rouses the villagers to rebel against his tyranny by killing him, alongside his pimps and henchmen. In contrast to the commander's selfish amorality that threatens social and political harmony, the villagers exhibit compassion, honour, integrity and solidarity. As such, the play offers a stout defence of democratic processes and celebrates the potential of collective will to overcome despotism – subject matter which, MacColl argued, 'was a reflection in microcosm of what was actually taking place in Spain'.[28]

Littlewood and MacColl's performance choices stressed group identity and social conscience. They orchestrated intricate crowd scenes where the mood of resentment and defiance prevailed as the conflict between the powerless, but socially strong, and the powerful, but morally bankrupt, escalated. The set design by Bill Sharples, a sculptor and engineer, also involved the work of the artists Barbara Niven, who designed the costumes, and Ern Brooks, who painted a large backcloth in colours and textures associated with Spain. The set emphasised communal space through the central image of the circular drinking well around which the villagers congregated to debate their circumstance and action, with the visual reminder of a towering rampant sheep standing in for the domineering, malevolent presence of the commander/General Franco.

Balletic dance interludes, conceived and executed by Audrey Lloyd, underscored the moral struggle at the heart of each act, and MacColl threaded through stirring Republican battle songs, creating a chance to bring all the actors together in rousing collective voice. Critics warmly received the production, with the *Manchester Guardian* reviewer reassuring its readers that Theatre Union had created a show whose 'propagandist content will not inspire, convert, or offend the most susceptible of voters, but whose aesthetic qualities will be a delight to all'.[29] Littlewood revived *The Sheep Well* in 1955, a year dominated by successful classics such as *Richard II*, *Volpone* and *Arden of Faversham* at the Theatre Royal. Given the production's close proximity to *Arden of Faversham*, several reviewers understandably picked up on a welcome revival of another neglected classic, but the historical distance from the politicising frame of the Spanish Civil War resulted in a generally lukewarm reception.

Littlewood and MacColl followed *Fuente Ovejuna* with an adaptation of Erwin Piscator's 1927 version of Jaroslav Hašek's novel,

The Good Soldier Schweik (1923) produced at the Lesser Free Trade Hall in Manchester on 12 May 1939. Tackling the bumbling, verbally incontinent, inept everyman figure of Schweik, whose wide-eyed wonderment at the travails of the world provides a humorous and penetrating attack on war, proved a significant theatrical challenge. Without the technical and creative resources available to Piscator that enabled him to use moving platforms and escalators to convey Schweik's journey, Littlewood and MacColl relied on a simple revolving stage, exaggerated cartoon-like characters, amplified gramophone music between scenes and symbolic dance. According to John Falstaff, this final element was surprisingly successful: 'A ballet of two young men, presenting the attitudes of war to the beat of the drum, was exceedingly well done, and their symbolic fusion into the brotherhood of peace was the highest note of the show.'[30]

Most notably, Ern Brook's comic-strip-style black-and-white line drawings depicting Schweik's journey were back-projected onto a large screen using innovative technology designed by a group of young technicians at Metropolitan Vickers.[31] Critical reception of this rambling picaresque work suggests it suffered from excessive, but ultimately unrealisable, ambition. As the reviewer in the *Manchester Guardian* poetically surmised, 'To fashion a coat of such exotic cut from a meagre strip of homespun is beyond the scope of any tailor's art ... The result is, frankly, a failure – but a fascinating and almost a glorious failure.'[32] Adapting a piece that had previously appeared in *New York Life*, the programme note stressed Littlewood and MacColl's admiration for Hašek's humanitarianism, satirical wit and bitter anti-militarism and declared Schweik

> a symbol of tortured mankind; and pictured against this kindly imbecile is one of the most biting satires of the modern world ever penned. Here you see the pomposity of generals, the corruption of empire, the inanity of doctors, the frailty of priests, the brutality of police, the hypocrisy of society. No diatribe, however burning, could present half so sad and cockeyed a world as that seen through the eyes of the hilarious half-witted Schweik.[33]

Schweik's blundering ebullience and inability to self-censor comically exposes corruption, abuse, pomposity and injustice. Moreover, as he walks and walks in the opposite direction to the front, his pedestrian momentum highlights the humility of one man's inability to function in the barbarous circumstances of the First World War. Equally, his encounters reveal a wider community alienated from the moral depravity of war and warfare, but ultimately implicated in its consequences. By the end of the play, Schweik reaches the front and there is a sense of disappointment as the creativity and playfulness of Schweik's evasions give way to a horizon of barbed wire and the sounds of men wounded and dying. Before this lovable antihero dies in a hail of gunfire, in MacColl's translation he inarticulately announces his plans to desert, exclaiming,

> So long, brother. Brother ... brother ... brothers. We're going home, brother. Home! Beg to report you Generals ... Beg to report all you fine gentlemen who make wars ... beg to report you've killed my mates ... killed 'em you bastards. Beg to report I'm going home. Fight your own bleeding war.[34]

In the immediate run-up to the Second World War, Littlewood and MacColl designed this representation of despair and desertion to unsettle and destabilise the momentum towards war, to offer a pause, an interruption in the audience's mind as they contemplated the impending hostilities.

Littlewood held *The Good Soldier Schweik* in very high regard and vowed to revive the production. Initially, MacColl revised his earlier adaptation for a production at the Theatre Royal in November 1954, with George Cooper, adopting a Lancastrian dialect, in the title role. Notes surviving in the Lord Chamberlain's Collection assert, 'This adaptation is, I think, better than Irwin Piscator's one, licensed in 1939; but I should have thought that this kind of coarse satire on matters military with its obvious anti-militaristic angle, would attract small audiences in an age of bigger and better miseries.'[35] In fact, the production received a positive response from critics and the local Stratford audience. According to Peggy Soundy, who founded the Theatre Royal supporters' club, the local audience connected to the populist broad humour and knockabout style and 'they felt *Schweik* was, somehow, part of them'.[36]

This popular appeal instigated a further revival in November 1955, with Maxwell Shaw as Schweik. Interestingly, both productions transferred to the West End, but whereas the first run at the Embassy Theatre received scant critical attention, this changed considerably by the time Theatre Workshop presented it at the Duke of York's in March 1956. Pre-empting the production's success at the Théâtre des Nations in Paris later in the year, Harold Hobson harks back to the company's prior success there with *Volpone* and *Arden of Faversham*, writing that

> Theatre Workshop throws out of the window the naturalistic acting which is the staple of the British theatre, and which seems to French audiences indistinguishable from immobility. Its style is caricatural, charadelike, simplified and exaggerated . . . it resembles, in its flickering intensity, its play of muscle and feature, its slinky walk and fluttering eyelids, the grimacing figures one sees in early comic films.[37]

What is most striking about the critical reception that greeted these revivals is the emphasis on theatricality over theme, presentational style over substance, the comedic exuberance over the satire; as if the decade that had passed since the close of the Second World War had numbed critics to the play's sharp political critique.

Who is the real enemy?

The Nazi–Soviet non-aggression pact signed on 23 August 1939 caused a dilemma for many British communists as the deeply contradictory position of the Communist Party became clear. Following events in Spain, the Communist Party was widely associated with a committed anti-fascist stance; although subsequent revelations have brought to light the fact that Stalin worked to quell the Republican movement in Spain,[38] in the lead-up to the Second World War this dubious position was completely up-front as the Soviet Union seemingly kowtowed to Hitler's demands. Struggling with the ideological volte-face, Harry Pollitt, the British Communist Party general secretary, refused to advocate this new position and resigned, maintaining his view that fascism had to be fought with full force wherever it was found.

Referring to the Spanish Civil War, Littlewood admitted that 'the tragedy of non-intervention weighed heavily on us. It was clear that Hitler and Mussolini were using Spain as a rehearsal for the war they were preparing.'[39] It is clear that Littlewood and MacColl vehemently opposed the British government's attempts to contain the war in Spain through a passive non-intervention policy. But in the immediate run-up to the Second World War their position became compromised as they tried to hold the Communist Party line that presented this war as a misguided imperialist venture that worked against the interests of the working class.

In this climate, Littlewood and MacColl began work on *Last Edition*, a large-scale living newspaper described as 'the story of the deception and betrayal of a nation'.[40] With this piece they aimed to denounce what they viewed as an imperialist war that was part of an ongoing betrayal of international working-class interests. A document called 'Memorandum on Living Newspaper on the War' contains fascinating information on their thematic concerns with the interconnectivity between fascism, colonialism and an anti-Soviet and anti-working-class agenda. This outline plan for the piece contains reference to several areas, including 'The holy crusade against Hitlerism', 'Spain – Britain's part in betrayal of the Spanish people', 'Czechoslovakia – France and Britain's complicity', 'the anti-Soviet (therefore anti-working class – anti-democratic) role of British imperialism' and the 'state of affairs in British Colonies'.[41] Not all the themes outlined found a place in the final production, which eventually divided into three episodes – 'The Home Front', 'Spain' and 'Munich' – that collectively contained twenty scenes with such titles as 'Hunger', 'Jarama' and 'Who Is the Real Enemy?', but warmongering, civil liberties, workers' rights, an anti-Soviet conspiracy and the complicity of the British government in Hitler's increasing power remained central components.[42]

As Harker acknowledges, 'history catches up with *Last Edition* in the show's last half hour, which deals with events post-1939', when 'the pressure to make sense of recent events through the buckled lens of the party line manifests itself in theatrical diminuendo as multi-perspectival montage makes way for one-eyed plodding linearity'.[43] The result is a performance that disturbingly erases the ethical dilemma posed by Nazism and the genocidal policies pursued by Hitler, and omits Stalin from the narrative of pre-war history. These omissions undoubtedly explain MacColl's subsequent denouncement of his script in a letter dated 14 December 1983, written prior to the publication of extracts from the text in *Agit-Prop to Theatre Workshop*. It reads, 'It really is a dreadful script and every time I look at it I am overcome with embarrassment. In some odd way I have succeeded in combining mawkishness with belligerence and the result is nauseating.'[44] Theatre Union premiered *Last Edition* as a club performance, to avoid the Lord Chamberlain's censorship, on 14 March 1940 at the Round House in the Ancoats district of Manchester. Despite being a self-proclaimed living newspaper, far from being a dry articulation of information, *Last Edition* used dance, burlesque, song, comedy, naturalistic scenes, parodies of popular genres, radio voice-overs, narrators and documentary evidence. Inspired by companies such as the Blue Blouse troupes in Russia working with the living-newspaper format and by Hallie Flanagan's work with the American Federal Theatre Project (1935–9) trying to attract working-class audiences with entertaining and educational, politically motivated and satirical living newspapers including *One-Third of a Nation* (1938), Littlewood and MacColl felt the time was right to approach this direct form of communication from their perspective.[45] Their perspective ultimately fused topical political commentary with audacious theatrical experimentation.[46] Harker pithily refers to 'the interrogative, eclectic, multi-perspectival theatrical aesthetic' of *Last Edition*, and also signals the careful ideological negotiation that took place to enable 'an anti-fascist, anti-National Government political line that combined swingeing critique with an affirmation of "the people's" political and cultural resourcefulness'.[47] As this description indicates, *Last Edition* covered a lot of ground.

In addition to the central stage area, Littlewood used two platforms that ran down each side of the auditorium so that the eclectic, variety-style mix of sketches, song and dance would confront and engulf the audience as they played simultaneously or in carefully orchestrated counterpoint. A young Anthony Burgess saw the production and commented on the impact of its formal promiscuity in the following terms:

> She presented enormities like the 1935 Anglo-German naval agreement in lateral form, gossip spraying out of frank but anaemic love-making between members of the ruling class. Hitler and Mussolini pranced in a ballet as good as *The Green Table*. The lighting plot was complex and oiled like machinery. Amplified gramophone records swelled in on split second cues. All the actors were amateurs, but Joan Littlewood had drilled them to the screaming limit.[48]

According to Robert Leach, the intercutting scenes 'encouraged interruption – or "contrast" – as a dramaturgical device, and helped to create urgency and forward momentum',[49] a sense of momentum that captured the frenetic course of events that characterised the lead-up to the Second World War. Stage directions for the opening sequence set on the New Year's Eve ushering in 1934 illustrate the highly theatrical nature of the piece:

> Music, faint at first, builds up. The stage has begun to fill with people. Three girls with buzzers. A young man and women with parcels. Old man and woman. The dancing couple join them. Drunk enters with bottle, dances from couple to couple. Whore weaves round crowd. They all dance. Two unemployed men enter L&R, move at counter rhythm through the dancing crowd. Whenever the drunk moves to a new crowd there is a burst of laughter.[50]

The frenetic movement, energy and air of 'new-year' expectancy is undercut by the presence of the unemployed men who provide a counter-narrative to a radio recording of Ramsay MacDonald claiming that despite difficulties 'we are travelling on the right road', initiating eight Home Front scenes.[51] Drawing on extensive documentary evidence, the scenes present narratives of disillusionment, despair and suicide as men, women and families grapple with the divisive and demeaning human consequences of the Depression. Like *Miracle at Verdun* before it, the spectres of the dead haunt the stage, launching a politics of memory and inheritance that demands to be atoned. Jacques Derrida extolled the virtues of communicating with the dead in *Spectres of Marx* (1994) and his premise is illuminating in this context:

> No justice . . . seems possible or thinkable without the principle of some *responsibility*, beyond all living present, within that which disjoins the living present, before the ghosts of those who are not yet born or who are already dead, be they victims of wars, political or other kinds of violence, nationalist, racist, colonialist, sexist or other kinds of exterminations, victims of the oppressions of capitalist imperialisms or any of the forms of totalitarianism. Without this *non-contemporaneity with itself in the living present*, without that which secretly unhinges it, without this responsibility and this respect for justice concerning those who *are not there*, of those who are no longer or who are not yet *present and living*, what sense would there be to ask the question 'where?' 'where tomorrow?' 'whither?'[52]

In *Last Edition*, Littlewood and MacColl animated the dead of the Depression: 'William Castle of Leeds [who] cut his throat and James Armstrong of Burnley [who] hung himself in the kitchen of the house where he couldn't pay the rent'.[53] These spectres contextualise the Hunger March scenes and 'force them to see that we're human'.[54] The 'them' remain anonymous, the faceless bureaucrats and means-test assessors, whilst the dead and current victims of the failings of capitalism are provided the dignity of voice and presence. These images are productive because they signal a refusal to be brushed under the carpet – they confront the audience to listen to the plight of the individual in the morass and the wider social frames contributing to self-annihilation.

Throughout *Last Edition*, there is an interesting gender dynamic at play.[55] Capitalism and the war machine are seen to strip ordinary working men of their humanity, to reduce them to easily dispensable fodder not worthy of clean air, a decent standard of living or life itself, if these things eat into profits or 'national' interests. Writing in an early creative notebook, Littlewood explained how

> young men are forced into the war machine – and degraded by every indignity which the bourgeoisie has learned in its history. Young fellows from factory benches and mines and mills … live their lives by numbers, they learn to kill by numbers … they are going to be lead like sheep to the slaughter again and again.[56]

In contrast to the vision of emasculated working-class men subject to the forces of the state and capital, the women represented in *Last Edition* lament war and refuse to kowtow to narratives of heroism. Their bitter scepticism and narratives of loss and mourning stand as compelling emotional counterpoints to the chilling dissections of capitalism, government failings, corrupt policy and personal ambitions. These women narrate the consequences of male-led warmongering, profit-seeking and imperial expansion to provide an ethical core throughout *Last Edition*.

Addressing the run-up to war, the production undermined Britain's claims to moral superiority by likening Hitler's plans for Germany to England's imperial history. MacColl and Littlewood grounded their attack on the hypocrisy of the nation in extensive coverage of the controversial Munich Agreement and policy of appeasement.[57] Under the title 'Launcelot's Dream', the then prime minister, Neville Chamberlain, was satirically portrayed as a whimsical fairytale figure who dreams of wood nymphs in bathing costumes and gold haloes whilst he fishes for a 'four-power pact', but is unable to catch the 'big one with the red scales' (Communist Russia). Rather than a credible politician with the nation's best interests at heart, Chamberlain is a flawed knight in shining armour capitulating to Hitler's ambitions. Theatre Union also employed a spoof of an American-style gangster movie, 'Who Killed Johnny the Czech?', a classic gangster narrative of false allegiances, double-crossings and shoot-outs to capture the spirit and failure of the Munich Agreement.

Above all, *Last Edition* promotes the view that the aristocracy and the government were keen to support Franco in Spain as a stand against socialist Republicanism and content to condone Hitler's actions prior to the outbreak of war as long as he committed Germany to fighting the communist threat coming from Russia, a view that Goorney explained needed to 'be set in the context of the refusal of the Western powers to co-operate with the Soviet Union in the pre-war years when the outbreak of hostilities might have been prevented'.[58] In contrast to Chamberlain's fear of Russia, *Last Edition* calls for an international workers' revolt against the war and a refusal to condone attacks on Russia. A crowd begins to chant, 'Not a ship, not a man, not a gun, against the Russian Workers' Republic – stop intervention.'[59] Instead of inciting worker-versus-worker conflict in war, *Last Edition*, like *John Bullion*, ends with a transnational call for the workers of the world to condemn the war as capitalist profiteering and to embrace the class war as the only cause worth fighting for.

A particularly significant performance device in *Last Edition* involved the performers stepping out from the scenes to address the audience as themselves. At one point an actor explained how Theatre Union enabled him to learn a craft without 'letting my life become divorced from other peoples' lives', which is followed by the assertion that 'whether we wish it or not, politics play just as much a part in the theatre as in any other sector of human life'.[60] These performed interruptions asserted the function of *Last Edition* as public political discourse. The content of the interruptions implores the audience to see themselves as part of a wider body politic that has the power to question established authority as part of the healthy functioning of a democratic society. However, as the war effort escalated, their uncompromising stance drew the attention of the police, who set about intimidating members of the company and eventually arrested Littlewood and MacColl for giving an unlicenced public performance during a run at the Milton Hall on Deansgate. After their day in court, MacColl was fined, Littlewood was bound over and Theatre Union was thrown into chaos.

After these travails, Theatre Union opted for a safer antiwar vehicle by producing Aristophanes' seminal antiwar play *Lysistrata* (later adapted by MacColl and renamed *Operation Olive Branch*). The narrative of *Lysistrata* focuses on Lysistrata's decision to convince the women of Athens to resist their desires and sexual relations with their husbands until the men agree to a peaceful resolution to a war that has raged for sixteen years. The show opened at the Milton Hall, Deansgate, on 18 January 1941. Once again, Theatre Union stressed the forces of creativity and theatre's role as an interrogative cultural practice, declaring in the programme that 'as the war intensifies the work of the theatre becomes more important'.[61] And, 'a classical play about ordinary citizens resisting war was considered nicely in step with the Communist Party's current line'.[62]

The version renamed *Operation Olive Branch* first appeared at St John's Hall, Middlesbrough, on 6 January 1947. After reading MacColl's adaptation, the Lord Chamberlain's reader described it as 'a good clean version', a surprising verdict given its propensity for salacious innuendo and lewd stage business.[63] However, the programme note for its production at the Central Library Theatre in Manchester, where it ran throughout August 1947, frames the antiwar agenda the company were keen to promote:

> When Aristophanes' great comedy was written the power of Athens was already beginning to crumble; she was no longer mistress of the seas; her fleet, the finest the ancient world had ever known, had been destroyed at Syracuse; but war mongers still held power. Some of the colonies tried to break from Athens and make peace, but these attempts were put down with horrible brutality. War and famine had exhausted the people. Out of this grim situation the playwright spoke, he put forward his solution to the ever-lasting problem of war. The world has laughed at his play for 2000 years. But, underlying the laughter, there are deep beliefs, beliefs in life and love rather than hatred and war.[64]

MacColl's prologue, a scene between four soldiers set in an Athenian camp at the front, rests on conversational banter as the men play cards and one writes a letter home. The soldiers reminisce about women loved and lost, about the thrill of sexual contact, and offer satirical suggestions for the letter-writer, including:

> Dearest, last week we were billeted in a Megarian village and our sergeant was stabbed in a wine-shop brawl. The commander of the regiment cordoned the village off and burned the villagers alive. Hoping the Spartans are not doing the same to you. I remain, your ever loving Strepsiades.[65]

The prefiguring of *Oh What a Lovely War*'s trench scenes is unmistakable. Assessing *Operation Olive Branch* in a radio documentary, Littlewood stressed its topical references and popular cultural forms, concluding that 'Ewan has attempted to translate an archaic form into twentieth century idiom'.[66] MacColl used his extensive musical knowledge to parody twelve-bar blues songs: 'I've been in Athens, I've been in Corinth too. Been at Pylos, I've been in Persia too, But I never saw a woman who was half as sweet as you.'[67] He also employed his burgeoning skills as a folk singer to sing unaccompanied, apart from incantations provided by the bored soldiers in their camp.

Regional dialect was particularly important for localising, contemporising and politicising Theatre Workshop's adaptation in performance. MacColl wrote the women from the provinces with a strong Scottish dialect and the Spartans as Irish, and references to disputed territories and internal colonisation resonated with campaigns for Scottish and Irish independence. For instance, Lysistrata pointedly states, 'And as for those colonies bound by ties of steel to Athens – we say release them. Sever the ancient and corrupt imperialism which is strangling them.'[68] The comment takes on added local flavour when the character Myrrine claims in broad Scots dialect, 'Anagyre belongs to the folk o' Anagyre. It's oor ain land again.'[69]

The incongruity of merging classical references with a distinct Scottish idiom in performance added theatricality and humour as well as bringing the depiction of a war-torn community closer to home. Talking about the effect of the men's absence from their homes, Myrrine insists that 'mine's trauchlin' aboot the streets of Pylos eating his hair toot thinking aboot the hairvest he should be reaping noo. Zeus in heaven, he's been awa' sae lang he's almost forgotten his native tongue.'[70] The ineffectual, doddering chorus of old men took on contemporary political resonance by aping Winston Churchill's distinctive language traits, as when Strymadorus responds to the news that the women are marching on the citadel to demand peace:

> Monstrous! Oh, what degenerate times we live in, to be sure! Friends, the future is in our hands. The barbarians are at the gates.

1. *Operation Olive Branch* (1947).

> We must fight on the beaches; in the streets, in the clubs, in the barber's shops.[71]

The reviewer in the *Felixstowe Times* admired 'the skill and aptness with which [MacColl] fits in extracts from some of Churchill's most famous war speeches', but some reviewers found this addition clumsy and obtrusive.[72]

Talking about design for *Operation Olive Branch*, Bill Davidson made the interesting observation that the company 'approached the problem architecturally, that is in terms of space rather than colour', resulting in twelve planes of various sizes that could be arranged in various spatial configurations in order to 'give the action both depth and height'.[73] However, evidence is mixed regarding the success of this aspect of the production, with one reviewer calling on Littlewood to 'find a better means of expressing her ideas than by sending the cast capering up and down steps all evening'.[74] Nonetheless, this setting, an ambitious lighting design, the use of movement and creative ensemble playing impressed other critics. Recognising the importance of the ensemble and Littlewood's attempts to capture scenes reminiscent of a Greek frieze, one reviewer noted 'that the production of Miss Joan Littlewood ... was outstanding for beauty of effect in the composition of stage pictures'.[75]

The most extraordinary aspect of *Operation Olive Branch* involved the conflation of creative endeavour with everyday life as the damning consequences of the brutal, dehumanising and disturbing experience of war broke through the veneer of theatrical artifice. Reflecting his life in art, MacColl, a pacifist and conscientious war objector, had included a deserter character written in Lallans in his adaptation. He planned to play the part and, according to Littlewood, 'The deserter became an expression of his own isolation', as his own deserter status forced him to keep an uncharacteristically low profile.[76] Hence, during rehearsals for *Operation Olive Branch*, the company, many of whom had colluded in shielding MacColl from the authorities, were acutely aware of the harsh penalties faced by men who withdrew from the war effort as a way of untangling their personal or political conscience from the demands of the state. But nothing could have prepared them for the events to come.

A week before the production opened, military police arrested MacColl for desertion during the Second World War. He was transferred to detention barracks at Northallerton and then to Parkhall Camp on the Welsh border, where he spent a solitary Christmas and New Year awaiting his court-martial, scheduled for 17 February 1947. However, MacColl's court-martial was cancelled on spurious medical grounds after a psychiatric profile declared him to be suffering from a form of epilepsy and he was moved to Northfield Military Hospital in Birmingham. After eleven weeks in hospital he was released and on 4 June he was formally discharged from the army.[77] These events shrouded the production of *Operation Olive Branch*.

If this situation were not bad enough, the performer who took over from MacColl attempted suicide and suffered a nervous breakdown a few days before the first performance. He admitted he was 'living on a knife edge'[78] – a traumatised state brought on by his wartime experiences. Whilst it is impossible confidently to speculate on the reasons for any mental illness, Benedict Ellis had witnessed unimaginable scales of human atrocity, and had been caught up in a bomb blast on D-Day and invalided out of the army.[79] Suffering from what is now well known as post-traumatic stress disorder, he was committed to an institution and, according to Littlewood and Goorney, a progressive doctor advised that he should continue to perform in *Operation Olive Branch* for therapeutic reasons.

Recalling the first night, Littlewood wrote, 'Questioned roughly by soldiers, the deserter begins his great apologia. Ben spoke quietly, simply, but with passionate conviction – pale as he was, half-naked, the effect was profoundly moving. In the audience, absolute silence. It was as if they all held their breath'.[80] The journalist and Labour MP Tom Driberg attended the first night. Alluding to events with MacColl and Ellis, he recorded, 'Despite – maybe because of – this ... all the cast played on Monday with exceptional brilliance', and, 'One of the most moving scenes (not in the ancient Greek original) showed the capture and killing of a deserter from the Athenian army.'[81] The immediacy of personal experience ruptured and uniquely charged this theatrical event – a sense of urgency that had understandably abated by the time Littlewood revived the production for the Theatre Royal and the Edinburgh Festival in May and September 1953.

'And nothing of morality remained': theatre after Auschwitz and the atom bomb

Whilst embarking on a brutal and bloody war against Hitler's Germany, the allied forces could adopt a position of moral authority against the appalling sickness of the Holocaust. Nonetheless, air raids and mass bombing changed the nature of war as they diluted moral identification with another human being and a sense of culpability in their death. The gradual erosion of the moral imperative that prohibited the intentional killing of civilians in war reached an apotheosis with the allied bombing of Dresden and with the dropping of the first atomic bomb on Hiroshima on 6 August 1945 and another one on Nagasaki three days later. These actions changed the ethical landscape irrevocably.

The bomb was an indiscriminate weapon of mass destruction, a way of culling men, women and children not only immediately, but also in the slow collateral deaths inflicted by radiation poisoning and the decimation of internal infrastructure such as water supplies and hospitals. Whilst many would identify the Allied forces as participating in a 'just war', Hiroshima and Nagasaki were, for many, disproportionate acts that failed to observe the moral boundaries of the 'just-war' thesis. And, after the war, nuclear proliferation continued.[82]

As the Cold War dominated international affairs, the threat of nuclear war was a very real and present danger as people lived with the constant fear that any escalation of hostilities between the East and the West could trigger nuclear disaster. British political, economic and intellectual life 'had been transformed by wartime participation in the development of the atomic bomb, and by the decision – taken in secret by the first post-war Labour government – to establish an independent nuclear force'.[83] Throughout the 1950s the British peace movement gathered momentum until the formation of the Campaign for Nuclear Disarmament (CND) in 1958. The campaign largely took the position that following the decline of empire, Britain should assert itself as 'a great moral rather than a military influence in the world'.[84] In 1957, the dramatist J. B. Priestley joined the fray with a powerful *New Statesman* article, 'Britain and the Nuclear Bombs', that railed against the complacent acceptance of nuclear weapons and urged a retreat from the 'idiot game' of brinkmanship that characterised the arms race.[85]

The horrific implications and widespread anxieties generated by the discovery of atomic weapons provided source material for *Uranium 235* (1946). Spurred on by his colleagues, MacColl drew on the Smythe Report, which explained the process leading to the bombing of Hiroshima and Nagasaki, which ushered in an age dominated by the possibility of total annihilation and the acceleration of the arms race as Russia sought to equal and exceed America's nuclear capability. A generation who once had faith in science to alleviate, if not cure, the problems of mankind now faced the daunting reality that their political leaders were prepared to use science and technology for destructive purposes. It seemed that whilst scientists were perfecting the art of destruction, the art of living and responsibility for humanity was being lost – a fear articulated by Miroslav Pecujlic's term 'social exterminism', 'by which he means that the danger of the arms race is species destruction, not just through nuclear war itself, but equally through a slow process of what he calls social involution, the reversal of civilised progress'.[86] There was a widespread feeling that the very *possibility* of nuclear war ruptured humanity from itself and created a moral vacuum at the very heart of civilisation, as Jeff Nuttall encapsulates in *Bomb Culture* (1968):

> We had espoused an evil as great as the Nazi genocide, we had espoused the instrument for the termination of our benevolent institution, society, and our certain identity, human. We had espoused a monstrous uncertainty both of future and of morality . . . and nothing of morality remained.[87]

In *Uranium 235* MacColl explores the ethical implications of nuclear energy and warfare by creating a 'historical pageant for the Advancement of Science'.[88] As Jonathan Key notes, the historical focus surprisingly places 'the atomic bomb within a tradition of heroic scientific progress'.[89] Even so, the play's ominous opening words, 'Good night', followed by the firewatcher's portentous speech forewarning of 'a universe of endless desolation' amidst sound effects of planes, bombs and an air-raid siren, signals a less optimistic reading.[90] In the first half of the play, MacColl presents scientists pushing the foundations of knowledge into new directions as a largely sceptical populace maintain faith in religion and mysticism over scientific proof and reasoning. Focusing on how machinations of power and capital undermine the potentially liberating and democratic potential of science, MacColl begins in Athens in 470 BC with Democritus' challenge to the gods and Greek mythology through his discovery of atoms as the source of all material existence.

Working through the implications of John Dalton's atomic theory of matter, to the Curies' discovery of radium, to quantum theory and Einstein's theory of relativity, MacColl stresses the enrichment of society through scientific progress. However, this tenor shifts as he confronts the mid-twentieth century and begins to echo Albert Camus's 1946 essay in which he holds science to account, arguing that 'its latest theoretical advances have brought it to the point of negating itself while its perfected technology threatens the globe itself with destruction'.[91] Referencing the bombings in the Spanish Civil War, the death of millions in concentration camps and the threat of nuclear annihilation, MacColl questions the direction science has taken towards more efficient and effective modes of human annihilation. And, with strong links to Brecht's *Life of Galileo* (1947), he puts science on trial for generating the means to destroy the human race in the pursuit of profit and power. He also puts humanity on trial by accusing it of apathetic indifference to and disengagement from the political processes that could change the future.

MacColl indicated numerous theatrical styles and techniques in his script and Littlewood brought these to life in performance, helped by experimental lighting and an exhilarating soundscape. She admitted that the piece could easily 'become a sermon or an illustrated lecture',[92] and worked hard to foreground its fast-paced, episodic structure, which moves through agitprop, expressionism, contemporary dance and parodies of popular culture. Audience plants, recorded voices, actors as narrators and direct address sit alongside extended scenes that work through physical and popular comedic techniques, as well as hard-hitting visual imagery. The audience were discouraged from adopting a cosy, passive reflective stance by the abrupt shifts in style, tone and modes of address that invited connections across scenes and active participation. At one point an actor using a microphone admits that the play is 'an attempt to discover the location of the audience's conscience', an invitation for the audience to judge themselves in relation to the characters and to think about their own ideological stance and themselves in relation to their responsibility to a wider global community.[93]

Kirsten Shepherd-Barr states that the original ending of *Uranium 235* signalled hope as the actors invited the audience to choose which path the future of nuclear energy would take. This implies that there was a choice to be made that could harness science and technology to improve rather than debase humanity. At the time, MacColl believed that the presence of atomic weaponry itself was not intrinsically bad and that the idea of 'atoms for peace' could work in a large-scale Mexican stand-off. But by the time he had reworked the play for publication in

1986, MacColl had changed his position and captured the anger, despair and disillusionment of many when he added references to nuclear reactor incidents from Windscale in 1957 to Three Mile Island in 1979.[94] He was particularly fearful of nuclear power's impact on the environment and ecological infrastructure and had the publication come a little later he could have added the devastating events in Chernobyl during 1986.

Reviews of the production consistently picked up on a courageous theatrical eccentricity that included putting 'electrons in tights to explain the atomic theory [and] ... power and greed in a frock coat and smoked glasses'.[95] The reviewer for the *Glasgow Herald* found in this 'impressive and thought-provoking piece', that not only 'has [MacColl] something to say; he has an unusual method of saying it'.[96] In one scene, the central scientist figure encounters a chorus of dancing alchemists and, in another scene, the expressionistic figures of the Puppet Master, his secretary and a masked figure representing Death. In a radio documentary Littlewood explained how she was conveying Marie and Pierre Curie's key scientific discoveries 'as a waltz, moving through three acting areas, which symbolize three periods in the lives of the Curies. Perfect synchronisation of light, music, movement and speech are absolutely necessary.'[97]

Similarly, quantum theory was explained through Einstein's 'atomic ballet' that used bodies pirouetting, colliding and bouncing off each other to represent the activity of electrons, protons and neutrons in the generation of energy. Nonetheless, when the Puppet Master character announces that 'Ballet, I'm afraid, is a little too precious for what we're looking for. Ours is a mass audience',[98] he prefigures Littlewood, who appraised this section as 'looking marvellous but I doubt whether anyone was any the wiser at the end of it'.[99] In a metatheatrical move, the company replayed the scene as a parody of a 1930s gangster movie (seen previously in *Last Edition*), a deliberate attempt to relay the information in a more palatable way for its target audience.

First performed as a short play at the Newcastle People's Theatre in January 1946 and developed into a two-hour version first staged at the Community Theatre, Blackburn, on 24 April 1946, *Uranium 235* became a mainstay of Theatre Workshop's repertoire. It toured south Wales in late 1950 and Scandinavia in February and March 1951, and played a week-long run at the Edinburgh Festival in August 1951. Most famously, it played a week at Butlin's Holiday Camp in Filey, the commercial epicentre of working-class leisure, where the company were keen to test its appeal. Reviewing the show, Ian McKay commented on the 'experimental', 'revolutionary' and 'remarkable' nature of the production, but above all, stressed the incongruity of its surroundings:

> Of all the bizarre and unexpected things you come across in this amazing phantasmagoria of a place there is nothing quite so surprising – not even the legless man who dives into what looks like a saucerful of water from a seventy-five feet tower – as the brilliant band of young strolling players who have been packing the giant camp theatre this week.[100]

Facing competition from ballroom dancing, wrestling and bingo, the show was a great success, according to MacColl, who insisted that the audience reframed the piece in relation to cultural forms and knowledge with which they were more familiar: 'They treated the play as they would have treated an exciting game of football. They cheered, groaned, shouted their approval, and when one of the actors tried to make a planned interruption from the auditorium they howled him down.'[101]

Uranium 235 equally impressed the theatre impresario Sam Wanamaker, and the actor Michael Redgrave. They took it upon themselves to organise and support a twelve-day run of it at the Embassy Theatre in London during May 1952, which also led to a short run at the Comedy Theatre in the West End in June. Despite high-profile celebrity support, critical reception was mixed. The reviewer for *The Stage* drew attention to the way that the production was 'criticised on the grounds that its expressionistic style is now out of date', but argued that 'its form is, surely, much less threadbare and no less legitimate than the standard three-act domestic drama that is currently accepted as the theatre's norm'.[102] Unfortunately, rather than praising Theatre Workshop for being at the vanguard of theatrical experimentation and having important things to say, the London critics were largely dismissive and, according to Littlewood, 'The public who came couldn't make head or tail of us.'[103]

MacColl's *The Travellers*, the last show Theatre Workshop produced before moving to the Theatre Royal Stratford East, developed many themes from *Uranium 235*. First performed at Oddfellows Hall on 29 July 1952 as part of the Edinburgh Festival, this dark, intense political thriller captures the spirit of the Cold War by emphasising ideological divides and a culture of suspicion, secrecy, unease, recrimination and entrenched hostility. The play accuses the West of historical amnesia and of hurtling headlong into the path of further death and destruction. It rails against apathy and advocates the importance of ethical witnessing, responsibility and human agency through the choices the travellers face between communism and capitalism, individualism and collectivity, peace and war. On the front of his script MacColl typed a telling phrase: 'It will require heroism to be men as long as people are not truly human.'[104]

Harker situates the play in terms of MacColl's decision to rejoin the Communist Party and his reacquaintance with party activism. '*The Travellers* was a measure of his reintegration; in form and content it toed the party line with a discipline not seen since *Last Edition*'.[105] Certainly, the formal experimentation, direct address and sharp sense of humour of earlier plays is missing from this rather dry and moralising play and the themes of American imperialism, anti-individualism and collective responsibility are writ large. The glaring absence of any reference to the brutality of Stalinism, the recent purges or show trials is equally palpable in a one-sided attack on the Western side of the East/West Cold War divide. As a result, critical reception focused on the extent to which the play was a vehicle for propaganda. The reviewer in the *Scotsman*, whilst acknowledging the strength of the production and praising Littlewood for proving 'once again her masterly handling of grouping and movement', had reservations about the play, particularly the 'Marxist clichés' and 'open Communist propaganda'.[106] Interestingly, C. D. Heriot, from the Lord Chamberlain's office, offered a more nuanced reading of the play:

> The fact that the prime mover in the plot is an acknowledged Communist does not necessarily brand this play as Communist propaganda – though the Party will undoubtedly claim it for its

own. The play is undoubtedly anti-American, but that is, after all, a point of view not entirely limited to the Communists.[107]

Unfortunately, two members of the Edinburgh People's Festival committee found the implied communist propaganda deeply troubling and their insistence on an emergency committee meeting to discuss the subject had far-reaching consequences when the Scottish TUC withdrew funding and added the festival to its list of proscribed organisations, which also prompted the Scottish Labour Party to withdraw its association.[108] At this historical remove, it is easy to read these decisions as indicative of the Cold War climate the play investigates, but this narrow assessment of the play detracts from its important critique in the immediate context of nuclear proliferation and the Korean War. In fact, its antiwar stance prompted Donald Douglas of the *Daily Worker* to assert, 'If there was a Nobel Peace prize for dramatists, it is unlikely, things being what they are, that Ewan MacColl would win it. But he would deserve it on the strength of *The Travellers* alone.'[109] In an attempt to reappraise *The Travellers*, whilst not wishing to ignore its dogmatism, I want to draw attention to its intriguing portrait of displacement, exile, trauma and loss that provides a more complex reading of contemporary politics and individual psychology than a strict communist interpretation might imply.

Set in the immediate postwar period, the characters – persecuted people, the displaced, economic migrants and exiles, who all wish to relocate to a new life in America – come together for a train journey. Embarking from an unspecified European station, the international travellers represent a cross-section of Europe's nation states and the train provides a microcosm of the world they have in common. In bringing this eclectic group together, marking their national differences as well as their common hope that they are bound for a new life in the land of opportunity, it is as if MacColl were attempting to represent the kind of politicised literal and cognitive space Hannah Arendt describes in the following terms: 'By establishing a space between individuals, an in-between which connects and separates them at the same time, the world provides the physical context within which political action can arise.'[110] Daniel Pick has written extensively about 'the image of war as the unstoppable and all-consuming machine, the runaway vehicle',[111] and the image of the train provides the central theatrical metaphor in *The Travellers*, whereby 'it's racing away from life / Death is the engineer / And war is the destination'.[112] Theatrically, Littlewood's production relied on ambitious staging that involved a simulated train complete with compartments, guard's van and platform that extended from the stage out through the audience. She positioned the audience either side of the set so they were involved in the action but also aware of their fellow audience members on the opposite side. Littlewood used sound and motion to convey the rhythm of the train and sound effects such as raising the volume of the clatter of the wheels to heighten intensity and the sense of claustrophobia at key dramatic moments.

The train embarks a few minutes before midnight, which heightens the sense that it is about to cross a threshold into a new dawn. It inhabits a liminal space, in transit with no clear national affiliation. As such, the play emphasises the collective responsibility of the characters to decide what route the train (the world) will take – will they allow it to proceed towards war or will they take up their moral responsibility for the human race and literally stop it in its tracks. Ultimately, this is what occurs as the communist hero, Mehring, triumphs, but the collision between collective identification and individual experiences of abuse, trauma and exile complicates the narrative.

The Second World War uprooted, traumatised and irrevocably damaged many of the characters. The Jewish Mehring, Maillard and Kari Neilson, alongside Polish Anna Woytschek, are all former inmates of Nazi concentration camps. In his book *Ethics: An Essay on the Understanding of Evil*, Badiou captures the inconceivability of the Nazi project, the way that it transcends the bounds of imagination – the scale is unthinkable, incomprehensible.[113] The Holocaust functioned on the basis that ethnic and social groups lost their moral status as human beings through a vile process of dehumanisation that rendered humans little better than brute beasts to be exterminated, and MacColl attempts to dramatise the individual and collective consequences of this physical and psychological trauma.

Whereas the Holocaust is indelibly connected to disappearance and loss, *The Travellers* is about presence, survival and possible futures.

The characters are motivated by intense emotional states or dreams of utopia spurred by their experiences of war. Blind Maillard is seeking revenge against the concentration camp officer who stubbed a cigarette out in his eyes after he protested against the persecution and humiliating degradation of a heavily pregnant Jewish woman. Anna is seeking a new life after years of enforced hard labour, a consequence of her destitute status under the Nazi regime. Kari was repeatedly sexually and physically abused in the concentration camp brothel and since her release has been unable to pursue a life beyond prostitution because of her damaged sense of self-worth. She is seeking to free her physical and mental subjectivity from the persistent patterns of abuse the war cast for her. She is travelling with Enrico Goriano, her young Italian fiancé, who knows little of her past and is keen to pursue the American dream after years of war and financial hardship in Italy. What MacColl captures is both the difficulty and the necessity of remembering the past, but also the difficulty and necessity of moving forward into a new historical moment – the politics of the Cold War that, for him, necessitate the identification of a new enemy: aggressive American neo-imperialism.

Through the Marshall Plan, the establishment of the United Nations, its commitment to nuclear proliferation and its monopolisation of popular culture, America played a leading role in reshaping the postwar world. In turn, Britain worked hard to position itself as America's closest ally in Europe by championing NATO (the military alliance of North American and Western European states against Russia) and generally supporting US foreign policy throughout the Cold War. For many left-wing sympathisers this meant colluding in the USA's postwar neo-imperialism, and they 'were highly critical of what they saw not only as America's military but also as its cultural colonisation of postwar Europe'.[114] So, for instance, in George Orwell's *Nineteen Eighty-Four* (1949), 'Britain is Airstrip One, the forward staging post of America's Cold War engagement in Europe. The currency is the dollar, while Americanisms infiltrate the language.'[115]

In *The Travellers* MacColl bluntly represents the United States through the ignorant, prejudiced, callous, egotistical Rocky Stevens, a young American soldier who blames communists for all the ills of the world and myopically ignores the experiences and histories of his fellow travellers. His domineering presence and arrogant assertion of American supremacy are epitomised when he declares, 'We've got enough planes and bombs to flatten out the whole goddamned continent of Europe.'[116] MacColl couples this unsubtle characterisation with an explicit suggestion that United States hegemony and neo-imperialism are on a historical continuum with fascism, a view he supports with reference to the aggressive military presence of the United States in the Korean War (1950–3), where they made first use of the appalling napalm bomb; America's plans to develop a hydrogen bomb (H-bomb) more powerful than the atom bomb; and the assault on democracy and freedom of speech represented by Senator McCarthy's witch hunts against communist sympathisers in the government and in cultural industries.[117]

Two of the more interesting and complex moral debates in the play occur between the first-class travellers. The first takes place between English Katherine and her husband Paul Lorentz, an exiled Czech novelist. An artist who has been part of the communist opposition, Lorentz has enjoyed the cut and thrust of intellectual debate but recently grown disillusioned with and contemptuous of the communist emphasis on a workers' revolution. He believes in the right of the intellectual class to lead the revolution and decides, unbeknownst to Katherine, to denounce collective political causes in favour of self-imposed exile and personal liberation. Declaring, 'I am a writer, a novelist, I represent nobody but myself',[118] Lorentz rejects responsibility for others and commits himself to nurturing the individual spirit and pursuing personal freedom. For him, estrangement experienced through imposed exile and his decision to become an intellectual exile are to be a source of creativity, as they became for many artists and writers during and after the war.[119]

But just as Lorentz has become disillusioned, Katherine has grown increasingly politicised and dedicated to the communist cause and to her life in Czechoslovakia. Throughout the play, she provides the moral touchstone, commenting, before leaving her husband, 'for you life is a question of style / For me, a matter of content.'[120] Their impassioned pleas from the positions of the artist versus the activist, the stylist versus the ideologue, are engaging and intricately woven together. MacColl had already demonstrated his distaste for those he dismissed as bourgeois modernists, more interested in 'art for art's sake' than in writing 'in touch with the soul of the masses',[121] and I suspect that MacColl intended that the audience should despise Lorentz's ruthless individualism. However, rather than the cartoon villainy of Rocky Stevens's aggressive nationalism, Lorentz's attraction to the championing of the individual, an opportunity to redefine his sense of self in a turbulent world that America signifies, is all the more understandable given his recent experience of political persecution and exile.

Set against these debates sits the hero Mehring, a communist infiltrator smuggled onto the train with false papers and passport. Like Katherine, Mehring sees a very simple choice unfolding between the inexorable drift towards war and the struggle for peace. Whereas other characters, such as Goriano and Maillard, need to excise or avenge historical events, Mehring is rooted firmly in the present and draws on contemporary atrocities to inform his dedication to an active struggle for peace. 'There are men planning massacres and the train speeds on. In Korea children's bodies are being destroyed by jelly-bombs. They are dying in Malaya and Indo-China and the train speeds on.'[122] Driven by the ideological differences of the Cold War, Stevens kills Mehring as he attempts to lead a communist uprising. Nonetheless, Mehring achieves his aim as the remaining passengers, recognising the imminent perils of war, act collectively to stop the train. This is the underlying message of the play, that individual trauma and the pursuit of revenge should not jettison present political need. However, the personal traumas continually rupture the narrative, the past does infringe on the present, and historical progress is not smooth but, in line with Walter Benjamin, is littered with discontinuities and catastrophic moments of crisis.

Collective memory and remembrance: *Oh What a Lovely War*

Theatre Workshop relocated to the Theatre Royal after *The Travellers*, where the company intermittently tackled antiwar themes in its work until the seminal production of *Oh What a Lovely War* in 1963 that is widely acknowledged as one of the most important theatre pieces of the twentieth century. Arguably, its success derived from a particular confluence between subject, form and historical moment that seemed to capture a wider mood of distrust with and dissent from political authority. Interestingly, the company was not alone in turning to the First World War as an ethical marker at this historical juncture. In fact, *Oh What a Lovely War* joined a growing body of 1960s cultural practice revisiting the Great War and its aftermath, including biographies, anthologies of war poetry, radio programmes and a lengthy documentary series *The Great War* that BBC2 broadcast in 1964.

In particular, there emerged a specific historiographic concern to recuperate the ordinary soldier's story as a way of counteracting official narratives and examining and unsettling power relations based on class and national nostalgia for a lost empire. This was exactly the impetus that drove the genesis of *Oh What a Lovely War*. In order to engage in this revisionist history, Littlewood insisted that it be rooted in extensive research of historical records, documentary accounts and political analysis of the war. In particular, Derek Paget identifies three texts that provided crucial source material: Leon Wolff's *In Flanders Field* (1959), Alan Clark's *The Donkeys* (1961) and Barbara Tuchman's *August 1914* (1962).[123] The company also had access to Charles Chilton's research files and to Raymond Fletcher, who receives a credit in the programme as a military adviser. However, Littlewood chose to mediate this research material through a deliberately unsentimental variety format and the result, according to Sir Richard Eyre, 'was political theatre that, unlike most of the genre, neither patronised its audience, nor tried to reprimand or reform them. It sought to inform and to entertain, and it broke your heart in the process.'[124]

The ethical questioning underpinning *Oh What a Lovely War* is rooted in the clever use of juxtaposition and counterpoint, a form of aesthetic disturbance that attempts to translate to the stage cinema's ability to 'cut' between scenes in ways pioneered by earlier European practitioners such as Piscator. The disarming cosy nostalgia of the pierrot show and the show's capacity to entertain with jolly songs and exuberant wit was consistently complicated by the scalpel-like incision of facts and figures in the glaring red lettering of the tickertape newspanel, as well as heart-rending moments of pathos. Equally, John

Bury and Littlewood heightened the aesthetic incongruity by having twinkly fairy lights and colourful circus-style tubs remain throughout the action. 'More importantly, the direct and unambiguous address of the performer to audience immediately constituted the audience as sharer in, rather than observer of, performance.'[125]

The show's theatrical genealogy in agitprop and popular entertainment forms, its eclectic 'collision montage' style, documentary credentials and use of cutting-edge technologies, have received extensive attention elsewhere.[126] So in this analysis I want to focus specifically on how the work constructs an ethical response to war, to its originators, enthusiasts and victims, through its staging of both real and fictionalised historical moments and its call to collective memory and remembrance:

> Human morality can . . . be partly transcended by the durability of the world and the public memory of individuals' deeds. By building and preserving a world that can link one generation to the next and that makes possible forms of collective memory, we are able, in Arendt's words, 'to absorb and make shine through the centuries whatever men may want to save from the natural ruin of time'.[127]

Susan Sontag suggests that 'what is called collective memory is not a remembering but a stipulating: that *this* is important'.[128] As such, I want to argue that the force of *Oh What a Lovely War* is as an act of remembering the dead of the First World War and of *stipulating* their political and cultural importance – a force that made a significant ethical, as well as theatrical, impact.

Littlewood and her collaborators created a work that was at once about honouring the dead of the 'Great War' and also about its political reverberations in the present – a present dominated by the Cold War, arms proliferation, a burgeoning Campaign for Nuclear Disarmament and debates around the Labour Party's vote in favour of unilateral disarmament at the 1960 Labour Party conference, followed by its reversal the year after. As Paget recognises, this historical jump-cutting is most tellingly evident in the original theatre programme for *Oh What a Lovely War*, 'which contained anti-nuclear facts and figures

2. *Oh What a Lovely War* (1963).

as an integral part of its overall argument'.[129] One item reads, 'One atom bomb in 1945 caused as many casualties as the entire Battle of Arras. One Polaris missile is 25 times as destructive as the bomb that destroyed Hiroshima.'[130] As the show explicitly questions what could possibly rationalise the scale of slaughter seen during the First World War, information about the obscene proliferation of the machinery of war provides a disturbing interpretive context.

The origins of *Oh What a Lovely War* reside in the sublime scale of the First World War, which erased the identity of the individual in a spectacle of mass death that is impossible to assimilate. One of the show's originators, Charles Chilton, began work on *Oh What a Lovely War* after visiting Arras in 1958 to photograph his father's grave, where he found no grave but instead a list of '35,942 officers and men of the Forces of the British Empire who fell in the battle of Arras and who have no known graves'.[131] Writing a programme note for *Oh What a Lovely War* he questioned, 'What could have possibly happened to a man that rendered his burial impossible? What horror could have taken place that rendered the burial of 35,942 men impossible and all in one relatively small area?'[132]

Oh What a Lovely War has its origins in a profound sense of loss and shock at the literal erasure of bodies of men, which Chilton articulates. Throughout the piece, Littlewood bombarded the audience with the sheer scale of the death toll through unfeasible statistics presented via a tickertape newspanel and iconographic images projected onto a large-scale screen at the back of the stage that depicted the extraordinary network of trenches and mass graves that scarred the landscape and public consciousness forever.

Photographic images were crucial to the original impact of the piece and served several functions. At a basic level, they closed the gap between the theatrical spectacle and its historic inspiration and served to remind the audience, in a Brechtian sense, that what they were watching had its origins in actuality. Developing the narrative of *Miracle at Verdun* of dead soldiers rising from their graves, *Oh What a Lovely War* uses photographs to have the *actual* wounded and dead assert their presence within the theatrical space. According to Ivor Dykes, the sound engineer for the production, 'Joan was insistent that we get away from the idea that these people were old dim photographs long dead. These are young men and women full of life and ideals, they do not know they are to be wasted!'[133]

Photos have an authority that supplements and transcends statistics and verbal accounts. For many, the atrocities of war exist beyond the capacity of language to articulate experience and so the photographs provided evidence of the human waste the piece interrogates. As Sontag suggests, photographs acquire an immediacy and become a form of rhetoric as they simplify and crystallise a particular moment or mood, but they also serve an ethical function: 'Certain photographs – emblems of suffering ... can be used like memento mori, as objects of contemplation to deepen one's sense of reality; as secular icons, if you will.'[134] As *Oh What a Lovely War* progresses, earlier images of maps, recruiting posters and patriotic crowds give way to photographs of war personnel. Images of soldiers laden with wooden crosses on burial duty and fields full of symbolic white wooden crosses stretching out across the horizon are

> an invitation to pay attention, to reflect, to learn, to examine the rationalizations for mass suffering offered by established powers. Who caused what the picture shows? Who is responsible? Is it excusable? Was it inevitable? Is there some state of affairs which we have accepted up to now that ought to be challenged?[135]

This sense of moral probing was central to Littlewood's desire to use *Oh What a Lovely War* to document and honour ordinary men and women brutally betrayed and culled in a war driven by imperialist and capitalist agendas, a war managed by myopic and incompetent men who, the piece suggests, remained largely impervious to the human consequences of the atrocities they administered.

Generally framed as a battle between opposing nations, war primarily involves issues of national territory, pride and honour that Littlewood theatricalised at the beginning of *Oh What a Lovely War* through the circus parade. This scene depicts characters in national dress expressing imperialist and nationalist ambitions and vying for national supremacy. In his book *Humanity*, Jonathan Glover suggests that this attitude is a form of social Darwinism, with the nation state as the unit of 'evolutionary selection'.[136] However, in *Oh What a Lovely War* the enemy becomes not the opposing national forces but the politicians, arms manufacturers and military leaders whom Littlewood routinely ridiculed and undermined for their arrogance, incompetence and desire to protect their own reckless self-interest regardless of the human and environmental consequences.

The performance destabilised the obsession with polarisations into 'us' and the 'other side'; instead the enemy became more specifically 'us and them' in class terms, and this polarisation was played out theatrically through different means, such as uniforms, accents, diction and the occupation of space. For instance, the piece humorously depicted the distance, literally and metaphorically, of officers from *real* trench life, as shown by the order to remove an 'offending limb' from a parapet,[137] or in the careless indifference shown when transport for the wounded is restricted to the officer class. In contrast, soldiers of different nations stand side by side in several scenes that undermine war's reliance on a distancing and dehumanising of the enemy as a foreign *other*.

In war the veneer of civilisation is very thin and frequently punctured, hence moments that assert civilising processes are both precious and rigorously policed. Christmas truces were widespread in the First World War and widely frowned upon by political and military leaders because they signalled a moment when equal moral status was acknowledged between enemy combatants, when sympathy prevailed over tribalism and when the resources of mutual respect, co-operation and chivalry surfaced. Rather than being made to seem worthy of slaughter, in Littlewood's Christmas truce scene the 'enemy' is humanised through their physical presence. Through this moment of performance there was a simultaneous celebration of difference and common humanity as the men shared greetings, songs and gifts of food inflected by their national differences.

In performance *Oh What a Lovely War* developed a complex interplay between collective and individual identity. On the one hand, the adoption of pierrot-style costumes suggests a uniformity of identity for the soldiers, as does the decision to keep the soldiers undifferentiated in the trench scenes; but rather than the renunciation of personality or a lack of individuality, *Oh What a Lovely War* highlights the quirks of individual soldiers and communal living. In particular, the piece celebrates the creativity and theatricalising of everyday life. Fussell has written of the ways that the First World War promulgated a profound awareness and appreciation of irony and this sensibility is evident in the signage employed in the trenches such as Piccadilly, Regent Street and Marble Arch and the establishment of the *Wipers Times*, a spoof newspaper that conceived the war in theatrical terms by circulating 'facetious theatrical advertisements very close in idiom to the real ones in London'.[138] Littlewood depicts both in *Oh What a Lovely War* to highlight the persistence of creative resilience and mordant black humour in the face of catastrophic living conditions.

In *An Intimate History of Killing* (1999), Joanna Bourke records that the importance 'of comradeship in enabling men to "carry on" is at the heart of most histories of "life at the front": so much so that it has become a cliché of military, cultural history',[139] and *Oh What a Lovely War* is no exception. The show's ethical core is firmly located in the displays of collective solidarity and communal banter that characterise the trench scenes. Through improvisation, Littlewood worked hard to create a theatrical depiction of the rhythms and atmosphere of habitual familiarity as the soldiers talked, wrote letters and played cards.[140] In this subtle way, rather than Foucault's reduction of ordinary soldiers to 'docile bodies',[141] Littlewood suggests a steely resilience that speaks more movingly about the triumph of the human spirit than the preposterous heroic rhetoric of Sir Douglas Haig or the pompous pronouncements of the chaplain.

Whereas Haig is characterised as humourless, cold, obstinate, inflexible, self-serving and self-righteous, the ordinary soldiers are comradely, witty, warm, imaginative and creative. Of course, this is a partial representation born of a deep political commitment to the ordinary soldier and a burning scepticism towards the motivations and competencies of those that ruled them. Rather than scenes of heroic action, the men's strength is in their stoical ability to co-exist in conditions of extreme physical discomfort with death hovering around the corner. In a sense, they adhere to Badiou's conception of ethics as reduced to 'Do all that you can to persevere in that which exceeds your perserverence. Persevere in the interruption.'[142] In conceiving and constructing textual, visual and verbal comedic moments the soldiers do not only persevere, they exceed the limits of their surroundings and this suggests an intensely ethical response. Clive Barker supported this reading when he pronounced that having

> been in the production, it is quite clear to me that *Lovely War* is a celebration of human resourcefulness in the face of the most appalling catastrophic conditions. So Joan celebrates courage, humour, comradeship, the triumph of life over death and the international solidarity between soldiers.[143]

As much as possible, the stage was to be given over to the real soldiers who experienced the war, a commitment that culminated every night in the company redirecting the applause they received back to the images on the screen. This was made all the more poignant the night the veteran philosopher and antiwar campaigner Bertrand Russell attended the show, when Raffles arranged for all the usherettes to come on at the end of the show and lay white flowers at his feet as he was hailed by Victor Spinetti as one of the 'original pierrots'. In a letter to the company, Russell testified to the piece's impact:

> As you know, the First War was an event which has a vital place in my thinking and in my life. All the people concerned with resistance to the war were my intimates. The great horror which affected us as the war interminably dragged on was something none of us have ever fully outlived. If there were any way in which I could make people understand how true and important your play is, I should wish to do it. I wonder it has been allowed on a London stage. After it, there was much that I should have wished to have said to you and to the performers I was fortunate enough to meet. The experience of the production had drained me, and I could only speak of ordinary things when I wanted to convey to you that I thought all that had happened to me that evening to be most extraordinary.[144]

For many, seeing *Oh What a Lovely War* was a deeply moving experience, as the act of remembrance it offered triggered individual recollections, spurred family histories and provided important contemporary political reverberations in the wake of the Cuban Missile Crisis and the lead-up to the Vietnam War. The show moved at least two families to gift Theatre Workshop the Christmas parcels their ancestors received during the First World War as a mark of their appreciation for its honouring of the ordinary soldier and its committed act of remembrance.[145]

In London, Paris, New York and Philadelphia, reviewers praised the show's political ambition and ability to entertain. The reviewer for *The Times* welcomed 'this savage humanitarian document'; the *New York Times* reviewer, Howard Taubman, claimed, 'it keeps reminding you of so-called civilization's monstrous fatuities'; and *Time* magazine's reviewer found that the show 'has the accumulative impact of an artillery barrage ... [that] leaves the playgoer purged, mute and strangely strengthened'.[146] These reviews capture the moral imperative at the heart of *Oh What a Lovely War* that saw the theatrical and thematic accumulation of thirty years' antiwar work.

It would be relatively easy to reduce the body of work explored in this chapter to passionate pacifism in action, but the collective impact is more complicated than this. Through this output, Littlewood, together with her collaborators, questioned how war comes about and, more importantly, how it keeps happening. There is a deep ethical core and moral questioning running through these works that cannot be reduced to a simple expression of communist values or pacifist agendas. Yes, these aspects are evident, and important, but they are not all that is apparent. It is not just capitalism, imperialism and the war machine Littlewood puts under scrutiny, but the value we place on life itself and what we are prepared to do to preserve it. The overarching call in all these works is for transnational humanitarian values and moral courage against those that would belittle, traumatise, harm and kill others directly or by implication – whether that be in the pursuit of war, profit or national expansion. Through this creative output, Littlewood addressed what it means to be human, to share common public space, not limited by national borders or political ideologies. But, above all, she expressed her belief that she could most defiantly express what it means to be alive, in communion with others, through the collaborative creative act.

This creative and ideological impetus also drove Littlewood's work on the Renaissance classics explored in the next chapter.

3 Controversial classics: resisting cultural authority

Prior to their move to the Theatre Royal, Theatre Workshop largely concentrated on new writing and contemporary classics. In 1949, they did school tours of *Twelfth Night* and *As You Like It*, followed by *Henry IV* in 1951, but these were rarely seen beyond the school halls of the north-east of England and Scotland. Shakespeare was a last resort turned to when the company needed to shore up their finances with productions designed for schools where they could guarantee an audience, regular payment and a chance to avail themselves of free school dinners. This attitude was largely down to MacColl's deep-seated aversion to the classics, which he perceived as counter to the company's aim to attract a popular working-class audience.[1] In fact, it was a fluke that Theatre Workshop announced its arrival at the Theatre Royal in January 1953 with a production of Shakespeare's *Twelfth Night*. The company had been doing a schools tour of the play between September and November 1952, so this show needed little rehearsal as the company concentrated on making the crumbling old theatre habitable.

Yet, cut adrift from MacColl's influence, Littlewood rediscovered an earlier passion for the classics ignited by a school trip to *Hamlet* at the Old Vic with Sir John Gielgud, Donald Wolfit and Robert Speaight, which she remembered 'had me on the edge of my seat all afternoon'.[2] As a young girl, Littlewood became a regular visitor to the Old Vic where Lilian Baylis 'presented the plays as an austere, evangelical alternative to lasciviousness and drink' as part of a socially reforming agenda to attract the working class to Shakespeare.[3] Seeing Gielgud's *Macbeth* on a subsequent visit prompted a school production with Littlewood taking the title role and acting as producer, in a staging she described as a blaze of lightning flashes, music, drum rolls and the sinking of knives into meat to elicit spurts of blood.[4]

Littlewood's reading of classical theatre was completely different from MacColl's and was more in tune with many on the humanist left at this time who regarded the Renaissance as a high point in popular culture. Whereas he worried about the bourgeois associations of the classics, Littlewood found 'an anti-establishment voice, an unruly, vibrant theatre connecting with and speaking for the people'.[5] In an early lecture titled 'Education and Understanding', she passionately enthused,

> The middle class have no past, no future – they have no understanding even of the great artists they themselves have produced. It has been said that the bourgeoisie have raised monuments to the classics – if they'd read them then they'd have burned them. We can find the truth of this statement when we go to the great writers of theatre like Aristophanes, Aeschylus, Marlowe, Shakespeare, Webster – these men by reason of their deep perceptions and understanding were the outstanding critics of their day. And then theatre was a theatre of the people. The Elizabethan theatre was the place where the stinkards as they were called paid their pennies to watch the players 'with passion in their eyes'.[6]

Believing in 'the politicised cultural traditions of continental Europe, in which mass working-class parties established or supported socially engaged drama',[7] Littlewood took inspiration from Federico García Lorca's work with La Barraca, which toured plays from the Spanish Golden Age as a means of promoting cultural and national regeneration.[8] In sympathy with Lorca's aim to repopularise classic national texts, Littlewood aimed to reanimate the social and political significance of English Renaissance classics and the Theatre Royal became the site for this ambitious campaign.

In many ways, Renaissance classics were an illogical choice for the Theatre Royal and its local, largely working-class, community. Commenting on the company's decision to mark their first anniversary at the Theatre Royal with a production of *Richard II*, the local paper admitted, 'It takes courage to present Shakespeare in Stratford – which has absolutely nothing in common with its more famous counterpart on Avon – but this is a quality which Theatre Workshop possesses to marked degree.'[9] Between 1953 and 1964, Littlewood produced work by Shakespeare, Ben Jonson, John Marston and Christopher Marlowe, with a particularly concentrated period of classics appearing between 1954 and 1957. During this period, she set about reimagining and framing her productions for an audience less accustomed to the classics than to the cinema and television for its entertainment. For instance, *The Stage* review of *Twelfth Night* commented that it is 'as though the Crazy Gang have invaded Illyria',[10] and the flyer for *Arden of Faversham* billed it as 'an unusual and exciting thriller', not hailing it as a long-neglected Renaissance classic, but adopting the language of pulp fiction or film to stress its accessibility and contemporary appeal.

According to Elizabeth Schafer, Littlewood 'offered a distinctly alternative vision of the Renaissance classics from that available in the mainstream theatre of the time',[11] and in a relatively short period, as Dymphna Callaghan recognises, 'Stratford East became literally and symbolically a site for counter-hegemonic Shakespeare'.[12] And whilst the local audience largely failed to materialise, Littlewood developed a formidable critical reputation for her iconoclastic and controversial approach to rehearsing, interpreting and staging classic plays. This chapter examines the nature of these transgressive productions, their innovative theatricality and the reasons why critics deemed them so controversial. My readings of these productions and their critical reception is inevitably tied up in the issues of tradition, heritage, legitimacy, authority, status, cultural hegemony and gender politics that shroud understandings of the classics and their place in defining a particular sense of national cultural identity, particularly in English-speaking countries and in relation to Shakespeare specifically.

W.B. Worthen, amongst others, has drawn attention to the 'authority' of Shakespeare, what he refers to as 'the stabilizing, hegemonic functioning of the Author in modern cultural production'.[13] Throughout history, some critics, academics and directors have colluded in an ideal of preserving a stable Shakespearean text that adheres to the authority of an elusive 'original' in performance, even if what the 'original' might be remains contested. This conception certainly motivated many reviews of Littlewood's productions that sought to distance her performative practice from their original source. So a review of her *Richard II* asked 'if this can possibly be Shakespeare's play at all', concluding that 'it is not, all in all, an interpretation of *Richard II* in which we can recognize the play that Shakespeare wrote'.[14] Similarly, the *Theatre World* review of *Macbeth* declared, 'no beholder who came fresh to the play could have supposed he had seen *Macbeth*. The text was subjected to alteration, interpolation and transposition, resulting in almost a new work'.[15] According to Dennis Kennedy, this kind of critical reception is evidence that critics not only 'privilege the written text above its performance, they also assume that standards or boundaries of interpretation must exist for its performance, usually determined by the critic's analysis of the playwright's objectives',[16] objectives seemingly immune to historical change and shifting theatrical tastes. Littlewood laced her productions with a keen desire to dislocate and contradict the authority of tradition and this sensibility inevitably courted controversy.

Worthen meticulously destabilises notions of a stable Shakespearean authority by emphasising the historical, cultural, social, theatrical and linguistic schism between the production of Shakespeare's texts and the material conditions of contemporary performance. He draws attention to the fact that the whole history of Shakespearean production relies on the instability of the text and its availability for reassessment and refashioning. A performance is always in dialogue with the *now*. However intentionally, or unintentionally, performance histories, political conditions, social concerns and the cultural zeitgeist all play a part in framing productions and their reception – a cultural negotiation takes place. 'To see performance in this way, however, is to see the question of a production's fidelity – to "the play," to "Shakespeare" – as purely tautological.'[17] Instead, the text only becomes fully significant when performatively embodied through staging, movement, speech and gesture, and its significance shifts according to the material conditions of performance, as well as in relation to different national cultures. Hence writers including Graham Holderness, Charles Marowitz and Gary Taylor have argued that the appeal of reinventing and recycling Shakespeare is common and complex as each new generation attempts to find their 'in' to Shakespeare: although this is not to suggest a neat trajectory as radical and conservative productions co-exist at any given moment and in any given culture.[18]

Contemporary classics

Littlewood created her productions of the classics to be in dialogue with the prevailing material and cultural conditions of her time. As Raffles explained, 'When we produced the classics we refused to regard them as sacrosanct museum pieces but, instead, tried to read them with fresh eyes and to weight the characters and their thoughts in the light of the modern world.'[19] As such, Littlewood used these productions to operate dialogically with the contemporary British nation, the national psyche and the anxieties of the present. She rejected the way that classic texts, particularly Shakespeare's, were often used to assert the glory of the nation and alternatively mined Renaissance dramatists to expose a nation in flux.

The 1950s witnessed incredible changes in the power dynamics that dominated national politics, and several conflicting images of Britain emerged. The electorate ousted the postwar Labour government in 1951 in favour of a Conservative government, although the return of Winston Churchill, the wartime leader, as prime minister undermined any impression of change. When he resigned from office in April 1955, rumours of alcoholism and ill health dealt Churchill's image as a strong national figurehead a crushing blow. The glamorous Anthony Eden, whose role in the Suez Crisis forced his resignation in January 1957, succeeded him. The Suez Crisis once and for all drew attention to Britain's loss of colonial power and an ever-increasing gulf between its self-perception as a major world player amidst the towering force of the new superpowers. The death of King George VI ushered in the coronation of Queen Elizabeth II in 1953, a chance to assert the longevity and grandeur of the state and Commonwealth rule at the same time as several British colonies sought and gained independence. On the global stage, the ideological battles of the Cold War continued and Khruschev's denouncement of Stalin and crushing of the

Hungarian uprising undermined the status of Russia as a beacon of hope for those on the left. Nuclear proliferation and the space race also contributed to the sense of a turbulent, uncertain world. Personal politics also gained momentum through the nascent second-wave feminism signalled by the publication of Simone de Beauvoir's *The Second Sex* in 1953 and the government-sponsored Wolfenden Inquiry (1954–7) put homosexuality under the spotlight.

This national and international context formed the backdrop amidst which Littlewood tackled plays dealing with the legitimacy of state, royalty, militarism, abuse of power, homosexuality, succession and fragile national and global politics. And coursing through her classic productions was a razor-sharp assault on the entrenched British class structure, an unquestioning acceptance of social hierarchy, respect for undeserved authority, rampant materialism and ruthless ambition. As Leach recognises,

> Not many critics – or even spectators – were looking, but Littlewood exposed a face of the age which the age probably did not much care to see. It was too smug, too complacent, too dull to wonder if indeed that which it deemed immutable – royalty, hierarchy, respect and so forth – was in fact fragile, in flux, only a constructed illusion. Theatre Workshop's was a brave examination through a series of productions of classic drama, of the shadows behind the shiny gloss of the New Elizabethan Age.[20]

Littlewood equally deployed these productions to lambaste the stuffiness, complacency and political conservatism of the British theatrical establishment that, largely speaking, generated productions of Shakespeare and his contemporaries that were conservative, reverent and archaic. According to Kennedy, in continental Europe the mass slaughter, political turmoil and moral uncertainty of the First and Second World Wars revoked the apolitical stance that characterised classic productions in the nineteenth and early twentieth centuries. Instead, in the inter-war years, directors such as Leopold Jessner in Berlin, Leon Schiller in Poland and Orson Welles in America began mining Shakespeare for contemporary resonances through his depiction of dictators, social turmoil and the dissolution of the state, and they played out their findings on experimental constructivist and expressionist stages. After the Second World War, theatre practitioners including Roger Planchon in Lyon and Giorgio Strehler in Milan, influenced by Marxist theory and Brecht's work, were even more concerned to use the classics to interrogate the trials, tribulations, humanitarian traumas and political machinations of the postwar world. The practice was further influenced by the publication of Jan Kott's *Shakespeare, Our Contemporary* (1964), in which he reread Shakespeare through the lens of postwar Europe and European theatre practitioners such as Samuel Beckett.[21]

However, Kennedy draws attention to the fact that this experimental visual and interpretive approach took time to catch on in Britain, 'where audiences and producers tended to be protective of Shakespeare's cultural status and defensive regarding his poetry'.[22] In the 1930s, Sir John Gielgud, with his design team Motley, heralded a new era of elegant and sophisticated commercial productions that privileged the spoken word as the primary signifier, in contrast to the extravagant Edwardian pictorialism of previous years. During the 1940s, Hugh 'Binkie' Beaumont's control of the West End did much to establish the ideological and aesthetic principles of classic productions, which involved 'the greatest stars in gorgeous classic revivals amidst the most sumptuous settings which taste and money could devise', as a glossy, excessively styled, antidote to postwar austerity.[23] There were exceptions. At the Cambridge Festival Theatre in the late 1920s and early 1930s, Terence Gray's overt theatricality relied on abstract shapes, minimal props and expressionist lighting that betrayed his influence by the European avant-garde.

In the late 1940s and the 1950s, directors such as Anthony Quayle, George Devine and Peter Brook began shaking up standards at the Royal Shakespeare Company with visionary productions. In 1951 Quayle set his cycle of history plays on a single permanent set to explore the tensions and anxieties at the heart of leadership rather than the more usual heroic portrayal of kingship. Devine's production of *King Lear* in 1955 employed a radically experimental design by the Japanese-American designer and sculptor Isamu Noguchi. Notably, Brook built up an impressive body of unconventional work that embraced the contemporary moment and a stunning visual aesthetic with productions of *Romeo and Juliet* (1947), *Titus Andronicus* (1955) and *King Lear* (1962), amongst others. Brook's productions were shocking because of his willingness to cut the text, as in his decision to curtail *Romeo and Juliet* after Juliet's death, and the clarity and inventiveness of their visual imagery. Who could forget Lavinia's wounds portrayed with blood-stained streamers pouring from her mouth and wrists in *Titus Andronicus*? Nonetheless, despite these visual experiments, the majority of these productions maintained an inherent conservatism, not least through their adherence to a rigid hierarchical 'star' system by employing actors such as Michael Redgrave, John Gielgud, Laurence Olivier and Paul Scofield and their address to an educated, elite audience.

Performative interventions

Arguably, whereas practitioners such as Gray, Devine and Brook experimented with style, Littlewood was concerned with substance and, in particular, the ways that she could appeal to a popular audience with an energised and vigorous approach to language, staging and textual interpretation. In order to popularise Shakespeare and his contemporaries, Littlewood had to provide a different perspective to the prevailing genteel, picturesque and poetic productions; she did this by stripping back the poetry, focusing on the action or the comedy and interpreting the work for a contemporary audience. The quality of interpretation is crucial here. It was not just about finding an exciting way of retelling a damn good story, but telling it in such a way that shed light on the contemporary political resonances of the text, and this often involved cutting, resituating scenes, radical rehistoricising or idiosyncratic character portraits.

To an extent, Littlewood invoked what Jonathan Dollimore has coined 'creative vandalism',[24] by which he and Susan Bennett refer to practitioners who take up 'a deliberately antagonistic relationship to their source text(s) as well as to the operations under which that source is generally produced and/or received'.[25] Rather than being antagonistic towards her chosen source texts, Littlewood refused to grant them the cultural authority they commanded in other quarters. Alternatively, she prefigured Marowitz's assertion that '"Shakespeare" is matter and matter can be reduced, expanded, transformed or reconstituted'.[26] Whilst radical approaches to classic texts are now very familiar to theatre audiences across the globe, in 1950s Britain this was exceptionally rarc and, as such, Littlewood gained a reputation for her willingness to cut, reorder and contemporise Renaissance classics. So her productions were not just 'versions' of Shakespeare, they also took the British Shakespeare cultural industry to task with their insistent modernity, global reach, theatrical experimentation and attitude.

It was crucially important for Littlewood that the language of the classics achieved contemporary relevance. According to Kennedy, Shakespearean verse has a problematic cultural authority on English-speaking stages that leads many theatre-makers, theatre-goers and critics to lament the loss of both Shakespeare's and their own cultural capital if the language is tampered with in any way. As he puts it,

> On the English-speaking stage the archaism and cultural status of the spoken text naturally grants it greater importance than in another language, and had led to frequent opinion that an audience should be permitted to hear it directly, to experience the play unmediated.[27]

Many directors have interpreted lack of mediation to mean an emphasis on the poetry of the verse at the expense of narrative or action. There is an assumption that their audiences know the stories being told and therefore they come to the theatre to hear the words spoken in rich, resonant vocal tones that bring out the 'beauty' of the verse through appropriate flow and melody. Gielgud was certainly an exponent of this school of thought. He was dismissive of 'a tendency to ignore the music of the verse and speak it like modern colloquial dialogue'.[28] He proposed that actors speaking Shakespeare 'need first to learn how to stand still and speak beautifully, without fidgeting and byplay'.[29] As an actor and director, Gielgud provided an exemplary model of elegant verse-speaking over action. But Littlewood 'couldn't stand the Gielgud voice, was always imitating it, and the worst thing she could say to you was "it's like Gielgud"'.[30]

In direct opposition to the 'Gielgud-school', Littlewood insisted that the 'poetry of Shakespeare's day was a muscular, active, forward-moving poetry, in that it was like the people to whom it belonged'.[31] She was adamant that classic texts should not be reduced to an archaic, long-lost language re-created as a pretty party-piece to satisfy the needs of an educated audience. For her, the language should be dynamic, alert to historical change and capable of being understood by a broad audience base. As Callaghan explains, 'Littlewood's objection to "poetry" was not a refusal to acknowledge the power of its aesthetic, but rather an attempt to reconsider the beauty of Shakespearean language from a nonhegemonic perspective.'[32] This was not a new strategy – as part of a popularising agenda, Barry Jackson, a pioneering director at the Birmingham Repertory Theatre during the 1920s, used contemporary settings and modern dress and played the text as if it were a modern play. He argued that 'period costumes and "poetic" vocal delivery were artificial barriers between the play and the spectator'.[33] So by stripping away the pomp he hoped to attract the ordinary man and woman to see the value of Shakespeare. Littlewood similarly saw language as a vital tool to aid accessibility.

In terms of delivery, Littlewood often worked to undermine the reverence actors accorded classic texts. The 'set' speeches in the classics are fraught with difficulty because they appear to be insulated from robust handling and their familiarity suggests a presentational, declamatory style that suitably marks reaching a 'high point' in the play with a kind of 'look, here it is' approach. Recalling work on Gaunt's 'This England' speech in *Richard II*, Goorney explained how Littlewood helped him overcome 'the feeling of respect and awe with which I approached it. I clowned it, put it into gibberish and generally sent it up.'[34] This playful, improvisatory mode was typical of her approach. During rehearsal of a classic play, 'dialogue would be adapted into colloquial speech or parts switched around or the entire company would perform a particular speech or scene'.[35] These techniques enabled Littlewood to explore the meaning behind the words and helped to make the plays live in the moment of performance. She also used regional dialects to capture the vitality and variety of the English language. During a defence of her 1964 production of Parts 1 and 2 of *Henry IV*, she asserted that 'I find the accents of Leeds, East London and Manchester as acceptable as those of St. John's Wood, Eton, Oxford or hangovers from Edwardian dressing rooms.'[36] And her decision to use these accents in productions of the classics captured her dismissive attitude towards the class politics that permeated responses to regional dialect, particularly when associated with the classics. However, those who worked most closely with her argued that this contemporising did not overlook the significance of the text's composition as verse:

> With a classical play in verse, once the improvisations have enabled the actors to grasp the tenor of the play and their characters, she will spend hours on the verse and its rhythms. She will not allow decoration – as soon as you spout 'poetry', you are stopped. The hard, driving rhythms which elucidate the meaning – and sometimes *are* the meaning – are all-important. Sometimes an actor is made to physically punch his way through a speech, beating out the metre with his fists like a shadow-boxer. This is making him physically move the verse – 'is this a dagger, which I see before me' – actually pacing it out. When you have the physical movement which underlies the verse, its meaning is brought right out. The movement might eventually be used in a modified way in the production itself.[37]

This quote draws attention to Littlewood's radical approach to rehearsing classic productions. Discussing his work directing Shakespeare, Laurence Olivier insisted, 'The actor must be disciplined. He must be so trained that he automatically carries out the director's orders. I expect my actors to do exactly what I tell them to do and to do it quickly.'[38] Rather than seeing actors as pliable servants under her expert tutelage, Littlewood viewed them as collaborators on a creative journey of discovery that involved experiment, intellectual engagement, physical play, discussion and improvisatory processes. Littlewood frequently asked the actors to improvise an analogous contemporary situation to one presented in a play in order to make a scene more real, more immediate, before returning to the text. She even invited the actors to invent scenes missing from the original. Working on *Macbeth*, 'the actors improvised the scene which Shakespeare never wrote, when Macbeth actually meets the murderers for the first time – in a pub; the murderers, two ex-R.A.F. types; Macbeth saying, "How would you boys like to do a job for me?"'[39] Whereas many directors view a Shakespeare play as the complete authoritative source, I would argue that Littlewood's lack of reverence helped her to expose the gaps in the texts that could help her actors gain insight and focus. It is interesting that Littlewood's willingness to play around with the textual authority of the classics, and with Shakespeare in particular, should have caused such consternation because even in Shakespeare's day,

> The conditions of production in the Renaissance playhouse militate against the final ascription of an ideal, coherent, work to a single animating *author*, and the texts of Shakespeare's plays are the result of dialogue and collaboration, of authorial and non-authorial revision.[40]

In many ways, Littlewood's productions of the classics adopted the same approach to making the texts work for the social and material conditions of performance through a creative approach to improvisation, cutting, reordering and embellishing. However, as usual with Littlewood, there was no definitive approach. Maxwell Shaw recalled that 'when we did *Volpone*, we sat around and discussed and analyzed for ten days'.[41] *Arden of Faversham* rehearsals began with an attempt to immerse the actors in the place and time of the play's inception with a trip to Faversham to see the house that Arden lived in and where he was murdered, and to receive a talk by a local historian. Working on *The Dutch Courtesan*, Littlewood brought the period to life through close attention to the materiality of surroundings and physical objects – the landscape, clothes, food and ornaments.[42] *Richard II* rehearsals emphasised physicality and revolved around Laban-based exercises and improvisation to explore how the actors could embody and communicate power relations, the hostility between characters and the ever-present threat of violence. As such, rehearsals initially abandoned the text and focused on proxemics, ways of moving, gestures and eye contact. As Goorney describes,

> How could we get the feeling of the period, the insecurity, the 'stab in the back,' the warring factions? Many hours were spent in actual movements – the look over the shoulder, the fawning of the favorites [*sic*], the hidden threat behind Bolingbroke's bow.[43]

Littlewood's preoccupation with getting the atmosphere and tone right underpinned Theatre Workshop's approach to staging. Steered by Bury's approach to design, Littlewood's productions used scenography as a theatrical signifier of attitude – a quality that corresponds with Kennedy's argument in *Looking at Shakespeare* (1993) that there is 'a clear relationship between what a production looks like and what its spectators accept as its statement and value'.[44] In the first instance, the 'look' of Littlewood's productions was deliberately counter-intuitive to the elegant approach of the Motley Theatre Design Group, Oliver Messel or Lila de Nobili that graced many mainstream productions of the classics during this period. Of course, it would be foolish to ignore the fact that many Theatre Workshop staging decisions derived from lack of money and restricted physical resources to build and store materials, but this should not detract from the fact that a very particular aesthetic was developed to frame Littlewood's productions of Renaissance plays.

Signalling a resolutely modernist sensibility, this aesthetic largely drew on Edward Gordon Craig's use of architectural shapes and on Adolphe Appia's innovations in evocative settings and lighting, in particular his ability to create psychological impressions of space through the atmospheric conditions of lighting and different spatial dimensions created by ramps, steps and slopes.[45] Bury's sets created environments evoking not a representational space, but rather atmosphere, tone and texture that related to the themes of the play. This often meant employing one significant visual signifier that offered a response to the play and exploiting the potential of different levels and shafts of light, darkness and shadow, to suggest mood and relationships. For instance, the production of *Arden of Faversham* in 1954 entailed two settings: a large open space interrupted by three massive tree trunks, around which lovers as well as their hired assassins could hide, fight and plot, and for the London scenes 'a cramped vista of London alleys'.[46] The reviewer for *The Times* accorded the black trunks a metaphorical function, writing that they served as 'an effective symbol of the tragic triangle of the tragedy'.[47] Lit from the back they also created a disturbing nightmarish quality as the murder plot unfolded encumbered by unforeseen delays, incompetence and fog before the final bloody denouement.

Courting controversy: queering the nation

Callaghan has written about 'the degree of oppositionality' Littlewood's productions posed',[48] which was no more apparent than in her productions of *Richard II* in 1954 and *Edward II* in 1956. I want to argue that in these productions she asserted a queer theatrical presence at the heart of the nation at a time when the state was placing the real presence of homosexuality under intense repression, surveillance and scrutiny. In this section, I want to explore how Littlewood employed framing devices, staging decisions and theatrical imagery to represent homosexual desire, subjectivity and its resistance to normative regimes and heterosexist power structures. In particular, I want to read these productions as strategic interventions that engaged in a highly politicised cultural dialogue around homosexuality that was taking place at the time.

Importantly, Littlewood staged these productions whilst homosexuality was still illegal in Great Britain but during the three-year government-sponsored Wolfenden Inquiry. The Wolfenden Committee was set up to investigate the laws governing homosexuality and prostitution. In 1954, conviction for sodomy still carried a life sentence, which had been on the statute books since 1533 (with the maximum sentence reduced from hanging to life imprisonment in 1861). In 1885, the Labouchere Amendment introduced the classification of 'gross indecency', which covered all sexual relations between men short of buggery and carried a sentence of up to two years with or without hard labour. The Wolfenden Committee was set up amidst growing concerns with the rise in 'gross indecency' cases from 316 in 1938 to 2,322 in 1955, the use of dubious police entrapment centred on 'agents provocateurs' lurking in public lavatories and a growing unease over the ethical implications of persecution and prosecution.[49] When the Wolfenden Report appeared in 1957, it recommended that consensual homosexual sexual activity between consenting adults over twenty-one should be decriminalised, although it took another ten years of parliamentary debate before decriminalisation finally occurred in 1967. This was the heated cultural climate surrounding Littlewood's decision to create two, very different, but specifically queer-orientated productions.

Littlewood's *Richard II*, originally produced in January 1954 to mark the first anniversary of Theatre Workshop's residence in the Theatre Royal Stratford East, was restaged to correspond with Michael Benthall's production of the same play at the Old Vic in January 1955. The productions could not have been more different in terms of their material resources, approach to the text, staging and attitude to language. She wanted critics and theatre-goers to confront the fact that there are many different ways of 'doing' Shakespeare and that her stripped-back aesthetic and political approach was as valid as Benthall's traditionally elegant, poetic version that functioned to 'exploit the tragic grandeur of the play'.[50] Schafer argues that Littlewood defiantly used comparisons with the Old Vic

> to define their [Theatre Workshop's] position as purveyors of an alternative, oppositional version of classical drama. With its perhaps inflated reputation for lyricism, *Richard II* was an ideal vehicle for Littlewood to make the point about her energised, iconoclastic Shakespeare, the antithesis of what was showing at the Old Vic and elsewhere.[51]

Robyn Bolam argues that

> *Richard II* is a play which generates questions. Trying to find answers makes it a challenging text in performance and may explain its continued popularity in the theatre. Textual instability can be a positive force on the stage as each director cuts, interprets and shapes the material anew.[52]

However, Bolam fails to historicise this openness to interpretation. Certainly, Littlewood suffered a censorious response to her directorial interventions into the textual instability Bolam recognises. Predictably, Littlewood's production offered an interpretation of the text as proto-socialist propaganda. According to Norman Marshall, 'Bolingbroke became the leading part, the typical Marxist hero, the revolutionary who overthrows a regime.'[53] Played by George Cooper, Bolingbroke became the brusque voice of the people, the figurehead of a popular uprising that deposes an arrogant, cruel, vain and selfish king who abuses his position:

> Needless to say, Miss Littlewood was not the first to see Bolingbroke as the hero of the play. The day before Essex's rebellion against Queen Elizabeth I, the conspirators bribed Phillips, the manager of the Globe, to put on *Richard II* as an example of how a weak and vacillating ruler can be deposed by the determined leader of an insurrection.[54]

However, rather than a Bolingbroke who grapples with the consequences of usurping an ordained king, Kenneth Tynan accused Cooper of tackling the job with 'the businesslike aplomb of a public executioner'.[55] He needed to depose the king in order to restore dignity to the people and Littlewood privileges this dignity over any dignity due to the king.

Littlewood clearly signposted her political allegiance with the inclusion of an extract from William Langland's famous poem *A Vision of Piers Plowman* in the programme for *Richard II*.[56] Most tellingly, the poem appears under the title 'historical data' that includes Richard II's dates and reference to the Hundred Years War with France. So Littlewood gives equal status to the royal, military and social history that Langland documents in poetic form. Written during Richard's reign in a West Midlands dialect, the poem narrates the story of a poor farm-worker and attacks the corruption of nobility and leading members of the church. However, Littlewood chose to draw attention to the devastating poverty faced by ordinary workers by quoting the following passage:

> His coat was of a clout that cary (course cloth) was called
> His hood was full of holes as he the plough followed
> Two mittens so scanty made all of patches
> The fingers were worn and full of mud hung
> Four heifers before him that weak had become
> You could count all their ribs so wretched they were
> His wife walked by him with a long goad
> Barefoot on the bare ice that the blood followed
> And at the field end lay a little bowl
> And on it lay a little child wrapped in rags.[57]

Yet it was not Littlewood's class politics but Harry H. Corbett's unorthodox portrayal of Richard that caused most consternation. Not only did Corbett emphasise Richard's abuse of his subjects through excessive taxation and land acquisition, which was used to indulge his extravagant tastes and court favour with his cronies; according to Goorney he played him as 'a less noble figure, slightly unbalanced, and with an effeminate streak'.[58] Indeed, Corbett provided a complex psychological portrait of a man caught between his public role and private homosexuality.

Confounded by Corbett's presentation of a man rather than a king, grappling with his sexuality and mental health, many reviewers found it easier to dismiss rather than explore Littlewood's interpretation. This dismissive response was especially apparent in relation to issues of sexuality. Whereas the more recent performance history of *Richard II* confirms that Littlewood's interest in this aspect was not especially aberrant, at the time, as Schafer confirms, 'in suggesting Richard might be homosexual Littlewood's production was taking real risks'.[59] A blatant queering of the 'national playwright' at this historical juncture was significant and calculated to contribute to a wider discourse and to thinking the unthinkable – that homosexuality had historical longevity, legitimacy and a place on the national stage. The very suggestion that homosexuality lurked at the heart of Shakespeare's troubled character caused uproar, and blatant homophobia fuelled several reviews of Corbett's portrayal. Norman Marshall referred to 'stripping [Richard] down until he was displayed as no more than a weak, treacherous, decadent pervert'.[60] Equally, Tynan regretted that the part

> is played in a frenzy of effeminacy. This Richard is a senile Osric, a flutter of puff-pastry, his voice a quavering falsetto which suggests Mr Ernest Milton as Andrew Aguecheek. Whimpering with rage he flies at Gaunt's throat and hurls him to the ground, recoiling at once with tremulous lips, like a child caught in the pantry and torn between defiance and contrition.[61]

Frank Granville Barker similarly pathologised Corbett's portrayal of Richard as a homosexual by describing 'a queenly pervert rather than a sickly, weak-minded king'. Despite acknowledging that Corbett 'played brilliantly according to this conception', Granville Barker reveals his disquiet with the interpretation by claiming that 'Richard's real tragedy was sacrificed, for the landslide from glory to utter ruin that Shakespeare depicts with gradual yet inevitable purpose had already taken place when the curtain rose'.[62] As such, Granville Barker suggests that Littlewood had already sacrificed Richard's hold on his reason, nobility and tragic appeal by this reading of his sexuality. Nonetheless, not all critics were dismissive, and for several theatre-goers Corbett's Richard II remained a highlight of their theatrical experiences of the period.[63] Harold Hobson, in particular, claimed that it was the 'more interesting, controversial and subtle' of the two performances of *Richard II* on offer, and that 'what Theatre Workshop aims at is an interpretation of the play, not a bravura performance'.[64]

Littlewood also courted controversy with her performative interventions. Critics praised the actors in Benthall's production for their cut-glass accents and skills as verse-speakers, with John Neville's mellifluous tones likened to Gielgud by Tynan and Hobson. In her version, Littlewood concentrated on the action that propels the words to move the play forward with energy, speed and fluency. Explaining their approach to the play, she wrote,

> Most modern productions of *Richard II*, for instance, sacrifice the meaning and activity in order to decorate the 'poetry' whereas vigorous action is inherent in the lines and, when they are spoken for their meaning, the poetry is not lost but gains by being active and the play moves with great speed.[65]

Several critics commended her reluctance to offer the usual declamatory style in favour of brisk narrative development, but J. C. Trewin found the verse 'mangled and minced'.[66] Littlewood underscored this physicality of language with a physicality of action and staging that proved revelatory of character traits, relationships and themes. For instance, Richard struck Gaunt with his glove as a climax to their confrontation and MacColl recalled, 'When Mowbray and Bolingbroke met they spat, literally. They spat in each other's faces. There was nothing gentlemanly about it.'[67] Equally, she brought Richard's final humiliation to the fore by replacing his opulent black velvet jacket, with its elongated white satin sleeves, with sackcloth and tethering his ankle to a stake positioned centre stage.

Benthall's production, designed by Leslie Hurry, emphasised the pomp, ceremony and spectacle of court life. 'On a stage full of light, coloured pennants flew, fanfares played, and the attendant Lords and spear-carriers manoeuvred into position, while everyone waited for the scenes to begin.'[68] This was presentational Shakespeare, announcing its importance, authority and regal status through appropriate visual signifiers. A quality enhanced by the fact that the Old Vic could draw on a cast of forty-five to create grandiose stage pictures, whereas Theatre Workshop had fourteen and a great deal of doubling, trebling and quadrupling of parts. Littlewood avoided any semblance of spectacle; there were no elongated fanfares or ceremonial processionals. She used light to break up an otherwise dour stage and scenes merged swiftly into one another. The staging was unremittingly stark and sombre. According to Goorney, it was 'conceived to emphasise fear and oppression, we aimed to bring out the hatred and cruelty of the period'.[69] Bury created a large oppressive multilevel symmetrical structure with a central tunnel, two plain turrets and two ramps that gave way to tunnels in raw, unpolished materials. The low roofs of the tunnels ensured that all the characters had to duck down to enter them; they were physically constrained by their environment. Whilst the set was unable to convey the geographical restlessness of the play, the structure created sinister shadows and spaces for concealment or clandestine meetings. The tunnels and ramps giving way to darkness promoted a sense of foreboding as characters entered them – where were they going, what would they find there, would they come back again? Equally, the multilevel, symmetrical quality of the set was ideal for creating group formations that commented on the brokering of power hierarchies central to the play's narrative. Littlewood's production not only broke new ground in terms of its interpretive audacity, it looked completely different from any other British production occurring at the time – it was stark, sombre, hard-edged and metallic.

In 1956, Littlewood produced Christopher Marlowe's *Edward II*, a play that has justifiably drawn comparison with *Richard II* due to its interrogation of national instability, patronage and power, as well as its treatment of sexual politics. For this production, Bury created an evocative set by tilting the entire stage on huge ramps to create a sharply sloped playing area. Goorney recalls the creative and financial ingenuity required to realise this staging in *The Theatre Workshop Story*:

> To make the huge ramps for *Edward II* we hired scaffold planking, scrounged off-cuts of hardboard from a local factory to cover the cracks, got out the old canvas rolls, and created, for about twenty-five pounds, a set which, even in those days, would have cost five hundred.[70]

Rather than deploying the much-used canvas rolls to create one of the scenic cycloramas that graced many of his contemporaries' settings, Bury used them for a massive stylised map of England that covered the floor. This map provided the central visual motif occasionally joined by an elongated throne at the summit, which lighting transformed into a stained-glass window or tombstone. All the action took place on or around the map, which continually reminded the audience that it was the future of the nation at stake, not just the tangled relationship between Edward, his lover Gaveston, his queen Isabella and the court. Several reviewers found the lighting particularly effective, with the reviewer for *The Times* commenting on how Littlewood used it to enhance intensity of focus and action:

> To reduce the echoing depths of her stage Miss Littlewood used barriers of light thrown from the wings, the murky recesses behind often growing into the lurid opening of the following episode. Light was also used as a commentary on the action, being especially powerful in the mime scenes that built a *montage* of the civil war.[71]

As this review suggests, by keeping scenery and hence interruptions to the narrative minimal, Littlewood was able to keep the pace of the action slick. As a scene unfolded, she was often 'gathering episodes in the murk upstage. Then, as the scene in play ends, she dissolves the one smoothly into the other.'[72] This technique created a modern filmic aesthetic rather than the traditional cumbersome scene-setting of many contemporaneous productions.[73] Music also took on a filmic quality to enhance the emotional impact. As Littlewood remembered it, 'My *coup de théâtre* was Edward's murder – only his face was seen above a cloak held across his body and as the red-hot iron was supposed to enter his bowels the music gave a terrifying shriek.'[74]

Whereas interpretations of Richard II as a homosexual rely on Bolingbroke's ambiguous reference to how his cronies 'Made a divorce betwixt his queen and him. Broke the possession of a royal bed', as Callaghan asserts, 'sexual practices which have been consistently persecuted, suppressed and marginalised since the eighteenth century (and intermittently prior to it) take centre stage in Edward II'.[75] Edward II's queer identity is a matter of historical record, explicitly treated in the play and overtly explored in Littlewood's production, which was billed in publicity materials as 'The wild and mighty tragedy of an irregular love affair'.[76] Despite the potential for accusations that this approach attempts to normalise queer relations through traditional ascriptions of romantic love, it is important to historicise the significance of this portrayal. In a pre-Wolfenden Report era, this wording granted legitimacy to Edward's rejection of the heterosexual consensus and the sexual conduct openly referenced in the play. In line with what we now theorise as queer politics, this tagline destabilised the normative associations with the 'love story' or 'love affair'. It immediately set up the production as not pleading tolerance for homosexuality but as refiguring the terms of debate. This was an 'irregular', non-normative, queer relationship.

The fact that Edward is reduced from ruling the nation (however badly) to being an incarcerated, tortured and brutally murdered figure is a telling image of the brutality inflicted on the homosexual body and consciousness by the church and state. There are interesting connections to be made here between Littlewood's production and the filmmaker Derek Jarman's return to *Edward II* during a period of state-condoned negligence of the HIV crisis and the homophobic Clause 28. Both engaged in a very specific 'outing' of Edward and Gaveston's sexual relationship in a totally non-apologetic, unambiguous way at a key historical juncture for the public and state-sanctioned treatment of homosexuality.

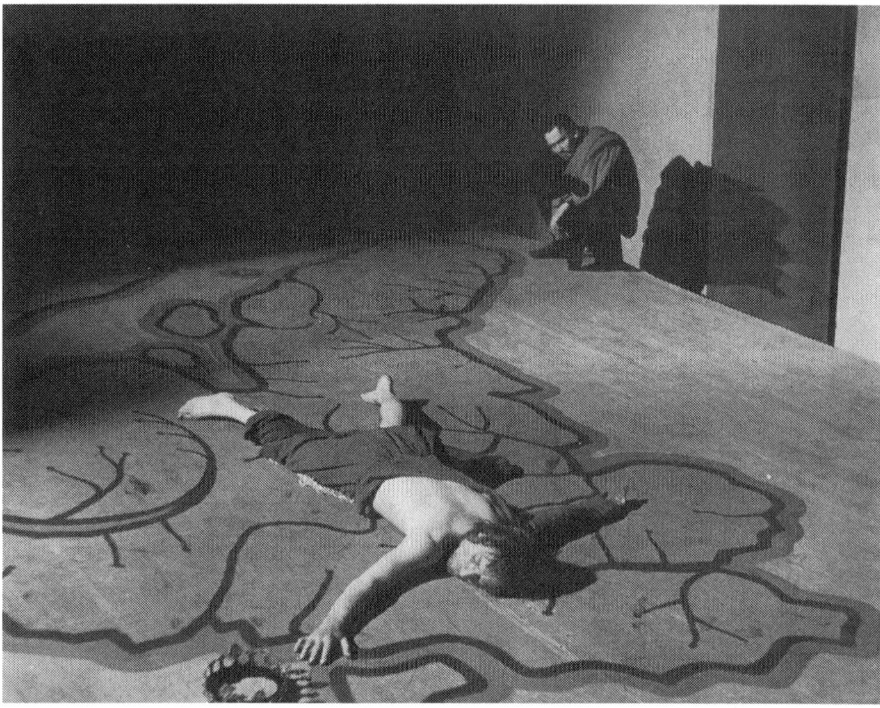

3. *Edward II* (1956).

In her production, Littlewood emphasised the crossover between the private and the public realms through Gaveston's intimate access to Edward and, as an extension, the nation through various visual signifiers such as Edward and Gaveston lying together across the map of England and Gaveston crouched behind the throne as Edward addresses his court. As such, Littlewood subverted the heteronormative space of the nation through the same-sex coupling that took place on the map. So, when a stripped-to-the-waist Edward dies, in a brutal parody of the act of sodomy, strewn across the map, there was a sense that the nation is both implicated in his murder and about to shift through the weight of Edward's literal and metaphorical presence – the nation is literally about to tilt on its axis. The image captured in microcosm what was happening in the public sphere. The Wolfenden Report would have not just a momentous impact on the personal relations of Britain's homosexual subjects, but also a profound impact on the political, social and cultural landscape.

The hostile climate surrounding issues of homosexuality also influenced Littlewood's decision to cast Peter Smallwood as Edward, as Clive Barker remembered:

> The superb performance of the actor playing Edward II for Theatre Workshop was achieved, through great pain, by having him confront his latent homosexuality, at a time when no great sympathy or tolerance could be expected from society at large.[77]

The personal investment inevitably led to a complex, nuanced performance of Edward's battle with dominant ideology, patriarchal authority and his own relation to his body and desire. Rather than Corbett's camp depiction of Richard II as a flamboyant, effeminate figure, Smallwood's dignified, sentimental Edward was full of pathos and vulnerability in the face of the masculinist status quo; certainly not the 'excitable, irresponsible King of history and Marlowe's play'.[78] The reviewer in the *New Statesman* claimed that Littlewood's 'Edward, Mr Peter Smallwood, by no means the gay, attractive king of legend, resembling as he did a willowy King Lear, was so intellectualised that he barely raised his voice above a well-bred, strangled cry'.[79] Taking Old Mortimer's description of Edward as 'mild and calm' as a starting point,[80] Smallwood's delivery was quietly unrhetorical, a feature that marked him apart from the overtly confident political bombast of the barons who ousted him and the manipulative verbal slipperiness of Maxwell Shaw as Gaveston. Smallwood's depiction subverted the portrayal of camp effeminacy that had come to stand in for homosexuality in many representations at the time (including Corbett's Richard II). It challenged fixed conceptions of the gay man, with its emphasis on ambiguity, fluidity and an alternative paradigm of the body, masculinity and sexuality. Smallwood as Edward found a way of embodying the duality of Edward's position as married/homosexual, compliant/defiant, desexualised/overtly sexualised, father/lover, victim/master of his own destiny.

As a king, Littlewood did little to suggest he was anything other than unfit for purpose due to his propensity for manipulation by

Gaveston, but Smallwood played this as a feature of his character as opposed to a feature of his sexual proclivities. This reading is borne out by *The Times* reviewer, who suggested that Littlewood interpreted the play as a 'sacrificial ritual', arguing that from the first entrance the King's demeanour and white robes marked him out as an victim.[81] The long, simple white robes and Edward's long hair also drew on Christian iconography of the martyred Christ – abused for his belief and activities. They also distinguished him from Gaveston, who wore black velvet and an extravagant red stole, which marked him as other from Mortimer and his henchmen, who were clothed in steel grey and black. Through his dress, language and deliberate flouting of his sexual access to the king, Gaveston stages a spectacle of power that belies his relatively lowly class status. He is a social climber and it is his and Edward's refusal to obey the rigid social hierarchy, as much as their sexual relationship, that infuriates the nobles. This is a play about both the lustre and the fragility of powerful allegiance. It exposes the villainy, hypocrisy and violence of the state as it seeks to maintain the status quo that advantages those in power and the heteronormative, but it equally highlights the fractures and ambiguities that reside within hierarchical social structures.

Although *Edward II* has since acquired iconic status in queer studies, Littlewood's blatant performative queering of the play was far too transgressive for the time. In comparison with the critical reception of *Richard II*, it is as if the critics collaborated in collective amnesia over the play's presentation of homosexual subjectivity and its resistance to normative regimes and heterosexist power structures. When sexual politics was deemed worth a mention in reviews, it was generally in the spirit of dismissal. For instance, the *Spectator* reviewer declared that the 'Edward–Gaveston *affaire* is given every textual licence to make it appear as un-becoming, and – more important for the plot – as politically inept'.[82] However, there is a sense that this textual licence was deliberately flouted by Littlewood's performative intervention. In presenting a sympathetic Edward, Littlewood critiqued the excessively patriarchal, masculinist and heterosexist culture governing his rule. This politicised reading also informed Littlewood's decision to cast Olive McFarland as Prince Edward. By casting a woman as the future monarch responsible for the death of Mortimer and the banishment of Queen Isabella, Littlewood drew attention to the juxtaposition of representations of femininity and homoerotic masculinity that would have resonated during the Renaissance, but also following the recent coronation of Elizabeth II. As such, she asked important questions about the role and function of those who did not subscribe to the dominant patriarchal and hetero-sexist order but had to function within it nevertheless.

Social satires

Littlewood steered clear of Shakespeare's comedies because she thought they were too safe, sentimental and distanced from contemporary life; instead she opted for the social comedies of John Marston and Ben Jonson who attacked human folly, greed and moral corruption with a sharp satirical bite. In 1953, she produced Jonson's *The Alchemist*, and in 1955 his *Volpone*, which caused a great stir both as part of the Paris-based Théâtre des Nations festival in 1955, where it received rapturous critical acclaim, as it did at the Theatre Royal. In contrast to the stark, elemental sets that relied on an overriding visual motif to draw out themes and atmosphere, *Volpone* employed an elaborate neoclassical Palladian set complete with marble columns, arches and a painted back-cloth of a Venetian street scene. However, the thematic emphasis was not lost as the opulent fakery of the set served as a poignant backdrop to the false, parasitic relationships and greedy lust for wealth the play satirises. Struck by the quality of the set and its ambition to be more than an attractively conceived and executed backdrop, Anthony Hartley of the *Spectator* stressed its originality for the time:

> How often is it that we see a really good set on the London stage? And by a really good set I mean a piece of stage achitecture [*sic*] and not the kind of chi-chi interior decorating which West End audiences tend to clap as the curtain goes up? The question is worth asking because it raises in a small way the whys and wherefores of the general decadence that has come upon the English theatre in recent years. This was started by the fact that Theatre Workshop have a really excellent Palladian set for their

> production of *Volpone*, designed by John Bury, and the shock of surprise was too much for me.[83]

What was particularly interesting about the *Volpone* staging was that it combined a mock eighteenth-century setting with a modern-dress production to create a strangely disjunctive set of images. Littlewood turned to modern dress for a number of her classic productions to underscore contemporary resonances in line with Worthen's assertion that 'modern-dress staging opens up the possibility of historical rupture' between the original and its contemporary production.[84] It urges audiences not to get lost in or seduced by the history of the play but to see how characters, situation and text can be related to the current climate. Despite earlier innovations by Jackson at the Birmingham Repertory Theatre, in the immediate postwar period many British directors expressed considerable suspicion of modern-dress productions, with several seeing them as an assault on the fidelity of the classics, and on Shakespeare in particular. But, as Worthen reminds us, 'despite the rhetoric of fidelity that undergirds modern directing, that fidelity is to "Shakespeare", a sense of the spirit or meaning of the play that transcends the concrete accidents of a particular version of the text'.[85] What is clear is that the 'Shakespeare' every director is trying to be faithful to is rooted in his or her own political convictions, social background, individual psychology, theatrical approach and attitude to history, and Shakespearean productions become the sites of contention where different perspectives are played out. In 1959, John Gielgud, for example, argued that the poetry, humour and manners of Shakespeare are distinctly of the Elizabethan age, frozen in a moment in time, and therefore that 'it is dangerous, too, and confusing, to play Shakespeare in costumes of a period later than his own'.[86] In contrast, Margaret Webster insisted on the universal applicability of Shakespearean 'truths' that rendered modern dress an unnecessary distraction:

> We shall not have to dress Hotspur in the uniform of the R.A.F. in order to invest him with life; we underrate both our author and our audience in supposing that they can only be dragged into accord by distorting Coriolanus to the image of General Franco; slyly insinuating that there have been abdications of the English

> throne more recent than those of Richard II; or claiming with gleeful shouts that Enobarbus is an anticipatory of Rudolf Hess. The truth of the plays is a timeless truth, and similarity of external circumstances no more than a fortuitous, though sometimes poignant, reminder that the returning paths of history have been trodden by many feet.[87]

In this quote, Webster reveals a particular understanding of history as a force doomed to repeat itself, a view that would have been complete anathema to Littlewood's understanding of dialectical history.

Without cutting or altering the text, Littlewood's *Volpone* transposed the action to present-day Venice to launch an attack on shallow materialism, greed and the obsequiousness of characters trying to ingratiate themselves for personal gain. Shaw played the disreputable Mosca as a sly, smooth-talking 'spiv' riding a bicycle whilst carrying pineapples and champagne, his changing fortunes reflected in ever more outlandish costumes. Corbett brought out the ridiculousness of Sir Politick Wouldbe by portraying him as a befuddled Tory backbencher and as the eternal bumbling Englishman abroad secure in only his suspicion of foreigners and his own self-importance, a self-image ridiculed by Corbett's deerstalker hat, swimming trunks and snorkel. Restricted to a wheelchair, Goorney's beret-wearing Corbaccio stressed eccentricity bordering on senility, and George Luscombe depicted Peregrine as an American tourist. In contrast to these larger-than-life characterisations, George Cooper's slick, carefully groomed Volpone was described as carrying 'considerable conviction', if 'insufficiently fruity and lecherous'.[88] Above all, Littlewood designed her production to bring out the human vanity and folly that Jonson exposes and the modern dress helped to signify the preponderance of these traits in the modern world.

The critics were overwhelmingly positive about this show, with many commenting on the resolutely modern quality of the piece. For Raffles, Theatre Workshop's contemporary approach meant that 'most of our audiences, both sophisticated and otherwise, thought they were seeing *Volpone* for the first time'.[89] Typical is Frank Granville Barker's review in *Plays and Players*, in which he insists that

> Littlewood's brilliantly imaginative production of *Volpone* blew the accumulated dust of ages off Jonson's savagely satirical masterpiece. Flinging crepe hair out of one window and moth-eaten costumes out of the other, the Theatre Workshop company showed us everything Jonson intended to bring home to us.[90]

Even those suspicious of modern-dress productions praised Littlewood's interpretive vigour. W. A. Darlington in the *Daily Telegraph* wrote,

> I have never been an admirer of the fashion of playing classics in modern dress. The incongruities always seem to detract from, rather than add to, the play. Last night, however, at the Theatre Royal, Stratford, Ben Jonson's *Volpone* was so beautifully brought off in this way that the sight of a bicycle, and strangely enough even the sound of boogie-woogie rhythm, failed to strike an incongruous note. The whole piece, in fact, played as freshly as if it had been written today.[91]

Theatre Workshop continued their relationship with Jonson in 1960 when they produced *Every Man in His Humour* at the Théâtre Sarah Bernhardt in Paris, as part of the Théâtre des Nations festival in 1960, before transferring it to the Theatre Royal. Failing to achieve the critical acclaim lavished on *Volpone*, the critics were still quick to praise Littlewood's lively, inventive approach that brought out the biting satire of Jonson's social comedy. She altered the text in places and, as Goorney recalled, 'Topical allusions had been included, and Joan's production carried it along at great speed and with a wealth of slapstick.'[92] The reviewers particularly noted how Littlewood had contemporised the performance style, with one recording,

> It is all throw-away, corner-of-the-mouth stuff, all wryness and self-irony. This may be the comic style now, but if so, it is because the cockneys have become just a bit Americanised. A great deal of the present production has more in common with *Guys and Dolls* than with *Every Man in His Humour*.[93]

As these quotes suggest, the production was closely allied to a popular end-of-pier slapstick that relied on bringing the material closer to its intended audience rather than being a faithful rendition of a classic that a purist might appreciate. This was due in large part to Littlewood's direction, but also to the comedic playing styles of Victor Spinetti, Roy Kinnear, Brian Murphy and Bob Grant. Although critics questioned 'whether we are left with Jonson or Littlewood',[94] they were primarily content to praise Littlewood's contemporising of Jonson's comedies and her insistence on overlaying them with her popular performance aesthetic.[95]

A positive response also greeted Theatre Workshop's production of *The Dutch Courtesan* in 1959. The company had originally staged this work in 1954 but it received scant critical attention. This production's profile benefited by following a year of critical and commercial successes with resolutely contemporary works including *A Taste of Honey, The Hostage* and *Fings Ain't Wot They Used T'Be*. In fact, Littlewood slotted it into a three-week gap in scheduling between revivals of *Fings Ain't Wot They Used T'Be* and *The Hostage*, and played the piece in dialogue with these recent social-realist depictions of seedy life to expose the thematic connections with the contemporary worlds they depict rather than the historical distance between the plays. Concerned with a sex worker's desire for revenge following her favourite client's decision to marry, Littlewood's brisk production exploited the play's wealth of dubious characters, crude vocabulary and salacious innuendo, which, according to one reviewer, left most of the audience 'in a state of stunned disbelief of their own ears'.[96] Several reviewers drew on Marston's reputation as a moralist and resituated the text in terms of the 1956 moment, describing it as an 'angry young malcontent's romp' and Marston as 'the A.Y.M. of Shakespeare's day' because of its keen sense of outrage against the socially disruptive force of prostitution.[97] But, rather than emphasising the conservative and misogynist implications of Marston's play, Littlewood framed Marston as 'the theatrical experimenter of his age – an Elizabethan James Joyce … he is noteworthy for his daring and extravagant vocabulary, for his innate sense of good humour: for his use of music: for his frankness'.[98] In particular, she relished the fact that the play offered complex psychological portraits rather than stock comic types, especially in his strong female characters. As she explained in a programme note,

> There are no lay figures, no heroes, no villains and no types to be found in most of Marston's work. Above all, there are real women . . . he was the only dramatist of the Golden Age of the English theatre who could write as women think.[99]

In producing *The Dutch Courtesan*, Littlewood wanted to present a social document, 'a kind of poor man's *Bartholomew Fair*'[100] that, much akin to Jonson's comedies, exposes the base desires, anxieties and propensity for violence lurking beneath the thin veneer of polite society.

Once again, critics praised Littlewood's ability to revitalise a neglected classic, with *The Times* reviewer claiming,

> Every now and then some fortunate or farsighted collector picks up a grimy object that turns out to be a treasure. Last night Theatre Workshop did something like that with a comedy by John Marston. Rubbing off the tarnish from the reputation of *The Dutch Courtesan* they made it shine like silver.[101]

There is a sense that whilst critics and audiences granted creative licence to Littlewood's popular approach to Renaissance and Jacobean comedy, especially comedy by dramatists other than Shakespeare, Shakespeare's tragedies and history plays were sacrosanct and ripe for preservation rather than regeneration. Indeed, the critics lambasted her modern-dress approach to Shakespeare's *Macbeth* in 1957 and her cutting and pasting of Parts 1 and 2 of *Henry IV* in 1964, which provide the focus for the next section of this chapter.

'Creative vandalism': cut-and-paste Shakespeare

After the rollercoaster success of her production of Behan's *The Quare Fellow* in 1956, Littlewood handed over the 1956–7 winter season to Bury, who took the opportunity to direct Shaw's *Captain Brassbound's Conversion*, J. M. Synge's *Playboy of the Western World*, and *School for Wives* by Molière. Littlewood returned after accepting an invitation to the World Youth Festival in Moscow, where she decided to take a play about 'the evil assumption of power' to comment on the immediate political situation in Russia.[102] Settling on *Macbeth*, with the title role played by Glynn Edwards, she 'set about stripping the play of the usual trimmings – no Highland mist, no bagpipes, no dry ice for the weird sisters, mine were three old biddies with a penchant for fortune-telling'.[103]

Rejecting the traditional Scottish setting, she referenced visual imagery from both the First and Second World Wars in a two-level set dominated by scaffolding. With khaki soldier uniforms, machine-guns rattling and the buzz of bombers circling overhead, the visual and aural *mise-en-scène* activated political parallels with recent events in Europe. Taking an approach in sympathy with Alan Sinfield's political reading of *Macbeth* which questions 'what is the difference between Macbeth's rule and that of contemporary European monarchs?',[104] Raffles admitted that the company considered setting the play in Europe, 'where the events of the play have been more or less re-enacted in real life in several countries in recent years, but Britain is not absolutely immune from power-hungry military men'[105] – a point chillingly brought home by the debacle in Suez in 1956. Presenting Macbeth as a Machiavellian British general who becomes a dictator, commentators were spoilt for choice for analogous twentieth-century political tyrants as the ghosts of Mussolini, Hitler and Stalin stalked the production. Robert Wraight used the tagline 'Hitler – Macbeth' for his review, T. C. Worsley referred to a 'poor man's Hitler' and Littlewood claimed that in Moscow 'the students seemed to grasp the parallel with their own political leadership'.[106] In February 1956, Nikita Khrushchev denounced Stalin as a despot whose repressive regime instilled suspicion and terror in all quarters through threats of humiliation, persecution and murder. The same year also saw the brutal Russian suppression of the Hungarian uprising. In the immediate aftermath of these tumultuous events, *Macbeth*'s depiction of rampaging generals intent on dominance and the wanton abuse of military power was bound to have resonance. In a programme note, Littlewood laid out the reasons for her approach to the text:

> In presenting MACBETH in modern dress we are not trying to be clever or experimental: the fundamental truth of a great work of

> art needs no decoration to make it acceptable. When we play the classics in our people's theatre we try to wipe away the dust of three hundred years, to strip off the 'poetical' interpretations which the nineteenth century sentimentalist put upon these plays and which are still current today . . . If Shakespeare has any significance today, a production of his work must not be regarded as a historical reconstruction, but as an instrument still sharp enough to provoke thought, to extend man's awareness of his problems, and to strengthen his belief in his kind.[107]

To help provoke thought and awareness, Littlewood adopted a Brechtian distancing mode. Her production began and concluded with Macbeth's execution. An image resonant with the executions administered after the Nuremberg war crimes trials that ensured that the production was as much an assault on wars of aggression and crimes against humanity as on the actions of one rogue general. By cutting and resituating scenes, Littlewood was able to present the rest of the play as a series of flashbacks in Macbeth's mind. Aware that Macbeth faces the ultimate punishment for his deeds, the audience was able to chart the journey and to understand how and why he meets this end. Rather than representing Macbeth as a weak character driven to inhumane acts by his manipulative wife, played by Eileen Kennally, Edwards drew on Littlewood's references to Eisenstein's *Ivan the Terrible* during rehearsals and portrayed him as an uptight macho thug, driven to mania by his ambition. The production explicitly asked questions about the relation between warfare and masculinity. To be known as a great warrior, as Macbeth is, requires an aptitude for killing that ultimately warps and destroys acceptable moral boundaries. Yet Littlewood explored how this moral dissolution connects to valorised versions of masculine success.

Above all, Littlewood stressed Macbeth's responsibility for his actions as a freethinking individual able to make ethical judgements and choices. Kott developed this interpretive line subsequent to Littlewood's production when he wrote, 'In *Macbeth* history, as well as crime, has been shown through personal experience. It is a matter of decision, choice and compulsion. Crime is committed on personal responsibility and has to be executed with one's own hands.'[108] To foster this reading Littlewood emphasised Macbeth's megalomania, but also his guilty conscience that grounded the whole production through the flashback structure and surfaced in frequent nightmare scenes. For instance, Macbeth's second encounter with the witches was staged as a nightmare, 'Macbeth tossing and turning in his bed, imagining the old women in the room with him and seeing pageants of kings only in his mind's eye'.[109] Similarly, Schafer has observed that a production photograph in *Plays and Players* 'confirms that Banquo's ghost was also a figment of Macbeth's imagination: a group of smartly dressed diners, the women in long white dresses and elbow length gloves, the men in dress uniforms, gaze in perplexity at the empty stool where Macbeth can see Banquo's ghost'.[110] Macbeth's guilt was unmistakable, but whilst Littlewood presented a flawed individual tortured by his actions, more important was her decision to situate him within a particular social structure and value system.

As Margot Heinemann recognises, 'The problem of presenting Shakespearean tragedy as usually conceived . . . is that it is based on the *acceptance* of evil and disaster as fated, unalterable, eternal.'[111] In *Macbeth*, this problem is rooted in the supernatural. In her production, Littlewood cut most references to the witches, as she was keen to steer away from a supernatural interpretation that absolved Macbeth of his crimes by seeing him as the passive victim of a dark metaphysical plot over which he had little control, or in relation to some abstract notion of 'evil'. Perturbed by this calculated omission, the reviewer for *The Times* argued that 'the exclusion of the witches robs Macbeth of heroic stature; he becomes merely an ambitious man', the 'life-size Macbeth' of his review title.[112] Similarly, Marshall regretted that 'her determinedly anti-poetic treatment of the play reduced Macbeth to no more than a craven killer'.[113] Issued as criticisms, these comments actually pithily capture Littlewood's approach to the text. As Sinfield proposes, the recourse to the supernatural

> suggests that Macbeth is an extraordinary eruption in a good state – obscuring the thought that there might be any proneness to structural malfunctioning in the system. It suggests that

> Macbeth's violence is wholly bad, whereas state violence committed by legitimate monarchs is quite different.[114]

Rather than adopting a reading of Macbeth as a usurping tyrant who disrupts an otherwise orderly absolutist state, Littlewood used *Macbeth* to explore the consequences of a hierarchical social order that ignites a lust for power in someone lower down the pecking order. Macbeth was a soldier in a chain of command who came to think he could do better than his superiors could. She exposed how Macbeth is seduced by and embraces naked personal ambition in a society that values success and how this social structure corrupts and destroys individuals and society. As Schafer acknowledges, 'Littlewood's determination to see Macbeth as a product of class, as a soldier and a thug does not seem so remarkable nowadays; however, in 1957, this line of thought completely shocked the reviewers.'[115]

Premiered at the Zurich Festival en route to Moscow, Raffles admitted that in both cities, 'it was received by the critics with considerable hostility and, although in Moscow the audiences were wildly enthusiastic, in Zurich there were cheers and boos'.[116] According to Goorney, the Moscow critics 'felt that the modernisation of the play undermined the belief of the audience in the truth of what was happening on the stage, and the need to abandon the mysticism destroyed Shakespeare's conception of the play as well as his poetry'.[117] In Britain, critics were aghast at Littlewood's audacious cutting and reordering of scenes, the relocation of the play to England rather than Scotland and the deliberate attempt to politicise the text. They were also concerned by a purposeful lack of grandeur. For instance, the reviewer for *The Times* stated that 'she seemed anxious to strip the titanic central figures of their dignity', and Caryl Brahms in *Plays and Players* accused her of taking the mickey out of the Macbeths.[118]

Severely disgruntled by the production, David Watt's review under the title 'The Relapse' accused it of 'arid doctrinaire aestheticism', and even went so far as to claim that it 'is an acute case of recidivism and ought to be seen by a great many people on the Chinese principle by which criminals are exhibited to the public under humiliating circumstances'.[119] The level of rancour is quite extraordinary and speaks volumes about the baggage attached to the classics and expectations of acceptable performative interpretations. Several reviews give the impression that Littlewood had tampered with a national treasure and in doing so had failed to show due respect for the cultural canon, the monarchy and the state. *The Times* reviewer concluded,

> The chief fault was not in individual performances but in the insensitive arrogance of the production which substituted for a coherent society a never-never land where staff-officers could chat to old men in the rain, where private executions were carried out by homburg-hatted hatchet men, and where coronation robes and the uniform of a commissar were jumbled together.[120]

A similar response greeted Littlewood's adaptation of *Henry IV* Parts 1 and 2, her first classic production since *Every Man in His Humour* in 1960, and the first since the phenomenal success of *Oh What a Lovely War* the previous year. Interestingly, Peter Hall had asked her to direct the plays for the RSC but as Colin Chambers put it, 'she did not like the Stratford set-up – which she nicknamed Stratford West – and departed'.[121] Tom Driberg, a lifelong friend and supporter of Littlewood recalled, 'Joan told me, "I'm tempted to do it largely because the plays are among my favourites. They are good for peace propaganda".'[122] The idea obviously stuck and Theatre Workshop premiered their controversial production at the Assembly Hall during the 1964 Edinburgh Festival, before transferring to the Theatre Royal. The main cause of critical disquiet centred on Littlewood's attempt to telescope the two parts of *Henry IV*, eccentric staging decisions, lack of fidelity to the verse and an interpretive approach that, once again, confounded expectations.

Littlewood's cavalier attitude to the textual authority of Shakespeare was apparent in her radical attempt to condense the two parts, which resulted in a carved-up creative collage that dispensed with some key scenes, characters and narrative development. Interestingly, in 1957, Planchon had chosen to combine the two parts of *Henry IV* in his inaugural production at the Théâtre de la Cité, where he hoped to establish a new popular dramaturgy that highlighted

4. Joan Littlewood rehearsing *Henry IV* Parts 1 and 2 (1964).

political relevance, social conditions and a combination of cinematic and Brechtian aesthetics. But whereas Planchon's Marxist interpretation focused on the conflict between church and state, Littlewood offered a revisionist history play that displaced the royal narrative in order to concentrate on the *other* England Shakespeare dramatises, 'its taverns, brothels and farms – which rivals the official history in importance and surpasses it in the sheer energy and copiousness of its detail'.[123] In Littlewood's version, there were no Cotswold scenes or renouncement of Falstaff, no ruminations on sleep by the King, and the combination ended with the death of Hotspur as if the intrusions of Part 2 had not occurred. Littlewood's deliberate dismembering of the text caused considerable consternation even amongst admirers of her work such as Simon Trussler, who was bewildered by the incoherent arrangement and noted the production's fixation on Part 1 'with odd portions of the second part obtruding like so many diseased growths on the healthy limbs of the first'.[124] Again, the ferocity of some reviews gave the impression that Littlewood had taken a machete to Shakespeare's corpse rather than to two of his history plays. Trussler's image of a mutant body is typical of the accusations levelled at Littlewood. *The Times* reviewer described it as 'an act of theatrical pillage which in its combination of muddled purpose and bungled execution rivals the expedition to the Bay of Pigs'.[125]

Bury's design and Littlewood's idiosyncratic staging ignited significant criticism. Rejecting the open stage Tyrone Guthrie had used at the Assembly Hall, Bury created an oblong traverse stage that bisected the entire audience down the middle – a design that led to unnecessary problems with communication as the action split focus between two audiences either side of the raised bridge-like platform, causing poor sightlines and audibility. Historical and geographical discontinuity characterised costuming that used modern dress with a period twist in accessories such as cloaks, hats and boots. The court was dressed in modern suits with cloaks; Hal in a pair of Mersey heels and Poins in slick Italian slacks, a velour bowler hat, an ear-ring, a leather jerkin and jaunty high-heeled blue suede boots. Falstaff came across as a timeless vagabond with string holding up his navvy trousers and a protruding gouty foot, but he also carried the trappings of warfare, 'a British-warm, splitting at the oxters; a water bottle, Service ribbons and other incidentals, all of which ally him with the old campaigner, perhaps still on the reserve'.[126] In the light of Theatre Workshop's recent *Oh What a Lovely War*, this portrayal is significant, as it connects Falstaff to the weary yet defiantly humane soldiers Littlewood honoured in that production.

Several reviewers expected Littlewood to sidestep the troubled relationship between Henry IV and his son Hal in order to concentrate on the Falstaff theme because of its propensity for rumbustious scenes, low-life action and ribald humour. But George Cooper's Falstaff confounded expectations for a number of reasons. To begin with, he was played much younger than was customary and without the usual ruddy complexion and beard. According to Ernest Bradbury, Cooper instead offered 'a kind of hefty Lancashire comedian with a Chaplin moustache'.[127] Rather than making him a larger-than-life endearing rogue, Cooper's Falstaff was flawed, an old campaigner given to brawls, lying, accepting bribes and denouncing the troops he is ashamed to be seen with. Refusing to excuse this aspect of Falstaff's character and, in fact, drawing attention to it, Littlewood and Cooper made him far more complex and less sentimental than usual depictions of a red-faced, whiskered, pot-bellied man given to high jinks and a love of good living. Equally, Littlewood cut the scene where Hal rejects his old carousing companion, leaving the relationship open-ended at the death of Hotspur, when Hal decides to forgo his right to claim responsibility for Hotspur's death in order to protect Falstaff. As James C. Bulman has observed, this moment

> achieves a morally complex and tentative resolution. On the one hand, Hal's defeat of Hotspur signals his assumption of royal responsibility and ensures reconciliation with his father; on the other, his protection of Falstaff intimates his potential for regression and a profound ambivalence about the role he is destined to play.[128]

Stephen Greenblatt has written persuasively on how Hal's 'low-life excursions' and mastery of 'tavern slang' stage a transgression 'for the pleasure of what Victor Turner calls "communitas" – a union based on the momentary breaking of the hierarchical order that normally governs a community'.[129] Greenblatt proceeds to examine how Hal's occupation of social space and linguistic proficiency is part of a politically strategic process of surveillance and control and crucial to his transition to effective monarch. Nonetheless, this reading relies on the renouncement of Falstaff that Littlewood chose not to stage, so in her version the vision of 'communitas' holds sway. In Littlewood's production, clear class dynamics were at work whereby the highway, tavern and rustic scenes were full of wit, vitality and a richness of experience completely absent from the court scenes populated by 'cold politicians, uniform in dress and clipped and unemotional in speech'[130] – an approach echoing Littlewood's work on *Oh What a Lovely War* discussed in the previous chapter. The King lacked stature, 'Hotspur's grandiloquence was *meant* to sound empty' and the career politicians were sketchily drawn out in austere grey and black costumes to highlight their lack of individuality.[131]

In contrast, the minor characters were given far more depth and colour in Littlewood's cut-and-paste script. They had rounded characterisations, meaningful exchanges and a capacity for quick-witted humour, loyalty and dignity missing from most productions of Shakespeare during this period, which still primarily employed 'low-life' characters for facile, cheap laughs. Discussing the production, John Russell Brown explained that at Stratford-upon-Avon, 'Francis was a gormless lout, kicked around for broad comic effect, but in the Theatre Workshop production, played by Jeremy Spenser, his scene with Hal revealed honesty, loyalty, ambition, ignorance – a small, conventional and intense imagination'.[132] Melvin played Gadshill as a sharp-talking street hustler compensating with language what he lacked in physical stature, and Richard Gurnock's Feeble impressed Russell Brown:

> Feeble's good nature was as firmly established, but his philosophizing was not produced as if it were philosophy; he was the sort of man who might quote Patience Strong in the barrack-room. 'Faith!, I'll bear no base mind' spoke of inexperience as well as bravery, self-concern as well as honesty; it was of a piece with the whole characterization.[133]

Nonetheless, the majority of critics were openly dismissive of Littlewood's method and outcome, which is interesting given its close proximity to the RSC's *Wars of the Roses*, staged the previous year during which John Barton 'cut about half the total text and added some 1400 lines of mock-Elizabethan verse as connective, tightening the political argument of the unfamiliar works'.[134] But this was not the epic political pageant staged by Peter Hall, it was a rough, bawdy theatre that relished the dirty squalor of Eastcheap and the lascivious antics of its inhabitants.

The response to the production was so negative that Littlewood called a press conference under the chairmanship of Lord Harewood, the artistic director of the Festival, during which she courted further controversy by claiming that they played for audiences rather than for critics, and, 'We have no respect for Shakespeare. In Scotland, England, the whole world they are bogged down with art and respect for the past. We are not.'[135] She also issued a statement, claiming, 'It is easier to attack the Royal Family than attempt to scrape off the patina of age and the dreary respect which stifles Elizabethan verse. Shakespeare's company was made up of leary misfits, anarchists, out of work soldiers and wits who worked at their ideas in pubs and performed them as throwaways to an uninhibited pre-Puritan audience.'[136] Interestingly, she also tried to align Theatre Workshop with her conception of Shakespeare's company as a bunch of outsiders collaborating and peddling their theatrical wares to a popular audience. She consistently referred to her actors as nuts, clowns and villains, and in this instance claimed that 'we're not directors or actors, we are just really a shower of bums. We came up here for a good holiday.' There are several things at play here: in line with her reputation as 'a walking paradox, a ragbag of contradictions',[137] Littlewood both asserted the importance of her endeavour to promote the relevance and popular appeal of Shakespeare and, simultaneously, undermined the seriousness of her theatrical experimentation.

Her production of *Henry IV* was about much more than trying to contemporise Shakespeare, it was part of a much wider aim to destroy the complacent, genteel, well-behaved theatre of the middle classes; it was an echo of the way Shakespeare employed his original *Henry IV* to critique the puritanical Lord Chamberlain and the Privy Council that had closed theatres the summer before in revenge for Jonson's seditious play *The Isle of Dogs*.[138] In her programme note for the production, Littlewood noted this transgressive quality, claiming, 'In the tavern scenes every phrase is a dig at the Puritans or a send-up of the styles and concepts of fellow poets.'[139] Coinciding with Littlewood's developing plans for a popular Fun Palace that could revolutionise leisure, education, entertainment and theatrical practice, this production was a call to arms, a blunt assertion of her refusal to take anything for granted. Theatre needed ripping up from the roots and returning to the pre-Puritan age, a sensuous and vital theatre of the streets, of ribald humour, of antisocial desires and anarchic potential that put play and pleasure at its heart. As Tynan recognised in her, 'she would like to revive the Elizabethan London of bear-pits and bordellos thronged with "delicious ruffians"'.[140] So in this production, without ignoring the concerns with kingship, succession, political rebellion and the wresting of the nation state from the claims of feudal warlords, she chose to emphasise the taverns of Eastcheap and their hedonistic inhabitants. In her reading, the excessive partying and creative word-play of Falstaff, the sexual innuendo of Mistress Quickly and the salacious banter of Doll Tearsheet were what the 'groundlings' would have relished and what constituted the riotous popular entertainment she was trying to reignite. An aim deliciously illustrated by the inclusion of a comic visual sequence that involved the transference of fleas from low-life character to low-life character that provoked intense laughter in the audience.[141] Flawed in design, incoherent in structure, and hastily brought together it may have been, but Littlewood's production had a definite purpose that only Ronald Bryden, a lone voice in a cluster of sanctimonious critics, could articulate:

> Not the epic of emergent Britain, as in Peter Hall's Brechtian cycle; not the emblematic verse-pageant of Tudor royalism. Instead, a neo-Elizabethan performance of a performance, an attempt to make us see what the Globe groundlings saw: a group of disreputable cockneys in cloaks and tinsel posturing through a thicket of incomprehensible baronial skirmishes for the sake of those rough, comic scenes which enshrined the folk-legend of the people's prince, the royal knave of Eastcheap and his cronies. As much as any Third Programme reconstruction of Elizabethan pronunciation, it was an essay in dramatic scholarship: a projection not simply of the play but of its audience.[142]

Littlewood's decade of experimentation with Renaissance classics drew to a close with *Henry IV* as she turned her attention to the much larger cultural project of the Fun Palace and the creative community activism explored in later chapters.

As I claimed in my introduction to this volume, these productions have received minimal prior scrutiny and her influence on, or synergies with, stagings of Renaissance plays by other companies has been largely unacknowledged.[143] By 1964, Tynan recorded that in productions of Shakespeare 'the new fashion is to excavate truth, no matter how many diamonds of elocution one may lose in the process',[144] a shift that owed a great deal to Littlewood's innovations at the Theatre Royal. Certainly, when

Peter Hall embarked on a reorganisation of the Royal Shakespeare Company in the early 1960s, he opted for a permanent core of directors, performers and designers working towards the goal of producing Shakespeare for a modern audience through vigorous textual analysis, as well as an emphasis on narrative thrust and visual economy. These qualities were evident at the Theatre Royal during the previous decade and undoubtedly had an influence on Hall's vision. In fact, in 1964, he persuaded Bury to join the company, and, as a result, the visual aesthetic honed at the Theatre Royal became a signature of the RSC's new approach.[145] At this time, the RSC was becoming *the* global reference point for ways of producing Shakespeare and it is interesting to speculate on how much this new theatrical orthodoxy owed to Littlewood's vision. It is also possible to see the defining traits of Littlewood's classic productions resurface in the work of contemporary European directors such as Simon McBurney, Declan Donellan and Calixto Bieito, who have continued to develop the physical and linguistic muscularity Littlewood helped pioneer.

4 Poetic realism: representing working-class communities

Throughout the 1930s and 1940s, Littlewood regularly stressed her commitment to the working class as the force for revolutionary social change in Britain. But she equally expressed her frustration with working-class apathy and materialism. In a letter to Raffles sent 9 March 1947 she confided,

> The masses of the workers, the vast majority in this country are at the moment smug, snobbish, stupid bourgeoises in outlook – they would wince at the name 'worker' – not hold it an honour and dropping any romantic twaddle I cannot see that there are any groupings, including the miners at the moment, who stand as exceptions to this.[1]

As such, Littlewood was aware, at a very early stage, of the conditions that had prompted one of the central debates within British society since the Second World War: the decline of the working class as a demographic formation and a distinct sociocultural entity. By the 1950s, when affluence replaced the rhetoric of austerity, commentators began to express anxieties about the impact of increasing educational opportunities, social and geographical mobility, material security, consumerism, mass culture, industrial change and suburbanisation on traditional working-class communities, politics and culture. As a result of these changes, during the 1950s and 1960s the working class was regarded as a topic of exceptional social, political and cultural importance.

In sharp contrast to a culture of working-class apathy and bourgeois sensibility she deplored, Littlewood argued, of her fledgling

Theatre Workshop group, 'We unlike many of them have not lost our class roots and ideology.'[2] She was determined to put her output as a cultural worker at the service of the working class as her inspiration, subject and target audience. Encouraged by Archie Harding, D. G. Bridson and Olive Shapley in the 1930s and 1940s, Littlewood, together with MacColl, had already made a significant contribution to the documentary radio movement through her location-based work in the north of England recording working-class people articulating their everyday life experiences in local idioms. And, when she was in a position to focus on theatre full time, a central strand of her early work explored the centrality and character of working-class communities in creating the conditions in which a proletarian consciousness could evolve and be politicised. And in her later work Littlewood increasingly engaged in a theatrical dialogue with wider sociological concerns around shifting patterns of working-class identification.

Before we go any further down this path it is worth dwelling for a moment on the problem of adopting the term 'working-class community'. Both 'class' and 'community' as viable descriptors have come under considerable scrutiny and reappraisal in recent years. For many, the terms are unacceptably essentialist and fail to account for the multilayered, often conflictual and contradictory, identities experienced by individuals and groups. Yet both remain persistent in social analysis and together they occupy a powerful place in the social imaginary of British culture, particularly when considering the mid-twentieth century, when Littlewood was working. This notion of the 'social imaginary' is important, because in this chapter the representation of working-class life and communities comes under scrutiny, rather than a focus on *actual* working-class communities.

In broad terms, the conception of class employed in this chapter refers not to the Weberian structural model that emphasises different strata or hierarchical social layers that define experience, but sees class as a 'social-relational' model that structures class dialogically and relationally. This perspective relies on a historical materialist understanding of class as embodied through lived experience, social phenomena and an elusive 'structure of feeling', to adopt Raymond Williams's famous phrase. As such, it is more about affiliation and identification than a quantifiable structural reality. Williams captured the elusive quality of this 'structure of feeling' when he described it as 'specifically affective elements of consciousness and relationships; not feelings against thought, but thought as felt and feeling as thought: practical consciousness of a present kind, in a living and interrelated community'.[3]

Commentators often describe working-class communities as tight and close-knit, metaphors signalling a particularly embedded set of social relations. Describing working-class communities in his study *The Working Class* (1978), Kenneth Roberts found that 'Residents feel a consciousness of kind. They share an awareness of facing common problems and mix with an effortless sociability. Neighbourliness becomes natural and is continuously cemented in pubs, streets, corner-shops, workplaces and homes.'[4] Joanna Bourke similarly refers to a sense of locatedness in a particular street or neighbourhood, close physical proximity with neighbours, a sense of shared perspectives and reciprocal dependency.[5] As this demonstrates, the working class is associated with a very particular geography and landscape of the street, immediate neighbourhood and locality, factors that consistently reoccur in Theatre Workshop productions that set out to represent working-class characters and communities.

In general terms, this geography suggests a sense of connectedness with others, a communal consciousness that engenders a sense of responsibility and co-operation with and for others. Like Richard Hoggart before her, Bourke argues that in the late nineteenth and early twentieth centuries, harsh material conditions forged traditional working-class communities as individuals sought solace and strength in the communal social relations offered by family, the workplace and community that provided a shared culture of support and resistance where reciprocity was crucial.[6] However, Bourke is quick to dispel easy romanticism by establishing that these communities were more often than not based on allies helping each other out rather than on close friendships and that the existence of conflict rooted in the failure of kinship networks, local rivalries and the complex nuances of differing social status, ethnic backgrounds and religious sensibilities remained persistent. Equally, the idea of working-class communities shifts according to different industries, regional variations, gender status and ethnic mix, for example, and it does not take too much of a leap for close-knit to become claustrophobic, lacking in privacy and stifling change or ambition.

Nonetheless, for Bourke, the social imaginary of the close-knit working-class community works as a powerful rhetorical device within two distinct discourses: 'one, a backward-looking romanticism, and the other, a forward-looking socialism'.[7] The former foregrounds open doors, friendly neighbours and shared resources as opposed to harsh living conditions and competition for jobs and housing, whilst the latter emphasises that horizontal relations with others suggest a conduciveness to class consciousness and serve as a form of 'innate socialism'.[8] Both of these discourses are crucial in understanding Littlewood and Theatre Workshop's representation of working-class communities. Littlewood consistently evoked representations, albeit often sentimental and nostalgic, of the traditional mythology of working-class life and community in order to celebrate it, to critique it and to chart the social cleavages irrevocably altering its make-up – all of which occurred within the broader ideological impulse of socialism.

This chapter addresses some of the representational strategies Littlewood used when approaching the social imaginary of the working class. One section addresses two early Theatre Workshop productions, *Johnny Noble* (1945) and *Landscape with Chimneys* (1951) to consider how they employ the street and ideals of a close-knit northern geographical community to tackle the treatment of communal struggles, agency and action. The second section explores the representation of exclusively male occupational communities in *The Long Shift* (1951) and *You Won't Always Be on Top* (1957) as a means of articulating a specific iconography of working-class life tied up in male work-based relations, trade union activity, and shared communal space. The third section begins an investigation of Littlewood's theatrical imagining of the East End of London, an iconic site associated with a vibrant working-class community and culture and one that became a touchstone for shifts in working-class communities following the seminal publication of Michael Young and Peter Willmott's *Family and Kinship in East London* (1957), which charted the impact of rehousing and relocation on family, kinship and community relations.[9] However, I begin by considering the ways in which Littlewood's work corresponded with and departed from the 'new wave' movement that emerged in British culture during the 1950s and 1960s as part of the wider social and political discourses taking place around the fate of the working class.

Littlewood, Theatre Workshop and the 'new wave'

Several writers have positioned Littlewood and Theatre Workshop within a broader postwar movement focusing on cultural representations of working-class life, experience and communities associated with the term 'new wave'.[10] Focusing on the socially marginal experience of the working class, the teenager and the geographical regions, 'new wave' practitioners, many of whom came from working-class backgrounds, sought to unsettle the postwar consensus by mapping other versions of social reality than those previously privileged in cultural discourse.[11] New themes emerged such as fluid social identities, tensions between individual and collective identities, working-class backgrounds and middle-class aspirations, gender antagonisms, the 'outsider' hero, entrapment and escape.

Novelists such as John Braine, Alan Sillitoe and Stan Barstow presented working-class antiheroes voicing 'a protest against the soullessness and conformity of "affluent" modern life'.[12] In the theatre, John Osborne's *Look Back in Anger* (1956) and Arnold Wesker's *The Wesker Trilogy* (1960) exposed the continuing significance of class in a deeply divided British society. The 'new wave' in cinema, associated with directors with notable theatre experience including Lindsay Anderson and Tony Richardson, drew heavily on adaptations of the novels and plays of the period, such as *Room at the Top* (1959), *Look Back in Anger* (1959), *Saturday Night and Sunday Morning* (1960), and *A Taste of Honey* (1961):

> The literature is suffused with a consciousness that the period represents a turning point in the history of class relations, and that it was important to document working class cultures and their social foundations before they were lost; hence the work has aspects of both celebration and lamentation.[13]

Formally, the 'new wave' was associated with social realism, the implication being that social realism had the potential to do more than merely replicate surface realities, but could provide a rhetoric of social responsibility, democratic principles and education by countering the absence of the working class from dominant discursive regimes and cultural output. As such, Andrew Higson illuminates the 'new wave' project with reference to the term 'moral realism', which suggests a degree of commitment to exposing social problems and issues or showing the dignity and achievements of the working class.[14] Prior to this movement the working class were generally viewed from outside and constructed by an educated middle class as lowlife stereotypes, comic foils, brave chirpy Cockneys or stoical brusque northerners, who lacked complexity, humanity and inner life. In contrast, the 'new wave' presented working-class characters as central protagonists undertaking complex social and emotional journeys.

However, unlike the documentary veracity of the Mass Observation movement that sought to authentically record working-class life and experience, Higson identifies a clear aesthetic which takes the representations offered beyond documentary realism into the realm of 'poetic realism', which 'involves a more perfect conjunction of surface realism and moral realism, a conjunction which in fact *transcends* ordinariness, which makes the ordinary strange, beautiful – *poetic*'.[15] According to Terry Lovell, the idea and practice of poetic realism 'allowed New Wave directors to stress the personal vision of the observer/film-maker as well as the authenticity of what was observed'.[16] Poetic realism relies on the presence of thinking practitioners composing images or developing heightened language that has a particular resonance or impact. As such, poetic realism draws attention to its own construction, theatricality and aesthetic strategies.

Arguably, Littlewood's work corresponded with this conception of 'poetic realism'. She maintained an ideological commitment to representing the richness and variety of working-class life and experience, but she also remained a passionate advocate of theatrical experimentation and sharply honed visual and aural imagery. There are, however, ways in which she departed from the 'new wave'. John Hill has observed that, 'Despite the ostensive commitment to represent the working class, the British "new wave", through their adoption of conventional narrativity and "realism", tend to have the opposing effect, that is, the creation of accentuated individualism.'[17] In contrast to individual characters dislocated from their working-class roots that characterised the 'new wave', Littlewood's productions marshalled ensemble playing to represent complex communities united by a shared geographical location or workplace in which characters negotiate the trials and tribulations of everyday life en masse. Yet this should not be mistaken for a romantic image of homogeneity, which bleaches out difference and alternative identities and lifestyles. In fact, Littlewood emphasised the variations, social cleavages and antagonisms in working-class communities as part and parcel of their vitality and innate theatricality.

Andy Medhurst argues that recourse to the experiential is a valuable way of facilitating awareness of the various ways in which class is located, embodied and lived.[18] In the 1950s, this mode was enshrined in Richard Hoggart's seminal *Uses of Literacy*, whose 'hybrid combination of the personal and the public, objective and subjective, individual and collective ... lend it acute insights on working-class life'.[19] And, according to Stephen Lacey, interpretive frameworks surrounding the 'new wave' often stress 'a particular relationship between author, text and social experience being represented that relied on the personal situation of the writers to guarantee the "truth" of the text, its sociological validity'.[20] Despite the fact that experience does not necessarily equate to reliable authority, the trope of autobiography for legitimating and authenticating depictions of working-class life featured prominently in the framing mechanisms employed by Theatre Workshop. As Dee Heddon reminds us, this recourse to the autobiographical is inherently political as it draws attention to the questions 'Who speaks? What is spoken? What sorts of lives are represented, contested, imagined?'[21]

Littlewood was determined to frame her representations of working-class life and communities as different, as legitimate, and she consistently drew on the autobiographical as an authenticating mechanism. So a programme note for Henry Chapman's *You Won't Always Be on Top* (1957) explained, 'The author has worked for a long time in the building trade and was a card steward of the National Federation of Building Trade Operatives. He writes of what he knows.'[22] Goorney claimed of *Fings Ain't Wot They Used T'Be* that 'Frank's own experience of two years in jail for bouncing cheques, and his first-hand knowledge of the seamier side of Soho life, had been used to good advantage',[23] and that *Sparrers Can't Sing* benefited by originating from a playwright 'drawing on a background he really knew. Stephen Lewis, then thirty years old, had lived in the East End all his life and had been a bricklayer before joining the Company as an actor.'[24] There is also no doubt that MacColl's working-class industrial northern roots and political upbringing informed his early playwriting. As his biographer, Ben Harker, acknowledges, *Johnny Noble* (1945) drew heavily on MacColl's memories of his childhood in Lower Broughton and Coburg Street, autobiographical resonances that may go some way to explain its nostalgic and romantic construction of community.[25]

A socially imagined community: the street, solidarity and collective action

MacColl's ballad opera *Johnny Noble* and *Landscape with Chimneys* (1950) adhered to Littlewood's desire, articulated in an early notebook, to 'reflect the life of the people – to give voice to their tragedy', but also her ideological impulse to promote the working class as a force for renewal.[26] Both pieces are set in the north of England: *Johnny Noble* in Hull and *Landscape with Chimneys* in Salford. This geopolitical space reflected MacColl's Salford upbringing, but it also significantly drew on the fact that 'ideas of the North in British culture lean towards the iconic'.[27] The north is the site of the Industrial Revolution, of heavy industry, the province of the working class and the organised trade union movement. It is shot through with a turbulent history of industrial decline, deprivation, the Depression years and a stoic, hard-edged survival mentality:

> In this way, it was set against the South, the centre of the new industries of the inter- and post-war years, and the symbolic as well as the actual centre of affluence. The North connoted

> 'working-classness' in a very direct way, helping to define a particular social and cultural landscape and to fix a pervasive stereotype, implying an authenticity of experience and attitude that could be contrasted with the narrow, shallow concerns of the South.[28]

Johnny Noble opened at the Girls' High School in Kendal on 13 August 1945, and subsequently toured community halls throughout the north-west of England and Scotland and Wales before going to Germany and Czechoslovakia the following year. Set in a small north-east fishing community, *Johnny Noble* begins by referring to 'a desolate land' created by the traumatic conditions of the 1930s.[29] But this bleak outlook is belied by the social imaginary of a close-knit, working-class geographical and occupational community where youths play pitch-and-toss; children play hopscotch; and neighbours gossip, argue and fall in love. The community, and the romantic and intergenerational relationships that reside within it, is the beating heart of the play. The subject matter drew on research Littlewood had conducted in Hull for one of her wartime radio documentaries. In fact, the piece is woven through with the north-east coast folk songs she recorded and MacColl rewrote, but it moves beyond a concern with local indigenous culture to situate the travails of the community within a wider international context.

Through the microcosm of a love story between Johnny Noble, a merchant seaman originally played by David Scase, and Mary, played by Rosalie Williams, the play explores the personal, political and social scars caused by the Depression, the Spanish Civil War and the Second World War. Johnny faces a political awakening ignited by his travels around Britain and then Europe, where he sees working-class men used as dispensable fodder for industry and war. When he returns he articulates a developed class and transnational consciousness and epitomises the postwar desire for social upheaval and regeneration. In a bruising agitprop sequence, two 'Roaring Boys', grotesque figures in black tights and bowler hats, herald a return to 'normality', by which they mean advanced industrial capitalism and the brutish pursuit of profit. Blowing whistles and shouting rhythmic reiterations of 'Time! Time! Time! Time!' as a chorus goes through the motions of clocking in and mechanically operating machinery, the 'Roaring Boys' welcome the return of a Darwinian social landscape. Unsure of how to respond, an unidentified figure reminds Johnny of the suffering of the past and that he, and his class community, must 'Take the world in [their] hands ... and wipe it clean'.[30] The world is at a crossroads. It can either cling to an ideal of mutually supportive networks and sense of common purpose symbolically present in the romantic 'imagined community' or go down the path of least resistance to a culture of individualism and social alienation.

Johnny Noble performatively embodied the significance of the group – the community – over the individual through the scenes of communal play and dancing, the presence of a chorus, and 'a cappella' singing. Played in simple black drapes, without any set or props, the onstage community comes under constant attack from an orchestrated soundtrack including factory noise, ships' sirens, artillery, aeroplanes and bombs, but they are resilient and survive to reconstruct their community. Above all, 'Johnny Noble re-imagines the 1930s as a process of striving for the community ideal'[31] as a way of speaking to the immediate postwar climate, and this process continued with MacColl's *Landscape with Chimneys*, which similarly combined narration, song, dance and social realism. Theatre Workshop first performed this play in January 1951 during a tour of south Wales and subsequently took it around the north-east in repertoire with *Uranium 235*. Whereas *Uranium 235* offers a far-reaching historical pageant, *Landscape with Chimneys*, set in 'a dockland street in Salford', provides an intimate portrait of the day-to-day struggles of 'ordinary' working-class people. In the programme for the tour of south Wales, Littlewood and MacColl framed it in line with Mass Observation's aim to retrieve and record working-class life and experience, writing that

> 'Landscape with Chimneys' is the story of a street and the people who live in it. There is nothing extraordinary about this street, its prototype could be found in Glasgow, Manchester, Cardiff ... anywhere in fact.
>
> And the people who live in it? Ordinary people; hard-working, patient, persevering, the men and women who's [*sic*] lives

> pass unrecorded ... dockers, housewives, engineers, factory hands.
>
> And yet, this compact community of ordinary people is rich in the raw material out of which drama is made. For the street is a world in miniature, and by recording a year of its life, its tragedy, its hopes, its humour, its flashes of gaiety, Theatre Workshop offers you a play full of truth and simple humanity.[32]

Interestingly, MacColl chose not to represent the domestic arena or workplace in the play, but the lived spaces of social encounters and discourse – neighbourhood, street, café – that shape and define working-class life and wider patterns of social reality. The narrative takes place over a full calendar year, beginning with the imminent arrival of Hugh and Frank, soldiers returning from active service, for whom members of the community are gathering to mark and celebrate their return. As they congregate in the street and prepare a welcome banner, as with *Johnny Noble*, a social imaginary of a close-knit community is established – the characters all know and greet one another, they exchange pleasantries and wait to welcome and reintroduce Hugh and Frank back into the communal fold through vocal greetings and physical embraces. Romantic reunions and blossoming relationships signal a mood of postwar euphoria and hope, but this mood is soon dashed by the bitter disillusionment caused by poverty and the housing crisis. A spiral of despair ensues that rocks the stability of the community and its faith in its ability to protect its members until an opportunity arises to redeem the community ideal.

The play draws on a tradition of Marxist historiography that sees the experience of the working class in terms of a constant process of struggle and resilience in the face of adversity and explores how poverty erodes trust, confidence and relationships. In *Landscape with Chimneys*, adversity is framed in terms of the class system, the war machine, the government and capitalist modes of production that rely on competition and exploitation in equal measure. It provides a site for considering the disillusionment of young, working-class males, returning from serving their country, who are unable to provide suitable material conditions in which to nurture relationships and bring up families. However, although the play tackles these challenges to working-class structures of masculinity, social despair emanates through the female characters. As in *Johnny Noble*, the men leave the community to fight and to search for work, whilst the women stay at home to fret and mourn. Even when the men return, the female characters exhibit psychopathologies by becoming mentally unstable, depressed and suicidal, another burden facing the men in this intensely patriarchal play.

As with many plays of this period, such as Robert Mcleish's *The Gorbals Story* (1946) and Ena Lamont Stewart's *Men Should Weep* (1947), the most immediate and pressing problem faced by the working class is the housing deficit. 'The population as a result of the war was crowded into 700,000 fewer houses than in 1939', a problem compounded by a rapid postwar increase in marriages and births that intensified the unsatisfied demand for more homes.[33] Returning from six years' active service, Hugh finds himself sharing four rooms with three other adults and four children and on a waiting list for social housing below 929 others. Recalling the 1946 Squatters' Movement when thousands of British citizens commandeered empty houses and disused military bases, Hugh takes matters into his own hands after his relationship with Claire begins to collapse under the strain of enforced cohabitation and decides to squat in a disused parsonage. The implied dispersal of faith only heightens the sense that the inhabitants need to pull together to nourish and strengthen the community. And they do. Moved to collective action by the encroaching authorities coming to evict Hugh and Claire, as she gives birth to their first child, the community literally creates and mans the barricades. This action, together with a rousing version of Florence Reece's 1930s trade union anthem 'Which Side Are You On?', presents an image of working-class mobilisation in order to construct an allegory of class consciousness and class unity. This theatrical image captured MacColl and Littlewood's belief in grass-roots activism and echoed the call in *Johnny Noble* for people to force through the radical social reconstruction that the postwar Labour government promised.

Even though the play is resolutely about evoking a community ideal that relies on a shared geographical location and mutuality, there is a welcome resistance to easy homogenisation. The community is eclectic in make-up and encompasses different generations and cultural backgrounds, including an Irishman, a Scotsman and a Jewish refugee from Nazi Germany. And the characters represent the full gamut of humanity from young girls drunk on the prospect of romance to eccentric figures such as Amos Mitchell, who has a loose grip on reality. Working against the overly saccharine potential of its ending, *Landscape with Chimneys* undermines romanticised views of community by referencing the frailty and volatility of human relations and the propensity for communities to be rife with tensions, feuds and conflict. It also presents a range of characters who dream of ways in which they can escape the limitations of their environment. Shaunnessey believes that education is the key to his eighteen-year-old daughter Kathy avoiding the poverty trap – a belief that generates a violent outcome as Kathy refuses to avoid relationships that might steer her away from this path. Swindels seeks solace and potential escape in his gambling and pools coupons and Jessie in her ability to dance like a Hollywood starlet. Frank dreams of becoming a dirt-track motorcycle racer, but this leads to tragedy as his wife, Trudi, commits suicide and infanticide because she thinks that their presence is hampering his ambition. Interestingly, as with *Johnny Noble*, Hugh acquires a burgeoning political consciousness from leaving the community, but importantly these characters return to redirect their newfound knowledge towards the improvement of their community.

Treating working-class life in a poetic, lyrical way and, as such, giving it a heightened status, MacColl insisted that the lives played out in the community are rich in desires and dreams. By furnishing his characters with a complex interiority, MacColl adhered to a 'prewar tradition of Marxist aesthetics which stress the importance of creating fully rounded working-class consciousness'.[34] Several characters display a propensity for engaging self-narration. For instance, Shaunnessey constructs a past persona of a hard-drinking swashbuckling adventurer and Ginger, a Celtic adolescent, fancies himself a libertarian working-class poet given to kissing girls at whim and expostulating on the beauty of manual labour. With strong echoes of MacColl himself, it is no surprise that Ginger sings MacColl's famous folk song

'Dirty Old Town', which knowingly romanticises the industrial north and Salford in particular:

> I found my love on the gasworks' croft
> Dreamed a dream by the old canal
> Kissed my girl by the factory wall
> Dirty old town, dirty old town.[35]

As with *Johnny Noble, Landscape with Chimneys* has a heightened theatricality that involves a chorus, an onstage street musician, dancing and several moments that disrupt the fourth wall. These interruptions largely emanate from a stage manager figure, played by MacColl in both the original production and the revival at the Theatre Royal in 1953, who narrates the action throughout. The play begins with a conversation between the stage manager, an electrician and the sound operator about the visual and aural signifiers employed to evoke an industrial town, before the stage manager speaks directly to the audience. Rather than addressing them as theatre-goers, he speaks to them as part of a community and thanks them for taking 'time off from the daily routine of living and dying, of eating, riding buses, making love, worrying about the rise and cost of living, procreating the species, visiting friends'.[36] He encourages them to imagine a street where 'eight tenths of the population of this sceptred isle live out their lives', and appeals to them that 'you know this street too well, some of you were born here, some live here now'. It is 'our street'.[37] In so doing, the narrator narrows the gap between the on- and offstage and blurs the boundaries between the real and fictional space.

Albeit well intentioned, these interruptions lead to an awkward narrational self-consciousness. MacColl adopted the autodidact role familiar from classic working-class novels such as *The Ragged Trousered Philanthropists* (1914) and *Love on the Dole* (1933). Unwilling to let the events of the play speak for themselves, MacColl literally inserted himself as a heavy-handed narrator to explain and elucidate. C. D. Heriot highlighted this fault in his report on the play for the Lord Chamberlain. With an unconsciously fascinating insight into the workings of class hegemony, he assesses *Landscape with Chimneys* thus:

> A pretentious, bad play about the poor – stylised and overemphasised to a neurotic degree – with no change in the expressionist set except the lighting, and a constant break in the dramatic build-up when the stage manager indulges in long 'poetic' addresses to the audience. There is no plot – just a group of assorted dummies in slum clothes . . . This is a play to make one angry because it is such a brutal libel on the inhabitants of slums, written by some ridiculous young man who imagines that the introduction of the word 'whore' confers the stamp of literature on his stale lucubrations. The play is being inflicted on miners all over South Wales in the New Year. I have never felt so sorry for them.[38]

Contrary to Heriot's misgivings, the reviewer for the *Western Mail and South Wales News* appreciated the play, which he proffered had 'in it truth and simple humanity'.[39] Perhaps it is worth speculating on the disjunction between the readings of the play configured in the confines of Kensington Palace against the reception that may have occurred in the venues toured, which included Easington Colliery, the Mechanics' Institute in Darlington and small community halls in Aberdare and Rhymney in south Wales, where the experiences presented in *Landscape with Chimneys* arguably had far more resonance.

Littlewood revived the play, renamed *Paradise Street*, at the Theatre Royal in March 1953. Here, the setting consisted of the bare back and side walls complete with peeling paint, wires and pipes. Bury added a single cement-textured flat made to look like the rear wall of the stage which contained a doorway, a street light attached to the upstage right wall, galvanised dustbins and a 'Paradise Street' street sign. But these were the only embellishments to an otherwise open stage space. The reviewer for the local paper welcomed the production as 'adventurous' and was able to see qualities of the local environment in the Salford 'dockland drama'.[40] The reviewer for *The Stage* referred to it as 'one of a number of working-class documentaries in Theatre Workshop's repertoire', but disparagingly commented, 'The trouble with this sausage-string kind of presentation is that, apart from a certain cumulative intensity, it has no dramatic effect.'[41] Nonetheless, the production provided an incursion into representations of contemporary working-class life that gained increasing prominence in the Theatre Workshop repertoire of the 1950s.

The male domain: work, men and community in *The Long Shift* (1951) and *You Won't Always Be on Top* (1957)

> Crucial to the idea of the traditional working class as it was developed in the 1950s and 1960s was the intimate relationship between work and cultural identity, the strong sense of identity and 'proletarian consciousness' characteristic of the 'occupational community'.[42]

Importantly, this conception promoted a very male-orientated image. 'Because work was seen as the defining feature of working-*men's* lives, characterizations of the traditional working-class community and its culture were masculine, work-related ones.'[43] Indeed, working-class life and culture have been heavily associated with the traditionally male-dominated industries such as mining, shipbuilding and steel. This work, which is hard, gruelling and dirty, functions as a stark antithesis of middle-class comfort. Also, its associations with particular geographical locations mean that industrial labour serves as a metonym for the kinds of close familial and community networks traditionally associated with working-class communities. As Huw Beynon has observed, the industrial worker 'who through physical strength, skill and endurance provides the basis for society's existence', offers a powerful image that 'has sustained many popular and political ideologies'.[44]

In the postwar period, when economic shifts saw increasing numbers of the working class redeployed to sites of mass production such as the factory, which 'less easily converted into heroic and romantic imagery',[45] there grew an understandable nostalgia for images of virile working-class male manual labour. Littlewood produced two plays in the 1950s that represented an exclusively male workplace. The first, *The Long Shift* (1951), the only original play written by her and her partner Raffles, is set down a mineshaft in Lancashire.[46] This play was followed in 1957 by Henry Chapman's *You Won't Always Be on Top*, which is set on a building site in the south of England. What is striking about these two productions is that they are by far the most naturalistic Littlewood ever produced. She was intent on authentically representing men and the workplace and worked extraordinarily hard to achieve a rare degree of verisimilitude on the British stage with these two productions.

Miners – the most highly politicised, emotive and contentious element of the working-class labour movement – hold a prominent place in imagery of the working class. In many ways mining communities epitomise the characteristics associated with working-class communities: industry-dominated social homogeneity, multigenerational quality and a densely interwoven work, social, family and community life. As Day writes, 'conventional assertions about working class community reach an apotheosis in accounts of mining communities'.[47] Equally, Mark Simpson argues, 'Unasked, the miners have been assigned the burden of representing authenticity in an inauthentic Britain; real British men from real communities doing real work. Their labour – hard, masculine and productive – is an antidote to failed, frivolous and "feminine" service industries.'[48] Simpson was writing in the aftermath of the 1984–5 Miners' Strike, but, arguably, miners seen as the forefront of proletarian class consciousness and action occupied a prominent space in the social imaginary of the working class throughout the twentieth century.

The miners' steadfast position in the 1926 General Strike, the socioeconomic turmoil of the 1930s Depression and the Gresford Colliery disaster of 1934 did a great deal to mythologise mining communities in Britain. During this period, many British intellectuals spoke out about the appalling conditions miners faced whilst championing them as epitomising the values of community solidarity and activism that would spearhead a new egalitarian politics. In a 1937 essay, George Orwell typified this response by situating miners and the mining industry at the heart of civilisation. Marvelling at the hardships faced by working miners, he likened their working conditions to his own picture of hell caused by the 'heat, noise, confusion, darkness, foul air, and, above all, unbearably cramped space'.[49] In one especially poignant paragraph, he captured their invisibility and indispensability:

> You could quite easily drive a car right across the North of England and never once remember that hundreds of feet below the road you are on, the miners are hewing out coal. Yet in a sense it is the miners who are driving your car forward. Their lamp-lit world down there is necessary to the day-light world above, as the root is to the flower.[50]

In cultural representations of the 1930s and 1940s, miners became a familiar trope for art, films and novels with a campaigning social agenda and a concern with representing working-class life and culture. Key examples include Lewis Jones's two mining novels *Cwmardy* (1937) and *We Live* (1939) and, in film, *The Stars Look Down* (1939), *The Proud Valley* (1940) and *How Green Was My Valley* (1942). In fact, the proliferation of films depicting miners led Graham Greene to comment in 1940 that the image of pithead gear against the sky had 'joined the Eiffel Tower and the Houses of Parliament among the great platitudes of the screen'.[51]

In 1940, Littlewood and MacColl included a section on the Gresford Pit disaster in their living newspaper *Last Edition*. In 1934, an explosion and fire ripped through the Gresford Colliery near Wrexham, causing the death of 266 men. After the bitter industrial disputes of the period, this traumatic event reminded the nation of the precarious conditions and personal risk faced by miners. The tragedy also came to signify a great deal for those with left-wing sympathies as the subsequent inquiry and court case threw a harsh light on the ruthlessness of capitalism. The pit manager with responsibility for health and safety allowed men to work double back-to-back shifts and falsified records on ventilation to ensure the continuation of operations to maximise profits. Intercut with several names of the dead, *Last Edition* offered a documentary-style enactment of the Gresford trial to draw attention to these issues. In writing *The Long Shift*, Littlewood and Raffles strove to honour and celebrate the individual and collective strengths and resilience of a small mining community.

Coming in the aftermath of the miners' fight to nationalise the industry and the implementation of the 'miners' charter' to address working conditions in the coalfields, *The Long Shift* offered a compelling mixture of social observation and political comment embedded in a social-realist framework. They based the play on Raffles's experience working down Pendleton Pit in Lancashire during the latter half of the Second World War. He worked as a 'ripper', one of the men who break up the stone, earth and rubble to create new tunnels, until he suffered a serious knee injury.[52] Raffles's first-hand knowledge helped create an authentic picture of life down a mineshaft, but Littlewood was keen that all the cast should 'experience the magnetism of the pit, always there despite the underlying sense of danger'.[53] To meet Littlewood's demand, Raffles arranged for the company to visit Pendleton Pit, which Littlewood recalled in the following terms:

> Nobody spoke as the cage plummeted into the depths. Our guide, a deputy, was waiting for us. We followed him along the rails, till we had to bend to avoid banging our heads and walk lopsided not to trip over the cables. Even so, despite the protecting helmets, we gave ourselves some sharp knocks.[54]

This experience gave the cast a sense of the cramped physical conditions, heat and dirt they were to replicate, but also the site's innate theatricality.

In the production, which toured to south Wales in November 1951 and the north-east throughout January and February of 1952, there was a strong emphasis on physical and aural accuracy. Littlewood remembered, 'We never ceased to check on details in our search for authenticity.'[55] The setting, designed by Harry Greene, involved a realistically cramped coalface tunnel held up by scaffolding poles, in which the actors could only crouch or kneel, and wherever possible a tunnel was constructed that ran the length of the theatre through which the actors had to crawl to enter the coalface. Greene was able to draw on his south Wales background and he dressed the set with real coal dust and the cast wore miner's shorts and hats and used miner's lamps donated by 'friendly South Wales ex-miners at Bargoed and Rhymney'.[56] Several of the cast stripped to the waist in line with real miners, who frequently worked in loincloths to combat the extreme heat of the pits, and they replicated spitting, chewing tobacco and sucking coal, techniques used to combat dry mouths. Sound effects were courtesy of the BBC sound archives and the production opened

5. *The Long Shift* (1951).

with the following: 'Morning sirens sound. The signal for lowering the cage of men is heard ... sound of the cage descending and arriving.'[57] This concern with authenticity was more than a stylistic flourish and can be likened to Margot Heinemann's argument regarding Brecht's productions: 'Respect for manual work and the people who do it is expressed in the conviction and accuracy with which a canteen wagon is fitted out, a chicken plucked, a sleazy bar-room mounted.'[58]

Littlewood and Raffles had a deep respect for the men they were representing. They felt a duty of care towards their subjects that prompted their concern with accuracy as anything less risked undermining the importance of the lives and work they were depicting. In performance, this meant mastering the appropriate rhythms of industrial labour. There are several sections in the play involving the careful enactment of pit duties, with one stage direction explaining,

'Work proceeds at a pace, shovelling, working with picks and hammers. In due course props arrive. The lights at the coal face dim, so that only the miners' lamps are lit. Work proceeds rhythmically and in shadow.'[59] As this quote suggests, the representation of industrial labour could be both realistic and intensely theatrical and, above all, there is a celebration, however nostalgic and sentimental, of the material reality of hard manual labour.

The narrative centres on five men, Elijah (Eli), Geordie, Stan, Harry and Walt, who work the treacherous Plodder seam, when most of their colleagues have been moved to the Trencherbone seam. The men are all very different: Harry is a heavy drinker and gambler and rather maudlin; Eli is elderly and suffers from severe short-sightedness; Stan is the stoical union man; Walt is a gentle soul who brings the men fresh produce from his well-tended allotment; and Geordie is a young, political firebrand from the north-east. Yet, despite their carefully individuated characters and generational differences, these men are mutually dependent on each other and find a collective voice through the common experience of work and local life.

The play divides into two halves. In the first half, a broken conveyor belt intermittently frustrates the men's attempts to work and the play captures the minutiae of life down the pit: the waiting, mechanical failures, close physical proximity, eating and banter about unseasonal weather, hobbies, their characters and relationships. The second half takes a dramatic turn after the roof collapses, trapping Elijah under a fallen slab. In production, the intensity of the action was enhanced by the sounds of a pneumatic pick cutting through the fallen rubble and expressionistic sound effects made to sound like 'the blood in the ears of the entombed men . . . or the thin trickle of sand and pebbles'.[60] The men assess their predicament and negotiate suitable action as the air turns foul and the roof threatens further collapse. The final part of the play alternates between the entombed men and those launching a rescue attempt, until the successful release of the men secures a happy ending.

For miners, the very act of going underground and the dangerous conditions they face intensifies the sense of social isolation and closed community. Charles Vaught and David L. Smith draw attention to the portal through which miners pass in order to carry out their jobs as marking a boundary, a moment of territorial passage that literally and symbolically marks the journey from one social world to another.[61] However, *The Long Shift* made it clear that the values of communality instilled down the pit can cross-fertilise into the wider world. The carefully constructed scenes realistically captured the ebb and flow of conversation as it shifts from the banal to the serious and prefigures the trench scenes of *Oh What a Lovely War*, as the men face falling rock, dust and potential suffocation as opposed to poisonous gas and artillery fire.

In the first half, the men banter about bad bets, dates, industrial relations and inedible sandwiches prepared by their wives and generally mock their working conditions. In adversity, the men share their histories, reminiscences and dreams and discuss the centrality and bonds of family, community and industrial traditions. The stress is very much on a group of men exhibiting the deep bonds of horizontal kinship characteristic of close occupational and geographical communities. The men join together to hunt for Walt's lost watch, a family heirloom, and Harry tells of his inevitable journey to the pit following his six brothers and eight uncles. Eli and Geordie, representatives of different generations, stress the importance of honouring the past, political activism and symbolism. Eli recalls his childhood:

> Childer i'white and wi' tableaux on carts; stirring bits of history that folks've forgotten mostly now. I remember once we had a collier riding a white horse; he were representing a chap that led the colliers against the police in 1874 before there were a union thought of.[62]

Geordie talks about the Big Meeting in Durham, an annual event celebrating mining communities that uses banners emblazoned with socialist heroes, parading and colliery bands to publicly mark occupational pride and the spirit of occupational communities. He describes how 'each pit has its own banner, a great embroidered banner, red or gold or purple, fine colours they are and all embroidered by the miners' wives', and how the dead are honoured by the placement of a black ribbon on a banner, which is duly revered by silence as it passes people who know what pit work means.[63] The stress on camaraderie and collectivity is emphasised by Geordie's self-confessed liking for the slogan 'united we stand, divided we fall', which sentimentally punctuates the play as Elijah is finally carried to safety.

An important strand in the play refers to the hobbies the men pursue outside the work environment. Rather than being seduced by the trappings of popular culture, the miners represented by Littlewood and Raffles pursue self-taught, largely pastoral activities that involve elements of discovery and nurture. Interestingly, they also involve a degree of solitary endeavour in contrast to the enforced collectivity of the workplace. As Ross McKibbin asserts, 'When other sides of life, working and domestic, were all too collective, the pleasure of an activity that emphasized privacy and solitude seems explicable.'[64] Walt is a keen gardener who demonstrates pride in his hobby through a magnificent greenhouse that he has lovingly created with dovetailed joints. Geordie collects specimens of wild flowers and Stan remembers finding a piece of coal with a leaf in it for Young Fairclough, who is interested in archaeology. All the hobbies involve a degree of intellectual curiosity, discipline, skill and knowledge and assert a rich and varied life beyond the constraints of the pit. However, whereas McKibbin fears that hobbies may detract from concentrated political activism in the working class, the characters are all variously politically aware, class-conscious and active.

Throughout the play, there is a sense in which an absent 'they' controls the men's lives by making decisions about work patterns, productivity levels, which seam to mine and for how long. It refers to a history of poor industrial relations but suggests that nothing has changed in terms of workers' rights since nationalisation – the machinery is still unreliable, the conditions dangerous, the work unrelenting and the profits enjoyed by others as most of the coal industry's profit during this time went to mine owners as compensation. As Martin Leighton explained, 'The mine owners who pre-dated nationalisation were never particularly solicitious about the social welfare of their workers, and the state made no provision to fill the gap'.[65] At one point Harry exclaims,

> Look, nationalisation's done nothing for me. Coal Board! Three blinking pimps doing a job that used to be done by one bummer.

> All the jumped-up clerks in creation walloping up to the pit yard in cars that our money's bought them.[66]

In many ways the play pre-empts concerns aired in *Coal Is Our Life* (1956), a study of a Yorkshire mining community conducted to investigate the impact of nationalisation.[67] This study found that miners still faced the same issues as before nationalisation:

> The idea that there has been a Hegelian 'break' at the end of the war is . . . illusory: the progression from the bad old prewar days of private ownership, the dole and the Spencer Union, to the brave new world of state ownership, full employment, and the NUM has brought about only cosmetic changes.[68]

In *The Long Shift*, the manager is still concerned with lack of yield, dirt on the coal and the workers' productivity, and he proposes docking pay for problems caused by circumstances beyond the men's control. A stance strongly countered by Stan's call for the importance of embedded unionisation that goes beyond dealing with the latest pay settlement. Reminiscent of the managerial negligence exhibited at Gresford, the manager dismisses his deputy's concerns about the safety of the Plodder seam roof and says that he will deal with it once he has conducted his executive duties, by which time it is too late. In production, Littlewood revealed her political sympathies by physically signifying the gulf between the management and the workers through a spatial divide with the manager's office located on a high rostrum above the coalface, isolated by spotlight. Where the miners are fully rounded sympathetic characters, the manager is a thinly drawn agitprop-style caricature of high-handed self-interest and corporate values.

The play initially toured the south Wales valleys to venues such as Swansea's Llewelyn Hall, the Miners' Institute at Gorseinon and Resolven Miners' Welfare Hall, where this way of life would have been all too familiar. During this tour, reviewers picked up on the realism of the piece, with one reviewer likening it to 'the film documentary or the dramatised radio feature, and reminiscent of the Army Bureau of Current Affairs theatre units of the last war'.[69] However, in retrospect, Littlewood was less convinced by the policy to take *The Long Shift* to the communities that lived the lives it represented and admitted that 'it was a mistake taking Gerry's play to the North-east: coals to Newcastle. "We'd sooner see how the other half lives," I was told.'[70] And, interestingly, given the close proximity of the production to Theatre Workshop's move to Stratford East, Littlewood never revived the production, unlike several others from this period.

Whereas *The Long Shift* offered an ambitious, if sentimental, attempt to honour the camaraderie and bravery of the mining community as a metonym for the wider working class, *You Won't Always Be on Top* celebrated an eclectic group of working-class men during a wet Monday on a building site in Hastings. Like *The Long Shift*, *You Won't Always Be on Top* is a classic ensemble piece. There are no leading characters and its power resides in the collection of finely drawn individuals sharing a common space. Nothing really happens in the play. 'The plot was a series of everyday incidents bound together by the job in hand, each incident developing easily into the next'.[71] A group of men arrive for a day's work, they eventually begin work, they stop for lunch, poor weather and a visit from a union official, two men fall out and one is threatened with the sack and the group rallies to secure his job. It has been described as a

> landmark in the history of recent English theatre, not only as a play about working men which actually shows them engaged in their daily work . . . but also as a play which succeeds in evoking the rhythms of ordinary life through subtly poetic use of everyday speech and action. Chapman's work is invaluable, not for any arguments contributed to a political cause, but for its picture of a group of men and the lives they lead – which is, after all, what politics is all about.[72]

In many ways, I think this overview underestimates the political ambition of the play and production. Inevitably, a performance representing building workers drew comparison with Robert Tressell's seminal play of working-class life, *The Ragged Trousered Philanthropists*.[73] Writing in the *Daily Worker*, Mike Myson approvingly claimed, 'Not since Tressell committed to paper the story of the ups and downs of his fellow workers in the ever-memorable "Ragged Trousered Philanthropists" has anybody depicted such a faithful picture of the men on the job.'[74] Indeed, Tressell's opening manifesto for 'a faithful picture of working-class life – more especially of those engaged in the building trade – in a small town in the south of England', could equally apply to Chapman's play, which makes several intertextual references to the novel.

Tressell's novel deals with the politics of culture and representation and the obstacles in the way of a socialist restructuring of society. It explores 'the relation between physical workers and their employers' and 'examines this relation as a function of capitalism and questions why those who are its victims nevertheless show little interest in criticizing this system, and even less in changing it'.[75] It is perhaps no surprise that the character in *You Won't Always Be on Top* who invites the union representative to organise the workers, who, incidentally, was played by the author, shares his Christian name, Frank, with Frank Owen, the voice of socialism in Tressell's novel. Yet after the union man turns up to impart pompous empty rhetoric, the men as a collective body, rather than Frank or the union man, politicise each other. Slowly they organise to meet their basic needs – more and better tea, a weatherproof shed, a bonus scheme and due financial reward for taking on extra roles and responsibilities.

Chapman very clearly delineates the characters in terms of their dispositions, ages and trades – carpenters, bricklayers and labourers – and at the bottom of the chain sits Fred, the put-upon tea-boy played by Dudley Sutton in Littlewood's production. Yet Fred has resistant strategies for subverting his lowly status. He plays numerous practical jokes on the group, such as when he brings peanuts instead of cigarettes for Jeff and when he tricks all the workers into stopping to listen for the approaching 'pooff pooff' of a boy's toy train.[76] Fred occupies an interesting position in the play. He constantly sings from Handel's *Messiah* and harbours ambitions to be a conductor, a level of aspiration that disturbs the other men by exceeding the symbolic boundaries of his class position.

Many studies have conceded that working-class communities can be restrictive, overbearing and hostile to education, ambition and signs of individuality that exceed traditional codes of behaviour. Fred claims he wants to 'make something of my life . . . I don't want to spend the rest of my time amongst a lot of ignorant old bloody labourers.'[77]

This outburst breaches the unspoken code of unity the men observe and musters a stern response. Bill tells him to 'learn to keep your place' and Jeff tells him to 'keep his mouth shut'.[78] This incident marks the dynamic shift in the play. When a misunderstanding leads the men to think that Jeff has orchestrated Fred's sacking, coupled with their unease over his failure to join the union, the men turn on Jeff. A telling domestic metaphor encapsulates the play's socialist impulse: 'It's like that bucket, Jeff, none of us can get a decent cup of tea out of it unless all of us does. And if one of us can't that means that none of us can.'[79] Ultimately, the power of the group, and Jeff's desire to be an integrated member, cajole him to join the union, at which point Fred rushes on to symbolically announce 'The Ragged Trousered Philanthropists' the winner of a recent horse race.

However, it was the striking staging and theatricality, as opposed to the political narrative, which made *You Won't Always Be on Top* such an unusually effective and exhilarating representation of working-class life. In his sketch of the design, Harry Greene referred to 'realism on the stage', but this does not quite capture the degree of verisimilitude Bury achieved in his set design, a particular feat given the company's lack of resources. It reproduced, in minute detail, a three-storey building in the course of construction surrounded by a full-size shed, scaffolding, a fully operational cement mixer, numerous filthy ladders, wheelbarrows, piles of bricks, sacks of cement, a large pile of sand, planks to walk on and the necessary tools for the job, including hods, trowels and buckets. Tynan referred to it as 'the most spectacular and elaborate setting I have ever seen in the legitimate British theatre ... an astonishing achievement'.[80]

Unusually for the time, Littlewood decided to have the curtain up for the audience's arrival. Myson accused this 'gimmick' of destroying the impact for the audience but it was crucially important to Littlewood as it set up the impression that the audience had happened upon the site, just as they would on the street. In his Lord Chamberlain's reader's report, Heriot dismissively wrote,

> It is difficult to see the point of this play. It is about a gang of workmen on a building site who grumble and squabble and

6. *You Won't Always Be on Top* (1957).

> complain and loaf through three acts. There is no plot and no development and has about as much entertainment value as a tape-recording of real workmen on a real job.[81]

The sentiment was echoed by Lisa Gordon Smith, who cautioned, 'The author might do well to remember that a play is a work of creative art. Mere reproduction shows talent for nothing more than observation and memory.'[82] But this completely misses the point. The production of *You Won't Always Be on Top* was precisely about creating the impression that the audience was voyeuristically eavesdropping on a group of men going about their business and, through this representation, giving the life and working relations of the men validity and capturing its innate theatricality. As Littlewood had long held,

> It seems to me more necessary now than it has ever been, for the young actor to go to life rather than to the theatre for his

> inspiration; to listen to the speech of the countryside, the back street, the factory; to bring to this work as the Elizabethans did, the raciness, tang and rhythm of democratic speech.[83]

And this is exactly what *You Won't Always Be on Top* achieved. In its highly inventive use of language, its set theatrical 'moments' and its enduring sense of rebellious fun, it is also possible to see the influence of another male-only production, Behan's *The Quare Fellow*, produced by Littlewood a year previously. In stressing the rituals and strict timeframe of the working day, Littlewood created a realistic depiction of the everyday and community-based structures that inhabit the workplace. The first few minutes of the production were wholly devoted to the ritual of arrival and greetings – the process of daily 'reunion' with the group in which the subtle variations of greeting establish different relationships and levels of status. The men variously prepared for work, some going straight to it, some procrastinating by smoking and chatting. It becomes clear that whilst the men do not socialise beyond the workplace they have a shared knowledge and cultural experience typical of their class status, revealed through conversations about the football, racing and the Saturday night fight on the television.

Above all else, the production captured the informal structures of the workplace that, for many, make work bearable – the joking, rites of initiation, banter and play. When a new member of the workforce arrives, Nick, played by Richard Harris, the group immediately embark on an unspoken initiation ceremony that involves tricking him into going into a deep wet muddy hole. Vaught and Smith write about the role of initiation in traditional workplaces as a provocative means of testing personality, degrees of self-control and sense of humour, all of which are vital in securing effective working relations.[84] In his aggressive but accepting response, the group recognise that Nick is one of the lads, able to take a joke and willing to see the funny side of his predicament. As such, the men can integrate him into the communal banter through which they predominantly communicate. Anthony Easthope explains,

> Outwardly banter is aggressive, a form in which the masculine ego asserts itself. Inwardly, however, banter depends on a close,

> intimate and personal understanding of the person who is the butt of the attack. It thus works as a way of affirming the bond of love between men while appearing to deny it.[85]

The random episodes of banter and horseplay underwrite the validity of the fictional narrative as they present a life lived in the present, and through the gentle mickey-taking and sharp witty retorts the characters depict a playful acceptance of each other's strengths and weaknesses and, above all, cement their solidarity as a group.

Littlewood's concern with authenticity extended to acting style. During rehearsals and production, she encouraged the cast to inhabit the set and they began to co-exist in the space in a way that established both their own and a collective rhythm. They created a casual conversational style amidst the frenetic action of breaking bricks, cutting wood, going up and down ladders, measuring and mixing cement. Each night members of the cast constructed a brick wall and Littlewood enlisted the help of local builders to teach the company their craft, showing due respect for a working trade in her desire to get the detail right. In the programme accompanying the production she thanked 'the real bricklayers and building workers at present working in West Ham who have so carefully and generously watched and criticised and helped us to avoid some obvious gaffes'.[86] Reviewers were generally astounded by the level of accuracy achieved, with Tynan connecting the play to a broader European tradition of art-house film-making, claiming, 'Admirers of the films of Fellini or the latter-day Polish cinema will know the kind of excitement to expect: the excitement of seeing actors who look and behave like unobserved, uninhibited human beings.'[87] The reviewer for *The Stage* similarly found that 'the actors seem indistinguishable from the men on any building site', and that the language 'sounds at times as if [Chapman] had made a tape recording of his mates in the building trade behind their backs'.[88]

In a radio interview, Littlewood admitted to being attracted to 'beautifully observed writing in which you really heard the authentic voice of the country building worker using a fine speech, which I had not heard in the theatre'.[89] Yet, typically, Littlewood augmented Chapman's original script through rehearsal, improvisation and visits to building sites, and by exploring the physical possibilities of the play.

As Chapman was part of the cast he was involved, as the causal logic of a traditional linear narrative became a meandering multivocal polyphony. The dialogue ebbs, flows and overlaps. Conversations interconnect, subside and re-emerge. Nonetheless, there is a clear theatrical structure and music-hall-style set pieces are contained within the naturalistic framework, as when the foreman and architect demand the cement be wet and then dry in short succession. Repeated refrains such as Bill's 'ruddy little teddy boy', Jim's 'I wish I was in bed with my missus' and Albert's 'ain't that cold then' punctuate the language and create a poetic rhythmic quality.

A clever use of language enabled thinly disguised expletives to remain, such as Nick's 'mouthy mucker' directed at Bill.[90] This quality enhances the veracity of earthy language spoken in a male-only domain during this period. And, according to Goorney, 'The exchanges that arise naturally between men working on a building site lent themselves readily to improvisation, and as the cast became more familiar with the situation and their relationships developed, the language became less restrained.'[91] Indeed, the Lord Chamberlain prosecuted the company for presenting new material not passed by the censor as the company allowed their improvisatory instincts to hold sway.

Improvisatory processes also generated a number of visual jokes, such as the placement of two planks of wood as a cross emblazoned with RIP. Another incident, which particularly troubled the censor, arose when Harris, playing Mick, imitated Sir Winston Churchill whilst pretending to open a public lavatory. The imitation of a living person was enough to get the company in trouble but Harris upped the stakes by pouring water from a watering can as if to imitate urination.

In their shared knowledge, easy banter and sense of shared purpose, the closed male communities represented in *The Long Shift* and *You Won't Always Be on Top* serve in many ways as theatrical microcosms of the ideal working-class community. The characters are predominately embedded in and emotionally identified with their occupational role, workplace and class status, and the patterns of daily interaction and supportive networks are suggestive of qualities that underpin the social imaginary of the working-class community.

But Littlewood was also conscious of the growing body of sociological analysis charting the decline of working-class identification and communities caused by factors such as a growing individualism, social mobility, rehousing, intergenerational discord and the intervention of welfare agencies. Some of these issues reside at the heart of two productions focused on the East End, *Van Call* (1954) and *Sparrars Can't Sing* (1960), discussed next.

The East End: dismantling the myth of community

During the 1950s and 1960s, myths and images of the East End exhibited a degree of schizophrenia. According to Ed Glinert, the Second World War generated the 'myth of the Blitz', an enduring idealisation of plucky East Enders banding together to gallantly defend communities as bombs devastated the landscape.[92] This picture corresponded with the mythical status of the East End as a key site for close-knit occupational and class-based communities sharing space, resources and a unique vocabulary. This social imaginary proved hard to shift despite evidence of opportunist looting during the Blitz and widespread social problems associated with poverty, gangsters and racial discord following the arrival of large diasporic communities in the inter-war and postwar periods.

On moving to the East End of London, Theatre Workshop hoped to capitalise on the predominately working-class character of the area for subject matter and audience. To celebrate their one-year anniversary of residency at the Theatre Royal, the company commissioned twenty-four-year-old Anthony Nicholson, a local journalist, to write *Van Call*, a play about the local railway industry whose title refers to the breakdown vans that clear railway lines after an accident.[93] After going through several drafts, the play ended up with two loosely integrated storylines. Bert, a devoted railwayman played by Joby Blanshard, is a company man who devotes his life and time to his work and to advancement up the ranks, to the detriment of his relationship with his wife Lily, played by Avis Bunnage, and their daughter Melanie. Whilst Bert refuses to engage in the social spaces associated with working-class culture, Lily refuses to abstain and during a night out with her friend Phyllis in the local pub, Lily is reacquainted with Johnno, an old boyfriend played by Nicholson, with whom she embarks on an affair.

This love triangle comes to a head when a train crash leaves Johnno trapped and Bert arrives as part of the rescue team. He only learns of Johnno's relationship with Lily after releasing him from danger and proceeds to agree an amicable separation so that Lily and Johnno can make a life together. The second strand centres on the male workers Dan, Joe, Sam and Bert, as they debate concerns in the railway industry around piecework, deskilling and the merits of union-orchestrated industrial negotiations such as managerial and employee tribunals as opposed to unofficial strike action.

Through its combination of domestic and industrial narratives, the play grapples with many of the themes that came to prominence in Young and Willmott's *Family and Kinship in East London*. This study documented the long-standing existence of a close-knit working-class community with strong kinship ties and a deep-seated identification with the locality. It presented a picture of neighbours sharing the resources and intimacies of everyday life, but also how this geographical and social character was being put under strain. They cited the regrettable intervention of planners and welfare agencies, but also the destabilising impact of a younger generation of affluent workers intent on loosening kinship ties, geographical mobility and an increasing individualism associated with enhanced materialism and values of self-advancement rather than community solidarity.

The overriding message of *Van Call* is that Bert, as representative of the new individually orientated worker, does not value the important things in life – family, community and his fellow workers – he is only interested in his own professional and financial progression. His longing for material success, epitomised by a desire to own a car he has no time to drive, as well as his aspirations to relocate to leafy suburbs away from the Stratford community, overshadow his interpersonal relationships. The audience sees all the other characters occupying the iconographic social spaces of London's East End such as the street and the pub, but Bert is located squarely at work or at home. Ultimately, Bert ends up alone and isolated from his family, community and fellow workers and, whilst he accuses the older generation of being out of touch and delusional, Nicholson implies that it is Bert who has made some poor choices that undermine the bonds of locality.

One of the most interesting aspects of Littlewood's production concerned its negotiation with the local community. Richard Findlater stressed that it was, 'ostentatiously and successfully, a local play', but this largely ignores the complex motivations and interpretive frames that drove the production.[94] Prior to *Van Call*, Theatre Workshop had provided a theatrical diet of Shakespeare and Molière, alongside modern classics by Sean O'Casey and George Bernard Shaw. The company commissioned Nicholson to get them on the local map and they relentlessly emphasised this aspect in pre-publicity and production materials. The programme stated, 'The action of the play takes place in Angel Lane, Stratford and the surrounding district', and stressed Nicholson's place within the community by announcing that he was drawing on his

7. *Van Call* (1954).

father, grandfather and great-grandfather's experiences as railwaymen in the local industry.[95]

To open the production with an authentic visual and aural spectacle, Littlewood populated the stage with real market stalls set up nightly by local street traders Grace Fisher, Maureen Daly, Israel Price and Bill Armond – a move reflecting Littlewood's desire to see the street literally represented on the stage. In pre-publicity in the local newspaper, Raffles claimed that 'Van Call has captured the spirit of Stratford and presents the kind of people which the audience will be able to recognize'.[96] By this he meant not only that the production geographically referenced the immediate locality but that it aimed to represent working-class life and experience as realistically as possible through depictions of social spaces such as the street, marketplace, railway station, pub and workplace. Within these spaces, Littlewood worked hard to capture both the banality and the theatricality of everyday encounters as characters variously chat, joke, backchat, debate, flirt and argue. She also stressed the collective nature of working-class life; whilst the central narrative rests on a classic love triangle, this relationship is consistently framed within a broader set of social relations. Reviewers particularly valued these qualities, with *The Times* reviewer claiming that

> *Van Call* is at its best in its report of the talk of the market, of the team of men working at night on the wrecked engine, and of the strikers who loiter in the street ... and almost every member of the company helps to create the impression that the life of the people rather than the fortunes of one or two individuals is the real theme of the piece.[97]

The company was also keen to use the production as a showcase and marketing tool for displaying its cultural relevance within and for the local community as a means of encouraging local council funding. According to Findlater,

> On the first night, the Mayor of West Ham made a speech after the curtain fell. In welcoming 165 councillors from 8 councils to the theatre, he remarked how true to life *Van Call* was, and how

> much it echoed his own experience in the railway shops (his house had been a strike headquarters in 1926). He was a sturdy, municipal testimony to the effectiveness and relevance of this kind of theatre.[98]

However, the national critics were far more convinced by the local efficacy of the production than the local audience was. Whereas several national critics praised its ability to capture a 'slice of life' and 'a fascinating glimpse of railwaymen's lives', the critic from the *Stratford Express* more cynically suggested that 'Stratford people may fail to find themselves reflected in what they see. There is, of course, plenty of local colour, and even some of Angel Lane's habituees take part and look rather out of place with their stalls on the stage.'[99] Indeed, evidence suggests that the locals did not come out to support the production because it flaunted its concern with local issues rather too mechanistically. As founder of the theatre's supporters' club Peggy Soundy recalled, 'you were trying to put across a line and you could feel it. If it doesn't come from somebody's gut, in a real sort of way, it shows, and I think the locals saw this.'[100]

Soundy's appraisal of *Van Call* raises issues of motivation, representation and authenticity that plagued Littlewood's attempts to theatricalise a particular mythology of working-class life that courted accusations of nostalgia and sentimentality. Littlewood did use theatrical representation to eulogise a working-class community that increasingly existed in the social imaginary rather than in the reality of East End life, but she also developed productions that undermined a romantic conception of community. This duality is no more evident than in her production of *Sparrers Can't Sing* (*Sparrers*), which emphasised gender-based, generational and familial fractures and conflicts at the heart of working-class life and community.

Set on the first warm day of the year, *Sparrers* meanders through a plotless sequence of encounters, flirtations and pointless conversations. Epitomising the 'slice-of-life' nomenclature, no major events occur and the characters end the day as they begin it. It centres on three generations of the Juggs family who live in a condemned slum in Stepney: Granny Miggs, her adopted son Charlie and his estranged wife

Maggie; her daughter Bridget and her husband Fred and their two children, Jimmy (Knocker) and Nellie. Alongside these central characters sit their lodger Jack, their neighbour Lily and her son Willie (Peanut), Nellie's suitors Joe (Chunky) and Georgie, and two other figures, Wilkins, who sells odd bits he finds to make ends meet and tries to avoid the man from the National Assistance Board, and Sid, a tramp, who loiters in the vicinity. The other central character is Stepney itself. The programme for the original production provided information about the borough's physical boundaries and its population shifts, as well as its social and political character. In the play, the narrative journey that this community is taking is of primary concern.

Described as 'gentle and nostalgic' by Littlewood, at first glance *Sparrers* would appear to construct a vision of a close-knit community

8. *Sparrers Can't Sing* (1960).

much the same as that seen in *Johnny Noble* and *Landscape with Chimneys*.[101] Littlewood and Bury signified the close physical proximity and interconnectivity of the characters' lives with a vividly realistic setting that comprised a communal alleyway that ran alongside the convergence of three properties. 'The alley formed a **T** running across the stage with the third arm of the **T** running upstage under one of the houses to make an archway'.[102] Bury designed the set to look as if one of the streets outside the theatre had encroached inside. The walls and houses looked like real brick, the windows were real glass and the houses had fully functioning electric lights that characters turned on and off as they entered and exited the space.

According to Graham Day, 'Descriptions of working class community are forever associated with images of back-to-back, terraced, accommodation or tenement apartments, and conversations conducted over garden fences or on the doorstep', and Littlewood brought this image alive onstage.[103] All action took place in this external shared space, and even when characters entered their private domestic space their exchanges spilled out across the thresholds of doors and windows. For instance, in the opening sequence, Nellie sang through an open window, Jack whistled inside but was heard outside, whilst Fred and Knocker discussed their relative betting prowess in the alleyway. As the scene progressed Lily and Bridget polished their front steps and exchanged gossip about their family and neighbours. This scene captures how the physical intimacy of the community is reflected through the characters' interpersonal relations, intimate knowledge of each other and spatial occupation.

However, it is clear that the community is in a period of massive change. The families are due to be rehoused and construction workers are building a block of flats offstage. This context chimed with the experiences of many in the East End during the 1950s and 1960s when local councils decided to address the problem of housing shortages and slum dwellings with enforced relocation to new housing estates, the erection of tower blocks and the demolition of old terraces:

> The planners put to one side notions that many East End communities, though slums, were successful socially, that

> people enjoyed where they lived, that they simply wanted better houses, not a new community. They decreed that since the old communities were slums they had to be wiped out: Clean it up! Remove the mess! Rid the East End of this chaos![104]

Young and Willmott's study 'contended that this was eradicating the valuable social bonds built up over several generations, and thereby undermining the values and collective solidarity of the working classes'.[105] But *Sparrers Can't Sing* offers a far more complex and finely nuanced account of community relations in the East End that complicates Young and Willmott's impressionistic sociological study. Utilising the classic dramatic narrative of a character frozen in a moment of time through incarceration, Charlie cannot even locate the street where he used to live due to the redevelopment taking place. From Lewis's account, it is not only the physical geography that is changing, but also the social character of the community as vertical living takes hold, as Granny Miggs articulates:

> It ain't natural, people balanced on top of one another like that. No, give me the little old houses everytime . . . You know, people all seem to get funny when they moves into them . . . and when they gets in them new flats, they don't want to know you anymore.[106]

Granny Miggs represents a sentimental, nostalgic vision of a mythical old East End. She has an intimate embodied knowledge of the 'deep maps' of the street and its inhabitants. 'She remembers which pork butcher's was previously an undertaker's after being a Chinese laundry, where anybody lives or ever has lived, what abortions and illegitimacies and Borstal sentences and diseases have marked any family'.[107] Like the sparrows of the title that she feeds and nurtures with breadcrumbs, she tries to look after her fellow inhabitants. She took in an orphaned Charlie as one of her own and welcomes his return after eight years in prison despite fearing his disruptive presence. She gives Wilkins her dead husband's trousers to replace his threadbare ones, even though she knows he will take them straight to the pawnbroker's. In production, Littlewood had Amelia Bayntun's Granny Miggs selling home-made toffee apples off a dilapidated crate mounted on an old pram, an image that drew attention to her poor socioeconomic status but also her resourcefulness and willingness to graft.

Yet Granny Miggs also exposes the impending threats posed to the community mythology she espouses. Her piano, a mythical hub of East End family life and community singsongs, is on hire purchase, nobody can play it since her son died and her family would rather she swapped the defunct object for a television set. Evoking the mantra of British prime minister Harold Macmillan's famous phrase 'You've never had it so good' in a humorous, self-consciously intertextual reference, she exclaims, 'I ain't never had it so good as them what's got it so good says, I've never had it so good though, never'.[108] Indeed, *Sparrers* resists the postwar rhetoric of affluence and communal consensus as the fractures that rupture the myth of community along the lines of relative social status, gender and generational difference soon become apparent.

Through *Sparrers*, Lewis and Littlewood depicted figures stubbornly resisting the postwar emphasis on the law-abiding worker citizen as the driving force of a successful economy and society. At a time of almost full employment, the majority of the male characters are work-shy layabouts who rely on National Assistance, gambling, the pawnshop and casual criminality to fund their existence. In contemporary terms, they occupy an underclass and inhabit in-between states of existence – men on parole, an ex-Borstal boy, the jobless and the homeless. Not the victims of inequitable social structures as seen in *Landscape with Chimneys*, but lazy good-for-nothings who survive on their wits. Also, unlike the vision of working-class horizontal kinship implied by the terraced housing community, complex social stratification pits the homeless, the lodger, the slum dweller and the council house tenant against each other. Yet despite the presence of socioeconomic difference, there still existed a problematic homogeneity whereby the religiously and ethnically 'mixed community' of Stepney referred to in the programme was absent in its theatrical staging. Arguably, Littlewood had retreated from the progressive depictions of racial difference apparent in productions such as *A Taste of Honey* and *The Hostage*.

The younger characters, representing the future, signal worrying prospects for the future of community ideals represented by Granny Miggs. Apart from Nellie, they have no regard for history, little respect for their elders and deeply flawed morals. Peanut and Knocker, whom Granny Miggs calls a 'vampire, Bloodhound, leech',[109] rob from their neighbours and Knocker steals family heirlooms to fund their social life. Knocker is more interested in cultivating a macho persona and an ostentatious display of fashionable clothing than in developing familial or community relationships. He is blatantly disrespectful to his elders, calling his dad a 'lazy old git', telling his mother to stop making an exhibition of herself when she tries to discipline him and telling Granny Miggs to 'shut yer old gag mag'.[110] In fact, Lewis consistently undermines the close-knit family, as a microcosm of a healthy functioning community in *Sparrers*, to the extent that Maggie, Charlie's wife, has had two children with a married man since Charlie has been in prison and has unsentimentally placed both in care.

The gender dynamics of *Sparrers* are equally fascinating, even more so because the spectrum of casual to violent misogyny was completely overlooked by critics. Charlie served eight years for staving in his wife's head with a poker and returns to stalk his prey once more. Bridget moans about how her mum adhered to traditional gender roles by nurturing and spoiling the boys and ignoring her girls, which has instilled in the men an underlying misogyny. Knocker informs Peanut that his girlfriend should have repaid her night on the gin and limes with sexual favours, menacingly suggesting that 'she wouldn't have got away with it, if it had been me, I can tell you'.[111]

In Littlewood's production *Sparrers* had a vivid theatricality. In his programme note, Lewis wrote, 'The world as seen through the bottom of a pint pot is much more entertaining than that usually seen through opera glasses, and less distorted.'[112] Before he produced *Sparrers* Lewis had been working as an actor with Theatre Workshop since *You Won't Always Be on Top*, under his real name Stephen Cato, and there is no doubt his script sparkles with the quick wit, observational comedy and deft use of rich working-class vernacular that had become the company's prototype. This quality prompted *The Times* reviewer to report, 'What they do and say is very funny, utilizing to the full the Englishman's delight in tartly abusive repartee, and if the verbal fun slackens, Miss Joan littlewood's production is highly inventive and provides them with farcical peripheral action.'[113] Recognising the working-class archetypes of music hall, Alan Brien called it 'a piece of Thirties music hall brilliantly preserved and pickled by Joan Littlewood'.[114] The music-hall influence was enhanced by the continuous piano accompaniment that Littlewood introduced.

Yet despite the production's playful theatricality, the majority of reviewers praised the extent to which Littlewood's production created a vision of everyday life on stage. Naomi Lewis referred to 'the truth of the Stepney life itself', *The Stage* reviewer sensed a 'documentary vividness' and the *News Chronicle* reviewer wrote that 'Joan Littlewood with, I suspect, more accuracy than ever before brings the East End streets that her playwright and company know so well into her pretty theatre'.[115] This reception was equally apparent when Littlewood made one of her rare incursions into the film industry and directed an adaptation of *Sparrers* in 1963 on location in the East End using many actors from the original cast, including Barbara Windsor and James Booth. According to Robert Murphy, the film 'hardly has a plot, but its characters – virtually created by the actors who play them – are solidly rooted in East End life'.[116]

This is all very well, but it is important to pause for a moment to consider the representation of East End life on offer in *Sparrers Can't Sing*. This is a piece that depicts brutal social division, a declining work ethic, violent misogyny and corrosive family breakdown, with two generations of children placed in care. Yet according to many reviewers, including Brien, the play 'manages to be an honest and impressive picture of the basic attitudes of the British working class'.[117] There was obviously something in this production that appealed to the educated professional class of critics that reveals a problematic set of value judgements about working-class life. For instance, according to *The Times* reviewer, 'Mr Lewis's Stepney Sparrows cannot sing; that is to say, they cannot be other than they are – noisy, work-shy, as law-abiding as they are made to be and devoting their turbulent vitality to the laudable object of having a good time.'[118]

The fact that these reviewers are able to offer such patronising glorifications of feckless characters and fatalism as an authentic depiction of East End working-class communities suggests that something went seriously awry from the politically engaged and driven representations of working-class life Littlewood championed earlier in her career. A few critics did question the veracity of Lewis and Littlewood's depiction of East End life, especially after a revival transferred to Wyndham's Theatre on 29 March 1961. Interestingly, one of the most forceful dissenting voices came from Heriot in the Lord Chamberlain's office, who commented in his reader's report, 'I cannot call myself an expert in East End behaviour, but I am convinced that all this is bogus and synthetic. I don't believe any of it – and I cannot think that Miss Littlewood does either.'[119]

Far from offering what Ronald Bryden referred to as the 'eternal nostalgic now of Joan Littlewood's never-never working class', a formulaic, problematically sentimental vision of working-class life,[120] *Sparrers Can't Sing* ruptured a cosy, backward-looking vision of working-class life by representing an 'underclass': those living on the margins of society due to their poverty, criminality or demeaned social status. In turning her attention to this 'underclass', Littlewood risked exoticising working-class communities, particularly when her productions became increasingly focused towards the West End in a bid for survival rather than touring to working-class communities or working to attract the local community to the Theatre Royal. As John Hill warns about the aestheticising of poverty and squalor in the 'new wave' movement, there is a danger of 'marking a separation between spectator and subject', and that 'the pleasures delivered may well rely less on recognition than the very sensation of class difference'.[121] Increasingly, Littlewood began to tout representations of working-class life designed to titillate and amuse as much as to drive home political commentary and a desire for social change. But this shift was complex and underpinned by a decision to engage with the politics of popular culture that is explored in the next chapter.

5 Popular theatrical communities: outsiders, misfits and miscreants

It is, perhaps, not too much of an exaggeration to say that everything changed for Littlewood and Theatre Workshop after Brendan Behan sent them a package containing his play *The Quare Fellow*. For Littlewood, his impact was profound. He embodied the unruly, spontaneous, witty, rumbustious popular approach to theatre she craved and their shared love of humanity, irreverence, foul language, ribald humour and joy in the communitas offered by theatre generated creative alchemy. Neither dithered in the realms of the traditionally acceptable and this allowed them to conceive a theatre practice where an execution could be narrated as a competitive horserace and the dead could rise again to sing a defiant, light-hearted song about cheating death. In other hands, these theatrical moments could have been woefully distasteful; executed by Theatre Workshop they were gloriously theatrical and life-enhancing.

In many ways, Behan's impact exceeded the bounds of the two plays Littlewood produced, *The Quare Fellow* (1956) and *The Hostage* (1958). According to Clive Barker, who played the Volunteer in *The Hostage*,

> Behan's influence on Littlewood was volcanic. Gone was the rigid Puritanism and in came 'fun'. She embarked on a run of productions that satisfied her and which were eminently commercial. The effects were manifold. The audience became paramount, which was simply an extension of previous policy, but now it was clearly articulated. The roles of music, song, and dance were heightened and extended.[1]

Prior to Behan's appearance on the scene, Littlewood had always asked her actors to prepare for an evening's performance in quite a formal way with vocal warm-ups and relaxation exercises culminating in an hour of silence before a production started. But during the run of *The Quare Fellow* Behan frequently arrived with a crate of Guinness to drink and share stories, songs and banter with the cast until the performance started. Murray Melvin remembers that henceforth the company congregated on the stage to sing, dance and tell jokes as they waited for a show to begin. As I have written elsewhere,

> This more informal approach similarly infused what was happening on the stage as Littlewood increasingly embraced her inclination to move beyond the constraints of the fourth wall to acknowledge the presence of the audience in ways that emphasised the *communion* of popular theatre.[2]

Excited by the dynamic interchange with a living playwright after several years focused on Renaissance and contemporary classics by those long dead or geographically distant, over the next five years Littlewood began fostering collaborations with emergent writers. More importantly, she embraced those who were on the periphery of British society because of their class, gender, age, criminal background, educational status or political sympathies. In the writers she chose to promote she took deliberate steps away from the structures of authority that had previously sanctioned entry into the British theatre system.

Uniting these writers was a commitment to vivid depictions of working-class life on the margins of contemporary British and Irish society: a brothel and an IRA safe house in *The Hostage*, a Salford back street in Shelagh Delaney's *A Taste of Honey* (1958) and a Soho gambling den in Frank Norman's *Fings Ain't Wot They Used T'Be* (1959). However, it was not the *what*, but rather the *how* of representation that made Littlewood's productions of these plays so theatrically charged and resonant. When they initially made contact with Theatre Workshop these writers were intent on depicting working-class life in a predominately realist mode akin to the works discussed in the previous chapter. Specifically, they relied on their ability to capture the idioms, dialects and language patterns of the class and region they portrayed. Yet, ultimately, Behan, Delaney and Norman colluded, to a greater or lesser extent, in Littlewood extraordinarily transmogrifying their work in performance. She took their texts and invested them with an exuberant theatricality that relied on and heightened the very qualities of performance – its liveness, unpredictability and moment of exchange between the performance space and spectator.

In *Rabelais and His World*, Mikhail Bakhtin explains that

> Rabelais' images have a certain undestroyable nonofficial nature. No dogma, no authoritarianism, no narrow-minded seriousness can coexist with Rabelaisian images; these images are opposed to all that is finished and polished, to all pomposity, to every ready-made solution in the sphere of thought and world outlook.[3]

It is my contention that Littlewood's theatre practice, from the late 1950s onwards, should be read in a similar fashion to Bakhtin's reappraisal of Rabelais as she sought ways to promote a non-official, anti-authoritarian, non-dogmatic theatre that revelled in its own subversive techniques, acknowledgement of the audience and wilful blurring of the boundaries of theatrical form and taste. Stephen Lacey has written about how 'renewed interest in popular, "illegitimate" and non-literary forms' challenged realism as a dominant representational regime in the 1950s, and Littlewood positioned Theatre Workshop at the vanguard of this aesthetic disturbance.[4] This cultural 'rebranding' was part of a very deliberate strategy to situate her practice as part of an 'illegitimate' theatre genealogy – to play on her status as marginal, anti-establishment, regional as opposed to metropolitan; concerned with the live event of performance rather than the supremacy of the written word. It also, importantly, set her work apart from the largely text-bound outputs produced at the Royal Court, which despite important departures remained 'the temple of social realism'.[5]

For inspiration, Littlewood looked back to popular cultural forms such as music hall and variety that had been such a vital part of the British theatrical landscape in its heyday in the late nineteenth and early twentieth centuries.[6] The East End had a long association with music hall as a cultural form, in fact the Theatre Royal's history was tied up in various aspects of popular entertainment and Littlewood became determined to draw on this history as well as the contemporary popularity of entertainers such as Max Miller and the Crazy Gang, who continued to attract large audiences with stage shows and the televised *The Gang Show* (1956). In her quest, Littlewood drew on a rather nostalgic assumption about the working-class impetus and popular ownership of music hall and variety acts that rather sidestepped the realities of commercial transaction and ideological complexity inherent in their patterns of production and consumption. And she was not alone.

Writing about the mythological status of music hall in the 1950s, John Harrop acknowledges that in that decade 'the belief flourished that it had represented an earthy uninhibited popular humor, a healthy response to life's energies, unhampered by the enervating politeness of middle-class culture'.[7] Inspired by the myth of wit, vitality and irreverence surrounding music hall and variety forms, Littlewood appropriated their strategies of song, direct address, set comic pieces and double entendre to rupture the social-realist undertones of the texts she produced in the late 1950s. And, as Lacey argues, this aesthetic shift 'sprang as much from an ideological impulse (to replace outmoded representations on the stage and to reach a working-class audience) as it did from aesthetic ones'.[8] Hence, in her move to embrace the popular, alongside, or increasingly over and above, the political, Littlewood both implicitly and explicitly engaged with the politics of the popular.

The politics of the popular

John Storey draws attention to how 'popular culture is a concept of ideological contestation and variability, to be filled and emptied, to be articulated and disarticulated, in a range of different and competing ways'.[9] Many theorists in the mid-twentieth century, particularly those associated with the Frankfurt school, argued that popular culture induced myopia in the working classes as it shielded them from the realities of their existence through complex ideological manipulations administered by the capitalist-driven culture industries. In contrast, Littlewood embraced a popular culture aesthetic as a resistant strategy closely connected to her radical politics and commitment to working-class life and experience, a decision that connected her to 'Gramsci's idea that folklore and popular arts could form the basis of counter-hegemonic cultural activism'.[10]

Choosing to align with the popular against the official, dominant culture, Littlewood set about confronting ideas around cultural 'taste' and spheres of legitimacy by unsettling an authorised hierarchy of cultural preferences by deliberately subverting Culture with a capital 'C' through a self-conscious adoption of popular cultural formations and techniques. Rejecting the distanced aesthetic gaze Pierre Bourdieu associates with high art and Culture, Littlewood promoted a form that was local, haphazard, bawdy and improvised and openly embraced the audience's role in the event. More importantly, whereas Bourdieu assumes the irreversible denigration of working-class culture and that 'the working-class aesthetic is a dominated aesthetic, constantly obliged to define itself by reference to the dominant aesthetic', Littlewood regarded popular culture on its own terms and in relation to its own merits and principles of aesthetic judgement.[11]

Ian Haywood writes that 'a rich vein of debunking, irreverent and often ribald humour has long been a hallmark of working-class culture', and Littlewood embraced this with gusto.[12] She hoped to revive qualities associated with Bakhtin's conception of the carnivalesque, whereby humour undermines power and authority in a moment of inversion from established rules. For Bakhtin, the moment of laughter is a collectivising moment – it facilitates a bringing together that temporarily dissolves hierarchies in favour of horizontal comradeship. In Littlewood's work, she deployed comedy to unsettle bourgeois decorum with bawdy innuendo, rebellious satire and general silliness. However romantically, Littlewood believed in the liberating potential of laughter as part and parcel of her socialist impulse. This took many forms. For instance, characters use ribald, self-deprecating and satirical humour to laugh at themselves and others in the face of adverse conditions. She encouraged moments of performer–audience exchange, 'corpsing' and improvised ad-lib that dissolved the distinction between the stage and auditorium in shared mirth that temporarily ruptured the narrative frame. And, for her, the affirming communal laughter emanating from the audience potentially created moments of temporary unification, shared values and pleasure that suspended hierarchical divisions apparent beyond the theatre space.

The perceived success or otherwise of the relationship between the authentic documentation of working-class life combined or set against the vigour of up-front popular theatricality dominated reception of the theatrical hybrids discussed in this chapter, and this forms a central narrative strand in the investigation that follows. In particular, I am interested in how the excessively theatrical, exuberant popular theatre forms can be read as either underpinning or undermining the social, political and ethical questions and concerns that reside at the heart of these works. I want to argue that in the heightened theatricality generated by Littlewood there resided an implicit faith in and celebration of life itself as a persistent critique of regimes that sought to contain, restrict and undervalue working-class life and experience. Connecting to the previous chapter, I also focus on the alternative communities represented in these productions that offer radical reconfigurations of family, class, community.

However, it is important to acknowledge that Littlewood's representations of working-class life and championing of the popular were not without their problems. Arguably, in Littlewood's later work, she peddled reductive cameos of illiterate, limited and immoral working-class characters problematically divorced from wider frameworks of family, community or social/ethical conscience. She also increasingly began to exoticise and romanticise criminality and to buy into some of the myths surrounding the criminal underbelly operational in the East End at the time. In one interview with Alan Brien she claimed, 'It's the layabouts that know best. I've always knocked about with gangsters and whores. As a young girl, I used to stand on a street corner and pretend to be a whore.'[13] This provocative statement is typical of Littlewood, but its flippant disregard for the social, material and personal consequences of gangsterism and the sex industry is very troubling. Hence, in this chapter, I explore how productions such as *Fings Ain't Wot They Used T'Be*, *A Kayf Up West* and *Make Me an Offer* demonstrated an uncritical populism that relied on a raucous, high-tempo theatrical 'good night out' divorced from wider social discourse and arguably reversed Littlewood's early political campaigning agenda. Rather than a rumbustious humour defying authority and unseating social hierarchy, I argue that the humour implicit in these productions reasserted hegemonic forces by laughing at rather than laughing in joyous communion with life's outsiders and underclass. However, my analysis begins with the productions of Behan's *The Quare Fellow* and *The Hostage*.

Theatrical disobedience: *The Quare Fellow* and *The Hostage*

The Quare Fellow began life as a one-act play in Irish ominously called *The Twisting of Another Rope*. After rejection by the Abbey Theatre, Behan rewrote a three-act version that premiered at the newly opened Pike, a small theatre in Dublin run by Alan Simpson and Carolyn Swift. The published text is based on Theatre Workshop's production, so in many ways it is hard to differentiate between that which originated with Behan, that which came about through the cuts and reordering instituted by Simpson and Swift and that which emerged through rehearsal and improvisation with Theatre Workshop.[14] Littlewood's production premiered at the Theatre Royal on 24 May 1956, only sixteen days after John Osborne's *Look Back in Anger*, but whereas Osborne petulantly bemoaned the lack of 'good brave causes', Behan belted onto the English theatre scene with a deeply humanitarian account of the brutal degradation capital punishment inflicts on individuals, the prison community and society. In *Discipline and Punish* (1977), Michel Foucault notes how the disappearance of torture and the death penalty as public spectacles became associated with a humanisation of the judicial process marked by the introduction of trial by jury, appropriate judicial procedure and strict guidelines on how to enact the death penalty.[15] Yet, like Foucault's work, Behan offers a disturbing meditation on how the continuing spectacle of death still resides in the largely hidden/unmarked act of execution. Equally, prefiguring Foucault's theoretical analysis, Behan explores how brutal punishments enacted on the body of an individual are as much about social control and power as about retribution.

Set on the night before an execution, *The Quare Fellow* addresses the perennial question whether it is ever morally justifiable for the state to kill a human being as a punishment for crimes committed. In Behan's play there is no suggestion that those facing the death penalty are innocent, so, leaving aside issues of proving guilt beyond doubt, the play considers the broader ethical dilemmas posed by state-sanctioned murder and its impact on a closed community of men. For *The Quare Fellow*'s audiences, capital punishment was a vivid reality. The campaign against the death penalty had been raging throughout the 1950s, propelled by a series of high-profile cases such as the execution of Derek Bentley in 1953, a young man with learning difficulties who was an accomplice rather than a murderer, and of Ruth Ellis, the last woman hanged in Britain, in 1955. The play opened just two months after the House of Lords had overruled Parliament's attempt to abolish the death penalty.[16] As such, the production was intensely topical and generated a great deal of public interest, a situation bolstered by Behan's ebullient public persona, which attracted the attention of millions after his drunken, incoherent appearance on the Malcolm Muggeridge show during the play's run.[17]

Behan 'avoids both human sentimentality and the problem-play approach which one might expect from abolitionists'[18] by exploiting his experiential knowledge of the mordant humour and rituals at Mountjoy Prison on execution day, an embodied knowledge sensationally highlighted in the programme note for the Stratford East production:

> Brendan Behan has spent 8 of his 33 years in British prisons for political offices connected with the liberation of Ireland. A man of acute observation and perspicacity, he has known many men awaiting execution; in some cases he has talked with them until the day before their deaths.[19]

Behan's own close proximity to the death penalty for IRA terrorist offences made him more aware than most about the arbitrary nature of the sentence. Both the arbitrary nature and ideologically loaded enactment of the death penalty are apparent in the play as two men are due for execution but one receives a last-minute reprieve. The reprieved Protestant man beat his wife to death with a silver-topped cane, whereas the remaining 'quare fellow' killed his brother and cut up his corpse with a meat cleaver. Behan cleverly insinuates the class, religious and gender politics pervading the outcome in which a domestic murder of a woman is not deemed worthy of the death penalty and a 'real bog-man act' by an inarticulate Catholic boy is. Despite these details, Behan refused to individualise the quare fellow, and his absent presence stands in for all killed in the name of punishment. Yet Behan's focus is not on the nearly dead but on those barely living in incarceration and their ways of coping with and articulating the consequences of the death penalty – through sardonic humour, collective volubility and objectifying commentary. The discourse that 'life is cheap' results, as John Brannigan has noted, in a culture of subversive conversion whereby a hanging becomes a source of entertainment and communitas, the letters of a dead man become highly regarded currency and pages of the Bible are ripped out for cigarette papers.[20] In her staging, Littlewood exploited this very quality of 'subversive conversion' and its implicit performative playfulness.

In performance, Littlewood emphasised an obsessive preoccupation with the grim minutiae of preparation for and the rituals of execution – the last meal, the removal of watches and the brutal calculation of height, weight and neck strength to ascertain the required length of rope. Failing to collude in the government and media spin of a quick, clean death, Warder Regan refuses to hide behind the scientific euphemism of 'execution' by referring to neck breaking, throttling and the grizzly practice of cutting open the back of the neck to reveal the broken vertebrae. There is no attempt to shy away from the gruesome reality of the death penalty and the traumatic impact it has on the people exposed to it who seek alcoholic solace, retreat into religious rhetoric, faint or avert their gaze. The text relating to the material reality of execution is shocking, visceral; it jolts the audience into body consciousness and a relation with an event carried out in their name. As such, Behan articulates a vociferous attack on the complacency that facilitated the continued issuing and enactment of the death penalty, whilst the highly visible sign demanding SILENCE that greeted the audience on curtain up further implicated their complicity. The hanging temporarily collapses hierarchical boundaries between the prisoners and the warders, and the audience is similarly implicated when Regan states, 'It's a bad night for all of us.'[21]

Likening the play to Gorki's *The Lower Depths*, the reviewer for *Theatre World* announced the production as 'a prison documentary, a transcript from life at the lowest human level'; Tynan similarly noted 'a model of restraint, integrity and disciplined naturalism', whereas Maurice Richardson admitted that 'there is more to *The Quare Fellow* than good reporting, to say nothing of the ingenious stagecraft'.[22] Alongside the pressing subject matter, what distinguished Littlewood's production was her ability to create a mood of 'absolute realism', whilst simultaneously generating an aesthetic space for frequent performative interruptions, many of which were added during rehearsals. Songs, dances, jokes and comic set pieces disrupted the flow of the narrative by inserting a Rabelaisian jocularity that asserted the theatrical and excessive alongside stark social observation and commentary. The co-existence and blurring of these parallel theatrical modes proved shocking and prompted Tynan to claim that *The Quare Fellow* deserved a place in 'theatrical history'.[23]

Bury's design established a provocative environment to capture 'the aridity of confinement'.[24] The prison yard was a bleak bare space framed by the unconcealed brickwork at the back of the stage, a concrete plinth and railings. Photographic documents of the production reveal Littlewood's mastery of social interaction and grouping as the men huddle around the edges of the space to avoid the brutal exposure of centre stage. The male actors did not command the space, but tried to dissolve into it as they shared thoughts and banter on the event looming large on their horizon. References to the markers of time and time passing are prevalent in the play and Littlewood theatricalised the intense claustrophobia and boredom of prison life in restricted spatial areas such as the prison yard and corridors. Rehearsals started on this even before scripts arrived. As Goorney remembered, 'The day to day routines were improvised, cleaning out cells, the quick smoke, the furtive conversation, trading tobacco and the boredom and meanness of prison life were explored.'[25]

In performance, Littlewood emphasised the mundanity of everyday prison life with activities such as cleaning out chamber pots and sweeping corridors. However, this quotidian existence was interrupted by several comic moments that resonate with the set routines of music-hall theatrics such as the heightened chorus greeting the condemned man's last meal or the intermittent presence of two young prisoners singing and sweeping in unison. When two prisoners, Dunlavin and

9. *The Quare Fellow* (1956)

Neighbour, contrive to steal swigs of the methylated spirits used to rub their rheumatic legs and Dunlavin, suffering from the after-effects, humorously refers to himself as 'a methylated martyr', these characters morph into stock comic types.[26] A key comic set piece occurs when Mickser, an inmate, conveys the quare fellow's walk to the gallows as a quick-fire racing commentary:

> We're off, in this order: the Governor, the Chief, two screws Regan and Crimmin, the quare fellow between them, two more screws and three runners from across the Channel, getting well in front, now the Canon. He's making a big effort for the last two furlongs. He's got the white pudding bag on his head, just a short distance to go. He's in. [*A clock begins to chime the hour. Each quarter sounds louder.*] His feet to the chalk line. He'll be

> pinioned, his feet together. The bag will be pulled down over his face. The screws come off the trap and steady him. Himself goes to the lever and . . .[27]

In this moment, the tension that has been ratcheting up explodes in a highly theatrical piece of, literally, gallows humour. In line with the rest of the production, the condemned man was absent, yet his death becomes a mordant spectacle marked, as the prison bell tolls, by a rattling and banging of bars and an eruption of 'ferocious howling'.[28] In this unified moment of dissent, marking and mourning the death of a fellow human being, the production reached its apotheosis. In its woeful repetition, this prison ritual re-enacts the banal inevitability of another state-sanctioned death. Hence, as with the entire play, the form and subject interweave in productive relation to avoid maudlin sensationalism and emotional manipulation in favour of a Brechtian distancing effect.

The language of *The Quare Fellow* is robust, a factor Vincent Trowbridge of the Lord Chamberlain's office connected to authenticity when he acknowledged that 'I hope justifiably, I have allowed this play much latitude over numerous "bloodys" and lesser oaths. To cut them out would make nonsense of the speech of a lot of low Irish'; however, he also let slip a loaded comment that 'the language will cause no offence whatever in Stratford East'.[29] Yet *The Quare Fellow*'s language far exceeded realism in its heightened creative theatricality. After encountering the play, Tynan wrote, 'The English hoard words like misers; the Irish spend them like sailors; and in Brendan Behan's tremendous new play language is out on a spree, ribald, dauntless and spoiling for a fight.'[30] In Behan's hands, and undoubtedly drawing on reality, a hanging becomes a 'haircut and shave' and a bleak prison cell a 'flowery dell'. He carefully crafts language to function in performative counterpoint to the barren surroundings. Hence the first time a warder speaks Behan laced his utterance with alliteration that heightens it into a theatrical realm as opposed to the realm of naturalism: 'The screw is listening as well as peeping, and you'll be bloody well weeping if you don't give over your moaning.'[31] In Littlewood's production, voice and sound actively transgressed the stagnant atmosphere. A burst of song announced the opening of the play:

A hungry feeling came o'er me stealing
And the mice were squealing in my prison cell,
And that old triangle
Went jingle jangle,
Along the banks of the Royal Canal.[32]

Its eruptive rebellious presence, its refusal to obey the constraints of confinement in the face of a large sign demanding SILENCE, set in motion a train of performative acts of defiance designed to counteract a repressive regime. 'The Brechtian counterpoint of aural and visual signs serves to highlight the notion that the prison regime is not total in its power, and can be cheated, however contingently.'[33] The men find ways to experience the stuff of life that the disciplinary apparatus of incarceration seeks to expunge. Hence banned communication between prisoners takes place through an elaborate form of Morse code carried by the hot-water pipes and the men are given the chance to experience heterosexual desire after catching a glimpse of the women prisoners hanging out their washing.

When she revived the play in 2004 for the Oxford Stage Company, Kathy Burke decided to excise some of the songs, explaining, 'I think the songs were absolutely right for the 1950s, to soften the blow of a hard-hitting play, but I think that now they're a bit twee and "diddly-dee".'[34] But I think this underestimates the importance of the songs as a multilayered structural and thematic device. On one level, their skeletal structure conveys the passing of time, on the other their presence is a defiant affirmation of a powerful life force and the prisoners' ability to transcend pleasurably the limits of their immediate environment. For example, the first song emanates from a prisoner in solitary confinement. As such, through song the production mocks the brutality and inhumanity of his prescribed isolation, which connects him to the wider community and symbolically breaches his containment.

Several visually inscribed moments similarly have a complex function beyond the immediate theatrical frame. The physical presence of the grave and its 'bringing to life' is a constant reminder of impending death. The fact that the prisoners dig the grave suggests their own close proximity to death and their complicity in the event itself. That the warders and prisoners embark on an economic transaction to reward a clean-cut grave only enhances the sense of moral bankruptcy. At the same time, the grave becomes a site of humour when Neighbour, a curmudgeonly inmate, is thrown in it for transgressing the bonds of communal solidarity. Yet ultimately the unmarked grave is the site of the condemned man's erasure. The prisoners, like society, will become oblivious to the existence of the executed; he will fade from memory as his body decomposes and those mourning his loss will have no meaningful place to grieve. What *The Quare Fellow* offered was a space in which to contemplate the ethical questions surrounding the death penalty, a moment of pause in which the absent and soon-to-be-forgotten man had a presence in the here and now. Moreover, the intricate splicing of authentic representation and music-hall-style theatrics initiated by Littlewood shifted the spotlight onto life itself and sharpened an ethical probing of the death penalty at the very point when its future was being widely debated in British society.

Behan's next play for Theatre Workshop, *The Hostage*, opened on 14 October 1958. The action is set in a Dublin boarding house owned by Monsewer, a mentally unstable Republican campaigner, and managed by Pat, a former IRA 'hero', who unknown to Monsewer runs the building as a brothel to make ends meet. Populated by outsiders, sex workers and petty criminals who congregate to sing, dance and tell stories, the brothel doubles as an IRA safe house. The narrative hinges on the kidnapping and threatened execution of an apolitical eighteen-year-old Cockney soldier called Leslie as a reprisal for the imprisonment and imminent hanging of an IRA prisoner in Belfast. The play traces Leslie's interaction with his captors, including a burgeoning love affair, and ends with his accidental death during a raid by Civic Guards, who are supposed to rescue him.

The Hostage's complicated theatrical geneaology began with *An Giall*, an O'Casey-influenced Irish play commissioned by Gael Linn, the Irish-language organisation, and first performed at the An Damer, Gael Linn's theatre in Dublin, on 16 June 1958. Littlewood persuaded Behan to translate the play so that Theatre Workshop could produce the English-language premiere, but conflicting accounts remain of the creative process that followed. Failing to successfully negotiate and prioritise his multiple identities as writer, social commentator, alcoholic, story-teller, public-house raconteur and one of Ireland's most famous exports and nationalists, Behan proved elusive. The slipperiness caused Raffles to take drastic action to gain Behan's compliance:

> Brendan was going round the Covent Garden pubs in the morning, taking a kip in the afternoon and drinking again at night, so he wasn't taking too much notice of rehearsals. The actors were improvising a second act and Joan was getting desperate, so one night, Gerry sat Brendan down, pointed a gun at him and told him to write.[35]

When such measures failed, Littlewood worked on coaxing a verbal translation of *An Giall* from Behan in the absence of a more formal textual body of work. She also augmented the 'script' with material derived from improvisation and Behan's infamous bonhomie.[36] Hence the text first published by Methuen in 1958 was a fluid combination of translated text, Behan's orality, improvisatory processes and Littlewood's performance intuition. Revisions continued throughout the production's history. A new version appeared at the Paris Théâtre des Nations Festival on 3 April 1959, where it won the coveted prize and Littlewood received the award for directing alongside long-overdue support and recognition from the Arts Council and the British Council.[37] She also reworked the production once it transferred to Wyndham's Theatre in the West End on 11 June 1959, followed by tours to New York, Toronto, Montreal and San Francisco, so that by the end of 1962 Methuen had published three editions of the 'definitive' text and, according to Barker, none of them were an accurate record of the performance.[38] Importantly, Theatre Workshop holds the copyright for *The Hostage* rather than Behan, a clear acknowledgement of the play's multiple authorship.

Whilst there is no doubt that Littlewood retrospectively exaggerated her contribution to *The Hostage*'s subject matter, she played a significant role generating its theatrical style. In a telling curtain speech on the opening night, Behan claimed Theatre Workshop had performed a better play than he had written, a statement acknowledging Littlewood's deft navigation of Behan's uproarious comedy and moving pathos, incisive political commentary and anarchic theatricality. As Littlewood admitted, 'the most difficult part was holding on to the theme and sustaining the tension behind the jokes and laughter'.[39] Writing to congratulate her, Terence Rattigan similarly picked up on Littlewood's direction when he admitted,

> I think 'The Hostage' is the best directed modern play I have ever seen. I think the play is pretty wonderful too but it's you who have made it just as wonderful as it is, and it's you I must humbly and sincerely thank for an evening of excitement and joy.[40]

So where did these qualities of excitement and joy reside?

Despite thematically dealing with the consequences of intransigent political ideologies, the production managed to celebrate the bodily, sensual pleasures derived from conversation, dancing, song, humour and love over and above difference, dissension and conflict. When the kidnapped soldier has his blindfold removed, he tells the group to carry on dancing and pursues amicable and romantic relations with his captors rather than animosity. As Harold Hobson enthused, 'Life is what "The Hostage" is rich in; it shouts, sings, thunders and stamps with life.'[41] Hence, in a marked departure from earlier Theatre Workshop productions in which form and content connected to the politics of class struggle and radical social change, in *The Hostage* the politics of pleasure held forth and this largely emanated from its use of popular theatre strategies.

As with *The Quare Fellow*, the main stylistic differences from the Irish original involved a reconstitution of a largely social-realist form through the addition of a pianist; a fiddle player; Republican, folk and music-hall songs; wild dances; obscene profanities; and Cockney slang. Littlewood also inserted topical references to immigration and race relations, the atomic bomb, Suez, the Wolfenden Report on homosexuality and the Lord Chamberlain. Above all, the production, like its originator and those charged with bringing it into being, refused to behave. Both on- and offstage the disruptive presence of Behan generated a remarkable frisson with his notorious impromptu interjections from the auditorium – and occasionally the stage.

Discontented with the 'silent' role of writer, Behan deliberately inserted himself into the performative role of action through speech, song and dances. However, what should have been embarrassing incidents of failure, a lapse in performance discipline, became joyously extra-theatrical moments, which invariably seduced audiences. On one notable occasion when Behan interrupted proceedings, 'the play stopped completely, the actors unable to continue because of their own laughter'.[42] The thin veneer between real life and theatrical representation dissolved in this moment as the writer and performers temporarily annihilated the play in favour of their own shared mirth. Arguably, for Littlewood, these interruptions were more valid than the play because they offered unbounded, impromptu evidence of popular pleasure unfurling in the moment. Hence there was no attempt to disguise the moment or embarrassment because the 'proper' order was unsettled; instead the performers and audience were encouraged to celebrate and enjoy the playfulness. In *Stage Fright, Animals and Other Theatrical Problems* (2006), Nicholas Ridout draws attention to the multiple theoretical and performative implications of 'corpsing'. He writes, 'Corpsing, then, is something that both happens and is done, is intentional and unintentional, has to be connected with death, as well as with the irruption of the real and the suspension of proper order.'[43] In fact, the material that made up *The Hostage* (including its originator) constantly burst out from the confines of the narrative space into a performative space of action and interaction to suspend literally and metaphorically the 'proper order'.

Epitomised by the moment when Mulleady and Gilchrist's religious lament for 'our souls' is slurred into a repetition of 'arseholes', the production was defined by its irreverence, naughtiness, exuberance and excess.[44] Opening with pimps, sex workers, and their clients dancing a wild Irish jig, the actors gave the impression that they were out on a drunken spree and they were taking the audience with them for the ride. Onstage, there was no carefully defined 'fourth wall' as the actors invited Kate, the pianist, to start a tune and frequently addressed the audience to explain plot developments. As well as breaching the stage/auditorium divide, the action also breached the demarcated spatial confines of the boarding house when the actors needed more room to dance or fight. There is a sense in which the material was unruly and uncontainable. The loosely structured plot ebbed and flowed; Pat served as an informal

Master of Ceremonies; characters drifted in and out, hung around for a drink and a chat and were as likely to burst into or join in with a song or raucous Irish dance as to further the narrative. Real-time mundane conversation collided with the theatrical time of heightened story-telling, linguistic play and Rabelaisian partying. Even for the cast, 'it all seemed a mess, if a glorious one, and quite lacking in form'.[45]

Reviewing the production for the first time, Tynan admitted that 'conventional terminology is totally inept to describe the uses to which Mr. Behan and his director, Joan Littlewood, are trying to put the theatre. The old pigeonholes will no longer serve.'[46] Defined by naturalistic standards, its construction was 'faulty'; it exhibited a 'babble of styles, devoid of form'.[47] Tragedy, comedy, vaudeville, music hall, love story, political drama, farce and satire collided in *The Hostage*, a theatrical promiscuity that prompted Tynan to reach back into history to pluck out 'commedia dell'arte' as a descriptor. Yet, mirroring the production itself, there was no critical consistency – Robert Brustein called it a 'vaudeville whirligig', whilst Alan Brien found it 'Brechtian' in *The Threepenny Opera* mode.[48]

Littlewood's intervention in *The Hostage*'s reconstituted style and content led many Irish commentators to accuse her of a neocolonial disregard for the authenticity and integrity of the original and of undermining its Irish nationalist rhetoric. Tom MacIntyre argued that Behan had been 'diminished by gimmickry', and Ulick O'Connor called it 'a blown-up hotch-potch compared with the original version ... *An Giall* had its roots in Ballyferriter, the Blaskets and the Atlantic; *The Hostage* in a commercial entertainment world Brendan had no real contact with'.[49] However, this reading conveniently overlooks Behan's professed admiration for the music-hall form and his complicity in Littlewood's production. In fact, they self-referentially embedded concerns with the politics of appropriation, commodification of the self, nationalism and cultural tourism in a telling exchange directly referencing Behan's IRA past, his reputation for excessive drinking and his willingness to adapt his Irish text in collaboration with English artists for consumption by an English audience. In other words, they pre-empted and mocked those critical commentators who would put nationalist rhetoric over and above a theatrical 'good time' in a direct echo of the play's overriding impulse.

Rather than championing an uncritical nationalism, throughout the production nationalist rhetoric, songs and symbolic emblems such as 'anthems, flags and banners denoting political identities are made the objects of farce and ridicule'.[50] Instead, *The Hostage* indicates the close proximity between the legitimate fight for national autonomy and blinkered violent sectarianism in which 'an eye for an eye' is a zero-sum game. Also, as Nicholas Grene observes, by inserting references to Kenya and Cyprus, Littlewood's aim 'was to internationalise the play's theme, to turn it from a play about Republicanism and the continuing Irish question to a play about colonialism and armed conflict throughout the world'.[51] The point is underscored by several mentions of the H-bomb, which according to Pat had transformed the landscape of terrorism. Yet, within this international agenda, the Irish question looms large. The degeneration of a Republican stronghold into a seedy site for sexual transactions speaks volumes about Behan's biting attack on the inconsequential state of the IRA at the time of the original production – a point brought home by the kidnapping of a British soldier on national service on his return from a dance rather than a career soldier on official duties. Indeed, rather than heroic political activists, the IRA sympathisers in the play either are ludicrously petty and vindictive, immersed in historical amnesia, or have a fragile grasp on reality.

In *The Hostage*, the characters strategically employ role-play, disguise and constructed narratives to blur the distinction between fact and fiction, illusion and reality. Monsewer, dressed as a hybrid Celtic/French revolutionary in Littlewood's production, is ironically the upper-class English son of a Protestant bishop who romantically and self-consciously adopts the Irish Republican cause, a kilt, the Irish language and bagpipes, after discovering his Anglo-Irish heritage. Described as thinking 'he's still fighting in the Troubles or one of the anti-English campaigns before that', he leads a delusional life, fuelled by Pat, whose political past is undermined by his present 'role' as an infirm, domestic brothel-keeper complete with carpet slippers, battered corduroys and a walking stick.[52] He looks after Monsewer by disguising the sexual as opposed to political economy that drives the place and even gathers a motley assortment of inhabitants, ironically including the hostage, for Monsewer to scrutinise on his rounds inspecting the 'troops'. The theme of falsity and role-play is equally evident in the ridiculously pious IRA officers guarding the hostage, who, it transpires, are a schoolteacher and a railway ticket collector. This element of disguise and duality is similarly evoked in the building itself – as a former safe house turned brothel becomes a holding room for a political prisoner, this informal prison becomes a site for dancing, drinking and sexual activity and a dirty cellar becomes a potential escape route.

In *An Giall*, Leslie's death marked the tragic conclusion of the play. Yet in Theatre Workshop's version, 'when it seemed the boisterous and brilliant carnival was about to surrender to death',[53] Littlewood had Leslie literally leaping to his feet to sing a defiant, life-affirming, final song.[54] Grene has drawn attention to potential readings of this final image in the following assessment:

> This *can* work, as it is intended to work, to deliberately undermine the catharsis achieved in the emotional moment of death, and to remind us that 'it's not in the play-world that people are dying, but out there in the real life of the audience and the distressful country beyond'. But it can also act as a last let-off, a release for the audience into the reassurance that it has only been make-believe after all, and that the violent forces at work in the Irish–English situation can be dissolved into a jolly Irish–English song-and-dance routine.[55]

Rather than an either/or, I contend that the qualities Grene identifies are co-existent. The defiant theatricality of Leslie's refusal to take it 'lying down' ruptures the empathetic potential of the moment but it also, rather than being a 'let-off', reminds the audience that the sensual values, desires and resilience of the body and the carnivalesque hold sway in this production.

Simultaneously disguised and enriched by *The Hostage*'s overt theatrical playfulness and music-hall sensibility was a complex meditation on the politics of identity and allegiance that mocked the black-and-white demarcations of sectarianism. Adding Miss Gilchrist, a lascivious social worker; two female sex workers, Colette and Ropeen, who are only mentioned in the original; and two queer characters, Littlewood extended Behan's Irish community to create a community of marginalised 'Others'. Lacey refers to the group as 'sub-proletarian',[56] but this class-bound term fails to encapsulate the different classes, ages, political allegiances, sexualities and ethnicities that inhabit the stage space. More importantly, the production used a variety of playful strategies to destabilise fixed and immutable boundaries of identity. For instance, the exotically named Rio Rita is a British male prostitute, and his black client, Princess Grace, references the notoriously blonde American film star, Grace Kelly, who married the prince of Monaco in 1956. Princess Grace and Rio Rita, alongside other couples in the play, meet and develop platonic and sexual relationships across the borders of class, religious, national and racial identities. So a Cockney prostitute has sex with a Russian sailor at the height of the Cold War and an Irish Catholic girl falls in love with a British Protestant soldier in the midst of a violent sectarian incident. As such, the production overturned ideological and identificatory fixity in favour of a playful blurring and splitting of distinct gender, sexual, racial, socioeconomic and geographical markers of identity. Refusing to observe binaries such as black/white, male/female, Catholic/Protestant, heterosexual/homosexual and Irish/British, Littlewood alternatively presented a vision of simultaneity and overlap in which love and pleasure have the potential to rupture divides.

Interestingly, Theatre Workshop extended this split identification to Behan in a carefully crafted programme note that depicted him as both an Irish nationalist preoccupied with English colonialism and Irish subjugation, and also as a potential defender of Britain:

> [Behan] has a hatred for the political forces who divide and subject Ireland: but for people – even if those people are the instruments of antagonistic political forces – he has only love and understanding. If a stranger attacks Britain, no-one will support this country more strongly than Brendan Behan, but when he talks of Ireland – of a country where, outside the cities, there are almost no young and active men left, where the villages are now but rows of empty houses, where Irish butter and meat are dearer than they are in England, and where partition gives such a sense of continuing betrayal and defeat that the brilliant and useful ones

> leave for abroad to escape the internecine quibbling and denigration – he grows angry with the anger of a man who loves his native place as passionately as Shakespeare loved his.[57]

Nonetheless, the framing and interpretation of *The Hostage* considered above was wholly reliant on a particular historical circumstance in which Irish sectarianism was in a lull and open to humorous scrutiny. By 1972, when Littlewood revived *The Hostage*, sectarian violence and battles between the IRA and the British state were increasingly brutal and bloody. Littlewood's annotated copy of *The Hostage* from this period indicates that a desire to keep step with the current political situation in Ireland motivated many of her proposed cuts and additions.[58] She added references to solitary confinement, hunger strikes, armies of occupation and suggested that the names of the 'Derry Dead' should be read out. It is unclear whether these changes occurred in the actual production, but this revival could not escape the consequences of radically altered circumstances. Whereas in 1958 the stress on common humanity was both welcome and celebrated, by 1972 it seemed ill-conceived, reductive and vacuously sentimental, qualities that led Benedict Nightingale, amongst others, to accuse Littlewood of 'an astonishing insensitivity to the temper of the times'.[59] Critics levelled no such accusation at Littlewood's production of Shelagh Delaney's *A Taste of Honey*, which they hailed as a triumph of contemporaneity.

'Real people ... joking and flaring and scuffling': *A Taste of Honey*

At first glance, *A Taste of Honey*, which received its first production at the Theatre Royal in May 1958, before transferring to the West End and Broadway and becoming an iconic film in 1961, epitomises the social-realist tradition. Its industrial northern setting in Manchester, the drab 'comfortless flat' in which the narrative unfolds, the poverty of its characters and its 'gritty' depiction of social issues are all suggestive of a classic 'kitchen sink' drama. Certainly, many reviewers connected Delaney to the 'angry young men' movement and praised what they saw as the play's documentary veracity. Lisa Gordon Smith claimed it 'records what actually is, shedding upon the theme a clear and dispassionate light'; Tynan hailed Delaney a 'portent' for presenting 'real people ... joking and flaring and scuffling'; and, more disturbingly, Alan Brien applauded it as 'not so much dramaturgy as anthropology demonstrated by a genuine cannibal'.[60]

The intriguing figure of Delaney, a nineteen-year-old Salford factory worker who wrote this, her first play, in ten days after seeing Terence Rattigan's *Variations on a Theme*, helped to promote the authenticity of the piece. The programme note accompanying the production declared,

> Shelagh Delaney is a nineteen year old Salford girl who works in an engineering factory. Her father works on the buses, and her brother is an apprentice engineer ... With a fierce independence of mind and an integrity which is part of the classic Lancashire tradition she is typical of many of today's young people in the North of England.[61]

As the writer Kay Mellor explained in a radio documentary marking the fiftieth anniversary of the play's first production, Delaney's class, gender, age and educational background made her seem like 'the real deal'.[62] Equally, her daring depiction of taboo subjects, including a dysfunctional mother–daughter relationship, mixed-race coupling, unwanted pregnancy and homosexuality, ensured that her play would make an impact. According to Lindsay Anderson, Delaney created a work

> of complete, exhilarating originality ... it has all the strength, and none of the weaknesses, of a pronounced, authentic local accent. Going north in Britain is always like a trip into another country, and *A Taste of Honey* is a real escape from the middlebrow, middle-class vacuum of the West End.[63]

A Taste of Honey is brutal, uncompromisingly unsentimental, and challenges the rhetoric of affluence and many of the mythical representations of working-class family and community life prominent at the time. According to Terry Lovell, 'Helen and Jo exist on the margins of working-class culture and community'.[64] Undercutting the classic representation of the extended working-class family and close intergenerational relations, they are single parents and the traditional family unit is a disruptive force. Rather than the middle-aged, asexual, overly protective, nurturing working-class 'mam' who became a common female trope of the working class in the British 'new wave', Helen is a heavy-drinking, highly sexual 'semi-whore' who is steadfastly impulsive in her actions and resolutely non-maternal. In fact, Helen's neglect and abandonment of Jo defines their mutually antagonistic relationship. In contrast to a stable home life and a close-knit community, Jo's young life has been characterised by emotional and geographical upheaval. She is unaware of her father's identity and accustomed to Helen's geographical restlessness as they regularly flit from one run-down bedsit to another, a practice that literally dislocates her from any sense of community belonging. Helen's priority is her own welfare, and her repeated phrase 'it was good while it lasted' mirrors her transient approach to life.

It is possible, however, to detect a degree of nostalgia for a more communal way of life. Helen recalls a pub she used to work in where it was 'a real get-together at weekends. Everybody standing up and giving a song'.[65] Also, the children singing and playing outside the flat occupy a particular role in the social imaginary of community. According to Lovell, they 'represent the past: the childhood, as well as the childishness, of the young people of the story, and an earlier, more "authentic" way of life which has been lost'.[66] Helen articulates and romanticises this past when she retreats into childhood memories towards the end of the play:

> You know when I was young we used to play all day long this time of the year; in the summer we had singing games and in the spring we played with tops and hoops, and then in the autumn there was the Fifth of November, then we used to have bonfires in the street, and gingerbread and all that.[67]

But this sentimental vision is a far cry from Jo's experience of childhood. Delaney also undercut notions of a homogeneous community identity through her radical (for the time) representation of different ethnic backgrounds, sexualities and miscegenation. She also dismantled the myth of the rallying community, as despite the evidence of a neighbour making her a crib, Jo has no faith in her local community or work colleagues to do anything other than point and stare at her unmarried pregnant status, so she takes refuge in her flat and shuts out the wider world.

The spaces the characters inhabit are bleak, and in many ways Delaney metonymically reduces them to the poverty and dilapidation of their environment.[68] The audience learns that the tenement bedsit is located in close proximity to a canal, cemetery and slaughterhouse, and the metaphor of stagnant water and death pervades the action. Yet, unlike *Johnny Noble*, *Landscape with Chimneys* and the later *Sparrers Can't Sing*, *A Taste of Honey* is stripped of public space. All the action takes place in the domestic environment with its shared bathroom and a naked bulb that shines a harsh light on the inadequacy of the fixtures and fittings.[69] In Littlewood's production, the unmade bed remained centre stage throughout, a visual reminder of the multiple sexual transactions that drive the play's narrative, not least the inference that Jo is regularly required to vacate the bed she shares with her mother to make way for the latest 'gentleman caller'. Yet within these inauspicious surroundings, Delaney offers the potential of an alternative family model based on friendship between marginal social outcasts.

Implicit in the play, as Lacey argues, is the presumption that

> happiness can only be found in a 'family' that is constituted on a different basis to that of the traditional family, one which breaks all the rules, and in which the central role, that of the mother, is detached from the biological mother and becomes the subject of negotiation.[70]

In Act One, Jimmie, a black nurse and sailor, is both surrogate mother and lover to Jo as he makes her hot milk and seduces her. In Act Two, Geoff, a homosexual art student, shares his meagre resources and takes on the domestic and maternal role by cooking, cleaning and caring for Jo as her pregnancy progresses. All of these relationships rely on complex gender and generational reversals that disrupt codified notions of appropriate social roles. In particular, *A Taste of Honey* defied the image of the confident, affluent consumer-conscious teenager at the vanguard of social change prominent in the 1950s in novels such as

Colin MacInnes's *Absolute Beginners* (1959). Jo, Jimmie and Geoff are not fashionable, brash young things confident of their place in the world – they are insecure and in the process of becoming adults. So Delaney simultaneously infantalises Jo and Geoff through cultural signifiers such as the teddy and balloons they export from the fair and their exchange of nursery rhymes, but they are also impressively independent and resourceful. Even more importantly, for the time, the play presented a positive representation of homosexuality. Geoff's queer status is never explicitly stated, but revealed through a series of coded signifiers. Nonetheless, this character marked a turning point in the relaxation of the censorship laws that previously banned depictions of the 'forbidden subject'.[71]

During the production, questions circulated around how much of the performed text was down to Delaney or Littlewood. Lisa Gordon Smith in *Plays and Players* wrote, 'the author may be a "natural" and a jolly good thing for British theatre if she is; but I still maintain that the finished article owes plenty to Miss Littlewood – and more power to her akimbo elbows'.[72] Actually, the subject matter and narrative of Delaney's original text are remarkably similar to the final published text, which used the performance as source – the setting is the same and the central relationships are clearly established. Key alterations centred on the transformation of Delaney's rather romantic portrayal of Helen's lover Peter to a drunken, aggressive, lecherous figure. Littlewood also tried to iron out the naivety surrounding Geoff's sexuality and whereas the original ends with his imminent suicide, the final version leaves his position far more ambiguous. Littlewood did, however, make significant changes to Delaney's social-realist form with the addition of music-hall-style asides to the audience, an onstage jazz band and characters dancing on an offstage to improvised music. In *Anger and After* (1962), John Russell Taylor admires the way Littlewood sustained and drew out the spirit of Delaney's original text to create 'a sort of magnified realism in which everything is like life but somehow larger than life',[73] but he is dismissive of the theatrical additions, claiming that

> the only modifications which one might find out of keeping are very minor: the introduction of a few lines addressed, music-hall

> style, straight at the audience, and the slight fantastication involved in having the characters dance on and off to the music.[74]

In his appraisal, Taylor echoed the mixed reception Littlewood's production elements encountered. Milton Shulman called it 'jittery and stylised ... out of key with the author's simple realism', the *Punch* reviewer found 'the production uncertain of its style', and Brien described it as 'a boozed, exaggerated, late-night anecdote of a play which slithers unsteadily between truth and fantasy, between farce and tragedy, between aphrodisiac and emetic'.[75] Frances Stephens found the asides to the audience irritating and even Tynan admitted, 'I don't know that I like all of Miss Littlewood's production tricks: I don't see why the mother should address all her lines to the audience, like a vaudeville soloist.'[76]

These reviews reveal unease about the tensions that emerged between the social-realist qualities of the text and the qualities of theatricality Littlewood added. Reviewers, it seems, were more than happy to accept *A Taste of Honey* as an acerbic 'slice of life from up north', but they were less happy to endorse the way Littlewood lifted the play 'out of its naturalistic mode on to a plane where it vibrates with a rather different kind of life, an eminently theatrical but still a wholly unrealistic life'.[77] In his *Antitheatrical Prejudice* (1981), Jonas Barish discusses 'anti-theatricalism', the suspicion towards overt practices of role-play, exaggeration and theatrical excess that the more hostile reviews of *A Taste of Honey* clearly exhibit.[78] They imply that the production's overt theatricality either masks a lack of depth or undercuts the seriousness of the content, which Littlewood would have better served with unadulterated social realism. For example, *The Times* reviewer argued that 'Miss Joan Littlewood's handling of the author's music-hall manner has the paradoxical effect of making us suspect that she is brilliantly contriving to conceal a lack of genuine character content'.[79] Far from seeing these modifications as minor irritants, these theatrical qualities – the eclectic, disjunctive style, the music-hall elements, the jazz band and the choreographed entrances and exits – were crucial to the production's impact. These additions functioned to destabilise the primacy and authority of the social-realist text in favour of the collaborative creative act and the live, communally encountered performance event.[80]

Championing the possibilities that arise from the chance encounters, accidents and explosive dynamics activated through improvisation, Littlewood used this creative approach to augment Delaney's text in rehearsal. As Avis Bunnage explained, 'We did a lot of improvisation. When we came to bits that didn't seem to work we ad-libbed around the ideas, made it up as we went along.'[81] So, in effect, the performers became co-authors, honing and shaping Delaney's text as it came up against their craft as performers. From this approach a hybrid emerged that combined the essence of the script with a performance-orientated theatricality. Hence a rather wordy line, 'Listen! I'm the sole financial support of our little combination and until that happy day when you contribute to the family income you'll leave disposal of said income to me', became 'when you start earning you can start moaning', which has a far more music-hall-style comedic quality.[82] Through this process, Littlewood edited, reshaped and redistributed the text amongst characters.

Rather than adhering to the rather even social-realist characterisations presented by Delaney's original text, Littlewood encouraged the co-existence of different theatrical genealogies and disjunctive elements. During the rehearsal process, each of the performers began to carve out a distinctive performance style for their character. Hence Bunnage, encouraged by Littlewood to find the humour, was hailed for her larger-than-life, music-hall-style turn as Helen, and Murray Melvin as Geoff was credited with 'a quietly convincing portrayal' that Anderson found 'a miracle of tact and sincerity'.[83] These characters sat alongside John Bay and later Nigel Davenport as Peter, who both interpreted him as a drunken, lecherous cartoon villain. In Littlewood's production, visual signifiers aided this slightly surreal collision of character tropes: whereas Jo wore casual clothes or her school uniform and Geoff wore an understated shirt and jeans, Peter sported a pirate-style eye patch and Helen appeared in some extraordinary outfits. On one occasion, when Jo stood in her uniform, complete with sensible flat pumps and buttoned-up shirt and tie, Helen appeared in an exaggeratedly huge puff-ball dress in shimmering material, a pill-box hat with an over-sized flower on top, long satin gloves, high heels and a long chiffon drape.[84] The contrast is striking and clearly deliberate – these characters inhabit the same social space, but they inhabit completely different theatrical conventions.

One of the most striking elements of the play and its original production was its language. The characters converse in a curious hybrid of everyday demotic language and a heightened music-hall-style back-and-forth as they incessantly bicker. This was not the chirpy Cockney dialect or dour northern brogue normally associated with working-class characters, but 'a rich expressive dialect, and it came as a welcome relief from the rigid, stereotyped dialogue which had, over the years, become the hallmark of traditional character acting'.[85] In itself, the language conveyed a heightened poetic realism, a celebration of working-class creativity through language, but Littlewood augmented this through direct address. Jo, rather than directing her 'I hate living off your immoral earnings!' to Helen, as occurs in the original text, moans, 'what a place ... and we're supposed to be living off her immoral earnings', directed towards the audience.[86] This is followed by numerous asides, primarily from Helen, such as 'She'd lose her head if it was loose' and 'Wouldn't she drive you mad?'[87]

As Thomas Postlewait and Tracy C. Davis observe in *Theatricality* (2003), 'When the spectator's role is not to recognize reality but to create an alternative through complicity in the "heightening" of the breakthrough into performance, then both performer and spectator are complicit in the mimesis.'[88] In Littlewood's production of *A Taste of Honey*, the words spoken in these incidences of direct address are pretty meaningless – they do not provide new insight or drive the narrative forward – but the fact of how they are expressed is crucial as they rupture the authority of the text (in which the characters only speak to each other) to assert a theatrical presence that breaches the theatrical frame. They acknowledge and engage with the audience to create a moment of exchange – a shared joke, understanding, observation that happens in the here-and-nowness of performance. As such, these performative speech acts are not expressive of a reality, but they constitute a reality through their utterance and the performance attitude they enact.

In these disruptive moments, something happens to the nature of the exchange between the stage and the auditorium. Anderson credited them with establishing both a genealogy with earlier popular theatre forms, describing them not only as 'sudden patches of pure music hall, panto-style', but also as a means to avoid 'soppy "identification"', a Brechtian-style alienating device that points up the artifice of theatrical practice.[89] Philip Auslander argues that in the 1950s, when television was the new kid on the block, the status of live performance was put under scrutiny. He writes that 'descriptions of drama on television from this period emphasize that television's immediacy and intimacy make the experience of drama entirely comparable to that of drama in the theatre'.[90] In direct contrast to this assessment, Littlewood made the production do exactly what television could not – it talked back and as such acquired a distinct energy and commitment to the moment in which the stage acknowledges a process of dynamic interaction taking place.[91]

In her autobiography, Littlewood glosses over her decision to add an onstage jazz band as merely a strategy for linking disjointed scenes – but it was far more important than that. Having made the transition from a minority cult interest in the 1940s, in the 1950s jazz occupied a particular place in the social and cultural imagination. According to George McKay, jazz was uninstitutionalised and 'part of a new, alternative proletarian culture', but also connected to a globalised culture, what he calls 'a restless internationalism' in its hybrid, syncretic mixture of European, American and African influences. Viewed as a transgressive and subversive form, jazz became associated with intellectuals, art school students, beatniks and CND supporters. Importantly, according to Robert Hewison, 'a taste for jazz remained one of the touchstones of contemporaneity', a view evident in Anderson's review of *A Taste of Honey* which states that the 'jazz interludes by the Apex trio gave the whole evening a friendly, contemporary and hopeful air'.[92]

In the 1950s, jazz began to appear in plays and films as a key signifier for characters who wanted to challenge the status quo and look to a new, bright future. It is no surprise, therefore, that Jimmy Porter in *Look Back in Anger* plays solo jazz trumpet offstage whilst the radio music he listens to is Vaughan Williams, 'something strong, something simple, something English'.[93] Whilst this depiction keys in to Jimmy's imperial nostalgia, the jazz trumpet is suggestive of his restlessness, and Osborne connects his love of jazz to his call for feeling to reanimate British culture. However, whereas jazz is a largely participatory ensemble cultural form, Jimmy plays alone and his banjo-playing friend never turns up – a further sign of his curious estrangement from other people, as well as from political and cultural movements.

In contrast, in *A Taste of Honey*, the jazz band was an integral part of the overall ensemble playing, with the band directly addressed by the performers. At one point, in a departure from Delaney's original script, Helen reminisces about working in a pub and begins to sing. After singing a verse, she says to the band 'come on, vamp it in with me', after which Jo, in an attempt to undermine Helen, retorts, 'You can't play to that. It's got no rhythm.'[94] The call to 'vamp it in with me' also points to another important signifier of jazz – its credentials as an improvised form that thrives on spontaneous invention and creative exchange. The theatrical nature of this moment relied on its liveness – the music is not left to a disembodied recording but played live in the theatre in real time. Littlewood also enhanced the theatricality of the production as the performers danced on and off the stage. This element was unfixed and the performers responded to what the band played. This oddity provided further evidence of Littlewood's desire to promote the rough edginess of theatre over a smooth, polished interpretation of text.

To understand Littlewood's staging of *A Taste of Honey* it is crucial to frame it within the broader tradition of 'poetic realism' discussed in the previous chapter. Whilst maintaining the level of social impetus and enquiry evident in other 'kitchen sink' plays of the period, it acted as a rebuttal to these examples of text-bound social realism. It refused to denigrate working-class life and culture, as plays such as *Look Back in Anger* and Arnold Wesker's *Roots* (1959) did, as inferior and lacking credibility, but also largely managed to avoid nostalgic sentimentalism. Rather than presenting an extended lament for a lost culture of extended families and close-knit communities, it maps a different experience of individuals who live wholly in the present moment as they collide to create alternative, often temporary, family units. Through its heightened music-hall-style theatricality, vital language and sharp wit it lifted what could have been a drab and tragic story of poverty, neglect and wasted talent into another realm. Reviews of the production invite us to dismiss these elements as weird misjudgements, theatrical excesses that do the text a disservice, but ignoring these attempts to erase the range of theatrical vocabularies Littlewood employed reanimates Littlewood's genius. Without ignoring the social impetus and the desire to represent the previously unrepresented, she turned this story of lives played out in an ordinary Salford back-street setting into an effervescent evening of theatricality.

From Cockney to mockney: class, culture and criminality

Unfortunately, it is very difficult to discern a complex relation between the politics of working-class representation and theatricality when it comes to Frank Norman's *Fings Ain't Wot They Used T'be*. This production, described as a 'play with music' rather than a musical, but widely credited with ushering in 'a new era in British musical theatre',[95] premiered at the Theatre Royal in February 1959 and, after being fought over by several managements, transferred to the West End's Garrick Theatre in February 1960 for a two-year run. With a cast including George Sewell, Barbara Windsor, Miriam Karlin, James Booth and Yootha Joyce, it was one of Theatre Workshop's most successful productions critically and commercially, securing the *Evening Standard* best-musical prize in 1960. But, for many, *Fings* signalled an ideological weakening of purpose in its representation of working-class life. Norman had already achieved a degree of notoriety as the author of the prison memoirs *Bang to Rights* (1958), before he was encouraged by the theatre critic Penelope Gilliatt to send his first playscript to Littlewood. Thrilled to 'discover' someone completely untainted by any theatrical training, Littlewood embraced Norman's script as a project to develop in collaboration with the company and the composer Lionel Bart, who had recently achieved success writing pop songs.

With his pronounced facial scar and well-known history as a Barnardo's boy who had drifted into criminality, Norman cut an interesting figure on the theatre circuit. Certainly, Littlewood was keen to exploit Norman's background and there emerged a problematic exoticisation of his criminal past and associates. According to Goorney, 'Frank's own experience of two years in jail for bouncing cheques, and his first-hand knowledge of the seamier side of Soho life, had

10. Programme for *Fings Ain't Wot They Used T'Be* (1959)

been used to good advantage.'[96] And not just in the script. Publicity material and the programme used the defining image of spilt blood, and Norman's background was touted as a marker of authenticity, which arguably did box office receipts no harm at all, but suggested an ethical dilemma at the heart of Littlewood's enterprise as criminality became glamorised.

During the 1950s and 1960s, widespread social problems with gangsters and rival gangs profiting from racketeering, the sex industry and protection rackets that relied on the threat of violence meted out by heavies with flick knives and knuckle-dusters threatened to dismantle the myth of the East End as the epitome of a working-class community ideal. According to Gareth Steadman-Jones, 'the "cockney" is a figure successively constructed and reconstructed by different types of discourse'.[97] From the late 1950s, Littlewood abandoned the discourse of the financially deprived but socially rich, proud and resilient Cockney figure embedded in their local geographical community to contribute to an alternative discourse of a criminal fraternity intent on self-advancement through dubious and often violent means.

According to Ed Glinert, the East End of the 1950s lacked credible public figures and the void left by respectable social campaigners such as Thomas Barnardo was filled by the presence of glamorous, charismatic gangsters epitomised by the notorious Kray twins. The Krays still maintain a prolific presence in the social imaginary of the East End, fuelled by a relentless stream of articles, biographies, confessions, cultural works and walking tours capturing their old haunts for curious voyeurs. The Krays' reign of terror was contemporaneous with Littlewood's work at the Theatre Royal and she had an association with them that led her to invite them to the launch party for her film of *Sparrers Can't Sing*, held at the house she shared with Raffles in Blackheath, and the post-premiere party for the film was held at the Kentucky Club, a nightclub owned by the Krays.[98]

The problematic romanticising of criminality and aberrant behaviour associated with the powerful symbolic presence of the Krays arguably underpinned Littlewood's production of *Fings* and several other productions that appeared in its wake. In these works, Littlewood resorted to representing an exoticised criminal underbelly rather than recognisable everyday domestic and working lives as seen in *Van Call*, for example. And, in these instances, theatricality, in particular the use of songs, only served to heighten the sense that Littlewood had resorted to exploiting a very real social problem for its comedic potential and popular entertainment value.

The loose plotting of *Fings* centres on Fred Cochran, a down-at-heel gangster who owns a run-down 'shpieler' (gambling den). This site provides refuge for various low-life characters who fail to make their mark in the criminal underworld: Lil Smith, his moll and long-standing sex worker; Paddy, a gambling addict; Redhot, a useless burglar; and Tosher, a pimp, who is led a merry dance by sex workers Betty and Rosey, until he threatens them with physical violence. They all rely on Fred for their livelihoods but Meatface, a rival gangster, is squeezing him out of the market. Events turn when Fred's unexpected win on the horses provides the money to employ an over-the-top, camp interior decorator, Horace Seaton, to lavishly refurbish the shpieler into a vision of contemporary design. Determined to win back the ascendancy from Meatface, Fred challenges him to a razor fight and slashes him, but then decides to go straight by marrying Lil and handing over the shpieler to Sergeant Collins, who has long harboured a desire to join the criminal fraternity from whom he has previously taken bribes. For many critics, *Fings*'s brash, colourful irreverence epitomised the cultural shifts about to emerge in the 1960s. According to Tom Valance, 'Like Norman's libretto, Bart's songs perfectly captured a time of change – of the Wolfenden Report, massage parlours replacing street-corner pick-ups; and a time when "ordinary people" had started going to Paris for the weekend instead of Southend.'[99]

Littlewood was most attracted to the language in Norman's script. East End vernacular is characterised by its inventiveness and performativity. An ability to converse through this idiom defines belonging within and identification with the local community and Norman's script captured this organically mutating language as it appeared on the streets. The script is written phonetically to demonstrate slipped words, vowels and consonants such as 'wotcha want' (what do you want), 'nuffink' (nothing) and 'culcher' (culture) and is liberally sprinkled with local phrases and rhyming slang such as 'boat' (boat race = face) and 'rabbit' (rabbit's paw = jaw = conversation). For the critic Alan Brien this meant that 'the dialogue is jammed with apparently surrealist images which add a kind of wild, gutter poetry to the simplest interchange'.[100] In this description, Brien reveals his cultural distance from the play's language register, whereas Littlewood recalled that when Bart, an East Ender, encountered the script, he announced that it was the 'First time I've heard cockney as she is spoke'.[101] However, Brien's response indicates the potential for an audience to voyeuristically objectify the representations offered.

Littlewood relished any chance to highlight the reductive, false, class-bound strictures of the Cockney stereotypes peddled at drama schools, where 'the voice of the Cockney was one long whine of blissful servitude [and] no play was complete without its moronic maid or faithful batman'.[102] In Norman's script, the language was vital, energetic, playful and anything but subservient. In performance, Norman's language forcefully announced its presence through its theatricality. As one observer notes, 'Frank's renditions of cockney speak is real like the New York slang of Damon Runyon's New Yorkers is real – colourful, exaggerated and humorous, catching the spirit of the language better than any dry transcription could.'[103] Importantly, Littlewood refused to water the language down or translate it for the uninitiated. Reviewing the play, J. C. Trewin postulated that the play 'might be translated one day into English', and *The Times* reviewer found 'little or nothing in the way of conventional English'.[104] This *was* English, just a version of it with which many reviewers were unfamiliar. On this occasion not only did Littlewood succeed in representing the street on the stage, but *Fings* seeped into a broader consciousness and, according to her, 'entered the language'.[105]

Intended as a straight play, Norman's script treads a fine line between romanticising the criminal underworld he inhabited and undercutting romantic illusions. Fred keeps a scrapbook of newspaper cuttings documenting his glory days as a hoodlum terrorising the community with antisocial behaviour and knife crime that earned him the mantle 'razor king of the manor'.[106] He nostalgically longs for this macho-inscribed power and authority again and his lament for a lost world is captured in the very title *Fings Aint Wot They Used T'Be*. However, the characters are all rather pathetic and the menacing presence of violence is never far away. Several characters carry the scars of razor fights and the reality of criminality seems to be lots of hanging around and little rewards. Prostitution fares little better. Rosey admits she needs a 'cast-iron stomach' in her line of work and Betty keeps a brick in her handbag as security.[107] Despite these rare moments of rupture puncturing the nostalgic veneer, Littlewood's theatrical embellishments to the text seriously undermined any semblance of satirical social critique intended by Norman. As he explained of rehearsals, 'With every day that passed my original conception of the play seemed to drift further and further away, until eventually I was hardly able to identify with the antics on stage at all.'[108] In this case, the popular theatrics introduced by Littlewood, such as the light-hearted songs, undermined the critical impetus of the playwright.

Unlike the audiences who flocked to the show, the critics largely found the piece purposeless, a position summed up by Caryl Brahms's description of 'a rudderless gas-inflated air-ship'.[109] Trewin described the antics as a 'go-as-you-please, not very uplifting musical smash and grab', and T. C. Worsley described it as a 'harum scarum, helter-skelter, rag-bag and bob-tail musical'.[110] Above all, the production had a relentless feel-good quality that emanated from the larger-than-life characters, frequent extemporising from the stage, a chorus of jiving teddy boys and girls, jolly songs, music-hall-style exchanges and exuberant stage business. There were no reflective moments; instead the characters seemed to be shouting, look-at-us, fun social misfits and loveable rogues, factors that understandably drew criticism for their potential to create a thinly disguised freak show around violence, criminality and the misogynistic sex industry. As Goorney argued,

> A more valid criticism of *Fings* was expressed by those who questioned the morality of using razor gangs, crooks and, in particular, prostitutes and their ponces, as subjects for humour and comic songs, an issue that went deeper than good or bad taste. In some people's minds, it wasn't far removed from poking fun at physical deformities.[111]

By far the worse culprits are the songs. According to the website eastlondonhistory.com, 'Bart took the language of the East End and cranked it to within an inch of parody in his songs.'[112] Having achieved considerable success with pop songs including 'Living Doll' and 'The Young Ones' for Cliff Richard, Bart allowed his creativity to run riot in *Fings* to generate 'vigorous, idiomatic "sing-along" music'[113] such as the grisly 'carve-up', which celebrates a great razor fight that results in twenty-seven stitches from ear to ear and the infamous title song, which nostalgically laments the passing of a 'golden age' when 'ponces killed a lazy whore'.[114]

Littlewood chose to frame *Fings* as marking a return to a long-lost popular tradition she associated with the commedia dell'arte, Shakespeare, Jonson and Marston. She argued,

> If the West End theatre now follows the lead of the East End theatre and finds its amusement in the liveliness that is under the surface of Britain, perhaps this is a sign of the resurgence of a popular theatre in England and not a regression but a step forward.[115]

But, arguably, *Fings* provided evidence of what Jim McGuigan refers to as 'an *uncritical* populist drift' whereby popular culture receives an uncritical endorsement rather than being a representational process that instigates an investigation and critique of cultural formations, attitudes and values.[116] *Fings* marked a departure from the social enquiry and privileging of community and class consciousness exhibited in early work such as MacColl's *Johnny Noble* and *Landscape with Chimneys*. Indeed, *Fings* began with a visual joke that strikingly captured the distance Theatre Workshop had travelled from its earlier incarnation. With the company dressed in service uniforms, wildly dancing the 'hokey-cokey', a banner is unfurled saying 'WELCOME HOME FRED'. Whereas the welcome banners that greeted Hugh and Frank in *Landscape with Chimneys* marked their return from service to a country that demanded investigation and critique, *Fings* undercuts the image with a second banner proclaiming 'FROM DARTMOOR'. Fred has not been serving his country, but serving time for knife crime. More importantly, the embedded historical materialism of MacColl's work is lost as Fred embarks on a path back to his criminal life having learnt nothing from the past.

Littlewood returned to ethically tenuous representations of working-class criminality in several other works that followed *Fings*. In October 1959, she produced Wolf Mankowitz's *Make Me an Offer*, a musical cynically produced with a West End transfer in mind. It tells the story of a young antiques dealer in Portobello Road market who overcomes his honest streak to embrace more profitable criminality. Amidst a flurry of praise for an exuberant, light-hearted production, Alan Pryce-Jones sounded a warning bell that 'there is by now some danger of the Theatre Workshop technique becoming a formula'.[117] In March 1964, the corruption-of-innocence theme resurfaced in *A Kayf up West*, Norman's follow-up to *Fings* that again featured his 'tirelessly colourful' Soho low-life layabouts, prostitutes, drug addicts and petty criminals.[118] Hugh Leonard complained, 'As a piece of observed life, it is untruthful, dehumanising its characters and betraying its own terms of reference'.[119] The programme is very clear, once again, to establish these terms of reference as Norman's criminal background and experience of prison life, but there is a sense in which, as happens with his central character, Littlewood was problematically parading him in front of guests at a sophisticated party. It seems extraordinary that this flimsy piece of popular entertainment appeared just one year after the ground-breaking politically serious, yet popular, *Oh What a Lovely War*.

Returning to her roots: community activism

In her final productions at the Theatre Royal in the early 1970s, Littlewood returned to the themes of community with the productions *Forward up Your End* (1970) and *The Projector* (1970). Whilst Ken Hill's burlesque pageant *Forward up Your End* humorously treated local government corruption in Birmingham, *The Projector* dealt explicitly with local concerns in its satirical treatment of the partial collapse of a twenty-two-storey residential tower block at Ronan Point in the London Borough of Newham. The disaster, which killed four people and injured seventeen others, was caused by an explosion of leaking gas in a flat on the eighteenth floor, which led to a massive structural failure that collapsed the whole south-east corner of the building. London boroughs had seen a disproportionately high rate of high-rises built in their locality due to the shortage of available land for new housing. Welcomed as a way of addressing squalid housing conditions, meeting housing needs and preventing urban sprawl, little attention was paid to the social implications of the high-rise, which exacerbated problems with social isolation, children's development through play and family breakdown.[120] Littlewood was not against high-rise flats per se, as long as architects and builders conceived buildings 'with design and beauty, and with a feeling for the other person, for their scales, their life'.[121] But she saw in the Ronan Point disaster a repeat of the scandalous corruption and high-level cover-up she had previously explored in relation to the Gresford Pit disaster.

Once again revisiting her agitprop roots, Littlewood attended the Ronan Point Tribunal of Inquiry with a view to producing a drama documentary on the subject. She left the trial appalled that the local authority had accepted the Ronan Point builders' offer of a 'package deal' which meant they 'offered not only the customary building work but also professional services of architectural design and engineering consultancy which had hitherto been provided separately'.[122] Describing the practice of outsourcing to subsidiary firms as 'a cancer in society',[123] she determined to expose the cover-up of explicit culpability and inept penny-pinching that had led to a devastating failure of safety standards.

Denied the right to use trial material and threatened with legal action, Littlewood, together with the renowned satirist and *Private Eye* journalist John Wells, created a draft of a play that historicised the events of Ronan Point to 1733. To get the play on, Littlewood and Wells billed it as a newly unearthed work, *The Mock Mason*, by the eighteenth-century playwright William Rufus Chetwood.[124] The play centred on a crooked Dutch property developer, Van Clysterpump, played by Bill Wallis, who bribes and dodges his way through a series of deals and mishaps including the collapse of one of his buildings. Stylistically cross-fertilising an eighteenth-century pastiche with music hall, the *Singspiel* style of *The Beggar's Opera* and the biting wit of Hogarth's paintings, the production introduced an atmosphere of amoral lasciviousness to accompany the political intrigue surrounding the Ronan Point incident. Described by J. W. Lambert as a return to the 'good old recipe, derisive high spirits with a dash of pathos … cooked up with slapdash gusto',[125] the performance also had an important political point to make.

To underscore the topical inspiration for the piece, Littlewood filled the theatre foyer with photographs of and items concerning Ronan Point, and the programme announced the newly discovered play's 'many similarities to the 1968 story'.[126] Unfortunately, critical attention largely focused on the elaborate theatrical hoax, a necessary gimmick, which backfired by undermining the sincerity and severity of the intended critique. Indeed, Irving Wardle claimed that 'it is better to forget about the politics and take the production for what it is: an exceptionally inventive and sometimes brilliant pastiche'.[127] Only Ronald Bryden fully articulated the interpenetration of text, form and context:

> When you walk out of the theatre you step into a desert of developer's mud and hoardings, across which twinkle cliff-faces of towering flat blocks, each window lonely as a lighthouse beam ... the greatest Littlewood productions have never been artistic events complete in themselves, but deliberately tawdry, spangled dance-hall globes of mirror fragments which sent blizzards of light dancing and stabbing over the society around them.[128]

This interpenetration between text and context continued with a reworking of *Sparrers* as a musical called *The Londoners* (1972). With music by Bart played by Bob Kerr's Whoopee Band, who added to the fun by producing old standards on kazoos, football rattles, teapots, motor horns and saws, the production was an exuberant revival of the rowdy music-hall comedy of cheerful comic Cockneys laughing in the face of adversity. There was more than a hint of nostalgia in the reviews for the style of theatre and for Littlewood herself, but even more so for the surrounding district gutted to make way for an unremarkable supermarket and office block. The context for the original play was the growth of suburbanisation and the encroachment of the high-rise in place of the terraced housing community; twelve years later the area had become a desolate building site. Amidst this sea of corporate development, the critics lovingly referred to the theatre as 'a small floodlit mauve and scarlet knickerbocker glory', 'a lighthouse in a desolate sea' and a 'Christmas tree in a bombsite'.[129]

This nostalgic rendering of the Theatre Royal as standing in for the light and colour that had been lost in the demolition of a community of terraced houses, a street market and local pubs was equally present in the show itself. However, after all the gaiety of the singing, playing and comic exchanges, the show slipped into a mood of mournful melancholia, as the band played a haunting lament to accompany the audience back into a desolate landscape which had once housed the community that inspired Lewis to write *Sparrers*. This elegy to community life, however imagined, marked the end of Littlewood's long history of celebrating the spirit, and the communal consciousness, of working-class communities through the armoury enabled by popular cultural formations. Nonetheless, just as Littlewood extricated herself from the theatre, there emerged a new generation of British practitioners such as John McGrath and Roland Muldoon, who, having been inspired by Littlewood, were equally intent on reanimating popular theatre traditions as part of their commitment to working-class representation and to encouraging working-class audiences to participate in theatrical encounters. But, as the next generation of practitioners was emerging, Littlewood turned her attention to her Fun Palace project, explored in the next chapter.

6 Cultural democracy and spatial encounters: the Fun Palace project

Increasingly alienated from theatre as an institution, from the early 1960s Littlewood largely withdrew from making traditional theatre productions, and instead threw herself into an ambitious scheme to create a temporary arts complex in the East End of London.[1] Inspired by a desire to democratise the arts and to animate community-based activity and values, Littlewood developed her Fun Palace project dedicated to pleasure, entertainment, communication and learning. Proposals for the Fun Palace are particularly interesting for the way they hark back to traditional forms of popular entertainment such as the Vauxhall Pleasure Gardens and the funfair, whilst providing a radical reconceptualisation of what entertainment could encompass in the modern age. Littlewood's plans also linked in some ways to the impetus behind settlement houses that originated in Victorian England, where reformers lived and worked in disadvantaged areas to facilitate social and educational improvement.[2] The dialectic between these social and cultural traditions and a contemporary imagining of how cultural and everyday life could merge characterised Littlewood's plans for the Fun Palace. Analysing the documents, designs and descriptions drawn up to promote the Fun Palace, the following chapter will discuss the ideas driving this ambitious project and the reasons behind its failure.

As with her other works, the Fun Palace relied on collaboration. In particular, Littlewood developed her ideas in conjunction with the architect Cedric Price. Introduced by their mutual friend, Tom Driberg, it was an extraordinary meeting of minds. Like Littlewood, Price was an iconoclast, vehemently anti-authoritarian and happy to fly in the face of convention, and together they produced a groundbreaking vision for a space that would draw on all the technological advancements of the age to house Littlewood's grand plans for a place of limitless educational and entertainment possibilities.[3] As their ideas developed, they also drew on discussions with a range of individuals excited by their plans. Ideas committees formed around a diverse group of politicians, scientists, architects, academics and creative artists, including the cybernetician Gordon Pask; historian Asa Briggs; the artist and theorist of telematic art Roy Ascot; and Ian Mikardo, a Labour member of Parliament, who gathered to discuss the project and strategies for its implementation.

The project equally captured the public imagination. After Littlewood launched the project on BBC's *Monitor* programme on 28 April 1963, she and Price received a huge response from individuals and businesses keen to offer support or to exploit the potential of such a venture for their own ends. The media certainly picked up the story and the trials and tribulations encountered by Littlewood and Price, as they tried to get the project off the ground, received regular newspaper coverage and commentary.[4] Mindful of the need to generate a groundswell of public support if the Fun Palace had any hope of becoming a reality, Littlewood and Price courted media attention at the same time as soliciting support from industry, political power-brokers, influential cultural figures and patrons of the arts and education. In 1964, Littlewood assembled a board of high-profile trustees comprising R. Buckminster Fuller, Lord Ritchie-Calder, the Earl of Harewood and Yehudi Menuhin to lend weight and credibility to the project. In 1964, Calder sent a letter to the *Sunday Mirror* that vibrantly captured his passion for the forward-thinking nature of the project:

> It is so imaginative that there is nothing in the world with which to compare it. It breaks through convention the way the rocket broke through gravity and is as uninhibited as free-fall in Space. Why don't you show that you are also 'with it' and give us an international 'Festival of Living' – to convince the younger generation that life is not just a delayed action H-bomb?[5]

As the project's initiator and primary champion, Littlewood wrote articles, spoke at numerous conferences and lobbied local councils, arts organisations and residential associations in an attempt to galvanise people to see the social and cultural benefits of her proposal. In fact, the sheer verve with which Littlewood pursued her dream of a Fun Palace mirrored her attempts decades earlier to get her fledgling theatre company on a sound footing. Yet whereas in the 1930s and 1940s the young Littlewood had little power in the wider cultural arena and even less money, by the early 1960s she had an enviable address book to call on and to generate funds to support her campaign she made six television commercials and agreed to direct the disastrous musical *Twang!* in the West End in 1965. But all this was still no guarantee of success.

The Fun Palace and the 1960s 'moment'

The conceptual underpinning to the Fun Palace intrinsically related to the political, social and cultural agendas that arose during the 1960s around participatory democracy, freedom, popular culture, new technologies, changing conceptions of time and the pursuit of pleasure. The Fun Palace was conceived as a utopian agent of change for the individual, community and environment and, as such, corresponded with the questioning of theatrical and cultural orthodoxies and the progressive sensibility that emerged during this period – above all, Littlewood dared to imagine new spatial possibilities, new modes of social organisation and new possibilities for cultural encounters. This leap of imagination connected her to a long tradition of utopian thought that contemplates an imaginary place of possibility. 'To count as a utopia, an imaginary place must be an expression of desire.'[6] To exhibit desire is to contemplate what is yet to come; it is a projection of something that might be, and not what is; and this is exactly what the Fun Palace offered, a projection of a new way of relating to leisure time, culture and community that was responsive to its particular historical moment.

During the 1960s, there was a great deal of speculation about the increased leisure time people would have due to shifting work patterns and the impact of new technologies. The Fun Palace was conceived as a cultural manifestation of the acceptance of new scientific developments and their cultural consequences; a social shift captured by the then prime minister Harold Wilson's references to the 'white heat of technological change'. Social commentators argued that people would soon be free from the drudgery of work as computers and robots took over the bulk of the manufacturing process and labour-saving devices freed people from the tyranny of time-consuming domestic chores. Writing in the *New Scientist*, Littlewood proposed that those who

> at present work in factories, mines and offices will quite soon be able to live as only a few people now can: choosing their own congenial work, doing as much or as little of it as they like, and filling their leisure with whatever delights them.[7]

Littlewood really believed in the potential dissolution of the work–leisure binary and thought that a Fun Palace would be a fitting response for a moment when '"work" and "leisure" overlap and merge: life becomes a whole'.[8]

However far-fetched this romantic faith in the potential unleashed by new thinking and technologies seems now, in the 1960s there was a general belief that technological advances would enable leisure to become the primary aspect of everyday life. This belief prompted politicians, educators, sociologists and those concerned with the physical and cultural environment to debate the consequences of such a radical shift. For example, in 1966 the Massachusetts Institute of Technology hosted a conference called Inventing the Future Environment that explored the possible implications of new technologies and different social structures for urban planning, the environment and the architecture of the future. During the conference, Pardon E. Tillinghast contributed the following:

> In 1900 the work week averaged about 60 hours; today it varies from 40 to 36 hours, except for those with two jobs. By 2000 it may be 15 hours. How will society then keep people from each other's throats when most of their waking time is at their own disposal? How will a profoundly technological culture use this time in an intelligent and creative way?[9]

These concerns corresponded with British social and cultural theorists drawing attention to what they argued was stagnation and passivity initiated by the widespread success of welfare state educational and cultural policies, alongside the increasing presence of American-dominated commercially produced consumer culture and mass-media communications. Taking inspiration from ideas emanating from the Frankfurt school, there was a general concern that the 'levelling of social experience – not to be mistaken for the levelling of the class structure – and the anaesthetization of society was perceived by some intellectuals as a situation nearing crisis'.[10] For example, Richard Hoggart's *The Uses of Literacy* (1957) lamented the threat posed to indigenous, communal and organic forms of working-class popular cultural traditions by an externally imposed commercial culture and the 'dumbing down' heralded by the frivolous and vicarious pleasures of mass entertainment.

In her Fun Palace, Littlewood proposed something very akin to an 'uncensored network of communications' that can be likened to the central hypothesis of Stuart Hall and Paddy Whannel's seminal cultural studies text *The Popular Arts*, published in 1964. Rather than adopting the view, which permeates Hoggart's work, that high culture and popular cultural traditions are mutually exclusive, Hall and Whannel proposed instead that people could find valuable, socially enriching and pleasurable material in both. They encouraged people to discriminate within a range of cultural practices and to appreciate the value accorded to a particular pursuit at the point of use and on its own terms. The ideas that 'welfare state passivity had to be countered through motivated, self-willed learning',[11] and of discriminating participants exerting choice across a range of popular cultural forms, science-based activities and arts and crafts, were central to the Fun Palace project. This culturally inclusive ethos distinguished Littlewood's plans from the other major cultural initiative that emerged in the 1960s, Arnold Wesker's Centre 42.[12]

Employing various strategies such as touring concerts, poetry readings and short plays around provincial clubs and pubs, Centre 42 activists hoped to reinstate cultural activity as an intrinsic part of individual and community life.[13] At first glance, Centre 42 appears to have much in common with Littlewood's Fun Palace proposals; however, there are acute ideological differences centred on the high art/popular culture debates that raged in the postwar era.[14] Launching his ideological rallying cry for Centre 42 in an article, 'Let Battle Commence!', for *Encore* magazine in 1958, Wesker echoed his character Beattie from *Roots* (1958) when he argued for participation and appreciation of the arts to provide vital humanitarian 'tools for living'.[15] Drawing on a tradition exemplified by Matthew Arnold and F. R. Leavis, Wesker sought to enable access to 'good' art that could promote an understanding of the human condition, civilised values and 'stirring the human spirit'.[16] Whereas Littlewood championed access to a broad base of cultural activity that spanned the high art/popular culture divide, Wesker maintained an unswerving faith in the empowering potential of high art. This cultural positioning led others, including Littlewood, to accuse Wesker of problematically promoting biased values of what constitutes 'good' art and of preaching to the working class about what cultural practices they should appreciate.[17] As Reyner Banham observed at the time, Centre 42 had the aura of 'a cultural soup kitchen approach for the under-privileged, hand-outs of free art for those "unlucky" enough to escape a grammar-school education'.[18]

A university of the streets/a laboratory of pleasure

Described as both a 'university of the streets' and 'a laboratory of pleasure',[19] Littlewood envisaged the Fun Palace as a multi-use space housing a series of short-term, frequently updated activities that could provide an ever-changing focus for people's leisure time. In a period of increasing social fluidity, geographical mobility and the resulting erosion of close-knit communities, Littlewood saw the Fun Palace as a twenty-four-hour, large-scale community centre that could foster mass participation and communal identification. Importantly, she wanted the Fun Palace to be responsive to the needs of the local community and to function in collaboration with pre-existing activities: 'Local clubs, gangs, societies, will be approached and activists from among them invited to assist in programming. Local schools, libraries, art galleries, museums, can extend their activities by using the site.'[20] As such, Littlewood's proposals were inclusive rather than exclusive, about sharing and democratising space, knowledge, skills and culture.

By eroding the borders between everyday life and the theatre, education and entertainment, work and play, observation and participation, pleasure and intellectual pursuit, the attainment of new skills and joy of doing nothing, Littlewood resisted official notions of carefully packaged cultural products that obediently sit within their disciplinary boxes – the educational institution, the theatre, the arts and crafts workshop. The central premise of the Fun Palace was to offer multiple modes of stimulation that could be educative in the traditional sense or could simply trigger the imagination or the development of new interests. For Littlewood, cultural activity was not something to be enshrined in elite institutions, behind plexiglass cases, or consumed in the comfort of the domestic environment, but was about engaging in public discourse and a social, hands-on approach that could become part and parcel of everyday life. She also recognised the importance of self-fulfilment and, as Mary Louise Lobsinger notes, one of the aspirations to galvanise the Fun Palace was to 'pry the subject free from the stifling repetitions of everyday convention and to nurture an emergent individuality'.[21]

By providing opportunities to experiment with different modes of entertainment and education, Littlewood hoped to stimulate people to make active decisions about what inspired them and ignited pleasure. As Price recalled of his initial introduction to Littlewood's plans, 'She talked about what she thought, not "theatre", she didn't use the word "theatre", but about how she'd like to give people a chance to activate their own lives, in learning and appetites and how to behave.'[22] She appreciated the complex and ever-changing tastes, motivations and desires of people, and wanted to represent and cater for this polymorphous quality. Above all, 'This new, relaxed and permissive sense of an egalitarian culture provided a space where issues of value could be decided on a pragmatic and provisional basis'.[23] This emphasis on choice infiltrated all aspects of design and content, as promotional literature makes clear:

> Arrive and leave by train, bus, monorail, hovercraft, car, tube or foot at any time YOU want to – or just have a look at it as you pass. The information screens will show you what's happening. No need to look for an entrance – just walk in anywhere. No doors, foyers, queues of commissionaires: it's up to you how you use it. Look around, take a lift, a ramp, an escalator to wherever or whatever looks interesting. Choose what you want to do – or watch someone else doing it. Learn how to handle tools, paint,

> babies, machinery, or just listen to your favourite tune. Dance, talk or be lifted up to where you can see how other people make things work. Sit out over space with a drink and tune in to what's happening elsewhere in the city. Try starting a riot or beginning a painting – or just lie back and stare at the sky.
>
> What time is it? Any time of day or night, winter or summer – it really doesn't matter.[24]

Content was described in the following terms:

> Joan Littlewood, with architects, designers, engineers, cyberneticians, cooks, topologists, toy-makers, flowmasters, think clowns, offers you the occasion to enjoy, 24 hours a day, space, light, movement, air, sun, water, in a new dimension.
>
> **For your delight**

Juke Box Information	Observation Decks
Adult Toys	Nurseries
Star Gazing	Music
Scientific Gadgetry	Theatre Clownery
News Service	Instant Cinema
Tele-communication	Fireworks
Swank Promenades	Recording Sessions
Hide Aways	Kunst Dabbling
Dance Floors	Gala Days and Nights
Drink	Genius Chat
Rallies	Gossip Revues
Battles of Flowers	Laboratories
Concerts	Food
Learning Machines	Ateliers[25]

The activities proposed illuminate Littlewood's engagement with contemporaneous debates on community, education, culture, information technology and new scientific systems. A 'science playground' holding illustrated lecture–demonstrations by day, by night was to become a space for sharing new theories and ideas, 'an agora or *kaffeeklatsch* where the Socrates, the Abelards, the Mermaid poets, the wandering scholars of the future, the mystics, the sceptics and the sophists can dispute till dawn'.[26] Anticipating recent developments in participant-centred museum culture, Littlewood also envisaged an interactive learning centre full of computers, calculating machines, language laboratories, scientific apparatus and large-scale puzzles, and a 'fun arcade' 'full of the games and tests that psychologists and electronics engineers now devise for the service of industry or war'.[27] Fundamental to these areas was the desire to democratise knowledge and to engage in knowledge transfer as the latest scientific gadgets, technological systems and groundbreaking ideas were to be released from the confines of universities and laboratories and 'brought to the street corner'.[28]

A 'plastic area' would enable people to experiment in arts and crafts including woodwork, clay, textiles, painting and metalwork, the idea being that somebody could pick up an activity and discard it in a day or return to develop skills and techniques over a longer period. Similarly, a 'music area' would provide access to instruments, free instruction, recording facilities, a music library and places to listen during the day, followed by jamming sessions, music festivals and dancing in the evening. As Banham enthused,

> What Joan and her team of 'younger creative nuts' (as she calls them) are trying to create here is an entertainment kit that the non-institutionalised aspects of leisure can improvise upon, a gigantic junk-playground for sophisticated grown-up people to whom the handling of mechanical tackle is nowadays as natural as breathing.[29]

Whilst Banham stresses entertainment in his assessment, B. N. Lewis, a member of the Fun Palace Committee, argued that there should be no distinction between education and entertainment. To encourage not just participation, but critical engagement with cultural practice, Lewis suggested discussion and debate about pop lyrics, television commercials and contemporary social themes. As he explained, 'Its overall aim is to meet people's need for play and to leave them, if possible, a little wiser and better informed. Its only covert purpose is to get people thinking occasionally and to widen their perspective.'[30]

Theatre, drama therapy and reality TV

Even when more traditional theatre events were proposed, the emphasis was on audience participation over passivity. In an essay, 'Theatre Workshop and Systems Research: Proposals for a Cybernetic Theatre', Pask provided complex, experimental plans for how a fairly traditional script could be augmented with opportunities to activate audio channels, preference buttons, seats equipped with mechanisms for recording reactions and a backstage computer to calculate and relay audience input and responses.[31] In fact, Pask likened the process of writing a play to writing a computer programme in which playwrights and actors rehearse various pathways and outcomes that they could use in the live event.

This democratic approach to play-making would have appealed to Littlewood's desire to challenge the autocracy of the playwright, but she was more interested in other aspects of the theatrical process. In fact, she proposed an 'acting area' dedicated to the 'therapy of theatre'. Rather than performing to an audience, she proposed a theatre of everyday life in which people would use the medium of theatre to explore ideas, events and dilemmas that directly affected them, arguing,

> Men and women from factories, shops, and offices, bored with their daily routine, will be able to re-enact incidents from their own experience in burlesque and mime and gossip, so that they no longer accept passively whatever happens to them but wake to a critical awareness of reality, act out their sub-conscious fears and taboos.[32]

Her intention was to use enactment and follow-up discussion to activate personal and political awareness of relationships and social structures. This was not a particularly new idea. In the early twentieth century, Jane Addams was writing on the value of drama for education and self-development and Dr J. L. Moreno had been using psychodrama techniques to explore interpersonal relations and private traumas from the early 1920s.[33] What was new, and potentially problematic, was the attempt to resituate this kind of activity away from a therapeutic context. There is an underlying principle here that drama therapy could be beneficial for everybody and therefore should be freely available within a progressively conceived contemporary cultural centre. But, because Littlewood frames this as just another facility within a massive cultural centre, there remains a troubling naivety about the level of training, supervision and aftercare required when employing drama therapy and psychodrama techniques.

In a remarkably prescient move, Littlewood proposed an extensive use of large television screens to transmit local and national news as well as popular events, including concerts and cup finals, and state occasions such as weddings and funerals, to a large communal audience. To facilitate this aim, the Fun Palace Trust spent £11,000 on a state-of-the-art eidophor, a television projector used to create large-scale images in cinemas and lecture halls. This was not a completely unique idea, as when John Glenn took off in the Friendship 77 capsule to outer space in 1962, a four-by-five-metre television screen in New York's Grand Central Station tracked his progress, and these screens were becoming an increasingly common part of the cultural landscape of major public, sporting and entertainment events.

Benedict Anderson has drawn attention to the way print media such as newspapers and novels can help create 'imagined communities' as people unknown to each other can feel bonded by engaging with national markers of identity and belonging. In his words, the shared experience means that 'in the minds of each lives the image of their communion'.[34] In Littlewood's plans for the Fun Palace, she wanted to encourage public reception of events to bring the 'image of their communion' much closer to home – an aim providing further evidence of Littlewood's enthusiastic, if rather naive, faith in the potential of technology to foster a sense of belonging and identity. Littlewood also anticipated the current cultural obsession with reality television and fly-on-the-wall observation in her extensive plans for closed-circuit television. Rather than CCTV being used as a vehicle for surveillance and control, Littlewood planned to co-opt this technology as a democratising resource for allowing access into other worlds and transmitting an appreciation of the performativity of everyday life. She imagined screens projecting,

> without editing or art, whatever is going on at a number of places in and out of London, and in the complex itself: it will be

> possible to see coal-mines, woodmen and dockers actually at work; Monkey Hill, the aquarium or the insect house at the Zoo; the comings-and-goings outside a local authority rest-centre, a Salvation Army hostel, the casualty ward of a hospital, or a West End club.[35]

In *Theatre and Everyday Life: An Ethics of Performance* (1993), Alan Read asserts the way theatre functions in direct relation to the quotidian, arguing, 'Everyday life is the meeting ground for all activities associated with being human – work, play, friendship and the need to communicate, which includes the expressions of theatre',[36] an idea that echoes Littlewood's insistence that 'theatre is not just the putting on of plays: it is everywhere – the transformation scene – in the markets, processions, meetings, partings, in the clothes we wear, our manners and mores and the front we put on'.[37] She also aimed to bring together all aspects of everyday life and 'being human' within one cultural complex. For her, the ultimate goal would be that people could use the Fun Palace to fulfil basic needs such as eating and drinking, to carry out domestic tasks such as visiting the on-site launderette or having their car serviced, to indulge in a cultural pursuit or, indeed, to combine all of these elements in one visit.

Play, pleasure and the joy of doing nothing

Joel Schechter recognised that the Fun Palace originated in 'an experimental, inquisitive attitude towards pleasure'.[38] Rather than the self-denying culture embedded in the British Protestant work ethic, Littlewood and Price stressed the importance of fun, play and pleasure. Johan Huizinga's influential *Homo Ludens*, first published in English in the late 1940s, had reasserted the importance of play for emotional and cognitive development. Moreover, the centrality of pleasure was a dominant feature of the challenge to normative social and moral values embedded in the revolutionary impetus of the 1960s. The Fun Palace acknowledged both positions and 'offered a focus to the optimism of the time, when it seemed possible to remake society around the potential for delight and opportunity'.[39] For instance, Littlewood regarded fun as an integral part of the learning process and encapsulated this in the interactive tests and games planned for the 'science' and 'fun' areas. It is clear from proposals that

> the idea of *fun* was not interpreted as passive entertainment as in the *amuse-me* ethic later to be adopted in the Walt Disney pleasure grounds. For Joan Littlewood and Cedric Price, it would be *fun* if the visitor could be stimulated or informed, could react or interact, but if none of these suited, had the freedom to withdraw'.[40]

By forwarding a shift in the traditional balance between work and leisure, the Fun Palace also challenged the social structures and values that drive the capitalist machine forward. As Lobsinger puts it,

> Reiterated in the Fun Palace brief is a soft leftist critique arguing that the disciplinary regime of time is dictated by a market-place that artificially divides a worker's life into work-time and leisure-time, a regimentation of time that is materially enforced through the zoning of work and leisure in urban space.[41]

Littlewood and Price believed that technological advancement and cybernetics would dissolve the stringent time constraints of industrial and domestic labour and that people would adapt to a new self-managed twenty-four-hour clock. Hence the Fun Palace would provide around-the-clock stimulus that could cater for all manner of needs and ways of inducing pleasure. Certainly, the project is interesting for the way it respected pleasure as polymorphous – activated in numerous ways from a bombardment of the senses to the excitement of intellectual curiosity, the application of practical skills, the process of learning, the feel of unfamiliar objects, the active participation in a public or communal event or simply the joy of doing nothing.

Alongside opportunities for activities and cultural encounters, Littlewood wanted a space that would enable casual strolling and observation as well as physical passivity that could activate contemplation and daydreaming, a space where the mind would be free to wander and imagine beyond the boundaries of possibility and materiality.[42] According to Stanley Mathews, the Scottish beat poet, Alexander Trocchi introduced Littlewood and Price to the creative possibilities of 'aimless urban wanderings (the *dérive*)', and they tried to create an environment to enable this.[43] They were concerned with broadening the horizons and capabilities of the populace that participated in the Fun Palace and part of this was opening up an inner world. Connected to this quest was Littlewood's desire for a riverside setting for the Fun Palace, as if the presence of the ungraspable, fluidity of water would provide the perfect visual metaphor and trigger for imaginative and expansive mental processes.

Place, space and the physical environment

> An ethical theatre cannot be produced in the purpose-built design of another time. It can only be built as a response, and with a responsibility, to its traditions with constant attention to a vocabulary drawn from the frontier disciplines that press upon its borders, new ways of describing the problematic of place, aesthetic value and audience that are central to its continued existence.[44]

Questions of how spaces and spatialities can contribute to the formation of new social meanings and identities have become widespread following Henri Lefebvre's seminal *The Production of Space* first produced in 1976 and translated into English in 1991. Lefebvre explores how spaces are never empty but always loaded with meanings actively produced and recirculated through dynamic social practices. Whilst Lefebvre draws attention to the ways that space regulates and governs behaviour, he also proposes that affective spatial resistance can occur that generates its own social practices. In the case of the Fun Palace, Littlewood and Price were proposing a radical reconceptualising of cultural democracy and participative learning, and to facilitate this social change they needed to rethink the spaces for these encounters.[45] In other words, they were engaged in 'spatial play', a utopian project to allow 'the free play of the imagination in the search for alternatives'.[46]

Littlewood's ideas for the physical environment that would house her Fun Palace had as much to do with what she was rejecting – conventional theatre, the trappings of a permanent building – as they did with activating her 'laboratory of fun'. In *Joan's Book*, she writes about leaving the Theatre Royal in 1961 because she 'could not face the prospect of passing the rest of [her] life in that crumbling old slum'.[47] As an antidote to the dated, dilapidated Theatre Royal that required substantial funds for maintenance, she envisaged a modern structure whose temporary status would ensure it never suffered the ravages of age and neglect. She stressed, 'There will be no permanent structures. Nothing is to last for more than ten years, some things not even ten days: no concrete stadia, stained and cracking; no legacy of noble contemporary architecture, quickly dating; no municipal geranium-beds or fixed teak benches'.[48] Read observes that 'the architectural solidity of certain theatre buildings steadfastly refuses the impermanence of their trade',[49] a view with which Littlewood would have had great sympathy as she sought to harness a flexible structure that stressed its own mutability and ephemerality. Meeting Price, she found the ideal person to realise her vision as he embodied the qualities the social theorist David Harvey assigns to the socially conscious architect. He writes,

> The architect has been most deeply enmeshed throughout history in the production and pursuit of utopian ideals (particularly though not solely those of spatial form). The architect shapes spaces so as to give them social utility as well as human and aesthetic/symbolic meanings. The architect shapes and preserves long-term social memories and strives to give material form to the longings and desires of individuals and collectivities. The architect struggles to open spaces for new possibilities, for future forms of social life.[50]

Price became known as an architectural innovator after designing the aviary at London Zoo in Regents Park in the 1960s with Lord Snowdon and Frank Newby. However, he became most influential for his ideas on the social role of architecture, obsolescence, responsive environments and flexibility, and his unrealised designs for projects such as the Fun Palace (1961) and the Potteries Thinkbelt (1964) held more sway than the buildings he actually built such as the Inter-Action Centre in 1977.[51]

Flying in the face of the postwar obsession with erecting permanent structures such as new housing estates, universities and municipal buildings as signs of widespread commitment to Britain's future development and prosperity, Price championed planned obsolescence and believed that a building should only exist for as long as it was socially useful. He argued that the

> existing built environment, however well designed and rebuilt in the future, will not provide the humane servicing it should to the urban community until it is wholeheartedly recognised that a high rate of destruction of the existing fabric is a positive contributor to the quality of beneficial social change.[52]

Above all, Price wanted to explore 'architecture's potential to nurture change, intellectual growth and social development rather than to offer a definitive aesthetic statement'.[53]

The design historian Royston Landau located Price's principles in the term 'a philosophy of enabling', which captured his ethical and social concerns to utilise the best in architecture, technology, science and the arts, as a means of fulfilling idealistic, humanist and ultimately utopian concerns with improving the human condition. In particular, he believed in the importance of unleashing individual potential for the ultimate service of society and believed in architecture as a generative force that could influence social responses and ultimately a new social order. Hence he believed in innovation over conservation and reconceived a building's worth not in terms of its durability or the quality of its construction material, but in terms of its use and social force:

> Price's view of architecture has a deeply ethical dimension, at the centre of which is *the effect an architecture may have upon its occupants or observers*. He has often stated that architecture can too easily be constricting and damaging for those who use it (socially, psychologically or even physically). But the obverse of this must certainly also apply, for architecture can be liberating, enhancing and supportive, and in his projects and writings Price has consistently asserted and demonstrated the importance of this awareness.[54]

Both Littlewood and Price optimistically embraced the possibilities made available by developments in contemporary design and technology and wanted a structure that was able to respond to a rapidly changing environment. During the 1950s and 1960s, there was an overwhelming acceleration of change as old institutions, frontiers of knowledge and conceptions of physical, social and political space faced challenges from new discoveries, ways of thinking and ideas for radically transforming social configurations. In 1951, the Festival of Britain celebrated all that was new in contemporary design, but in the ensuing years massive technological achievements such as space travel and satellite communication systems widened everybody's conception of what was feasible, and dreams of a space-age utopia, together with futuristic design, became commonplace. The USSR launched Sputnik into outer space in 1957; the USSR's *Luna 3* sent back the first photos from the dark side of the Moon in 1959 and in April 1961 Yuri Gagarin became the first astronaut launched into space. 'The space age spanned the demise of the industrial era and heralded the start of the new age of information',[55] as well as a new age of transformation as the discovery of new worlds and other horizons prompted designers and architects to think outside usual patterns of creation, consumption and use.

Hasan Ozbekhan described technology as generating an 'event of the mind' and initiating 'a generalized phenomenon of expansion: expansion in numbers, expansion of possibilities, knowledge, information, ambitions, the boundaries of mobility, relationships, needs, requirements, and wants'.[56] Littlewood and Price wanted to capture this dynamic change in and through the Fun Palace, a concern that connected them with wider architectural demands and movements that emerged in the 1960s.

Whereas the predominant British post-Second World War architectural dialectic focused on the empiricist-versus-formalist debate as architects drawn to romantic neo-Georgian influences battled it out with architects associated with new brutalism, Price associated with a wider group of radical architects who circulated around the Independent Group in the 1950s and *Archigram* magazine in the 1960s. Founded by the design historian Reyner Banham, the Independent Group started meeting at the Institute of Contemporary Arts (ICA) in 1952 to debate and challenge established values in the theory and practice of architecture and design. Running counter to a dominant nostalgia for romanticism and a folksy pre-industrial culture, the Independent Group enthusiastically embraced technology, American popular culture and 'the ever-intensifying assault of visual information from the mass media'.[57]

Rejecting the modernist search for authenticity and the history-orientated or formalist approaches of many of their contemporaries, architectural practices and groups such as Archigram, Haus-Rucker-Co and Coop Himmelb(l)au were similarly characterised by their questioning of elitist values and overriding acceptance of the vagaries of modern life. They embraced technological culture and the impact of an increasingly consumer-dominated society, and recognised the trend towards disposability, a throwaway society of cheap convenience documented so powerfully in Alvin Toffler's *Future Shock* (1970). They promoted the idea of buildings as temporary and explored ways, such as through pneumatic technology, of achieving structures that could respond to the new cultural condition of restlessness. Rather than forcing people to live their lives according to predetermined, standardised buildings, they stressed the importance of choice, flexibility and expendability in their speculative and experimental design concepts.[58]

The stress on impermanence had practical implications as production method and speed of assembly and disassembly became design factors. As a result, inflatable technology became a key area for exploration in design because of its lightness, durability and mobility. In 1964, the Ministry of Public Building and Works appointed Price to investigate the potential for pneumatic structures and he proceeded to present his findings and ideas in lectures to other architects and engineers. The concept of temporary, placeless architecture promoted by Price subverted the postwar concern with 'brutal concrete edifices'[59] and connected to the increased social presence of geographical mobility and the ultimate aim to create structures that were flexible enough to collapse and rebuild anywhere. Archigram's plans for Plug-in City (1964), Living Pod (1966) and 1990 House (1967) provide prime examples of this preoccupation with indeterminacy.

The inflatable was also popular due to its association with cheapness, fun and colour, qualities that connected it to the bright pop-art-inspired aesthetic pioneered by the artist Richard Hamilton, a sensibility similarly captured by *Archigram* magazine, an occasional journal/manifesto which spanned the 1960s, with its cheap offset litho, xerography and use of comic strips alongside collage and polemics. Increasingly, artists such as Eduardo Paolozzi and Hamilton were exploring ideas around the mass media, urban life and impermanence as ways of challenging the elitist aura that persisted around fine art. Adopting the term 'pop art', Hamilton provocatively declared this encompassed work that was:

> Popular (designed for a mass audience)
> Transient (short-term solution)
> Expendable (easily forgotten)
> Low cost
> Mass produced
> Young (aimed at youth)
> Witty
> Sexy
> Gimmicky
> Glamorous
> Big business.[60]

Many artists also sought to reject the commodification of the marketplace and the confines of the traditional gallery space through transgressive practices that emphasised cheap materials, accessibility and ephemerality.

Price's designs for the Fun Palace anticipated and corresponded with many of these artistic and architectural preoccupations by 'patently challeng[ing] the idea of architecture as shelter, as enclosure, or as a permanent signifier of social values'.[61] As Landau appreciated, Littlewood's proposals 'called for an architecture which was informal, flexible, unenclosed, and impermanent; the architecture did not need to be simply a response to the program, but also a means of encouraging its ideas to grow and to develop further'.[62] Rather than a central location, Price proposed a physical network of zones that could house multiple activities. According to Price, centrality promoted physical and intellectual isolation, led to self-congestion and disallowed expansive thought processes. In contrast, a network would offer flexibility and the possibility of infinite connections between the different zones.[63]

Capable of housing numerous adjustable units, the Fun Palace would provide 'a provisional stage to be continuously set and reset, sited and resited',[64] which could include small workshop spaces, as well as large-volume enclosures to house rallies, concerts and major exhibitions. Above all, the Fun Palace was to offer a democratic space that opened itself up for negotiation by the user, a deliberate attempt to redefine the standard relationship between people and institutions. Movement between different zones was to be part of the overall experience of freedom and the activation of individual agency. John Clark claimed this negotiation would contribute to the joy of the structure, as people would experience 'the self-fulfilment that comes from controlling environment instead of being crushed by it'.[65] Price embedded the importance of accessibility and mobility into his design through a large, unenclosed steel frame, together with multilevel ramps, moving walkways, catwalks and radial escalators, as well as large unobstructed spaces. The space was designed so that people could enter and leave from anywhere and so that they could have complete freedom of movement once inside the structure.

Through the Fun Palace, Price answered the polemical challenge posed by Banham in *Theory and Design in the First Machine Age* (1960) to exploit and harness the potential of technology to revolutionise architectural practice beyond simply utilising the aesthetics of the machine age. By proposing a radical use of cutting-edge technology to divide the spaces and ensure modification according to climatic conditions, Price and Littlewood hoped that technology would enable the public to have unprecedented control of their environment, as Littlewood proposes: 'If it's too wet the roof will stop the rain but not the light. The artificial cloud will keep you cool or make rainbows for you.'[66] Included in Price's designs are hanging auditoria; inflatable enclosures; moving walls, floors, ceilings and walkways; static vapour zones; optical barriers; fog dispersal units; and warm-air curtains, together with lightweight vertical and horizontal blinds. Each unit would be capable of reconfiguration and, according to Banham, 'the kit of service towers, lifting gantries and building components exists solely to produce the kind of interior environments that are necessary and fitting to whatever is going on'.[67] Ultimately, Price was trying to achieve an intelligent environment with the capacity to learn, memorise and respond according to Pask's cybernetic theory.[68] Emphasising the stress on flexibility, Price explained:

> All such equipment is capable of rearrangement – allowing multi-directional movement and random pedestrian grouping, yet capable of programming. The complex itself, having no doorways, enables one to choose one's own route and degree of involvement with activities. Although the framework will remain a constant size, the total volume in use may vary, thus presenting a changing scene even to the frequent user.[69]

Apart from the actual materials, equipment and construction techniques planned for the Fun Palace, Littlewood and Price recognised that other site-based factors were crucial if the project was to be successful. To achieve a transformational impact Littlewood and Price ideally wanted to convert a desolate wasteland into a vibrant cultural centre. To extend the site, Littlewood proposed, 'Existing derelict property and wasteground should be used as observation aprons. "As found" urban landscape is illuminated or obscured to extend the visual limits of the site.'[70] They also highlighted the importance of being part of a wider communication network to enable local, regional and national access through efficient transport. To encourage 'random time usage'[71] the communication routes also needed to be consistently available, cost-effective and capable of dropping off at several points around the site.

Anxieties, failure, impact and legacy

Throughout the 1960s, Littlewood battled to raise awareness of, interest in and financial support for the Fun Palace that Price estimated would cost two and a half to three million pounds. There was a general sense that support for the arts would increase during the 1960s as local authorities accessed the provision made in the 1948 Local Government Act for cultural activities, a viewpoint prompting William Taylor, a London-based librarian associated with the long-running St Pancras Arts Festival, to assert that 'in this respect we shall move much closer to European countries, where the maintenance of orchestras and opera and theatre companies by local municipalities is accepted without question'.[72] Littlewood sought direct subsidy from the local authority levy, as well as private donations and Arts Council funding. She also hoped indirect funds would come from commercial firms donating equipment, tools and materials and from local authorities through their ability to supply teachers and demonstrators.

Unfortunately, funding bodies greeted the project with the same scepticism that Littlewood's work received at the Theatre Royal, and local authority money proved impossible to release. Indeed, a survey of local government expenditure on municipal entertainment in England and Wales during 1961 and 1962, carried out by the Institute of Municipal Entertainment, discovered a worrying trend. The survey 'reached the conclusion that the average nett expenditure of municipal entertainment is a fraction over a 1d. rate, or little more than a sixth of the 6d. rate permitted under Section 132 of the Local Government Act of 1948'.[73] Lack of public money, coupled with the fact that Littlewood and Price proposed to provide free access to the Fun Palace, meant that the project was always financially unviable. Nonetheless, there are many other reasons why the Fun Palace failed which relate to the implications of an essentially ephemeral venture, public anxieties over potential social disruption and the political reorganisation of London in the mid-1960s.

Alongside the question of finance, timorous individuals and local bureaucracy blighted the project. Caught in a vicious administrative cycle of plans, proposals, feasibility studies, council meetings, local resident groups, muted support and eventual rejections, the project never received sustained support despite the identification of several potential sites. Aided by her friend Daniel Farson, Littlewood identified Glengall Wharf, on the Isle of Dogs, as a potential site, and in 1963 Price applied to the London County Council for use of the land. The council communicated its negative response in the following terms:

> The chairmen of the committees concerned have considered the possibility of leasing the five and a half acres of land (including Glengall Wharf) in the Isle of Dogs for the Fun Palace project, but because of certain legal and planning difficulties, the Council is unable to make it available for this purpose. The chairmen were, however, impressed by the imaginativeness and potentialities of

> the project and the possibility of finding an alternative site is being explored.[74]

Sidney Melman, Chairman of the London County Council Parks Committee that reached this decision, was particularly enthusiastic about the project and became centrally involved when Littlewood and Price began to pursue the possibility of combining plans for the Fun Palace with the Civic Trust's intention to regenerate a large area of green belt along the Lea River Valley. According to Littlewood, Leslie Lane, director of the Civic Trust, sent Price 'a map of the Lea Valley with a site at Mill Meads ringed in red' and a query as to whether it would be a suitable site for a Fun Palace.[75]

Unfortunately, the 1963 London Government Act initiated an upheaval in local government and a transfer of power from the London County Council (LCC) to the Greater London Council (GLC) in April 1964 put ideas for the Fun Palace, once again, on the back burner.[76] During this period of uncertainty, Littlewood and Price set up the Fun Palace Charitable Trust to enhance the prospect of securing financial backing. Hope returned in October 1964 following the election of a Labour government and the appointment of Jennie Lee as minister of arts, as she had shown some interest in the Fun Palace proposals. But this hope was short-lived as Lee's rhetoric around innovative arts policy translated into a more conservative sustenance of the status quo. In addition, Lee became immersed in plans for the Open University after becoming minister for the Department of Education and Science and, for many, plans for the Open University superseded the Fun Palace as a more tangible social experiment that could have lasting benefit for a broader spectrum of the national population.[77]

In 1965, the GLC informed Price that Newham Council were planning to use Mill Meads for storm water tanks and that this would leave no room for a Fun Palace.[78] The Fun Palace Committee lodged an appeal and a public inquiry was set for 22 March 1966. Several weeks before this date, the Fun Place committee withdraw its appeal and issued the following statement:

> It is felt that it would be unfortunate if the Council (the GLC) were to appear at the public planning inquiry in opposition to

> even a part of the proposals for the Lee [*sic*] Valley regional development, since this might tend to encourage other objections and even prejudice the passage of the bill.[79]

In the period between the identification of potential sites and the ensuing disappointment of rejection, Littlewood and Price sought out any temporarily available land where they could maintain momentum by running pilot schemes centred on educational and social activities. They assessed various types of site for suitability: riverside, railway, commercial, public parkland, new development and pre-war city housing areas. According to Littlewood, each of these possibilities offered potentially dynamic sites for a temporary complex as many were in a state of flux as postwar development and new technologies took hold. For instance, railway sites were documented as follows:

> With the continual re-organisation of rail communications, dismantled marshalling yards, cleared or redeveloped forecourts and derelict depots have been investigated. Such sites with their built in communication links and services are well suited to such temporary development during the time that a long-term plan is being considered.[80]

Similarly, Littlewood felt that new developments might offer 'areas which are suitable for experimental development of a temporary nature'.[81] In 1964, Price and Littlewood identified a two-acre site of slum clearance land in Hawley Road, Camden, controlled by the LCC Parks Division, but lack of faith and imagination from local residents blighted the project. They 'protested so noisily before anything happened that it seemed pointless to go ahead. It was, after all, meant to provide pleasure, not stir up rancour in the neighbourhood.'[82]

There are many reasons for the reticence encountered by the Fun Palace, the most obvious relating to the fact that the project was way before its time and demanded a leap of faith and imagination from potential funders, local councils, town planners and local residents, which few were able to meet. Whilst social theorists such as Toffler were happy to refer to 'the death of permanence' associated with an increasingly consumer-driven society, the atomic age and technological advancements, the general public were only gradually coming to terms with the implications and consequences of the rapid social changes inaugurated by these cultural shifts, a phenomenon Toffler described in 1965 as 'future shock – the stress and disorientation induced by subjecting an individual or a society to too much change in too short a time'.[83]

No matter how exciting the Fun Palace looked on paper, it proposed a revolutionary reshaping of local cultural activity and the 'shock of the new' proved difficult for many to contemplate. According to John Clark, a supporter and member of the Fun Palace committee, the insistence on flexibility and multiple uses meant that there was nothing concrete for town planners and funding bodies to support as the proposal 'presents no tangible reality to the uninitiated. It is undefined possibility and potentiality.'[84] Littlewood and Price were asking institutions to commit funds to a project they insisted would be determined at the point of use and, even then, that had obsolescence built into it. If town planners and local councillors could not even look forward to having their names immortalised in association with a successful permanent building, no wonder municipal art galleries and sports centres appeared the more attractive options. It is also easy to see that the need for permanent infrastructure, such as transport links and public amenities, to support a temporary venture simply did not stack up practically or financially. Newham Council aired these concerns regarding the Mill Meads site:

> It would attract large numbers of people from a wide area. The site was remote from public transport, access by public highway would be inadequate, improvement to the road pattern could have no priority. Remedial measures would be impractical and unjustified in view of *the temporary nature* of the project and the prior claims of other improvements.[85]

The fear that the Fun Palace would attract an undesirable *other* also proved problematic as local residents worried about escalating antisocial behaviour and noise, as well as increases in traffic volume and litter. Reporting on plans for the proposed Camden pilot, the *Hampstead and Highgate Express* quoted a local vicar giving reasons for his objections which included the destruction of 'existing church youth organizations, whose members would be weaned away and lost to church teaching', and that 'the building would attract the most undesirable type of rowdy and hooligan from other areas. We have quite enough of our own to put up with'.[86] Connected to these fears, Clark outlined how the non-prescriptive nature of the Fun Palace and the frivolous emphasis on pleasure-seeking sat uncomfortably within a utilitarian society more comfortable with notions of social function and application. He wrote, 'At the moment the Fun Palace appears to tower like some isolated island of guilty pleasure. It naturally offends the Puritan ethic it is dedicated to transform and yet its only chance of establishment lies in the extent to which it can relate its plans to a Puritan set of values.'[87] Melville Mark, a public relations consultant Littlewood and Price employed to improve the public image of the Fun Palace after a series of negative reports threatened to undermine the project with accusations of impracticality and unsustainability, agreed:

> Mark felt that the rather loose concept of 'fun' trivialised the Fun Palace image. He advised that it was important to sell the project as an extension of the Theatre Workshop idea, particularly in relation to its educational and sociological value.[88]

This was exactly the kind of prescriptive social engineering Littlewood and Price fought against, even if their ultimate aim rested on aspects of individual and social improvement. Ultimately, the resistance to easy categorisation was part of the Fun Palace's strength, but also a reason behind its failure, as people found it hard to reconcile the seemingly contradictory elements of education and entertainment, activity and passivity, frivolity and seriousness. Even though all these qualities are part and parcel of everyday life, Littlewood planned to bring them together in one multipurpose arena, a proposal that proved unworkable.

In his introduction to Price's *The Square Book* (2003), David Allford writes that the Fun Palace 'would have been a seminal building. It is, even so, one of the influential projects of the last twenty years.'[89] At the time of its conception, architecturally and culturally, it was part of a wider, global movement of experimentation. Whereas the Fun Palace was never built, other organisations in America and continental Europe had more success realising their ambitions for new-style entertainment centres. For example, the Ant Farm collective in America 'rejected the industrial city and created temporary shelters, with names such as Dreamcloud and Flagbag, to house concerts, conferences and happenings in the American deserts'.[90] Richard Rogers and Renzo Piano's Pompidou Centre, built in Paris in 1977, 'would have been inconceivable without the Fun Palace',[91] and draws on much of the Fun Palace's high-tech aesthetic in its unenclosed steel frame structure, external walkways and multifunctional spaces; although the social impetus of the Fun Palace is absent, as 'any transgressive challenge to social conventions posed by the Centre Georges Pompidou is purely symbolic and has been safely incorporated into institutionalised culture'.[92] Alan Parkinson's ephemeral architecture, such as the pneumatic works Archipelago and Luminarium IV from the mid-1990s that create total environments for artistic encounters, also hark back to the Fun Palace as a reference point.

In Britain, Price's austere concept for Ed Berman's Inter-Action Centre (1977), a multipurpose community resource that relied on a free-form interior adaptable for a variety of cultural and recreational functions such as workshops, rehearsal rooms, childcare facilities and studios, owed much to the Fun Palace.[93] More recently, the Millennium Dome (1999), also designed by Rogers, and Will Alsop's The Public (2008), a participatory community arts building in West Bromwich, are the closest manifestations of Littlewood and Price's desire to combine regeneration, entertainment and education. It may well have been that had the Fun Palace been built, like the Millennium Dome and The Public, it would have been blighted by a negative image, financial mismanagement and a sense that the architectural innovation far outweighed the content within its radical structure.

But what is clear is that the very proposal excited and promoted debate and continues to do so. In 2004, a conference called Fun Palace Berlin 200X was held in the partially demolished Palast der Republik in former East Berlin. Here, architects and social theorists inspired by the Fun Palace explored it as a possible model for a twenty-first-century cultural centre. In broader terms, the social impetus behind the Fun Palace is present in the now-fashionable themes of lifelong learning, brownfield regeneration and intelligent environments. The educational and entertainment aspects are equally echoed in participant-centred museum culture and numerous leisure complexes that house film theatres, games arcades, bowling, restaurants and nightclubs in close proximity, whilst the stress on participation is evident in developments such as interactive television and multiperson game-playing facilitated by new computer technology. The fact that her ideas are still stimulating and informing cultural agendas in the twenty-first century is a testament to the strength of Littlewood's vision, her willingness to contemplate 'spatial play' and her ethical concerns with how cultural and educational processes might be activated within the community. These qualities similarly informed the small-scale, local projects that I explore in the next chapter.

7 Spaces to play/playing with spaces: young people, play and citizenship

> I've finished with putting on plays. I don't like the theatre . . . At the moment I'm more interested in my children's playground.[1]

In the late 1960s, Littlewood struggled to find the financial resources to facilitate her work at the Theatre Royal or to make her Fun Palace a reality. Instead, she increasingly used the Fun Palace Trust to develop projects dedicated to imaginative intervention in and a sense of ethical responsibility for the local environment of Stratford East. Together with Raffles and other close collaborators such as Carole Christensen, Gaye Brown and Christine Jackson, Littlewood initiated several local schemes that emphasised cultural democracy, creative encounter, active citizenship and the animation of community-based activity and spaces with and for local residents, specifically children and young people. These projects continued the spirit and social impetus of the Fun Palace, if not its architectural ambitions. In a bitter account of the failure to see her Fun Palace materialise, Littlewood lamented that 'allotment holders, loving couples, rat hunters, ideas kids will have to find somewhere else to play', and she mused, 'could theatre royal be demolished and balloons go up on ½ an acre of rubble?'[2]

This chapter explores projects that centred on the creation of spaces for play, educational workshops and drama activities in order to illuminate Littlewood's approach to creative community activism and tussle with the questions they raise around space as a political and social agent, young people's citizenship, social capital, empowerment and the spaces of theatricality in everyday life. In accordance with Baz Kershaw's study of community-based performance, I argue that these performative interventions had the potential to ignite 'more extensive socio-political efficacy'[3] as they promoted an enhanced understanding of how active citizenship could address real material and social needs within the community.

The opening quote from Littlewood suggests that she perceived these projects to be distinct from her other, *theatrical* life, but, drawing on ideas articulated in Read's *Theatre and Everyday Life* (1993) and Nicolas Bourriaud's *Relational Aesthetics* (2002) I want to argue that these projects make up a distinct yet unwritten and undervalued aspect of Littlewood's theatrical output. In his inquiry into an ethics of performance, Read asserts the need to retrieve work that emerges from the politics of place and local relations and persuasively argues for the political value of work that highlights the interconnectivity of theatrical activity with the practices of daily life. This sentiment resonates with Littlewood's community-based projects that did not tackle a specific issue or cause as such, but reached out and temporarily altered the spaces of daily life as a means of contributing to a complex nexus of social relations.

Bourriaud's work on 'relational aesthetics' similarly champions the importance of socially situated art rooted in human interaction and encounter rather than the creation of autonomous objects or products for passive and private consumption. Bourriaud, as a curator, is interested in museum- and gallery-based practices but, as Gwen Robertson acknowledges, his 'ideas about the potential (even inevitability) of relational art to change the way we understand art ... can be used as an interpretive tool beyond a museum context'.[4] Bourriaud's assertion that artistic encounters have the ability to tighten the 'space of relations' in communities increasingly characterised by anonymity and technological mediations is particularly useful when thinking about Littlewood's urban regeneration and playground projects and their efficacy.[5] Like Read, Bourriaud's work facilitates a discussion of the local spaces, activities and dialogues Littlewood activated as legitimate artistic practices in their own right that deserve critical attention and reflection.

Citizenship and spaces of action

Ideas of what citizenship actually entails are contested and contingent on their immediate historical and cultural milieus, as well as different political perspectives and theoretical discourses. In the 1950s and 1960s, ideas of citizenship largely revolved around T.H. Marshall's seminal essay 'Citizenship and Social Class' published in 1950.[6] In this essay, he identified the triumvirate of civil, political and social rights as crucial to effective citizenship and his conservative vision of a top-down bestowal of rights from the state remained central to conceptions of citizenship during this period. According to John Hoffman, by the 1960s and 1970s the term 'citizenship' was generally denounced by those on the political left who found the term too 'bourgeois' and associated with those able to assert power due to their wealth, property or business interests.[7] However, it is clear from documents that Littlewood employed the term 'citizen' to refer to much more than a person who has rights just by virtue of being a member of a society or due to their material or cultural capital. For her, the term implied a much more democratic set of processes that involved an intellectual and practical engagement with society and the opportunities to activate this engagement within the available educational, cultural and community outlets . For instance, she refers to the fact that 'a nation's prosperity depends on the educational level of its citizens',[8] which implies that the state's responsibility to educate its members will be repaid in the actions that its educated members perform. And this is not just restricted to participation in the economy, but refers to the acquisition and utilisation of a range of social skills and competencies.

Arguably, Littlewood's conceptions of the terms 'citizen' and 'citizenship' were incredibly forward-thinking and have far more in common with recent shifts from Marshall's conception of citizenship as being primarily about rights to notions of 'active citizenship' which stress responsibilities as well as rights, alongside the crucial aspect of democratic participation. Chantal Mouffe (1992) argues for the importance of 'embodied citizenship' that takes steps beyond an abstract notion of individual social responsibility to collective identification that results in social action – a principle that was coming to the fore in the 1960s as political activists, social reformers and educationalists stepped up campaigns based on access and equal opportunities, for example, even if they were not necessarily framed in terms of the citizenship and social-capital agendas that have gained prominence in recent years.

Central to my argument in this chapter is a belief that Littlewood appreciated how young people require access to and creative engagement in local spatialities if they are to develop skills of effective citizenship. A number of recent studies have begun to utilise Lefebvre's work on space introduced in the previous chapter to open up questions of how young people inhabit and reinflect domestic, urban and rural spatialities as a vital part of identity and citizenship formation. For instance, Liisa Horelli has drawn on Lefebvre alongside research in environmental psychology and ideas concerned with collaborative planning and governance to explore how young people might establish environmental competence, which refers not only to knowledge and skills, but also to a willingness to take responsibility for an environment both individually and as part of a wider community.[9] She argues,

> The conditions for inculcating environmental competence in children and young people presuppose a physical and social space of action for children and young people, including such things as opportunities to move around, to manipulate the milieu and to take on meaningful roles in the community.[10]

Horelli stresses the importance of overturning the hierarchical expert-based mode of planning in favour of a polyphonic model that encourages collaboration and involves young people as creative producers of ideas. As such, she advocates a horizontal rather than a vertical model of planning and posits the inclusion, agency and empowerment of the young person through their negotiations with other partners (business, the local council, community groups, artists and so on) as vital to emergent citizenship. Taking a slightly different approach to Horelli, Susie Weller writes about how young people devise 'creative spaces of citizenship' and, in particular, explores 'geographies of hanging out within the community' whereby young people identify, occupy and claim particular spaces as theirs and enact various forms of participant, active and radical citizenship.[11] She found that 'through the shaping of micro-geographies, many ... challenged the notion of teenage apathy, and instead established themselves as committed political actors through developing and redeveloping areas within their communities'.[12] All of these ideas inform my understanding of Littlewood's decision to prioritise various strategies to generate physical and social spaces of action for young people and to facilitate their participation, ownership and agency within the various Fun Palace Trust projects she initiated. Whereas concerns with emergent citizenship are now part of the mainstream, as evidenced by the state-sanctioned enshrining of citizenship within the under-sixteen educational curriculum in Britain, when Littlewood was creating these projects her impetus was far more politically resistant and counterintuitive to dominant conceptions of young people's role in society.

A community under duress: Stratford East

Throughout this chapter, the term 'community' is defined by location, which in this case refers to Stratford East in the London Borough of Newham, one of the poorest boroughs in London. Moreover, I am concerned with a very small area of Stratford East, specifically the neighbourhood in the immediate vicinity of the Theatre Royal that, at the time, was characterised by a mix of owner-occupiers, private tenants and social housing. It is very easy to romanticise communities of location by envisaging a homogeneous group sharing common ideas and ideals that serve the geographical area. In reality, blurred borders, eclectic interests and many different economic, social, cultural and political agendas and identities define communities of location. However, a community of location coming under attack from wider political, social and economic forces activated the projects under scrutiny here, even though I am not suggesting an inclusive response to events in the locality. Only a small self-selecting group from within the community decided to get involved in the projects under discussion and they did so for a wide variety of reasons. Some participants were parents keen to provide a better environment for their children, some were activists keen to participate in grass-roots political action, some were artists interested in embedding arts-based practices in the local community and some were all three and more.

Whatever local anxieties and agendas prompted people to become involved, evidence drawn from the local *Stratford Express* newspaper suggests that Littlewood's adventure playgrounds, city gardens and workshop programme made a significant impact on the local community. Like Helen Nicholson, I am seduced by an understanding of community as 'a dynamic social practice, an identity that is constructed through networks of identification, open to change and renewal, rather than a fixed and immutable legal state'.[13] Because of this understanding, I am suggesting that Littlewood's small-scale creative interventions contributed to a dynamic resituation of community relations at a historical juncture when the community was dealing with the economic and social consequences of myriad factors such as commercial redevelopment, the shift from terraced housing to low- and high-rise flats, mass migration and geographical mobility.

During the mid-1960s and early 1970s, the area around the Theatre Royal Stratford East was subject to extensive redevelopment that involved Newham Council issuing compulsory purchase orders and agreeing to the destruction of Victorian terraced streets, the site of the local street market, a pub, small local shops and a local school. The developers placed the Theatre Royal itself under threat for many years and damage caused to the building meant the loss of its production office, workshop and wardrobe.[14] These places of public congregation, social encounter and discourse were to be replaced by low-rise flats, office blocks, a shopping complex and a multistorey car park – a capitalist-driven respatialisation designed to foster efficient living, production and consumption. Issued in the early 1960s, the plans were highly contentious and the redevelopment became a long-drawn-out process. The Council waited several years to attain ministry approval and then suffered a series of setbacks and delays caused by several financial crises, a public inquiry in 1962, local government restructuring in 1964 and interventions by the then housing minister, Richard Crossman, in 1966.[15] All the while, local people were uncertain about their futures and the area became increasingly run-down as residents and traders refused to invest in properties that faced imminent erasure. In 1967, the redevelopment began in earnest.

Raffles and Littlewood worried about the wider consequences of this redevelopment for the local area and its inhabitants in terms of community cohesion, social exclusion and associated problems of antisocial behaviour. Raffles feared that a development focused on retail and business would result in 'a purgatory with neon lights' after the shops and offices closed for the night. Without adequate leisure facilities, he feared 'a generation of vandalism caused by young people with nowhere to go and nothing to do' and 'a collection of lonely tower-block dwellers who can have no satisfaction from living in the area but only regard it as a dormitory for the men and a prison for their wives and children'.[16]

Littlewood and Raffles recognised that location plays an essential role in fostering self-worth and general wellbeing. If people are physically alienated from their neighbours or have daily encounters with abandoned, neglected and vandalised spaces, then this says something to them about the way their lived experience is valued and whether they should value it too. A particular bone of contention involved the way Newham Council declared many homes unfit for habitation in order to ease the passage to compulsory purchase orders and reduce the council's financial outlay as owners with homes designated slums only received site value as opposed to full market value.[17] It is easy to see this as a crude bureaucratic decision rooted in market capitalism, but the explicit downgrading of people's homes had far-reaching personal and social implications as homes declared 'unfit for habitation' *were* inhabited for many years as the redevelopment stalled. The frustrations associated with continual delays were acute. One letter sent to the local paper from a resident in the area tells of squalor, rats and the dangers of living amongst deserted houses. She concludes, 'If only the people responsible for the "on" "off" decisions of this project could live there for a week or so they would see and feel the despondency these tenants feel.'[18]

Young people, education and play

Like many in their community, Littlewood and Raffles were particularly concerned with the consequences of local government decision-making and urban planning to alienate and limit the opportunities available to young people in the area for productive educative and social outlets. Throughout the 1960s and 1970s, the *Stratford Express* raised serious concerns about the local education sector, identifying problems caused by lack of funds, school closures, staff shortages and dilapidated facilities. For some children these difficulties meant they were temporarily without school places, and others faced part-time education.[19] Coupled with the difficulties faced by the formal education sector, the *Stratford Express* also raised significant questions about the lack of adequate amenities for children to play in the area. The paper took this on as a campaign issue throughout the 1960s and responded forcefully to local government cutbacks or decisions that hampered provision. Typical is an 'opinion' column that appeared in July 1966 in response to Newham Council's decision to ban children over eleven using a playground after complaints of noise. The report concludes,

> Of course children can be a nuisance. Of course they can upset people by too much noise, but that doesn't make them delinquents to be banished from a proper place of pastime and pleasure. Most of the children live in flats. They need to play to breathe.[20]

This was not an isolated incident. The following month a news item reported a fight by local residents to have an area of grassland allocated as a play area during the school holiday period. According to the report, 'Over 300 residents appealed to Newham Council to have a fence around the open space taken down'.[21] The council refused. The following year, the paper reported the closure of another park, wryly commenting, 'The "Keep Out" sign is flanked by Fort Knox style battlements. Even 007 would have a job to steal past the giant concrete posts, barbed wire and alsatians'. But this is not the new resting place for the crown jewels. It is a – PLAYGROUND!'[22] In several stories, the paper makes connections between the lack of spaces for play and effective social and cognitive development in the young. It also speculates on the correlation between inadequate provision and rising criminal and antisocial behaviour in several items documenting problems with truancy, gang culture, vandalism and petty theft. In addition to these stories of social disorder are a disturbing number devoted to personal tragedies as young people were injured or killed as they played on the roads, or through misadventure in inappropriate sites such as derelict factories and building sites. The overwhelming message is that the immediate environment and its spatialisation had a deleterious effect on the young people of the borough that required urgent attention.

In *Growing up Absurd* (1962), Paul Goodman predicted that the immediate social and physical environment, predominately in urban areas, would increasingly work against children due to factors such as traffic, the weakening of neighbourhood identity and social networks, the lack of unstructured play spaces and increasingly hectic family time schedules.[23] In 1968, Littlewood intervened in these wider social debates and the specific circumstances of the Stratford East community in a Fun Palace Trust document called *Bubble City*. In this publication, she highlighted the connection between lack of spaces for social and creative encounter and the consequences for perceived and active citizenship amongst the young. Against a picture of a young boy, Littlewood asks, 'What will I be? Tinker, tailor, soldier, sailor, richman, spaceman, con-man, thief?'[24] and speculates on what might happen to 'young citizens' growing up in a run-down environment where previous intergenerational and intracommunal social relationships were being broken down by increasing geographical mobility, the loosening of kinship ties and environmental shifts to high- and low-rise flats. The document emphasises spatial and physical factors through images of children isolated against low-rise flats, empty fenced concrete spaces, a burnt-out car, a child trying to play in a narrow corridor of concrete, a deserted park and vandalised swings. The images conjure with isolation, restriction, community breakdown, alienation and limited opportunity – but specifically the lack of spaces for play.

Throughout the twentieth century, campaigners such as Jane Addams, Caldwell Cook and Johan Huizinga had been promoting the importance of play for emotional and cognitive development, so this was not a new agenda.[25] Littlewood also had in the East End a number of predecessor social innovators and reformers who sought to use education and play as a form of social altruism geared towards improving the lives of individuals and community-building in the late nineteenth and early twentieth centuries. For instance, Octavia Hill (1838–1912), a social and housing reformer supported by John Ruskin, championed the provision of playgrounds and access to common lands and green space, whilst Henrietta Barnett (1851–1936), who worked alongside Hill for a time, developed initiatives to take poor children for holidays in the country. Together with her husband, Samuel Barnett, she was also pivotal in founding the Hampstead Garden suburb and promoting university settlements such as Toynbee Hall, both of which thrived on the potential of social mixing across socioeconomic groups and democratic access to social amenities. Similarly, the dedicated Christian socialist and political campaigner Margaret McMillan (1860–1931) dedicated herself to improving the material and intellectual welfare of the poor by campaigning on issues such as nursery education, free school meals and health-care provision.[26] Although Littlewood's projects were largely divorced from wider campaigns for social reform, there are clear connections between these earlier initiatives concerning play, education, access to green space and democratic social participation and her local community-building and cultural activism.

Littlewood proposed that 'the young need to participate in living'[27] and that they require outlets (spatially, socially and creatively) to be stimulated and developed to become effective citizens:

> Low standards of education, a run-down environment, the break-up of old patterns of social relationship, leave children ill-equipped to face adult life; drifting from one menial job to another, bored and semi-literate, no outlet for their natural intelligence, no training in decision making, they burn up their energy in smash-ups, in stealing and outwitting the adults who mostly hate and fear them.[28]

Littlewood keenly felt the quality of dispossession occurring in the area and saw a need to foster a sense of agency and empowerment through the temporary occupation and creative animation of spaces. Rather than sitting by and lamenting the social and material conditions she witnessed around her, she decided to intervene, a move that further reiterates her connection to a radical strand of utopian thought that dares to imagine other possibilities. Importantly, she recognised that there was a temporal gap between developers demolishing buildings and subsequent redevelopment. Lefebvre draws attention to how spaces vacated by power can enable a different social imaginary to take effect before the logic of capital reappropriates it, and Littlewood determined to take advantage of this temporary crack in the spaces of capital. As Harvey writes,

> There are, Foucault assures us, abundant spaces in which 'otherness', alterity, and, hence, alternatives might be explored not as mere figments of the imagination but through contact with social processes that already exist. It is within these spaces that alternatives can take shape and from these spaces that a critique of existing norms and processes can most effectively be mounted.[29]

Before she got involved, sites designated for redevelopment became dumping grounds for the detritus of contemporary consumer culture and dangerous playgrounds for children with nowhere else to go. In *Joan's Book* she describes walking around the corner of the Theatre Royal and being confronted by 'broken mattresses, tin cans, wrecked prams, ruined refrigerators and unspeakable muck'.[30] Alternatively, she proposed to inhabit and reimagine abandoned spaces with a mixture of semipermanent and ephemeral structures dedicated to opportunities for play, pleasure, learning and communication for young people. As such, in Foucault's terms she was creating a heterotopia, a physical space in which she was determined to offer an alternative way of being and doing. The heterotopic potential was more apparent given Littlewood's occupation of abandoned public spaces that were more suggestive of the qualities of localism, communitarianism and playfulness that she was keen to harness, as opposed to the more restrictive regimes associated with institutional spaces such as schools, theatres and other public buildings. As such, Littlewood's alternative action and its imaginative terrain provided an overt political critique of the failures of local government and its policies to address the needs of children and young people in the area.

Writing to local people and potential backers, Littlewood explained,

> Everywhere land is becoming temporarily derelict while local authorities wait for the go-ahead on new building schemes. There

is insufficient money for schools, nurseries, modern youth clubs and clubs for people of all ages. At the same time, talented people are prepared to give their time and skill to direct practical solutions to this problem.

Pleasant, temporary structures to house these activities can be erected on the old debris instead of giving it over to dumping and dirt. When rebuilding starts, the structure can be moved on.

Meanwhile, we may find out how to enjoy ourselves and even enrich ourselves a bit more. The talent, which in the old days seemed to belong only to the 'stars' in society, is in each child. It just needs cherishing.[31]

Whilst these projects were responsive to local community needs, Littlewood was not alone in her endeavours. Across Britain in the 1960s and 1970s, community action escalated and many activists set up youth clubs, under-five groups, community centres and residential associations.[32] During this period, the Make Waste Space Playspace campaign grew and turned into the City Farm and Community Garden Movement (inspired by the Community Garden Movement in America and the Children's Farm Movement in the Netherlands). Also, the Woodcraft Folk educational movement continued to promote skills and activities connected to the environment and natural resources. All these activities were galvanised by a desire to increase qualities such as community identification and cohesion and to provide accessible productive and creative spaces where people could improve their skills, knowledge, local relations and, in turn, hopefully their physical and mental health.

Littlewood's 'direct action' began with the generation of an adventure playground on a deserted bombsite in Salway Road, Stratford East, in 1967, and by 1975 the Fun Palace Trust had turned waste ground into sites for community gardens, a temporary zoo and a small-scale city farm, as well as more playgrounds. At the same time, Littlewood co-opted and reconceived various buildings. A disused warehouse became a youth club; a primary school vacated by the education authorities was transformed for summer holiday activities and the Theatre Royal became a hub for various educational and drama-based workshops. Certainly, these projects functioned in line with Alan Filewood's assertion that the best community theatre consists of temporary, mobile 'strategic ventures' that have the flexibility to adapt to shifting circumstances.[33] Financial support came from the Fun Palace Trust and events were subsidised personally by Raffles and Littlewood, but above all they relied on local fundraising, donations and volunteers drawn from the neighbourhood, the theatre and the wider creative community. This facilitated the coming together of a diverse socioeconomic cross-section who might never have interacted in other circumstances and contributed to a redefinition of what and who constituted the local community as actors joined with gardeners, carpenters, doctors, plumbers, students and artists to reclaim and remake the immediate social and physical environment.

In Salway Road, a group of local residents started by clearing the site of rubble and rubbish, a process signifying that the spaces and those who inhabited them were of value. Littlewood applied for a temporary

11. Joan Littlewood helping to clear derelict ground.

planning order and galvanised local firms and individuals to donate sand, bricks, cement, turf, scaffolding, tools, paint and toys. For instance, she persuaded the construction firm Taylor Woodrow to bulldoze two sites, Moore's Plant Hire loaned a roller to flatten a site, Mills provided scaffolding to make a climbing frame, Galt Toys donated a swing and the Cement Marketing Board offered cement and resin paint. The successful promotion of altruistic principles of donation and volunteering provides a potent image of the active citizenship Littlewood was keen to foster. In donating goods, companies worked against the logic of market capitalism in favour of more socially orientated practices, although clearly the companies could also benefit from the positive publicity. By volunteering, people offered their time, skills and resources to facilitate temporary respatialisations after recognising their place in a broader set of communal relations beyond their immediate friends and family. In this sense, Littlewood contributed to the creation of what Victor Turner calls 'communitas', by which he refers to a process that stresses relationality, an awareness of the live presence of other human beings living in communion with one another.[34]

Active citizenship and the young

One of Littlewood's primary objectives was to counter 'a powerful ontology of childhood [which] delimits young people's opportunities for activism, framing them as adults-in-waiting . . . rather than as social agents capable of bringing a uniquely valuable perspective to civic discourse'.[35] According to Weller, the young are very often characterised as in an 'inbetween' state and this 'incompleteness' means that they are seen as vulnerable, dependent and passive, to be acted upon or for, in the 'best interests of the child'.[36] As such, the young have a problematic relationship to dominant conceptions of citizenship. There is a sense that young people, by virtue of the fact that they are still growing up and acquiring the emotional and cognitive resources to engage in competent decision-making, are not ready to take on the responsibilities of citizenship until they reach adulthood. Yet Littlewood recognised that good citizens are not made by accident but through a process of learning and exercising citizenship rights and responsibilities. Therefore, rather than dismissing the young as emergent citizens – caught in a process of becoming – Littlewood valued their current state of being. She viewed young people as competent social actors and stressed their agency by mobilising them as collaborators, clearing, designing, acquiring materials and constructing spaces.

Above all, Littlewood wanted to create spaces that functioned very differently from the unimaginative municipal parks, gardens and playgrounds provided by the local council that were epitomised by signs such as 'keep off the grass', 'no cycling', 'no ball games', 'closed at dusk'. Rather than emphasising restricted access and excluded activities, Littlewood wanted spaces to be enabling and reflective of young people's needs and concerns. Once she secured temporary planning permission, she invited the young to submit drawings of what the spaces could become or to record their ideas on tape. It was important that these innovative processes became more than just 'a tokenistic exercise in legitimising adult decisions',[37] so even though adults initiated and facilitated this involvement, the younger generation were free to propose whatever they wanted. In recent years, there has been a surge of interest in how to involve the young in democratic decision-making within their communities, but this was a relatively new idea in the 1960s. It mirrored Littlewood's progressive acceptance that youth 'not only have a right to participate in social decision making, they benefit from such inclusion and can make valuable contributions to playful, transformative thinking'.[38]

Young people from Stratford East were encouraged to explore what they wanted from social spaces and to redefine the boundaries that were put around them and that they put up around themselves by negotiating with different generations and authority figures such as youth leaders, planning officers and local entrepreneurs – a strategy that functioned in line with Horelli's work on collaborative planning and governance discussed earlier. These initiatives, therefore, had the potential to develop intergenerational relations as well as practical and social transferable skills. Invited to communicate their needs, the young learnt to articulate their concerns, a process that inevitably had an impact on their self-perception and self-esteem as inclusion validated their ideas and their action contributed to very real material, social and cultural change.

The young variously requested colour, a space for pets, grass to play on and a degree of privacy and respect. Recurring themes centred on dedicated spaces for play and the crucial aspect of ownership. During the creation of the Salway Road playground, young participants designed and produced banners and signs that proclaimed 'kid's village' and 'our place', items that simultaneously promoted membership and exclusion. The sense of ownership of and pride in the projects instigated several concrete examples of the young demonstrating active citizenship in the community. For instance, when the first Salway Road project began some local residents complained about bad behaviour and language and drew up a petition to try and stop the playground happening. In response, 'a group of older boys collect[ed the] electoral register, address[d] envelopes and distribute[d] explanatory letters to 400 neighbours to counteract the petition'.[39] Rather than conforming to the stereotype of juvenile delinquents with an underdeveloped sense of social responsibility, the group explained the rationale for the playground and resolved to address fraught community relations with a positive response. Those previously opposed to the project stopped their petition. The *Stratford Express* also recorded another incidence of the projects instilling positive community action after a deputation of children from another local area visited the Salway Road project and requested their own playground, after which, 'the Salway-street kids . . . offered to go and build it for them'[40] – evidence that the young people were prepared to disseminate the skills and knowledge they had developed through their participation.

The sites evolved in different ways. People working on the sites effectively improvised them according to available skills and resources, and the sites' planned obsolescence imbued the projects with the ephemeral nature of the performance event. Nonetheless, rather than limiting the scope of their ambitions, the volunteers worked to create images of permanence. During the construction phases, young people helped lay crazy paving, turf and block-paving in a spirit of bricolage. The sites became a chequerboard of different surfaces, a childlike aesthetic unrestricted by the design sensibilities of adults. This is not

12. Joan Littlewood with her young gardeners.

to suggest that adult agendas of education and symbolic resistance to local council plans were not pivotal. Littlewood was particularly keen to import vegetation into the sites. Grass, plants and trees were used to replace the gardens lost by the removal of terraced houses in favour of tower blocks. The placement of organic, living materials on the sites took on oppositional resonance in the face of plans for more concrete edifices.

In May 1968, Littlewood planted six ten-year-old lime trees donated by the National Coal Board opposite the first Salway Road adventure playground. Planting the trees with her young helpers she declared, 'It doesn't matter if they're all uprooted in five years' time . . . at least the local kids will have seen a bit of green in this rather barren stretch of the wilderness.'[41] Later, she reiterated the symbolic function of the planting, claiming, 'it's not a royal park but a symbol that their place will keep on growing'.[42] On another site, she planted thirty-six trees, with a sympathiser donating 'straps, stakes and topsoil for the trees "because you're doing something to brighten it up round here"'.[43] The Fun Palace Trust also began running Sunday outings to places such as Epping Forest and Canvey Island, to give young people experience of a different environment away from the congested confines of the city. One site also became a temporary farm after several local residents allowed the young people to keep their animals on one of the sites during the day. As a result, donkeys, goats, a tortoise, pigeons, chickens and rabbits were brought to the site. According to Littlewood, Jimmie Winston, a member of the band the Small Faces, was also involved and arranged for a baby lion, Horace, to be brought to the site.

Once sites were cleared of debris, resurfaced and made safe, they were available for young people to use through a series of structured and unstructured activities. A vision of creativity emerged that was not individualistic, elitist and located in institutions but open, inclusive, communal and as much about process as about product. Regular structured activities included drama and music workshops, maths games, gardening, sport, painting and picnics – alternative forms of pedagogy that existed outside the more rigid and authoritarian modes encountered in the classroom. Evidence suggests that at various points the young participants had access to individuals highly skilled in their fields. For instance, Bart, who composed the musical *Oliver* and *Fings Ain't Wot They Used T'Be*, ran music workshops. The mathematician Michael Holt designed games and puzzles and Martin Goodrich and Barbara Wheeler-Early, founders of Free Form Arts Trust, which experiments with how public art has a role to play in urban revival and community regeneration, ran various creative workshops in art and creative construction. Unstructured activities included chances to 'let off steam' – impromptu mud fights and parties whereby a group would arrive with makeshift furniture, food and drink to listen to music and dance. These activities may have been less welcome for local residents concerned by noise and adults charged with clearing up the mess.

Activities designed to reanimate the local environment also spilled out from the designated sites to the wider community. For instance, in August 1967, a team of young people began painting the walls and shop fronts along Angel Lane, the site where local traders and the street market were facing obliteration that ran adjacent to the Theatre Royal. Using paint donated by a local firm, the young people transformed Angel Lane with psychedelic hues of purple, pink and blue. The *Stratford Express* recorded that

> as the youngsters worked the shopkeepers beamed. They are convinced it will bring trade to the area. Mr Harry Shingler, who has kept a second-hand clothes shop in The Lane for 28 years was full of praise for the young painters. 'It can do nothing but good', he said. 'It will bring more people to The Lane. It's about time something like this happened. Good luck to the Theatre Royal'.[44]

Equally, Littlewood arranged social events to celebrate achievements and to encourage community-building. Between 1972 and 1975, the Fun Palace Trust hosted Autumn and Easter Fairs for the community and used these to widen the reach of the projects by inviting parents and other local residents to come and experience what the spaces had become and how the young people in the community used them. Using the collective title 'Stratford Fair', Littlewood conjured with images of the classic fair or fête that is typically associated with village life and occasions traditionally staged as opportunities for community members to gather in a shared public space to participate in fundraising activities such as raffles, a tombola and games. As such, the Stratford Fairs were reinflected by their presence in a down-at-heel inner-city area.

The Easter Stratford Fair staged on 31 March 1975 began with a processional element that took participants from the local railway station to the Salway Road site. This performance strategy required people to come together to walk the streets of their neighbourhood blighted by redevelopment before they were welcomed to the transformed sites, which functioned in accordance with Bruce McConachie's reminder that parades provide 'potent performative symbols of "communities of location"', but also as a political framing device.[45] Once at Salway Road, participants found a traditional fair complete with stalls and various performative acts including stilt-walkers, fire-eaters and an escapologist. There were also displays from the Boys' Brigade band and girl pipers and a staged re-enactment of a battle between the Cavaliers and the Roundheads. The day culminated with a cabaret at the Theatre Royal hosted by Victor Spinetti, and the local press favourably reported that the fair was a 'fabulous success' for adults as well as children.[46] These fairs demonstrated a commitment to and celebration of the locality, its spaces and inhabitants by effectively saying, look, see what we can achieve when we pull together, when we assert our agency to act and to have fun together.[47]

Antisocial behaviour, villainy and making good

Some young people reported that the spaces and activities provided them with an outlet away from petty crime, such as the following testimonies recorded in the *Stratford Express*:

> I've been coming here for about ten years. If this place hadn't existed I reckon I'd have been inside by now.
>
> At one time I used to hang about in the streets. When I got really bored, I'd smash windows. I was the best window smasher in Stratford. But I don't need to do that anymore.[48]

A volunteer who organised sporting activities similarly recalled a moment when 'a big gang came down to where we were playing volley ball. They asked our children "do you want to fight?" Our kids just turned around and said they'd rather play volley ball.'[49] This is not to suggest that everything was plain sailing. Some of the young people who used the sites still found themselves in detention centres following criminal activity and several young people used the sites when truanting from school, to which one of the organisers, Gaye Brown, responded by saying, 'we don't encourage it, but at least we're here so they're not smashing things up'.[50]

Sites also suffered regular petty theft and vandalism from the young people who used them. Nonetheless, they were encouraged to view themselves and to be viewed as part of a community of location, a social network – not in terms of a romanticised conception of homogenised identity and unity, but as citizens sharing the same social space. This identification led them to hold and respect court-style 'mock trials' to interrogate antisocial behaviour and to enact their versions of social justice, which ranged from fines to community service. Interestingly, Littlewood recalls that 'the worst punishment was banishment', a fate that befell one boy whom she remembers 'standing on the pavement outside the promised land, afraid to set foot on it. He'd been banished for three days for nicking an apple pie which some girl had baked for our Sunday picnic.'[51] On another occasion, an unknown culprit smashed the windscreen of a volunteer's lorry, leading Littlewood et al. to record in a project diary:

> A three-line whip has gone out for this evening. Two of the worst villains go to Martin's house and ask him to come. The assembly is serious, it's held in the 13–17 club. We stand round our only table, in the light of two butane gas lamps. Everyone turns up. The bill for the windscreen is passed round, £23.50.[52]

So whilst these activities did not erase antisocial behaviour, the projects did nurture a sense of accepting culpability and responsibility for activities detrimental to shared resources. In this case, the group agreed to raise money with a sponsored walk to St Paul's Cathedral, complete with songs, costumes and banners proclaiming, 'we pay for our kicks' and 'villain's pilgrimage'. This event required sensitive negotiation with the local police and St Paul's and received positive coverage in the local press.[53] The event was recorded in a month-long project diary and the extended extract below reveals a great deal about the complex interplay between mundane and performative activity that the Fun Palace Trust encouraged. It also highlights some of the difficulties of allowing the young freedom, whilst maintaining boundaries of respect and appropriate behaviour:

> The great day. The sky is blue and the sun clearly shining. Mike claps on a troubadour hat and strums his guitar. Jenny arrives wearing a tweed piss pot. Villains hats issued. Jimmy S. has a heavy moustache and a patch over one eye . . . Joan is particularly troublesome, complaining that there are not enough banners . . . Banners are raised. The pilgrimage sets off, the Sunday army gets on with usual chores, hut, paving, clearing as usual. Joan busies herself clearing rubbish. Allan Klein has agreed to meet the merry band at Bow Road . . . and sings with them. Joan shoots down to

> Paternoster Square in Mayfly for 4.00pm. It's cold, the sun's gone in – there they are – playing 'he' to keep warm. She rushes round to Cathedral . . . we see the one who was to meet us but he takes one look and disappears like lightning. What to do? . . . They've all been looking forward to getting in. J.L. practically kidnaps a passing verger and gives him the story. The kids are waiting at the door. He says bring them in. Two worst villains whirl through revolving door f . . . ing and blinding. Ringleader is admonished . . . The verger looks appalled. The nearest gets a surreptitious wallop and the rest walk towards the centre aisle and a miracle – THEY ARE IMPRESSED.[54]

This event was typical of the ethos underpinning the Fun Palace Trust and its activities. It encouraged young people to take responsibility for their actions, to negotiate productively with others and to engage in spatial reimaginings by inviting them to see the terrain beyond their immediate habitat and an iconic building such as St Paul's as somewhere they could temporarily inhabit, whilst being mindful of the social and political codings etched in any public space. These principles also galvanised Littlewood's decision to open up the Theatre Royal to young people, to open up a space where they might 'find ways of telling their own stories behind the security of locked doors'.[55] As such, she confronted and opened up the meanings associated with this Victorian theatre space, a building situated in the epicentre of Stratford East that many of these young people had probably never entered. Rather than perceiving the theatre as an exclusive space for adult artistic experimentation and cultural encounter, she allowed the young to occupy the space and reinterpret it as a site for their own experimentation and events. She invited the young to engage in radical spatial practices by challenging the social purpose that they perceived for the theatre by turning it into a representational space for their own alternative educative, social and dramatic interactions.

Improvisation, enactment and playing the citizen

It is important to stress that the activities conducted inside and outside the theatre were not separate but interconnected – both part of a creative engagement with self, space and community, both facilitating skills development and knowledge through collaborative social processes. In fact, Littlewood first invited young people into the theatre at the same time as the first Salway Road regeneration project so that the children and young people had somewhere to go after dark. Drawing on local expertise and skills, the children could take workshops in woodwork, typing, kendo (a form of Japanese sword fighting), basic electronics and using tools. Whilst these opportunities inevitably served a pragmatic purpose of keeping the young occupied and off the streets, they also had the potential to develop a range of competencies. By taking kendo classes, the young had access to a highly disciplined martial art that enhances bodily awareness, physical acumen, concentration and personal confidence. Opting for typing, woodwork or basic electronics, the young were enhancing their employability and gaining confidence from accomplishing a useful life skill.

As you would expect, there were classes devoted to theatre games and improvisation. The games were fun and helped develop concentration, co-ordination, spontaneity and imagination, as well as the skills required for effective group working such as communication and problem solving. One of the important aspects of this work for Littlewood was the opportunity for young people to work with guidance, but largely autonomously so that they could experiment with their own way of interpreting, rehearsing and presenting ideas. As in her theatre work, she resisted imposing a set view of how material should evolve and preferred to facilitate an organic set of processes that relied on trial and error, creative exchange, dialogue and playfulness. For instance, on one occasion she invited a group up to her office to listen to a tape of Allan Klein's 'Crazy World' songs:

> Me father's doing five years – grandad's doing ten,
> Me uncle came out just last week, now he's back again,
> Me cousin just done six months for petty larceny,
> Oh what a family . . .

She then encouraged them to transcribe the words, learn them and find ways of presenting them theatrically – an active learning-and-doing process that serviced cognitive and creative development, whilst also acknowledging the very real social circumstances that some of the young people were negotiating on a daily basis.

The blurring of performance and everyday life was also apparent during the Friday night 'posh nights' that merged role play, performance and the traditional party on the Theatre Royal stage. The young created environments through the use of screens, lighting and music and raided the props and costumes stores to find hats, dresses, sharp suits and fake moustaches to wear. Littlewood described these nights in the following terms:

> On Friday evenings, the Nutters were invited to take over the stage at the theatre, from six o'clock till eight, for their 'posh night'. They were a scruffy lot and declared themselves proud to be so, but on Friday nights they'd be wearing lighting-up ties, polka-dot cravats, embroidered waistcoats and decorated dance shoes. You wouldn't have known them. Each Friday the Nutters would choose a different theme – and we would invent the appropriate décor with them. They also chose their own dance music and in time formed their own band. The girls held off to the last minute, attending to their own appearance and strolling in, heavily made up, often half crippled in their mothers' high-heeled shoes.[56]

Evenings included: 'Buck House', 'A Gambling Hall', 'French Fete' and 'Flower People Pad'.[57] But this was more than just an elaborate game of dressing up. Through these theatrical processes of staging and enactment, the young were able to play with other versions of themselves and invert narratives of poverty, class, exclusion and powerlessness by temporarily occupying their own narratives of success that relied on their ability to imagine, create and play, a practice that works in terms of Nicholson's observation that 'the aesthetics of self-production is built on the convergence and interplay of different narratives, and that constructing narratives of selfhood is both an ethical and creative process'.[58] These 'posh nights' were not just escapist play, although this element should not be underestimated, they were opportunities to define and redefine a sense of self by creating different worlds both connected to and detached from the 'real world'. Young people adopting the guise of hippy dropouts or royalty were self-consciously performing social roles and negotiating these in relation to their own physicality, bodily responses, gestural patterns, language use and vocal inflections.

Improvisatory work took on a more socially therapeutic dimension as the young were encouraged to see how dramatic narrative could organise, articulate and negotiate complex social relations encountered during their daily experiences – a process that raised ethical issues about whose stories had found a narrative voice at the Theatre Royal. Whilst the theatre had made important inroads into representing local histories and experiences, the narratives of the young had been conspicuous by their absence. This opening up of the theatre allowed the young a legitimate space to share their stories with each other. Littlewood described these sessions in the following terms:

> First, the day's troubles, fights and mis-understandings would be re-enacted; the boys changing roles, playing the foreman who sacked them, the shopkeeper who turned them away, the headmaster who punished them. Not acting in the sense of exhibiting themselves or exaggerating, but remembering facts and moves, identifying themselves with their 'enemy'. If there had been a fight with the 'wogs' the boys who'd attacked played the victims and others, uninvolved, played the attackers. 'Who is the wog?' The answer turned out to be the stranger, often feared. Then, as the evening wore on fantasy would enter in. Ambitions, hopes, dreams and fears would be acted out.[59]

This description is extremely illuminating of the kinds of social processes explored. To begin with, it indicates recognition and consideration of the various power relations that operate in work-based, educational and social spheres and the ways in which intrapersonal and interpersonal skills are a necessary component of effective citizenship. It also presumes the need to accommodate and negotiate issues raised by differentiated citizenship in terms of age, class, race and gender identities. In her discussions of community relations, Mouffe stresses the importance of difference embedded in social discourse and the need to confront rather than ignore antagonistic relations. As the above quote suggests, Littlewood invited her young participants to narrate and assess their fractious community encounters in order to identify the triggers and consequences of their own antagonistic relations and wider community tensions in a non-threatening and non-judgemental environment. Workshop leaders, including Littlewood, paid particular attention to community changes wrought by postwar migration, with improvisations used to explore and interrogate some of the anxieties raised by the presence of *others*. Through drama, dubious cultural assumptions and prejudices could be held up for scrutiny and alternatives rehearsed and rerehearsed as issues of racial intolerance and misunderstanding continually resurfaced as Stratford East continued its journey to become one of the most ethnically diverse areas in Britain.

It is important that these young people demonstrated a willingness to re-enact their own stories and as such to view them as constructions capable of being replayed with different narratives, subject positions and outcomes. Moreover, it is significant that that they not only questioned their own position, but role-played the position of others, exercising the kind of 'active and creative participation in performance practices that dislodge fixed and uneven boundaries between "self" and "other"'.[60] The young person plays the adult, the young worker takes on the role of boss and the bully performs the victim to see another perspective and to gain insights into how the other's behaviour is also part of a performative social process. This actually suggests a radical engagement with notions of self and other that acknowledges how both are generated through interaction and how these relations are not fixed, but open to reappraisal and change. James Thompson expands on this idea in *Applied Theatre: Bewilderment and Beyond* (2003) by arguing that adolescents establish a sense of self by experimenting with 'fragments of action'; effectively they evolve by rehearsing their 'performance skills' to develop social competence:

> Theatre programmes working with adolescents are thus an intervention in an ongoing performance development process. They are no more likely to create pure role models (through characterisation) than the experiential marking moments that

> young people are already meeting. What they can provide are new interactions that positively carve new channels within and between young people. They offer a staging post between the modelling and the improvisation where the matter of action can be played with freely.[61]

Recognising that the creation of the self and the social citizen is a dynamic, evolving process, Littlewood invited young people to rehearse and reconfigure through imaginative and creative play their roles, interactions and responsibilities as emergent citizens. Importantly, this work was always about the process of exploring and never designed to be fixed for a definitive performance, a situation that provided the freedom to visit uncomfortable and difficult personal narratives and social relations.

In many ways, Littlewood's way of working with the young can be illuminated by reference to Paulo Freire's dialogical problem-posing educational model. Explaining traditional education as akin to banking whereby the teacher deposits knowledge in the minds of passive students who remain inattentive to the traditions and prejudices that reside in their learning, Freire's model encouraged original, critical thinking by overturning the traditional teacher–pupil hierarchy in favour of dialogue. In his foreword to *Pedagogy of the Oppressed*, Richard Shaull explains Freire's conviction that

> every human being, no matter how 'ignorant' or submerged in a 'culture of silence' he or she may be, is capable of looking critically at the world in a dialogical encounter with others. Provided with the proper tools for such encounter, the individual can gradually perceive personal and social reality as well as the contradictions in it, become conscious of his or her own perception of that reality, and deal critically with it.[62]

As a result of this critical enquiry and dialogical process, Freire believed that people could unsettle ideological structures of knowledge, develop self-determination and ultimately enact social change. Similarly, by inviting young people to engage in creative dialogues about their lives and attitudes, to discuss, defend and challenge their own ideas,

Littlewood hoped to encourage greater self-awareness and the young to take control of their daily lives by seeing themselves as responsible for their words and deeds rather than being passive onlookers going 'with the flow'. She also hoped to facilitate more harmonious community relations as different subject positions became familiar to the young through role-play rather than alien through antagonistic real-life encounters.

As Thompson makes clear in his work, it is impossible to quantify exactly what the impact of participation in theatre games, role-play and workshops might be because these activities operate in a complex nexus with other social processes, embodied histories and networks of human activity.[63] He argues that it would be

> wrong to say that we pick up skills, attitudes or roles from these experiences and display them later. I have argued . . . that action is not mechanistically (re)created this way. However, theatre, in being an explicit play with and around 'action matter', deals with the basic processes of how we learn to perform our lives. Actions undertaken or witnessed in theatre will leave emotional memories, behaviour fragments, characteristics, lines, gestures and images of self that will fit or conflict with an existing shape. In fitting, they become part of the material that can be recreated, reworked and displayed in later life.[64]

As such, the young people who participated in various theatre processes at the Theatre Royal were developing tools in their armoury of citizenship to join others activated in the home, the schoolroom and the street. And with each game, dialogue and theatrical encounter there was the potential that the participants would become more self-aware, reflexive and socially knowledgeable.

It is difficult to gauge the legacy of this kind of community-based work, but it certainly received predominantly positive support from people in the immediate locality. Parents were full of praise for Littlewood because her proactive approach created safer play environments and stimulating activities for their children. One mother said at the time, 'I've got three sons who didn't know what to do with themselves in the holidays before she came along last year. I think we should pay our rates to her – she's done more than the rest!'[65] The local paper similarly welcomed Littlewood's interventions and regularly reported Fun Palace Trust events in glowing terms. Belatedly, Newham Council began legitimising the projects with funding. In autumn 1974, it provided twelve pounds a week for youth leaders' salaries and in 1975 it supplied a grant of £800 pounds to fund a 'kids' village' run over Easter. Project funding came from other organisations such as the Gulbenkian Foundation, the Arts Council and the Greater London Arts Association. The International Volunteer Service also sent eight student workers from countries as far afield as Japan, Hungary, Sweden and Greece to work on the sites for three weeks in 1975. Unfortunately, no long-term financial strategy could be found to facilitate the work on a more secure footing. In 1975, the Gulbenkian Foundation offered £2,000 and applied for a seven-year extension to the lease of land opposite the Theatre Royal to allow work to continue, but Newham Council refused and, following the death of Raffles in April 1975, the activities slowly ceased to happen as Littlewood became increasingly remote from the theatre and its immediate surroundings.[66]

In many ways, it is the legacy of the processes involved in the temporary reconfigurations and occupations of sites that are important – the communal gathering, the shared purpose, the negotiations, the reimagining and creative engagement with space; the sense of belonging, ownership, agency, empowerment and self-esteem. These interventions could not hope to stop the redevelopment process but instead provided a series of interruptions, disruptions and ruptures that were suggestive of another set of social relations. There was a resituating of space away from the codified space of capital to a space reinscribed imaginatively, which through its materialisation, however temporary, however haphazard, spoke of an alternative world view based on a collective sharing of time, energy, skills and resources; a world view that recognised young people as active participants who demanded wider community recognition; a world view that promoted the ability to intervene and the necessity of doing so in community processes; and a world view that was ultimately oppositional and resistant to the pervasive economic capital of space that places office blocks and shopping complexes above nurseries, schools and youth clubs. As such, I would argue that Littlewood was able temporarily to intervene in the map of local history, culture and activity and to forge memories of participation that potentially people could reinflect in other situations. Above all, on a micro level, she facilitated some of the conditions and values necessary for an active citizenship culture: awareness of social, political and economic processes, engagement with the physical environment, self-scrutiny, accountability, problem solving and, above all, a sense of commitment to and responsibility for others, the local culture and community.

Notes

Chapter 1

1. K. Tynan, *Profiles* (London: Nick Hern Books, 1989), p. 178.
2. V. Spinetti, 'Still With Us: Joan Littlewood', *The Oldie*, 6 August 1993, p. 58.
3. Undated letter to Ewan MacColl, Ewan MacColl and Peggy Seeger archive, Ruskin College, Oxford.
4. J. Littlewood, *Joan's Book: Joan Littlewood's Peculiar History as She Tells It* (London: Methuen, 1994), p. 99.
5. See B. Harker, *Class Act: The Cultural and Political Life of Ewan MacColl* (London: Pluto Press, 2007), pp. 45–7.
6. Ibid., p. 57.
7. Letter from Joan Littlewood to Gerry Raffles, 21 October 1948, Michael Barker Collection, Harry Ransom Humanities Research Center, the University of Texas at Austin.
8. M. Bramwell, 'A Cup of Tea with Joan Littlewood', in Joannne Tompkins and Julie Holledge (eds.), *Performing Women/Performing Feminisms: Interviews with International Women Playwrights* (Brisbane: Australasian Drama Studies Association, 1997), pp. 103–9, p. 108.
9. Ibid.
10. J. Littlewood interviewed by A. Pitman, *The Oldie*, February 2002, p. 19.
11. Bramwell, 'A Cup of Tea with Joan Littlewood', p. 108.
12. J. Littlewood interviewed by A. Pitman, *The Oldie*, p. 19.
13. For a more detailed discussion of Littlewood's radio work see B. Harker, '"Was There Another England?" Joan Littlewood in Manchester', *North West Labour History Journal*, No. 28 (2003), pp. 36–41.
14. E. MacColl, *Journeyman* (London: Sidgwick and Jackson, 1990), p. 211.
15. Ibid.
16. Ibid.
17. Littlewood, *Joan's Book*, p. 93.

18. Harker, *Class Act*, p. 46.
19. Undated and untitled lecture contained in the Michael Barker Collection, Harry Ransom Humanities Research Center, the University of Texas at Austin.
20. D. Paget, 'Theatre Workshop, Moussinac, and the European Connection', *New Theatre Quarterly*, Vol. 11, No. 43 (August 1995), pp. 211–24, p. 212.
21. Cited in H. Goorney and E. MacColl (eds.), *Agit-Prop to Theatre Workshop: Political Playscripts 1930–1950* (Manchester: Manchester University Press, 1986), p. ix.
22. Promotional leaflet for Theatre Workshop produced as the company were planning to move to Kendal in 1945, Theatre Royal Stratford East archive, Pre-1953 File.
23. Joan Littlewood, in 'From Kendal to Berlin: The Diary of Theatre Workshop', script used for a recording on 30 July 1947 by Manchester Radio, Theatre Royal Stratford East archive, Pre-1953 File.
24. Programme for *Uranium 235* at St Andrew's Hall in Glasgow, 24–5 March 1952, Theatre Royal Stratford East archive, Pre-1953 File.
25. Harry Greene, 'Visions and Vicissitudes – the Story of Theatre Workshop', *The Stage and Television Today*, 31 January 1980, p. 103.
26. 'From Kendal to Berlin'.
27. MacColl, *Journeyman*, p. 254.
28. For a detailed discussion of this aspect of Littlewood's work see Nadine Holdsworth, 'Joan Littlewood's Working Method', in Holdsworth, *Joan Littlewood* (London: Routledge, 2006), pp. 43–75.
29. Littlewood, *Joan's Book*, p. 199.
30. G. Raffles, 'A Scheme for the Formation of an Experimental Theatre Workshop and Theatre School in Liverpool', 10 January 1948, Michael Barker Collection, Harry Ransom Humanities Research Center, the University of Texas at Austin.
31. Letter from J. Littlewood to G. Raffles, 4 March 1947, Michael Barker Collection, Harry Ransom Humanities Research Center, the University of Texas at Austin.
32. Letter from J. Littlewood to H. Goorney, 12 February 1947, cited in Harker, *Class Act*, p. 82.
33. Undated letter from J. Littlewood to G. Raffles, Michael Barker Collection, Harry Ransom Humanities Research Center, the University of Texas at Austin.
34. Undated letter from J. Littlewood to G. Raffles, Michael Barker Collection, Harry Ransom Humanities Research Center, the University of Texas at Austin.

35. Undated letter from Joan Littlewood to Gerry Raffles, Michael Barker Collection, Harry Ransom Humanities Research Center, the University of Texas at Austin.
36. Cited in Harker, *Class Act*, p. 76.
37. Letter from G. Raffles in *Stratford Express*, 24 April 1953, page unknown.
38. G. Raffles cited in J. Ennis, 'The Theatre Workshop Story Part I', *Reynolds News*, 9 October 1960, page unknown.
39. J. Littlewood, cited in H. Goorney, *The Theatre Workshop Story* (London: Methuen, 1981), p. 154.
40. Anon., 'Stephen Woos Girl – by Writing Play', *Stratford Express*, 4 February 1966, p. 10.
41. See V. Spinetti, *up front . . .* (London: Portico, 2006), p. 117.
42. H. Goorney, *The Theatre Workshop Story*, p. 103.
43. Nadine Holdsworth, 'Joan Littlewood', in Shomit Mitter and Maria Shevtsova (eds.), *Fifty Key Theatre Directors* (London: Routledge, 2005), pp. 75–80, p. 77. Faxing permission for Clwyd Theatr Cymru's 2003 revival of *Oh What a Lovely War*, Littlewood reiterated her antipathy towards 'bloody acting'. See D. Paget, '"The War Game Is Continuous": Productions and Receptions of Theatre Workshop's *Oh What a Lovely War*', *Studies in Theatre and Performance*, Vol. 23, No. 2 (2003), pp. 71–85.
44. M. Karlin, *Some Sort of a Life* (London: Oberon, 2007), p. 93.
45. Ibid., p. 94.
46. F. Norman, *Why Fings Went West* (London: Lemon Tree Press, 1975), p. 22.
47. M. Croyden, 'Joan Littlewood', in J. McCrindle (ed.), *Behind the Scenes: Theatre and Film Interviews from the 'Transatlantic Review'* (London: Pitman, 1971), pp. 1–12, p. 7.
48. Radio correspondent, 'Old Ladies of the Arts Council', *Daily Telegraph*, 25 July 1961, p. 12.
49. For a detailed consideration of this production see Nadine Holdsworth, 'Description and Analysis of *Oh What a Lovely War*', in Holdsworth, *Joan Littlewood*, pp. 77–115; and D. Paget, 'Case Study: Theatre Workshop's *Oh What a Lovely War*, 1963', in Baz Kershaw (ed), *The Cambridge History of British Theatre*, Vol. III (Cambridge: Cambridge University Press, 2004), pp. 397–411.
50. *Omnibus*, 'Joan Littlewood', BBC1, 19 April 1994.
51. M. Billington, *State of the Nation: British Theatre since 1945* (London: Faber, 2007), p. 26.
52. For a detailed discussion of Theatre Workshop's relationship with the Arts Council see Nadine Holdsworth '"They'd Have Pissed on My

Grave": The Arts Council and Theatre Workshop', *New Theatre Quarterly*, Vol. 15, No. 1 (1999), pp. 3–16.

53. Programme for *Macbird*, Theatre Royal Stratford East archive.
54. Holdsworth, 'They'd Have Pissed on My Grave', p. 5.
55. Letter from V. Trowbridge, 13 May 1961, concerning the need for a new licence to be granted for *Fings Ain't Wot They Used T'Be*, LC 1733B; and C. D. Heriot's reader's report for *A Kayf Up West*, 4 March 1964, Lord Chamberlain's Collection, British Library.
56. Letter dated 9 November 1957, LC 351, Lord Chamberlain's Collection, British Library.
57. Letter dated 27 October 1957, Lord Chamberlain's Collection, British Library.
58. Copies of these treatments and scripts are available in the Michael Barker Collection, Harry Ransom Humanities Research Center, the University of Texas at Austin, Box 1, Folders 7 and 2.
59. P. Kuppers and G. Robertson (eds.), *The Community Performance Reader* (London: Routledge, 2007), p. 4.
60. J. Littlewood, *Baron Philippe: The Very Candid Autobiography of Baron Philippe de Rothschild* (New York: Crown Publishers, 1984).
61. J. Littlewood, 'Home Fires Burning', *Guardian*, 28 December 1985, pp. 18–19.
62. C. Steedman, *Dust* (Manchester: Manchester University Press, 2001), p. 45.
63. R. Schneider, 'Archives: Performance Remains', *Performance Research*, Vol. 6, No. 2 (2001), pp. 100–8.
64. E. Schafer, *MsDirecting Shakespeare: Women Direct Shakespeare* (London: The Women's Press, 1998), p. 18.
65. See P. Hedley, 'Black Theatre Development at Theatre Royal, Stratford East', *Perfoming Arts International*, Vol. 1, No. 2 (1996), pp. 23–33, p. 25; J. Ezzard and M. Billington, 'Joan Littlewood', *Guardian*, 23 September 2002); and A. Strachan, 'Joan Littlewood', *Independent*, 23 September 2002.

Chapter 2

1. See G. M. Reichberg, H. Syse and E. Begby, *The Ethics of War* (Oxford: Blackwell, 2006), pp. 441–50.
2. Whilst theatre did respond to the cultural shock of the First World War, Mary Luckhurst, in 'A Wounded Stage: Drama and World War I', in Mary Luckhurst (ed.), *A Companion to Modern British and Irish Drama 1880–2005* (Oxford: Blackwell, 2006), pp. 301–15, rightly identifies that this amounts to a rather small body of work largely due to problems with

official censorship and audience antipathy as people sought uncontroversial entertainment as they struggled to assimilate their trauma and loss. Nonetheless, a number of plays did appear, such as Harry Wall's *Havoc* (1923), Alan Monkhouse's *Conquering Hero* (1924), J. R. Ackerley's *The Prisoners of War* (1925), R. C. Sherriff's *Journey's End* (1928) and Somerset Maugham's *For Services Rendered* (1932), that managed to negotiate significant antiwar sentiments without alienating audiences. In contrast, the Second World War and the moral abyss signalled by the Nazi genocide and atomic weaponry has remained a significant theme in postwar British theatre. In the immediate aftermath plays such as Noel Coward's *Peace in Our Time* (1947), Christopher Fry's *The Lady's Not for Burning* (1948) and John Whiting's *Saint's Day* (1951) explored moral issues raised by war. Several plays, including John Arden's *Waters of Babylon* (1957), Trevor Griffith's *Comedians* (1975) and Peter Barnes's *Laughter* (1978), picked up on Theodor Adorno's identification of a crisis in representation following Auschwitz. Other works, such as J. B. Priestley's *Summer Day's Dream* (1949), Doris Lessing's *Each His Own Wilderness* (1958), Robert Bolt's *The Tiger and the Horse* (1960), Howard Brenton's *The Genius* (1983), Edward Bond's *War Plays* (1985) and Michael Frayn's *Copenhagen* (2002) have grappled with the moral dilemmas posed by weapons of mass destruction. For more information see C. Barker, 'The Ghosts of War: Stage Ghosts and Time Slips in Response to War', in C. Barker and M. Gale (eds.), *British Theatre between the Wars 1918–1939* (Cambridge: Cambridge University Press, 2000), pp. 215–43; and P. Fussell and C. A. Carpenter, *Dramatists and the Bomb: American and British Playwrights Confront the Nuclear Age 1945–1964* (Westport, CT: Greenwood Press, 1999).

3. See B. Harker, *Class Act: The Cultural and Political Life of Ewan MacColl* (London: Pluto Press, 2007), pp. 79–83.
4. See J. Littlewood, *Joan's Book: Joan Littlewood's Peculiar History as She Tells It* (London: Methuen, 1994), pp. 632–3.
5. Cited in Reichberg, Syse and Begby, *The Ethics of War*, p. 663.
6. Recent scholarship, notably A. Richardson (ed.), *The Spanish Civil War: The View from the Left* (Monmouth: Merlin Press, 2007), originally published in 1992 by Socialist Platform Ltd, has complicated this simple binary opposition.
7. Anon., undated document, Pre-1953 File, Theatre Royal Stratford East Archive.
8. L. Hyde, *The Gift: How the Creative Spirit Transforms the World*, 2nd edn (Edinburgh: Canongate, 2006), p. 155.
9. Littlewood, *Joan's Book*, p. 64.

10. P. Fussell, *The Great War and Modern Memory* (London: Oxford University Press, 1975), p. 74.
11. Cited in R. Taylor and N. Young (eds.), *Campaigns for Peace: British Peace Movements in the Twentieth Century* (Manchester: Manchester University Press, 1987), p. 77.
12. *John Bullion* can be found in H. Goorney and E. MacColl (eds.), *Agit-Prop to Theatre Workshop: Political Playscripts 1930–1950* (Manchester: Manchester University Press, 1986), pp. 1–11.
13. E. MacColl inaccurately recalls the piece as *Hammer*, perhaps thinking of the play's producer John Hanmer. My thanks to Richard Boon for drawing *Slickers* to my attention and for providing me with a copy of the unpublished text.
14. Goorney and MacColl, *Agit-Prop to Theatre Workshop*, p. xxxiv.
15. J. Hanmer, 'Notes on the Production of Slickers', undated. My thanks to Richard Boon for providing a copy of this unpublished document.
16. A. Huxley, *An Encyclopaedia of Pacifism* (London: Chatto and Windus, 1937), p. 1.
17. Harker, *Class Act*, p. 44.
18. E. MacColl, 'Introduction', in Goorney and MacColl, *Agit-Prop to Theatre Workshop*, p. xxxv.
19. Huxley, *An Encyclopaedia of Pacifism*, p. 46.
20. Ibid., pp. 78–9.
21. Goorney and MacColl, *Agit-Prop to Theatre Workshop*, p. 10.
22. Barker has noted that 'ghosts walk the stage throughout the 1920s and 1930s' and in this play dead First World War soldiers rise from their graves to measure the extent of their sacrifice against the greed and warmongering of the present. See Barker, 'The Ghosts of War', p. 215.
23. S. Sassoon, *The War Poems* (London: Faber, 1983), p. 143.
24. Harker, *Class Act*, p. 39.
25. Anon., 'An Old Play', *Manchester Guardian*, 9 February 1939, p. 11.
26. See M. M. Delgado, *Federico García Lorca* (London: Routledge, 2008), p. 30.
27. D. S., 'Theatre Union: A New Manchester Movement', *Manchester Guardian*, 22 February 1939, p. 13.
28. MacColl, 'Introduction', p. xi.
29. D. S., 'Theatre Union', p. 13.
30. J. Falstaff, 'Theatre Union Disappoint in a Social Play', unsourced review of *The Good Soldier Schweik*, Theatre Royal Stratford East Archive.
31. See M. Melvin, *The Art of the Theatre Workshop* (London: Oberon Books, 2006), pp. 27–9.

32. D. S., 'The Good Soldier Schweik', *Manchester Guardian*, 13 May 1939, page unknown.
33. Programme note for Theatre Union's Production of *The Good Soldier Schweik*, Theatre Royal Stratford East Production.
34. E. MacColl, *Good Soldier Schweik* script, Lord Chamberlain's Collection, British Library, p. 64.
35. C. D. Heriot, reader's report, 23 November 1954, Lord Chamberlain's Collection, British Library.
36. Cited in H. Goorney, *The Theatre Workshop Story* (London: Methuen, 1981), p. 100.
37. H. Hobson, 'Good Soldier Schweik', *Sunday Times*, 18 March 1956, p. 15.
38. See L. H. Mates, *The Spanish Civil War and the British Left: Political Activism and the Popular Front* (London: Tauris Academic Studies, 2007); and Richardson, *The Spanish Civil War.*
39. Littlewood, *Joan's Book*, p. 106.
40. Programme for *Last Edition*, Pre-1953 File, Theatre Royal Stratford East Archive.
41. 'Memorandum on Living Newspaper on the War', 6 November 1939, Pre-1953 File, Theatre Royal Stratford East Archive.
42. Programme for *Last Edition*, Pre-1953 File, Theatre Royal Stratford East Archive.
43. B. Harker, 'Mediating the 1930s: Documentary and Politics in Theatre Union's *Last Edition* (1940)', in A. Forsyth and C. Megson (eds.), *Get Real: Documentary Theatre Past and Present* (Basingstoke: Palgrave, 2009), pp. 24–37, p. 35.
44. MacColl proceeded to ask John Banks at Manchester University Press to omit the script of *Last Edition* from *Agit-Prop to Theatre Workshop*. After further correspondence, a compromise was reached whereby it was agreed to publish the full text of *The Other Animals* and only extracts from *Last Edition*. The following analysis is based on the full script deposited in the Ewan MacColl and Peggy Seeger Archive at Ruskin College, Oxford.
45. See MacColl, 'Introduction', p. xliv. For an account of the Federal Theatre Project see B. B. Witham, *The Federal Theatre Project: A Case Study* (Cambridge: Cambridge University Press, 2003).
46. For an illuminating discussion of *Last Edition* see Harker, 'Mediating the 1930s', pp. 24–37.
47. Ibid., p. 34.
48. Cited in Harker, *Class Act*, pp. 58–9.
49. R. Leach, *Theatre Workshop: Joan Littlewood and the Making of Modern British Theatre* (Exeter: University of Exeter Press, 2006), p. 38.

50. E. MacColl and J. Littlewood, *Last Edition* script, Ewan MacColl and Peggy Seeger Archive, Ruskin College, Oxford, p. 1.
51. On 22 September 1934, the worst pit disaster for twenty-one years occurred when an explosion and fire ripped through Gresford Colliery near Wrexham. In all, 264 men lost their lives.
52. J. Derrida, *Specters of Marx*, translated by P. Kamuf (London: Routledge, 1994), p. xix, original emphases.
53. MacColl and Littlewood, *Last Edition* script, pp. 1–2.
54. Ibid., p. 5.
55. This aspect is omitted from the scenes reproduced in Goorney and MacColl, *Agit-Prop to Theatre Workshop*.
56. J. Littlewood, extract from an undated creative notebook, Box 1: Folder 5, Michael Barker Collection, Harry Ransom Humanities Research Centre.
57. On 29 September 1938, Germany, Italy, France and Britain signed the Munich Agreement, which secured the acceptance by Britain and France of Hitler's demand that the Sudetenland region of Czechoslovakia be ceded to Germany.
58. Goorney, *The Theatre Workshop Story*, pp. 22–3.
59. MacColl and Littlewood, *Last Edition* script, p. 88.
60. Ibid., p. 80.
61. Anon., programme for Theatre Union's *Lysistrata*, Pre-1953 File, Theatre Royal Stratford East Archive.
62. Harker, *Class Act*, p. 63.
63. Reader's report, 17 September 1946, Lord Chamberlain's Collection, British Library.
64. Programme note for *Operation Olive Branch*, Pre-1953 File, Theatre Royal Stratford East Archive.
65. E. MacColl, *Operation Olive Branch* script, Ewan MacColl and Peggy Seeger Archive, Ruskin College, Oxford, p. 2.
66. J. Littlewood, in 'From Kendal to Berlin: The Diary of Theatre Workshop', script for radio broadcast, 5 August 1947, North of England Home Service, Pre-1953 File, Theatre Royal Stratford East Archive, unpaginated.
67. MacColl, *Operation Olive Branch* script, p. 3.
68. Ibid., p. 32.
69. Ibid., p. 70.
70. Ibid., p. 10.
71. Ibid., p. 12.
72. See 'Arpeggio', 'Talented Company of Actors', *Felixstowe Times*, 7 June 1947, p. 1; and J.M.P.D., 'Operation Olive Branch', *Manchester Guardian*, 5 August 1947, p. 4.

73. Bill Davidson, in 'From Kendal to Berlin'.
74. J.M.P.D., 'Operation Olive Branch', p. 4.
75. 'Arpeggio', 'Talented Company of Actors', p. 1.
76. Littlewood, *Joan's Book*, p. 226.
77. See Harker, *Class Act*, pp. 79–82.
78. Quoted in Goorney, *The Theatre Workshop Story*, p. 57.
79. See ibid.
80. Littlewood, *Joan's Book*, p. 237.
81. T. Driberg, 'Tom Driberg's Column', in *Reynolds News*, 12 January 1947, page unknown.
82. Britain tested her first A-bomb in October 1952 and announced plans to develop an H-bomb in 1955, which received its first testing at Christmas Island in 1957.
83. A. Davies and P. Saunders, 'Literature, Politics and Society', in A. Sinfield (ed.), *Society and Literature 1945–1970* (London: Methuen, 1983), pp. 13–50, p. 31.
84. Ibid.
85. J. B. Priestley, 'Britain and the Nuclear Bombs', *New Statesman*, 2 November 1957, pp. 554–6.
86. Taylor and Young, *Campaigns for Peace*, p. 2.
87. J. Nuttall, *Bomb Culture* (London: Paladin, 1968), p. 19.
88. Littlewood, *Joan's Book*, p. 190.
89. J. Key, 'The Atomic Drama', in T. Howard and J. Stokes (eds.), *Acts of War: The Representation of Military Conflict on the British Stage and Television since 1945* (Aldershot: Ashgate Publishing, 1996), pp. 110–26, p. 110.
90. Goorney and MacColl, *Agit-Prop to Theatre Workshop*, p. 75.
91. A. Camus, cited in H. Zinn et al., *The Power of Non-violence: Writings by Advocates of Peace* (Boston: Beacon Press, 2002), p. 57.
92. Littlewood, *Joan's Book*, p. 185.
93. Goorney and MacColl, *Agit-Prop to Theatre Workshop*, p. 117.
94. See K. Shepherd-Barr, *Science on Stage: From Doctor Faustus to Copenhagen* (Princeton, NJ: Princeton University Press, 2006), p. 72.
95. A.G., 'Electrons in Tights', *Manchester Evening Chronicle*, 17 July 1951, p. 10.
96. Anon., 'The Message of Uranium 235', *Glasgow Herald*, 25 March 1952, p. 3.
97. Anon., 'From Kendal to Berlin'.
98. Goorney and MacColl, *Agit-Prop to Theatre Workshop*, p. 110.
99. Littlewood, *Joan's Book*, p. 191.

100. I. McKay, 'Red Bearded Playwright's Drama of the Atom', *News Chronicle*, 25 May 1946, p. 3.
101. E. MacColl, *Journeyman* (London: Sidgwick and Jackson, 1990), p. 251.
102. Anon., 'The Comedy: "Uranium 235"', *The Stage*, 26 June 1952, p. 9.
103. Littlewood, *Joan's Book*, pp. 426–7.
104. E. MacColl, *The Travellers* script, Theatre Royal Stratford East archive, Pre-1953 File.
105. Harker, *Class Act*, p. 100.
106. Anon., 'The Travellers: Brilliant Acting in New Play', *Scotsman*, 20 August 1952, p. 6.
107. Reader's report, 25 July 1952, Lord Chamberlain's Collection, British Library.
108. For a discussion of the controversy see H. Henderson, 'The Edinburgh People's Festival, 1951–54', in A. Croft (ed.), *A Weapon in the Struggle: The Cultural History of the Communist Party of Great Britain* (London: Pluto Press, 1998), pp. 163–71, pp. 169–70.
109. D. Douglas, 'Worth a Medal', *Daily Worker*, in Ewan MacColl and Peggy Seeger Archive, Ruskin College, Oxford, undated.
110. M. P. d'Entrèves, 'Hannah Arendt and the Idea of Citizenship', in C. Mouffe (ed.), *Dimensions of Radical Democracy: Pluralism, Citizenship, Community* (London: Verso, 1992), p. 148.
111. D. Pick, *War Machine: The Rationalisation of Slaughter in the Modern Age* (New Haven: Yale University Press, 1993), p. 189.
112. E. MacColl, *The Travellers* script, Lord Chamberlain's Collection, British Library, p. 62.
113. A. Badiou, *Ethics: An Essay on the Understanding of Evil*, translated by Peter Hallward (London: Verso, 2001), p. 62.
114. A. Davies and A. Sinfield (eds.), *British Culture of the Postwar: An Introduction to Literature and Society 1945–1999* (London: Routledge, 2000), p. 104.
115. Ibid.
116. MacColl, *The Travellers* script, Lord Chamberlain's Collection, p. 90.
117. See Harker, *Class Act*, p. 100.
118. MacColl, *The Travellers* script, Lord Chamberlain's Collection, p. 12.
119. See S. R. Suleiman (ed.), *Exile and Creativity: Signposts, Travelers, Outsiders, Backward Glances* (Durham, NC: Duke University Press, 1998).
120. MacColl, *The Travellers* script, Lord Chamberlain's Collection, p. 16.
121. J. Miller (E. MacColl), 'Capitalism, Writing and the War', *Our Time*, Vol. 2, No. 13 (July 1943), pp. 27–9. I am very grateful to Ben Harker for bringing this article to my attention.

122. MacColl, *The Travellers* script, Lord Chamberlain's Collection, p. 52.
123. For a detailed discussion of these sources see D. Paget, 'Popularising Popular History: "Oh What a Lovely War" and the Sixties', *Critical Survey*, Vol. 2, No. 2 (1990), pp. 117–27.
124. R. Eyre and N. Wright, *Changing Stages: A View of British Theatre in the Twentieth Century* (London: Bloomsbury, 2001), p. 269.
125. D. Paget, 'Case Study: *Oh What a Lovely War*', in B. Kershaw (ed.), *The Cambridge History of British Theatre*, 3 vols. (Cambridge University Press, 2004), Vol. III, pp. 397–411, p. 404.
126. See N. Holdsworth, *Joan Littlewood* (London: Routledge, 2006), pp. 77–113; D. Paget, 'Case Study: *Oh What a Lovely War*', pp. 397–411; and Leach, *Theatre Workshop*.
127. D'Entrèves, 'Hannah Arendt and the Idea of Citizenship', p. 149.
128. S. Sontag, *Regarding the Pain of Others* (New York: Picador, 2003), p. 86.
129. Paget, 'Case Study: *Oh What a Lovely War*', p. 398.
130. Original programme for *Oh What a Lovely War*, Theatre Royal Stratford East Archive (1963).
131. Ibid.
132. Ibid.
133. Undated manuscript, Theatre Royal Stratford East Archive.
134. Sontag, *Regarding the Pain of Others*, p. 119.
135. Ibid., p. 117.
136. J. Glover, *Humanity: A Moral History of the Twentieth Century* (London: Jonathan Cape, 1999), p. 197.
137. 'Dead horses and dead men – and parts of both – were sometimes not buried for months and often simply became an element of parapets and trench walls'; Fussell, *The Great War and Modern Memory*, p. 49.
138. Ibid., p. 194. For a more general discussion of the way the First World War was conceived in theatrical terms see Fussell's chapter 'Theater of War', in ibid., pp. 191–230.
139. J. Bourke, *An Intimate History of Killing* (London: Granta, 1999), p. 142.
140. See Holdsworth, *Joan Littlewood*, p. 97.
141. M. Foucault, *Discipline and Punish: The Birth of the Prison*, translated by A. Sheridan (London: Allen Lane, 1977), pp. 135–9.
142. Badiou, *Ethics*, p. 47.
143. C. Barker, cited in Goorney, *The Theatre Workshop Story*, p. 126.
144. Letter from Bertrand Russell to Theatre Workshop, 5 June 1963, Theatre Royal Stratford East Archive.

145. Two Christmas parcels are held in the Theatre Royal Stratford East Archive.
146. Anon., 'More Tears than Mirth', *The Times*, 21 June 1963, p. 16; H. Taubman, 'The Theater: Joan Littlewood's "*Lovely War*"', *New York Times*, 1 October 1964, p. 30; and Anon., 'Laughter in Hell', *Time*, 9 October 1964, p. 92.

Chapter 3

1. See K. Tynan, *Profiles* (London: Nick Hern Books, 1989), p. 182.
2. J. Littlewood, *Joan's Book: Joan Littlewood's Peculiar History as She Tells It* (London: Methuen, 1994), p. 51.
3. D. Kennedy, *Looking at Shakespeare* (Cambridge: Cambridge University Press, 1993), p. 122.
4. See Littlewood, *Joan's Book*, pp. 52–3.
5. E. Schafer, *MsDirecting Shakespeare: Women Direct Shakespeare* (London: The Women's Press, 1998), p. 18.
6. J. Littlewood, 'Education and Understanding', an undated notebook, Michael Barker Collection, Harry Ransom Humanities Center, the University of Texas at Austin.
7. C. Chambers, *Inside the Royal Shakespeare Company: Creativity and the Institution* (London: Routledge, 2004), p. 170.
8. See M. Delgado, *Federico García Lorca* (London: Routledge, 2008), pp. 28–33.
9. Anon., 'Shakespeare Again', *Stratford Express*, 22 January 1954, p. 10.
10. Anon., 'Twelfth Night', *The Stage*, 5 February 1953, p. 10.
11. Schafer, *MsDirecting Shakespeare*, p. 18.
12. D. Callaghan, 'Shakespeare at the Fun Palace: Joan Littlewood', in M. Novy (ed.), *Cross-cultural Performances: Differences in Women's Re-visions of Shakespeare* (Urbana: University of Illinois Press, 1993), pp. 108–26, p. 122.
13. W. B. Worthen, *Shakespeare and the Authority of Performance* (London: Routledge, 1997), p. 2.
14. See Anon., 'Theatre Royal Stratford', *The Times*, 18 January 1955, p. 5.
15. H. G. M., 'Macbeth', *Theatre World*, Vol. 53, No. 393 (October 1957), p. 9.
16. Kennedy, *Looking at Shakespeare*, p. 8.
17. Worthen, *Shakespeare and the Authority of Performance*, p. 15.
18. See G. Holderness, *Shakespeare Recycled: The Making of Historical Drama* (Hemel Hempstead: Harvester Wheatsheaf, 1992); C. Marowitz, *Recycling Shakespeare* (Basingstoke: Macmillan, 1991); and G. Taylor, *Reinventing Shakespeare: A Cultural History from the Restoration to the Present* (London: Hogarth, 1990).

19. G. Raffles, 'Theatre Workshop: A British People's Theatre', in H. Hobson (ed.), *International Theatre Annual*, Vol. III (London: John Calder, 1958), pp. 167–79, p. 171.
20. R. Leach, *Theatre Workshop: Joan Littlewood and the Making of Modern British Theatre* (Exeter: University of Exeter Press, 2006), p. 114.
21. Jan Kott's *Shakespeare, Our Contemporary* was not published in English until 1965, when it appeared in translation by Boleslaw Taborski.
22. Kennedy, *Looking at Shakespeare*, p. 109.
23. See R. Huggett, *Binkie Beaumont: Eminence Grise of the West End Theatre 1933–1973* (London: Hodder and Stoughton, 1989), p. 325.
24. J. Dollimore, cited in S. Bennett, *Performing Nostalgia: Shifting Shakespeare and the Contemporary Past* (London: Routledge, 1996), p. 1.
25. Bennett, *Performing Nostalgia*, pp. 1–2.
26. Marowitz, *Recycling Shakespeare*, p. ix.
27. Kennedy, *Looking at Shakespeare*, p. 133.
28. J. Gielgud, cited in T. Cole and H. Krich Chinoy (eds.), *Directors on Directing: A Source Book of Modern Theatre*, 2nd edn (London: Peter Owen, 1964), p. 406.
29. Gielgud, in ibid., p. 407.
30. M. Shaw, cited in 'Avis, Max and Philip on Theatre Workshop', undated interview transcript, Theatre Royal Stratford East Archive.
31. J. Littlewood, programme note, Theatre Royal Stratford East Archive.
32. Callaghan, 'Shakespeare at the Fun Palace', p. 115.
33. Kennedy, *Looking at Shakespeare*, pp. 109–10.
34. H. Goorney, *The Theatre Workshop Story* (London: Methuen, 1981), p. 167.
35. H. Goorney, 'Littlewood in Rehearsal', *Tulane Drama Review*, Vol. 11, No. 2 (Winter 1966), pp. 102–3, p. 102.
36. J. Littlewood, cited in Goorney, *The Theatre Workshop Story*, p. 130.
37. C. Goodwin and T. Milne, 'Working with Joan', *Encore*, Vol. 7, No. 4 (July–August 1960), pp. 9–20, p. 16.
38. L. Olivier, cited in Cole and Krich Chinoy, *Directors on Directing*, p. 412.
39. Goodwin and Milne, 'Working with Joan', p. 14.
40. Worthen, *Shakespeare and the Authority of Performance*, p. 8, original emphasis.
41. M. Shaw, cited in 'Avis, Max and Philip on Theatre Workshop'.
42. See Goorney, 'Littlewood in Rehearsal', p. 102.
43. Ibid.

44. Kennedy, *Looking at Shakespeare*, p. 5.
45. Ibid., p. 43.
46. K. Tynan, *Curtains: Selections from the Drama Criticism and Related Writing* (London: Longmans, 1961), p. 82.
47. Anon., 'Arden of Faversham', *The Times*, 29 September 1954, p. 2.
48. Callaghan, 'Shakespeare at the Fun Palace', p. 100.
49. See J. Weeks, *Coming Out: Homosexual Politics in Britain from the Nineteenth Century to the Present* (London: Quartet Books, 1977).
50. Anon., 'Richard II at the Old Vic', *The Stage*, 20 January 1955, p. 10.
51. Schafer, *MsDirecting Shakespeare*, p. 166.
52. R. Bolam, '*Richard II*: Shakespeare and the Languages of the Stage', in M. Hattaway (ed.), *The Cambridge Companion to Shakespeare's History Plays* (Cambridge: Cambridge University Press, 2002), pp. 141–57, p. 147.
53. N. Marshall, *The Producer and the Play*, 2nd edn (London: Davis-Poynter, 1975), pp. 299–30.
54. Ibid.
55. K. Tynan, 'Pair of Kings', *Observer*, 23 January 1955, p. 11.
56. Several versions of the poem appeared during Richard II's reign and Littlewood dates the extract she included to 1394.
57. Extract from William Langland's poem 'Vision of Piers Ploughman' in the programme for Richard II, Theatre Royal Stratford East Archive.
58. Goorney, *The Theatre Workshop Story*, p. 101.
59. Schafer, *MsDirecting Shakespeare*, pp. 164–5.
60. Marshall, *The Producer and the Play*, p. 300.
61. Tynan, 'Pair of Kings', p. 11.
62. F. Granville Barker, 'Richard II', *Plays and Players*, Vol. 2, No. 6 (March 1955), p. 20.
63. See interviews with J. Jones, G. Ayres and M. Melvin at the www.bl.uk/projects/theatre archive.
64. H. Hobson, 'Richard II', *Sunday Times*, 23 January 1955, p. 11.
65. J. Littlewood, cited in J. Corbett, 'Theatre Workshop: A British People's Theatre', *Meanjin*, Vol. 18 (September 1959), pp. 327–33, p. 330.
66. J. C. Trewin, 'The World of the Theatre', *Illustrated London News*, 29 January 1955, p. 192.
67. E. MacColl, cited in J. Lea Goodman, 'Joan Littlewood and Her Theatre Workshop', unpublished PhD thesis, New York University, 1975, p. 70.
68. Goorney, *The Theatre Workshop Story*, p. 101.
69. Ibid.
70. Ibid., pp. 93–4.
71. Anon., 'Edward II', *The Times*, 20 April 1956, p. 3.

72. M.C., 'Edward II', *New Statesman*, 28 April 1956, p. 451.
73. Roger Planchon also developed this technique for his productions of the classics at the Théâtre de la cité in Villeurbanne.
74. Littlewood, *Joan's Book*, p. 467.
75. D. Callaghan, 'The Terms of Gender: "Gay" and "Feminist" Edward II', in A. Oz (ed.), *Marlowe: Contemporary Critical Essays* (Basingstoke: Palgrave Macmillan, 2003), pp. 182–99, p. 183.
76. Flyer for *Edward II*, Theatre Royal Stratford East Archive.
77. C. Barker, 'Joan Littlewood', in A. Hodge (ed.), *Twentieth Century Actor Training* (London: Routledge, 2000), pp. 113–28, p. 121.
78. P. Squire, 'Edward the Second', *Plays and Players*, Vol. 3, No. 8 (May 1956), pp. 22–3, p. 23.
79. M.C., 'Edward II', p. 451.
80. C. Marlowe, *The Complete Plays* (London: Penguin, 1969), p. 460.
81. Anon., 'Edward II', p. 3.
82. A.V.C., 'Edward II', *Spectator*, 27 April 1956, p. 580.
83. Philip Hartley's review is quoted in 'Theatre Workshop: A British People's Theatre', a promotional brochure, Theatre Royal Stratford East Archive.
84. Worthen, *Shakespeare and the Authority of Performance*, p. 67.
85. Ibid., p. 61.
86. Gielgud, cited in Cole and Krich Chinoy, *Directors on Directing*, p. 406.
87. M. Webster, cited in ibid., pp. 419–20.
88. F. Granville Barker, 'Volpone', *Plays and Players*, Vol. 2, No. 7 (April 1955), p. 20.
89. Raffles, 'Theatre Workshop: A British People's Theatre', p. 172.
90. F. Granville Barker, 'Volpone', p. 20.
91. Cited in Raffles, 'Theatre Workshop: A British People's Theatre', promotional brochure, Theatre Royal Stratford East Archive.
92. Goorney, *The Theatre Workshop Story*, pp. 120–1.
93. A. Alvarez, 'The Price of Period', *New Statesman*, 9 July 1960, p. 46.
94. Ibid.
95. For a discussion on Littlewood's attitude to Ben Jonson and the critical response to her productions of Ben Jonson's plays see E. Schafer, 'Daughters of Ben', in R. Cave, E. Schafer and B. Wolland (eds.), *Ben Jonson and Theatre* (London: Routledge, 1999), pp. 154–78, pp. 160–6.
96. L. Gordon Smith, 'The Dutch Courtesan', *Plays and Players*, Vol. 6, No. 9 (June 1959), p. 15.
97. See A. Brien, 'Sophistication', *Spectator*, 1 May 1959, p. 616; and G. Smith, 'The Dutch Courtesan', p. 15.
98. Littlewood, programme note, Theatre Royal Stratford East Archive.

99. Littlewood, programme note, Theatre Royal Stratford East Archive.
100. A. Alvarez, 'The Dutch Courtesan', *New Statesman* (2 May 1959), p. 607.
101. Anon., 'The Dutch Courtesan', *The Times*, 24 February 1954, p. 12.
102. Littlewood, *Joan's Book*, p. 479.
103. Ibid., p. 480.
104. A. Sinfield, '*Macbeth*: History, Ideology, and Intellectuals', in A. Sinfield, *Faultlines: Cultural Materialism and the Politics of Dissident Reading* (Oxford: Clarendon Press, 1992), pp. 95–108, p. 98.
105. Raffles, 'Theatre Workshop: A British People's Theatre', in Hobson, *International Theatre Annual*, p. 178.
106. See T. C. Worsley, 'Wild Attire', *New Statesman*, 14 September 1957, p. 314; and Littlewood, *Joan's Book*, p. 488.
107. Littlewood, programme note, Theatre Royal Stratford East Archive.
108. J. Kott, *Shakespeare, Our Contemporary*, translated by Boleslaw Taborski (London: Methuen, 1965), p. 68.
109. Littlewood, *Joan's Book*, p. 480.
110. Schafer, *MsDirecting Shakespeare*, pp. 151–2.
111. M. Heinemann, 'How Brecht Read Shakespeare', in J. Dollimore and A. Sinfield (eds.), *Political Shakespeare: New Essays in Cultural Materialism* (Manchester: Manchester University Press, 1985), pp. 226–54, p. 213, original emphasis.
112. Anon., 'A Life-Size Macbeth', *The Times*, 4 September 1957, p. 3.
113. Marshall, *The Producer and the Play*, p. 299.
114. Sinfield, '*Macbeth*: History, Ideology, and Intellectuals', p. 99.
115. Schafer, *MsDirecting Shakespeare*, p. 150.
116. Raffles, 'Theatre Workshop: A British People's Theatre', in Hobson, *International Theatre Annual*, p. 178.
117. Goorney, *The Theatre Workshop Story*, p. 154.
118. See Anon., 'A Life-Size Macbeth', p. 3; and C. Brahms, 'Taking the Mickey out of Macbeth', *Plays and Players*, Vol. 5, No. 1 (October 1957), p. 13.
119. D. Watt, 'The Relapse', *Spectator*, 13 September 1957, p. 342.
120. Anon., 'A Life-Size Macbeth', p. 3.
121. Chambers, *Inside the Royal Shakespeare Company*, p. 33. Littlewood recalled that she declined the invitation after disagreements over casting (see Littlewood, *Joan's Book*, pp. 633–5).
122. Anon., item from *Reynolds News*, Theatre Royal Stratford East Archive, undated.
123. J. C. Bulman, 'Henry IV, Parts I and 2', in M. Hattaway (ed.), *Shakespeare's History Plays* (Cambridge: Cambridge University Press, 2002), pp. 158–76, p. 169.

124. S. Trussler, 'Edinburgh Drama 1964', *Plays and Players*, Vol. 12, No. 1 (October 1964), pp. 43–4, p. 43.
125. Anon., 'Scrambled Shakespeare', *The Times*, 18 August 1964, p. 11.
126. C. Graves, 'Shakespeare in the Oblong', *Scotsman*, 18 August 1964, p. 7.
127. E. Bradbury, 'Falstaff as a Lancashire Comedian', *Yorkshire Post*, 25 August 1964, p. 5.
128. Bulman, 'Henry IV, Parts I and 2', p. 166.
129. S. Greenblatt, 'Invisible Bullets: Renaissance Authority and Its Subversion, *Henry IV* and *Henry V*', in J. Dollimore and A. Sinfield (eds.), *Political Shakespeare: New Essays in Cultural Materialism* (Manchester: Manchester University Press, 1985), pp. 18–47, p. 36.
130. J. Russell Brown, 'Three Kinds of Shakespeare', *Shakespeare Survey*, Vol. 18 (1965), pp. 147–56, p. 153.
131. Ibid., original emphasis.
132. Ibid., p. 154.
133. Ibid.
134. Kennedy, *Looking at Shakespeare*, p. 179.
135. J. Littlewood, cited in Goorney, *The Theatre Workshop Story*, pp. 130–1.
136. J. Littlewood, cited in ibid., p. 130.
137. K. Tynan, *Tynan Right and Left: Plays, Films, People, Places and Events* (London: Longmans, 1967), p. 317.
138. Sir John Falstaff was originally Sir John Old-lad-of-the-Castle, a travesty of the puritanical Lord Chamberlain's respected ancestor. The Castle was a notorious brothel in Southwark.
139. J. Littlewood, 'Henry IV', *Edinburgh International Festival Souvenir Programme* (1964), p. 44.
140. Tynan, *Tynan Right and Left*, p. 319.
141. I am indebted to Murray Melvin for drawing this stage business to my attention.
142. R. Bryden, 'Within the Fringe', *New Statesman*, 28 August 1964, p. 291.
143. Colin Chambers has recently referred to the 'important if unacknowledged' influence of Littlewood's classic productions on the Royal Shakespeare Company in a book review in *Studies in Theatre and Performance*, Vol. 27, No. 3 (2007), pp. 308–10, p. 309. He also makes reference to Littlewood's influence on Peter Hall in *Inside the Royal Shakespeare Company*, p. 12.
144. K. Tynan, *Tynan on Theatre* (London: Pelican, 1964), p. 98.

145. For instance, John Bury designed the ambitious *Wars of the Roses* history plays cycle and descriptions of that production illuminate the debt owed to Littlewood and to Bury's earlier collaborations. 'Using then unusual materials of steel and wire-mesh (the tilted floor, in particular, was to be much copied by others), the team conjured up a dark, smoky world of ferocious tribal energy, constantly making the audience reassess the myths of history and kingship'. A. Strachan, 'Obituary: John Bury', *Independent*, 17 November 2000, p. 6.

Chapter 4

1. J. Littlewood, letter to G. Raffles, 9 March 1947, Michael Barker Collection, Harry Ransom Humanities Research Center, the University of Texas at Austin.
2. Ibid.
3. R. Williams, cited in J. Kirk, *Twentieth-Century Writing and the British Working Class* (Cardiff: University of Wales Press, 2003), p. 11.
4. K. Roberts, *The Working Class* (London: Longman, 1978), p. 73.
5. J. Bourke, *Working-Class Cultures in Britain 1890–1960* (London: Routledge, 1994), p. 137.
6. Ibid., pp. 148–9.
7. Ibid., p. 137.
8. Ibid.
9. M. Young and P. Willmott, *Family and Kinship in East London*, revised edn (Harmondsworth: Penguin, 1962).
10. See S. Lacey, *British Realist Theatre: The New Wave and Its Context* (London: Routledge, 1995); L. Kitchin, *Mid-century Drama* (London: Faber and Faber, 1960); and J. Russell Taylor, *Anger and After: A Survey of the New British Drama*, 2nd edn (London: Methuen, 1969).
11. Lacey, *British Realist Theatre*, p. 2.
12. I. Haywood, *Working-Class Fiction: From Chartism to Trainspotting* (Plymouth: Northcote, 1997), p. 94.
13. G. Day, *Community and Everyday Life* (London: Routledge, 2006), p. 65.
14. A. Higson, 'Space, Place, Spectacle: Landscape and Townscape in the "Kitchen Sink" Film', in A. Higson (ed.), *Dissolving Views: Key Writings on British Cinema* (London: Cassell, 1996), pp. 133–56, p. 137.
15. Ibid., p. 137, original emphases.
16. T. Lovell, 'Landscapes and Stories in 1960s British Realism', in Higson, *Dissolving Views*, pp. 157–77, p. 170.
17. J. Hill, *Sex, Class and Realism: British Cinema 1956–1963* (London: British Film Institute, 1986), p. 143.

18. See A. Medhurst, 'If Anywhere: Class Identifications and Cultural Studies Academics', in S. R. Munt (ed.), *Cultural Studies and the Working Class: Subject to Change* (London: Cassell, 2000), pp. 19–35.
19. Kirk, *Twentieth-Century Writing and the British Working Class*, p. 8.
20. Lacey, *British Realist Theatre*, p. 77.
21. D. Heddon, *Autobiography and Performance* (Basingstoke: Palgrave, 2008), p. 20.
22. Programme for *You Won't Always Be on Top*, Theatre Royal Stratford East Archive.
23. H. Goorney, *The Theatre Workshop Story* (London: Methuen, 1981), p. 114.
24. Ibid., p. 121.
25. B. Harker, *Class Act: The Cultural and Political Life of Ewan MacColl* (London: Pluto, 2007), p. 93.
26. J. Littlewood, undated manuscript, Michael Barker Collection, Harry Ransom Humanities Research Center, the University of Texas at Austin.
27. J. Kirk, *Class, Culture and Social Change: On the Trail of the Working Class* (Basingstoke: Palgrave Macmillan, 2007), p. 14.
28. Lacey, *British Realist Theatre*, p. 78.
29. E. MacColl, *Johnny Noble*, in H. Goorney and E. MacColl (eds.), *Agit-Prop to Theatre Workshop: Political Playscripts 1930–1950* (Manchester: Manchester University Press, 1986), pp. 35–72, p. 37.
30. Ibid., pp. 64–6.
31. R. Leach, *Theatre Workshop: Joan Littlewood and the Making of Modern British Theatre* (Exeter: University of Exeter Press, 2006), p. 67.
32. Programme note for *Landscape with Chimneys*, Ewan MacColl and Peggy Seeger Archive, Ruskin College, Oxford.
33. A. Sked and C. Cook, *Post-war Britain: A Political History*, 2nd edn (London: Penguin, 1984), p. 46.
34. Haywood, *Working-Class Fiction*, p. 107.
35. Unpublished *Landscape with Chimneys* script, Ewan MacColl and Peggy Seeger Archive, Ruskin College, Oxford, p. 23.
36. Ibid., p. 3.
37. Ibid.
38. C. D. Heriot, reader's report, 28 December 1950, Lord Chamberlain's Collection, British Library.
39. Twm O'R Nant, 'Acting Has Improved, but Welsh Drama Still Non-existent', *Western Mail and South Wales News*, 9 January 1951, p. 4.
40. Anon., 'Fascinating Drama of Dockland', *Stratford Express*, 6 March 1953, p. 17.

41. Anon., 'Paradise Street', *The Stage*, 5 March 1953, p. 10.
42. Hill, *Sex, Class and Realism*, p. 154.
43. Lovell, 'Landscapes and Stories in 1960s British Realism', p. 160, original emphasis.
44. H. Beynon, 'Images of Labour/Images of Class', in S. Rowbotham and H. Beynon (eds.), *Looking at Class: Film, Television and the Working Class in Britain* (London: Rivers Oram Press, 2001), pp. 25–40, p. 25.
45. Beynon, 'Images of Labour/Images of Class', p. 27.
46. In *Joan's Book: Joan Littlewood's Peculiar History as She Tells It* (London: Methuen, 1994), Littlewood attributes the play to Gerry Raffles but the version submitted to the Lord Chamberlain cites them both as authors and I will use this submission as the reliable source.
47. Day, *Community and Everyday Life*, p. 77.
48. M. Simpson, *Male Impersonators: Men Performing Masculinity* (New York: Routledge, 1994), p. 266.
49. G. Orwell, 'Down the Mine', in G. Orwell, *Inside the Whale and Other Essays* (London: Penguin, 1957), pp. 51–62, p. 51.
50. Ibid., p. 62.
51. G. Greene, cited in P. Stead, *Film and the Working Class: The Feature Film in British and American Society* (London: Routledge, 1989), p. 117.
52. In fact, compensation awarded by the Coal Board helped kick-start Theatre Workshop after the War.
53. Littlewood, *Joan's Book*, p. 417.
54. Ibid., p. 418.
55. Ibid., p. 419.
56. H. Greene, cited in Goorney, *The Theatre Workshop Story*, p. 87.
57. *The Long Shift* manuscript, the Lord Chamberlain's Collection, LCP1951/49, British Library, p. 1.
58. M. Heinemann, 'How Brecht Read Shakespeare', in J. Dollimore and A. Sinfield (eds.), *Political Shakespeare: New Essays in Cultural Materialism* (Manchester: Manchester University Press, 1985), p. 224.
59. *The Long Shift* manuscript, p. 7.
60. Ibid., p. 27.
61. C. Vaught and D. L. Smith, 'Incorporation and Mechanical Solidarity in the Underground Coal Mine', in D. Harper and H. M. Lawson (eds.), *The Cultural Study of Work* (Oxford: Rowman and Littlefield, 2003), pp. 96–115, p. 99.
62. *The Long Shift* manuscript, p. 37.
63. Ibid.
64. R. McKibbin, *The Ideologies of Class: Social Relations in Britain 1880–1950* (Oxford: Oxford University Press, 1991), p. 164.

65. M. Leighton, *Men at Work* (London: Jill Norman, 1981), p. 18.
66. *The Long Shift* manuscript, p. 18.
67. N. Dennis, F. Henriques and C. Slaughter, *Coal Is Our Life: An Analysis of a Yorkshire Mining Community*, 2nd edn (London: Tavistock Publications, 1976).
68. Haywood, *Working-Class Fiction*, p. 120.
69. Anon., 'Lights and Music: Two Plays of Our Time', *South Wales Evening* Post, 13 November 1951, p. 3.
70. Littlewood, *Joan's Book*, p. 419.
71. Goorney, *The Theatre Workshop Story*, p. 106.
72. Anon., 'Introduction' to H. Chapman, *You Won't Always Be on Top* (London: Methuen, 1965), unpaginated.
73. According to Littlewood, Chapman had been inspired by the novel and was intimately acquainted with it having been involved in its reissue in 1955. See Littlewood, *Joan's Book*, p. 494.
74. M. Myson, 'Workshop Well on the Job', undated cutting from *Daily Worker*, Theatre Royal Stratford East Archive.
75. G. Day, 'Highs and Lows: The Problem of "Culture" in *The Ragged Trousered Philanthropists*', in H. G. Klaus and S. Knight (eds.), *British Industrial Fictions* (Cardiff: University of Wales Press, 2000), pp. 71–83, p. 71.
76. Chapman, *You Won't Always Be on Top*, p. 57.
77. Ibid., p. 62.
78. Ibid., p. 61–3.
79. Ibid., p. 81.
80. K. Tynan, 'At the Theatre', *Observer*, 13 October 1957, p. 12.
81. C. D. Heriot, reader's report for *You Won't Always Be on Top*, 4 October 1957, Lord Chamberlain's Collection, British Library.
82. L. Gordon Smith, 'You Won't Always Be on Top', *Plays and Players*, Vol. 5, No. 2 (November 1957), p. 17.
83. J. Littlewood, programme note for *Arden of Faversham* tour of Sweden, Theatre Royal Stratford East Archive.
84. Vaught and Smith, 'Incorporation and Mechanical Solidarity in the Underground Coal Mine', p. 99.
85. A. Easthope, *What a Man's Gotta Do: The Masculine Myth in Popular Culture* (London: Routledge, 1990), p. 88.
86. Anon., programme for *You Won't Always Be on Top*, Theatre Royal Stratford East Archive.
87. Tynan, 'At the Theatre', p. 12.
88. Anon., 'You Won't Always Be on Top', *The Stage*, 17 October 1957, p. 12.

89. C. Wildman, 'Interview with Carl Wildman', *Talking of Theatre*, BBC Radio, 24 June 1958, British Library Sound Archive.
90. Chapman, *You Won't Always Be on Top*, p. 34.
91. Goorney, *The Theatre Workshop Story*, p. 106.
92. E. Glinert, *East End Chronicles* (London: Allen Lane, 2005), p. 236.
93. A copy of the play is available in the Lord Chamberlain's Collection, LCP1954/8, British Library.
94. R. Findlater, 'That's the Place for You!', *Tribune*, 12 February 1954, page unknown.
95. *Van Call* programme, Theatre Royal Stratford East Archive.
96. Anon., 'Theatre Workshop to Present Young Stratford Author's Play', *Stratford Express*, 15 January 1954, page unknown.
97. Anon., 'Van Call', *The Times*, 3 February 1954, p. 10.
98. Findlater, 'That's the Place for You!', page unknown.
99. D. Douglas, 'Crumbs from a Tasty Cake', Theatre Royal Stratford East Archive; and T.H.B., 'A Play about Stratford at the Theatre Royal', *Stratford Express*, 3 February 1954, p. 10.
100. Cited in Goorney, *The Theatre Workshop Story*, p. 100.
101. Littlewood, *Joan's Book*, p. 559.
102. S. Lewis, *Sparrers Can't Sing* (London: Evans Brothers, 1961), p. 14.
103. Day, *Community and Everyday Life*, p. 68.
104. Glinert, *East End Chronicles*, p. 244.
105. Day, *Community and Everyday Life*, p. 64.
106. Lewis, *Sparrers Can't Sing*, p. 46.
107. A. Brien, 'Casey's Court Rebuilt', *Spectator*, 26 August 1960, p. 309.
108. Lewis, *Sparrers Can't Sing*, p. 28.
109. Ibid., p. 53.
110. Ibid., pp. 20 and 53.
111. Harold Macmillan speaking at a Conservative rally in Bedford, 20 July 1957, see http://news.bbc.co.uk/onthisday/hi/dates/stories/july/20/newsid_3728000/3728225.stm; and Lewis, *Sparrers Can't Sing*, p. 14.
112. Programme note for *Sparrers Can't Sing*, Theatre Royal Stratford East Archive.
113. Anon., 'Stepney Sparrers Can't Sing', *The Times*, 25 August 1960, p. 12.
114. Brien, 'Casey's Court Rebuilt', p. 309.
115. N. Lewis, 'Without Nostalgia', *New Statesman*, 3 September 1960, p. 303; D.F.B., 'Sparrers Can't Sing', *The Stage*, 6 April 1961, p. 15; and M.G., 'This is East End on Any Friday', *News Chronicle*, 25 August 1960, page unknown.
116. R. Murphy, *Sixties British Cinema* (London: British Film Institute, 1992), p. 241.

117. Brien, 'Casey's Court Rebuilt', p. 309.
118. Anon., 'Stepney Sparrers Can't Sing', p. 12.
119. C. D. Heriot, reader's report for *Sparrers Can't Sing*, 19 August 1960, Lord Chamberlain's Collection, British Library.
120. R. Bryden, 'Up West', *New Statesman*, 13 March 1964, p. 423.
121. Hill, *Sex, Class and Realism*, p. 136.

Chapter 5

1. C. Barker, cited in J. Favre, 'Did Clive Barker Write *The Hostage?*', *New Theatre Quarterly*, Vol. 23, No. 4 (November 2007), pp. 326–30, p. 327.
2. N. Holdsworth, *Joan Littlewood* (London: Routledge, 2006), p. 61, original emphasis.
3. M. Bakhtin, *Rabelais and His World*, translated by Helene Iswolsky (London: The MIT press, 1968), p. 3.
4. S. Lacey, *British Realist Theatre: The New Wave and Its Context* (London: Routledge, 1995), p. 124.
5. Ibid., p. 110.
6. In November 1967 she even produced *The Marie Lloyd Story* by Daniel Farson and Harry Moore, which offered a theatrical treatment of one of music hall's most notorious stars.
7. J. Harrop, 'The Last Laugh: Comedy as a Political Touchstone in Britain from "The Entertainer" to "Comedians"', *Theatre Journal*, Vol. 32, No. 1 (March 1980), pp. 5–16, p. 6.
8. Lacey, *British Realist Theatre*, p. 136.
9. J. Storey, *An Introduction to Cultural Theory and Popular Culture* (Hemel Hempstead: Harvester Wheatsheaf, 1993), p. 202.
10. B. Kershaw, *The Politics of Performance: Radical Theatre as Cultural Intervention* (London: Routledge, 1992), p. 153.
11. R. Jenkins, *Pierre Bourdieu* (London, Routledge, 1992), p. 138.
12. I. Haywood, *Working-Class Fiction: From Chartism to Trainspotting* (Plymouth: Northcote, 1997), p. 114.
13. A. Brien, 'Interview with Joan Littlewood', *Vogue*, 15 September 1964, page unknown.
14. See C. Murray, *Twentieth-Century Irish Drama: Mirror Up to Nation* (Syracuse, NY: Syracuse University Press, 2000), p. 154.
15. M. Foucault, *Discipline and Punish: The Birth of the Prison*, translated by Alan Sheridan (London: Allen Lane, 1977).
16. The Abolition of the Death Penalty Act was finally passed in 1965 on a five-year trial basis and, despite widespread calls for its reinstatement, has remained as a permanent Act since 1969. The last execution in Britain took place in 1964.

17. See B. Behan, 'A Celebrated Interview', in E. H. Mikhail (ed.), *Brendan Behan: Interviews and Recollections*, 2 vols. (London: Macmillan, 1982), Vol. I, pp. 76–9.
18. A. Matheson Cain, 'Death's Jest Book', in E. H. Mikhail (ed.), *The Art of Brendan Behan* (London: Vision Press, 1979), pp. 75–6, p. 75.
19. Programme note for the Theatre Royal Production of *The Quare Fellow*, Theatre Royal Stratford East Archive.
20. J. Brannigan, 'Form and Ethics in the Comedies of Brendan Behan', in Mary Luckhurst (ed.), *A Companion to Modern British and Irish Drama 1880–2005* (Oxford: Blackwell, 2006), pp. 247–57, p. 251.
21. B. Behan, *Behan: The Complete Plays* (London: Methuen, 1978), p. 99.
22. H.G.M., 'The Quare Fellow', *Theatre World*, Vol. 52, No. 378 (July 1956), p. 5; K. Tynan, 'The End of the Noose', *Observer*, 27 May 1956, p. 11; and M. Richardson, 'The Quare Fellow', *New Statesman*, 2 June 1956, p. 624.
23. Tynan, 'The End of the Noose', p. 11.
24. Ibid.
25. H. Goorney, *The Theatre Workshop Story* (London: Methuen, 1981), p. 105.
26. Behan, *Behan: The Complete Plays*, p. 75.
27. Ibid., pp. 120–1.
28. Ibid., p. 121.
29. V. Trowbridge, 'Report on *The Quare Fellow*', Lord Chamberlain's Collection, the British Library, 2 May 1956.
30. Tynan, 'The End of the Noose', p. 11.
31. Behan, *Behan: The Complete Plays*, p. 40.
32. Ibid., p. 39.
33. Brannigan, 'Form and Ethics in the Comedies of Brendan Behan', p. 251.
34. D. Rosenthal, 'Borstal Boy', *Independent on Sunday*, 1 February 2004, p. 6.
35. Cited in Goorney, *The Theatre Workshop Story* (London: Methuen, 1981), p. 110. A slightly revised version of this story appears in J. Littlewood, *Joan's Book: Joan Littlewood's Peculiar History as She Tells It* (London: Methuen, 1994), p. 529.
36. See Littlewood, *Joan's Book*, pp. 520 and 531. Also see Murray, *Twentieth-Century Irish Drama*, pp. 156–7.
37. *The Hostage* was so impressive in Paris that Jean-Louis Barrault decided to stage his own version in 1962 with an all-star cast.
38. See Favre, 'Did Clive Barker Write *The Hostage*?', p. 330.
39. Littlewood, *Joan's Book*, p. 529.

40. T. Rattigan, undated letter from Terence Rattigan, Michael Barker Collection, Harry Ransom Humanities Research Center, the University of Texas at Austin.
41. H. Hobson, 'Triumph at Stratford East', *Sunday Times*, 19 October 1958, p. 21.
42. D. Foley, 'His London Appearances', in Mikhail, *Brendan Behan*, Vol. I, pp. 136–41, p. 138.
43. N. Ridout, *Stage Fright, Animals and Other Theatrical Problems* (Cambridge: Cambridge University Press, 2006), p. 135.
44. Behan, *Behan: The Complete Plays*, p. 152.
45. Goorney, *The Theatre Workshop Story*, p. 110.
46. K. Tynan, 'New Amalgam', *Observer*, 19 October 1958, p. 19.
47. L. Kitchin, *Mid-century Drama* (London: Faber and Faber, 1960), p. 23; and K. Tynan, *Tynan on Theatre* (London: Pelican, 1964), p. 89.
48. R. Brustein, 'Libido at Large', in Mikhail, *The Art of Brendan Behan*, pp. 128–30, p. 130; A. Brien, 'Political Pantomime', *Spectator*, 17 October 1958, p. 513.
49. T. MacIntyre, 'This Dying Lark', in Mikhail, *The Art of Brendan Behan*, pp. 63–7, p. 66; and cited in N. Grene, *The Politics of Irish Drama* (Cambridge: Cambridge University Press, 1999), p. 160.
50. Brannigan, 'Form and Ethics in the Comedies of Brendan Behan', p. 253.
51. Grene, *The Politics of Irish Drama*, p. 161.
52. Behan, *Behan: The Complete Plays*, p. 129.
53. R. Leach, *Theatre Workshop: Joan Littlewood and the Making of Modern British Theatre* (Exeter: University of Exeter Press, 2006), p. 154.
54. Without a clear script from Behan, Littlewood and her company struggled to find an appropriate ending to conclude this unruly production and it is possible that Littlewood remembered her work on Hans Clumberg's *Miracle at Verdun* when she proposed that Leslie should rise to his feet. I am grateful to June Favre for drawing this connection to my attention.
55. Grene, *The Politics of Irish Drama*, p. 165, original emphasis.
56. Lacey, *British Realist Theatre*, p. 79.
57. Programme note for the Theatre Royal Production of *The Hostage*, Theatre Royal Stratford East Archive. This statement was removed from the programme that accompanied the transfer of the production to Wyndham's Theatre.
58. A marked-up copy of *The Hostage* is held at the Harry Ransom Humanities Research Center, the University of Texas at Austin.
59. B. Nightingale, 'The Good Old Days', *New Statesman*, 9 June 1972, p. 801.

60. L. Gordon Smith, 'A Taste of Honey', *Plays and Players*, Vol. 5, No. 10 (July 1958), p. 15; K. Tynan, *Curtains: Selection from the Drama Criticism and Related Writing* (London: Longmans, 1961), p. 213; and A. Brien, 'First and Last Things', *Spectator*, 6 June 1958, p. 729.
61. Programme for *A Taste of Honey*, Theatre Royal Stratford East Archive.
62. K. Mellor, quoted during *A Taste of Honey*, Radio 4, 22 May 2008.
63. L. Anderson, 'A Taste of Honey', *Encore*, Vol. 5, No. 2 (July–August 1958), pp. 42–3, p. 42.
64. T. Lovell, 'Landscapes and Stories in 1960s British Realism', in A. Higson (ed.), *Dissolving Views: Key Writings on British Cinema* (London: Cassell, 1996) pp. 157–77, p. 175.
65. S. Delaney, *A Taste of Honey* (London: Methuen, 1959), p. 12.
66. Lovell, 'Landscapes and Stories in 1960s British Realism', p. 174.
67. Delaney, *A Taste of Honey* (1959) p. 85.
68. The film treatment of *A Taste of Honey* (dir. Tony Richardson) relied heavily on cameraman Walter Lassally's cinematography, which both captured and aestheticised the overwhelming presence of the Northern industrial landscape in the characters' lives.
69. A feature radically altered in Tony Richardson's film of *A Taste of Honey* (1961), which employs many location shots of Salford streets, the canal and the funfair.
70. Lacey, *British Realist Theatre*, p. 95.
71. D. Shellard, quoted during *A Taste of Honey*, Radio 4, 22 May 2008.
72. Gordon Smith, 'A Taste of Honey', p. 15.
73. J. Russell Taylor, *Anger and After: A Survey of the New British Drama*, 2nd edn (London: Methuen, 1969), p. 132.
74. Ibid., pp. 135–6.
75. Anon., 'At the Play', *Punch*, 11 February 1959, p. 235; and Brien, 'First and Last Things', p. 729.
76. F. Stephens, 'A Taste of Honey', *Theatre World*, Vol. 55, No. 410 (March 1959), pp. 7–8, p. 7; and Tynan, *Curtains*, p. 235.
77. T. C. Worsley, 'The Sweet Smell', *New Statesman*, 21 February 1959, p. 254.
78. Interestingly, there is still a tendency to erase the theatrical from discussions of Littlewood's production of *A Taste of Honey*. For instance, in a radio programme marking the fiftieth anniversary of the play, the focus was solely on the play's subject matter and documentary veracity.
79. Anon., 'Author's Two Manners', *The Times*, 11 February 1959, p. 3.
80. See also A. Patton, 'Jazz and Music-Hall Transgressions in Theatre Workshop's Production of *A Taste of Honey*', *New Theatre Quarterly*, Vol. 23, No. 4 (November 2007), pp. 331–6.

81. Goorney, *The Theatre Workshop Story*, p. 109.
82. Original line taken from Shelagh Delaney's original typed manuscript held at the Harry Ransom Humanities Research Center, the University of Texas at Austin, and the line as performed taken from Delaney, *A Taste of Honey* (1959), p. 7.
83. Gordon Smith, 'A Taste of Honey', p. 15; and Anderson, 'A Taste of Honey', p. 43.
84. A photographic montage of the original production can be found in *Theatre World*, Vol. 55, No. 411 (April 1959), pp. 13–15.
85. Goorney, *The Theatre Workshop Story*, p. 108.
86. Original line taken from Shelagh Delaney's original typed manuscript held at the Harry Ransom Humanities Research Center, the University of Texas at Austin, and the line as performed taken from Delaney, *A Taste of Honey* (1959), p. 7.
87. Delaney, *A Taste of Honey* (1959), p. 10.
88. T. C. Davis and T. Postlewait (eds.), *Theatricality* (Cambridge: Cambridge University Press, 2003), p. 6.
89. Anderson, 'A Taste of Honey', p. 43.
90. P. Auslander, *Liveness: Performance in a Mediatized Culture* (London: Routledge, 1999), pp. 17–18.
91. See M. Melvin discussing this antidote to television in Patton, 'Jazz and Music-Hall Transgressions', p. 335.
92. R. Hewison, *In Anger: Culture in the Cold War 1945–60* (London: Methuen, 1988), p. 134; and Anderson, 'A Taste of Honey', p. 43.
93. J. Osborne, *Look Back in Anger and Other Plays: Collected Plays*, Vol. I (London: Faber and Faber, 1993), p. 13.
94. Delaney, *A Taste of Honey* (1959), p. 13.
95. M. Coveney, 'Lionel Bart: Appetite for Destruction', *Independent*, 31 August 2006, p. 15.
96. Goorney, *The Theatre Workshop Story*, p. 114.
97. G. Steadman-Jones, cited in C. Brunsdon, *London in Cinema: The Cinematic City since 1945* (London: BFI, 2007), p. 165.
98. Littlewood, *Joan's Book*, pp. 646–7.
99. T. Vallance, 'Obituary: Lionel Bart', *Independent*, 5 April 1999, p. 6.
100. A. Brien, 'Anyfing Goes', *Spectator*, 27 February 1959, p. 289.
101. Littlewood, *Joan's Book*, p. 540.
102. J. Littlewood, 'Introduction', unpaginated, in F. Norman, *Fings Ain't Wot They Used T'Be* (London: Samuel French, 1960).
103. Cited on eastlondonhistory.com (accessed 23 February 2009).

104. J. C. Trewin, 'Putting It Differently', *Illustrated London News*, 28 February 1959, p. 358; and anon., 'Tealeaves and Tearaways', *The Times*, 18 February 1959, p. 5.
105. Littlewood, *Joan's Book*, p. 542. Interestingly, the phrase 'bang to rights' is attributed to the title of Norman's memoir.
106. Norman, *Fings Ain't Wot They Used T'Be*, p. 11.
107. Ibid., p. 20.
108. Ibid., pp. 46–50.
109. C. Brahms, 'Fings Ain't Wot They Used T'be', *Plays and Players*, Vol. 6, No. 7 (April 1959), p. 13.
110. Trewin, 'Putting It Differently', p. 358; and T. C. Worsley, 'Fings Ain't Wot They Used T'Be', *New Statesman*, 28 February 1959, p. 291.
111. Goorney, *The Theatre Workshop Story*, pp. 114–15.
112. Cited on eastlondonhistory.com (accessed 23 February 2009).
113. Coveney, 'Lionel Bart: Appetite for Destruction', p. 15.
114. Norman, *Fings Ain't Wot They Used T'Be*, p. 11.
115. Programme for *Fings Ain't Wot They Used T'Be*, Theatre Royal Stratford East Archive.
116. J. McGuigan, *Cultural Populism* (London: Routledge, 1992), original emphasis.
117. A. Pryce-Jones, 'Uplift and Downfall', *Observer*, 25 October 1959, p. 25.
118. R. Bryden, 'Up West', *New Statesman*, 13 March 1964, p. 423.
119. H. Leonard, 'A Kayf Up West', *Plays and Players*, Vol. 11, No. 8 (May 1964), pp. 41–2, p. 42.
120. See E. W. Cooney, 'High Flats in Local Authority Housing in England and Wales since 1945', in A. Sutcliffe (ed.), *Multi-storey Living: The British Working-Class Experience* (London: Croom Helm, 1974), pp. 151–80.
121. J. Littlewood, transcript of J. Littlewood interviewed by R. Sugarman, 13 January 1971, p. 5. I am grateful to Clive Barker for providing me with a transcript of this interview.
122. See Cooney, 'High Flats in Local Authority Housing', p. 168.
123. Littlewood, interviewed by Robert Sugarman, p. 5.
124. For details on the theatrical genealogy see G. Dorris, '*The Projector*, *The Mock Mason* and Miss Littlewood', *Modern Drama*, Vol. 16, No. 3 (1973), pp. 265–8.
125. J. W. Lambert, 'Raising the Roof', *Sunday Times*, 6 December 1970, p. 32.
126. Programme for *The Projector*, Theatre Royal Stratford East Archive.

127. I. Wardle, 'Dutch Lampoon and Music-Hall', *The Times*, 3 December 1970, p. 13.
128. R. Bryden, 'Mystery of Ronan Point', *Observer*, 6 December 1970, p. 25.
129. J. Mortimer, 'Nostalgia in the Mud', *Observer*, 2 April 1972, p. 27; H. Hobson, 'The Littlewood Touch', *Sunday Times*, 2 April 1972, p. 29; and I. Wardle, 'Superb Return by Miss Littlewood', *The Times*, 29 March 1972, p. 13.

Chapter 6

1. Between 1960 and 1973, Littlewood produced less than twenty-five shows at the Theatre Royal. Although Littlewood's plans for a Fun Palace centred on the East End of London, she also pursued the possibility of seeing her plans realised in Glasgow, Liverpool and New York.
2. One of the most famous settlement houses was cofounded in 1889 by Jane Addams and Ellen Gates Starr in Chicago. Named Hull House, over the years it developed a library, employment centre, gymnasium, swimming pool, kitchen and art gallery and held night classes in art, music and drama, as well as a kindergarten and clubs for older children.
3. For a detailed consideration of Cedric Price and his work, including the Fun Palace, see S. Mathews, *From Agit-Prop to Free Space: The Architecture of Cedric Price* (London: Black Dog, 2007).
4. For a selection of these media reports see H. Fielding, 'Nothing but Fun on the Isle of Dogs', *Daily Herald*, 30 April 1963, page unknown; H. Atkins, 'Something New: Just for Fun', *Daily Telegraph*, 6 June 1963, page unknown; and T. Driberg, 'The New Age of Leisure', *Sunday Citizen* (June 1964).
5. Letter from Lord Ritchie-Calder, cited in S. Mathews, *From Agit-Prop to Free Space*, p. 141.
6. J. Carey (ed.), *The Faber Book of Utopias* (London: Faber, 1999), p. xi.
7. J. Littlewood, 'A Laboratory of Fun', *New Scientist*, Vol. 22, No. 391 (1964), pp. 428–33, p. 432.
8. Cited in Mathews, *From Agit-Prop to Free Space*, p. 70.
9. P. E. Tillinghast, 'Leisure: Old Patterns and New Problems', in S. Anderson (ed.), *Planning for Diversity and Choice: Possible Futures and Their Relations to the Man-Controlled Environment* (Cambridge, MA: The MIT Press, 1968), pp. 143–54, pp. 143–4.
10. M. L. Lobsinger, 'Cybernetic Theory and the Architecture of Performance: Cedric Price's Fun Palace', in S. Williams Goldhagen and R. Legault (eds.), *Anxious Modernisms: Experimentation in Post-war Architectural Culture* (Cambridge, MA: MIT Press, 2000), pp. 119–39, p. 129.

11. Ibid., p. 120.
12. The project took its name from TUC Resolution 42 passed in 1960, which recommended greater participation by the trade union movement in a broad base of cultural activities.
13. Invited by the local trades council to help with a trade union recruiting drive, Centre 42 held its first festival in Wellingborough during 1961 and the success of this event led to five more festivals in Nottingham, Leicester, Birmingham, Southall, Bristol and Hayes during 1962. Each festival followed a similar format of local art exhibitions, jazz concerts, dances, plays and poetry readings, alongside political lectures and meetings. There was also an ill-fated plan to establish a permanent base in London. Artists hoped that a building-based initiative would allow them to seize control of their own means of production and distribution away from the constraints of commercial management in favour of a direct relationship with the local community. In 1963, Centre 42 acquired a sixteen-year lease on the Victorian Round House in Camden. Unfortunately, fundraising efforts with the Arts Council and trade union movement proved futile and, forced to function through a commercial imperative, the Centre gradually fizzled out.
14. Cedric Price organised a forum to discuss the aims and objectives of Centre 42 at the ICA.
15. A. Wesker, 'Let Battle Commence!', in C. Marowitz, T. Milne and O. Hale (eds.), *The Encore Reader: A Chronicle of the New Drama* (London: Methuen, 1965), pp. 96–103, p. 98.
16. A. Wesker, *Fears of Fragmentation* (London: Jonathan Cape, 1970), p. 35. See also M. Arnold, *Culture and Anarchy* (Cambridge: Cambridge University Press, 1960); and F. R. Leavis, *Mass Civilisation and Minority Culture* (Cambridge: Minority Press, 1930).
17. See a debate between John McGrath and Arnold Wesker on this issue in John McGrath, *Naked Thoughts that Roam about: Reflections on Theatre*, ed. Nadine Holdsworth (London: Nick Hern, 2002), pp. 34–9.
18. R. Banham, 'People's Palaces', *New Statesman*, 7 August 1964, pp. 191–2, p. 191.
19. Littlewood, 'A Laboratory of Fun', p. 432.
20. Anon., 'Camden Pilot Project Report', Clive Barker Personal Archive (January 1965), p. 6.
21. Lobsinger, 'Cybernetic Theory and the Architecture of Performance', p. 119.
22. Mathews, *From Agit-Prop to Free Space*, p. 66.
23. B. Curtis, 'Archigram: "A Necessary Irritant"', in D. Crompton (ed.), *Concerning Archigram*, 4th edn (London: Archigram Archives, 2002), pp. 25–79, p. 60.

24. J. Littlewood, 'Theatre or Fun Palace?', promotional material, Theatre Royal Stratford East Archive.
25. Cited in B. N. Lewis, 'Fun Palace: Counter-blast to Boredom', *New Society*, 15 April 1965, pp. 8–11, p. 8.
26. Littlewood, 'A Laboratory of Fun', p. 432.
27. Ibid.
28. Anon., 'Camden Pilot Project Report', p. 5.
29. Banham, 'People's Palaces', p. 191.
30. Ibid.
31. See Lobsinger, 'Cybernetic Theory and the Architecture of Performance', pp. 130–2.
32. Banham, 'People's Palaces', p. 191.
33. See J. Addams, *Twenty Years at Hull-House* (New York: Macmillan, 1910); and J. L. Moreno, *The Theater of Spontaneity: An Introduction to Psychodrama* (Beacon, NY: Beacon House, 1947).
34. B. Anderson, *Imagined Communities: Reflections on the Origin and Spread of Nationalism*, revised and extended edn (London: Verso, 1991), p. 6.
35. Littlewood, 'A Laboratory of Fun', p. 432.
36. A. Read, *Theatre and Everyday Life: An Ethics of Performance* (London: Routledge, 1993), p. 1.
37. G. Raffles and J. Littlewood, 'Uses for Land Awaiting Redevelopment, 1968–1975', ACGB/34/68, Arts Council of England Archives.
38. J. Schechter (ed.), *Popular Theatre: A Sourcebook* (London: Routledge, 2003), p. 177.
39. J. Melvin, 'Cedric Price', *Guardian*, 15 August 2003, p. 23.
40. R. Landau, 'A Philosophy of Enabling', in C. Price, *The Square Book* (Chichester: Wiley-Academy, 2003), pp. 9–15, p. 11, original emphases.
41. Lobsinger, 'Cybernetic Theory and the Architecture of Performance', p. 128.
42. This idea can be connected to the philosopher Gaston Bachelard's ideas on the power of daydreaming, in G. Bachelard, *The Poetics of Space*, translated by M. Jolas (Boston: Beacon Press, 1969), p. 183.
43. Mathews, *From Agit-Prop to Free Space*, p. 114.
44. Read, *Theatre and Everyday Life*, p. 7.
45. See also plans for Price's Potteries Thinkbelt (c.1964–7), which was designed to challenge the traditional conception of the educational institution.
46. D. Harvey, *Spaces of Hope* (Edinburgh: Edinburgh University Press, 2000), p. 163.

47. J. Littlewood, *Joan's Book: Joan Littlewood's Peculiar History as She Tells It* (London: Methuen, 1994), p. 626.
48. Littlewood, 'A Laboratory of Fun', p. 432.
49. Read, *Theatre and Everyday Life*, p. 4.
50. Harvey, *Spaces of Hope*, p. 200.
51. Price, *The Square Book*, p. 37.
52. See ibid.
53. Melvin, 'Cedric Price', p. 23.
54. Landau 'A Philosophy of Enabling', p. 11, original emphasis.
55. S. Topham, *Where's My Space Age? The Rise and Fall of Futuristic Design* (London: Prestel, 2003), p. 40.
56. H. Ozbekhan, 'The Triumph of Technology: "Can" Implies "Ought"', in S. Anderson (ed.), *Planning for Diversity and Choice: Possible Futures and Their Relations to the Man-Controlled Environment* (Cambridge, MA: The MIT Press, 1968), pp. 204–33, p. 205.
57. R. Hewison, *Too Much: Art and Society in the Sixties 1960–1975* (London: Methuen, 1986), p. 42.
58. See D. Green, 'Prologue', in Crompton, *Concerning Archigram*, pp. 1–6.
59. S. Topham, *Blow-up: Inflatable Art, Architecture and Design* (London: Prestel, 2002), p. 55.
60. Hewison, *Too Much*, pp. 41–2.
61. Lobsinger, 'Cybernetic Theory and the Architecture of Performance', p. 120.
62. R. Landau, *New Directions in British Architecture* (New York: George Braziller, 1968), p. 76.
63. The network appeared in many Price projects, such as the Potteries Thinkbelt proposed for Staffordshire. See Price, *The Square Book*, p. 13.
64. Lobsinger, 'Cybernetic Theory and the Architecture of Performance', p. 119.
65. J. Clark, 'Assessment of the Fun Palace Project', Clive Barker Personal Archive, 2 March 1966, p. 3.
66. Littlewood, 'Theatre or Fun Palace?'.
67. Banham, 'People's Palaces', p. 191.
68. Cybernetics, commonly defined as the study of control and communication in animals and machines, evolved during the Second World War to establish sophisticated radar tracking systems that could predict how pilots would react given specific circumstances in the field of combat. As a field of study, it involves interdisciplinary research, encompassing the social and psychological sciences, information

technology and environmental studies to explore how systems evolve and adapt to function most effectively. Pask was particularly associated with broad questions about the different types and nature of learning and skills acquisition; as such, he examined attention, memory, information processing, recall and the physical, psychological, environmental and genetic conditions that best activate these.

69. Price, 'A Laboratory of Fun', p. 433.
70. J. Littlewood, 'Non-Program: A Laboratory of Fun', *Drama Review*, Vol. 12, No. 3 (1968), pp. 130–4, p. 133.
71. Ibid.
72. W. Taylor, 'The St. Pancras Festival', in E. Hillman (ed.), *Essays in Local Government Enterprise* (London: Merlin Press, 1964), pp. 37–42, p. 37.
73. H. Jenkins, 'Towards the Civic Theatre', in Hillman, *Essays in Local Government Enterprise*, pp. 15–26, p. 16.
74. Littlewood, *Joan's Book*, p. 703.
75. Ibid., p. 711.
76. See Mathews, *From Agit-Prop to Free Space*, pp. 122–4, for a detailed consideration of the implications of the LCC changes.
77. Two former vocal supporters of the Fun Palace, Asa Briggs and Lord Ritchie-Calder, transferred their allegiances in 1967 when they joined the Open University Planning Committee.
78. The storm water tanks never materialised and in 2005 it was announced the Mill Meads would form part of the area developed for the 2012 London Olympics.
79. Cited in J. Hillman, 'London's Palace of Fun has Nowhere to Go', *Evening Standard*, 3 March 1966, p. 16.
80. Anon., 'Camden Pilot Project Report', p. 12.
81. Ibid., p. 13.
82. Hillman, 'London's Palace of Fun has Nowhere to Go', p. 16.
83. Cited in Topham, *Blow-up*, p. 79.
84. Clark, 'Assessment of the Fun Palace Project', p. 1.
85. Cited in Littlewood, *Joan's Book*, p. 739, emphasis in Littlewood.
86. Anon., 'Fun Palace Protests', *Hampstead and Highgate Express*, 26 February 1965, page unknown.
87. Clark, 'Assessment of the Fun Palace Project', p. 3.
88. Mathews, *From Agit-Prop to Free Space*, pp. 156–7.
89. D. Allford, 'The Creative Iconoclast', in Price, *The Square Book*, p. 7.
90. Topham, *Where's My Space Age?*, p. 93.
91. Melvin, 'Cedric Price', p. 23.
92. Mathews, *From Agit-Prop to Free Space*, p. 190.
93. See Price, *The Square Book*, pp. 62–3.

Chapter 7

1. J. Littlewood, cited in anon., 'I'm Quitting Plays – Joan Littlewood', *Stratford Express*, 14 July 1967, p. 9.
2. J. Littlewood, cited in S. Mathews, *From Agit-Prop to Free Space: The Architecture of Cedric Price* (London: Black Dog, 2007), p. 166.
3. B. Kershaw, *The Politics of Performance: Radical Theatre as Cultural Intervention* (London: Routledge, 1992), p. 2.
4. G. Robertson, 'An Art Encounter', in P. Kuppers and G. Robertson (eds.), *The Community Performance Reader* (London: Routledge, 2007), pp. 110–23, p. 118.
5. See N. Bourriaud, *Relational Aesthetics*, translated by S. Pleasance and F. Woods (Dijon: Les Presses du Réel, 2002), p. 16.
6. See T. H. Marshall, *Citizenship and Social Class and Other Essays* (Cambridge: Cambridge University Press, 1950).
7. J. Hoffman, *Citizenship beyond the State* (London: Sage, 2004), p. 1.
8. J. Littlewood, *Bubble City* (London: Fun Palace Trust, 1968), Theatre Royal Stratford East Archive, p. 9.
9. See S. Weller, *Teenagers' Citizenship: Experiences and Education* (London: Routledge, 2007); C. Spencer and M. Blades (eds.), *Children and Their Environments: Learning, Using and Designing Spaces* (Cambridge: Cambridge University Press, 2006); and H. Helve and C. Wallace (eds.), *Youth, Citizenship and Empowerment* (Aldershot: Ashgate, 2001).
10. L. Horelli, 'Young People's Participation in Local Development: Lip Service or Serious Business?', in Helve and Wallace, *Youth, Citizenship and Empowerment*, pp. 57–71, p. 60.
11. Weller, *Teenagers' Citizenship*, p. 99.
12. Ibid., p. 130.
13. H. Nicholson, *Applied Drama: The Gift of Theatre* (Basingstoke: Palgrave Macmillan, 2005), p. 27.
14. The theatre was only saved after Gerry Raffles contacted the Historic Buildings Council and they made it a listed building on 28 June 1972.
15. He demanded a substantial reduction to the scale of the project and reassurances that the Theatre Royal be left intact. See anon., 'Town Centre Plan Faces New Hitch', *Stratford Express*, 22 July 1966, p. 7.
16. G. Raffles and J. Littlewood, 'Uses for Land Awaiting Redevelopment, 1968–1975', ACGB/34/68, Arts Council of England Archives.
17. Several residents complained about their homes being designated slums. See anon., 'Couple Win Battle to Beat "Slum" Tag', *Stratford Express*, 16 December 1966, p. 2.
18. R. Dean, 'Still Living in Squalor', *Stratford Express*, 8 March 1968, p. 18.

19. In fact, Newham Council often used the poor state of education in the area as a counterargument to those opposing the redevelopment by claiming that it would use increased rates from shops and offices to improve facilities and the number of teachers.
20. Anon., 'Too Old to Play – at 11!', *Stratford Express*, 8 July 1966, p. 16.
21. Anon., 'So Keep off That Grass', *Stratford Express*, 12 August 1966, p. 2.
22. Anon., 'Kiddies Playground Is Banned – to the Kids!', *Stratford Express*, 22 March 1968, p. 6.
23. M. Francis and R. Lorenzo, 'Children and City Design: Proactive Process and the "Renewal" of Childhood', in Spencer and Blades, *Children and Their Environments*, pp. 217–37.
24. Littlewood, *Bubble City*, p. 2.
25. See J. Addams, *Twenty Years at Hull-House* (New York: Macmillan, 1910); C. Cook, *The Play Way* (London: Heinemann, 1917); and J. Huizinga, *Homo Ludens: A Study of the Play Element in Culture* (London: Maurice Temple Smith, 1970).
26. I am very grateful to Helen Nicholson for drawing these activists to my attention.
27. Littlewood, *Bubble City*, p. 8.
28. Ibid., p. 9.
29. D. Harvey, *Spaces of Hope* (Edinburgh: Edinburgh University Press, 2000), p. 184.
30. J. Littlewood, *Joan's Book: Joan Littlewood's Peculiar History as She Tells It* (London: Methuen, 1994), p. 754.
31. J. Littlewood, letter regarding Stratford Fair and progress on Salway Road children's playground, Theatre Royal Stratford East Archive.
32. Littlewood certainly saw her work within a wider network of operations and gave information and contact addresses for other movements in her *Bubble City* publication.
33. A. Filewood, 'Coalitions of Resistance: Ground Zero's Community Mobilization', in S. C. Haedicke and T. Nellhaus (eds.), *Performing Democracy: International Perspectives on Urban Community-Based Performance* (Ann Arbor: University of Michigan Press, 2001), pp. 89–103, p. 91.
34. See V. Turner, *From Ritual to Theatre: The Human Seriousness of Play* (New York: PAJ Publications, 1982), pp. 47–51.
35. S. E. Sutton and S. P. Kemp, 'Young People's Participation in Constructing a Socially Just Public Sphere', in Spencer and Blades, *Children and Their Environments*, pp. 256–76, p. 256.
36. Weller, *Teenagers' Citizenship*, p. 30.

37. E. Fahmy, *Young Citizens: Young People's Involvement in Politics and Decision Making* (Aldershot: Ashgate, 2006), p. 25.
38. Sutton and Kemp, 'Young People's Participation in Constructing a Socially Just Public Sphere', p. 256.
39. Littlewood, *Bubble City*, p. 12.
40. A. Constable, 'A Play Won't Stop Holiday Classes', *Stratford Express*, 1 September 1967, p. 17.
41. Anon., 'Touch of Kew in Salway-Rd', *Stratford Express*, 10 May 1968, p. 5.
42. Littlewood, *Bubble City*, p. 14.
43. J. Littlewood et al., 'January Diary', Michael Barker Collection, Harry Ransom Humanities Research Center, the University of Texas at Austin (1975), p. 3.
44. Anon., 'A Right Royal Splash!', *Stratford Express*, 25 August 1967, p. 3.
45. B. McConachie, 'Approaching the "Structure of Feeling" in Grassroots Theater', in S. C. Haedicke and T. Nellhaus (eds.), *Performing Democracy: International Perspectives on Urban Community-Based Performance* (Ann Arbor: University of Michigan Press, 2001), pp. 29–57, p. 38.
46. Anon., 'A Royal Rave-Up', *Stratford Express*, 4 April 1975, p. 49.
47. There were also attempts to extend this work throughout the country. In 1968, the Fun Palace Trust launched the Mobile Fair Project and secured a place at the City of London Festival held 8–20 July on Tower Place. Announced as a 'pilot for a developing series of mobile fairs presenting new toys, games, entertainment structures and events in the London area and elsewhere', it was presented as part of a wider 'campaign to foster improvement of local amenities both for adults and children'. Drawing on innovative practices in art, architecture and industrial design and expertise from the Archigram Group, the Royal College of Art and the Architectural Association, the fair included the 'humanoid', a giant model of a human body that could be walked through and played in; a fifty-foot aluminium musical windmill with electronic sound effects; and a 'chamber of bubbles' contained in a plastic house. It has proved impossible to find out whether the Mobile Fair appeared anywhere else in the country, although there were definitely plans to stage an event at Woburn Abbey in 1968.
48. L. Gill, 'Palace of Fun Casts a Spell', *Stratford Express*, 26 July 1974, p. 7.
49. Ibid., p. 7.
50. G. Brown, cited in ibid., p. 7.
51. Littlewood, *Joan's Book*, p. 758.
52. Littlewood, 'January Diary', p. 2.

53. Anon., 'Devious Hoodlums on Path to Money', *Stratford Express*, 24 January 1975, p. 7.
54. Littlewood, 'January Diary', pp. 5–6.
55. Nicholson, *Applied Drama*, p. 1.
56. Littlewood, *Joan's Book*, p. 756.
57. Littlewood, *Bubble City*, p. 13.
58. Nicholson, *Applied Drama*, p. 65.
59. Littlewood, *Bubble City*, p. 13.
60. Nicholson, *Applied Drama*, p. 24.
61. J. Thompson, *Applied Theatre: Bewilderment and Beyond* (Oxford: Peter Lang, 2003), p. 68.
62. R. Shaull, 'Foreword', in P. Freire, *Pedagogy of the Oppressed*, translated by M. Bergman Ramos (New York: Continuum, 2006), pp. 29–34, p. 32.
63. See Thompson, *Applied Theatre*, p. 73.
64. Thompson, *Applied Theatre*, pp. 73–4.
65. Anon., 'Touch of Kew in Salway-Rd', p. 5.
66. Anon., 'Minutes of a Meeting Titled "Future of Theatre Royal"', Clive Barker Personal Archive, 27 July 1975.

Select bibliography

Addams, J., *Twenty Years at Hull-House* (New York: Macmillan, 1910)

Anderson, B., *Imagined Communities: Reflections on the Origin and Spread of Nationalism*, revised and extended edn (London: Verso, 1991)

Anderson, L., 'A Taste of Honey', *Encore*, Vol. 5, No. 2 (July–August 1958), pp. 42–3

Auslander, P., *Liveness: Performance in a Mediatized Culture* (London: Routledge, 1999)

Bachelard, G., *The Poetics of Space*, translated by M. Jolas (Boston: Beacon Press, 1969)

Badiou, A., *Ethics: An Essay on the Understanding of Evil*, translated by P. Hallward (London: Verso, 2001)

Bakhtin, M., *Rabelais and His World*, translated by H. Iswolsky (London: The MIT Press, 1968)

Banham, R., 'People's Palaces', *New Statesman*, 7 August 1964, pp. 191–2

Banham, R., *Theory and Design in the First Machine Age* (Oxford: Butterworth Architecture, 1960)

Barish, Jonas, *The Antitheatrical Prejudice* (Berkeley: University of California Press, 1981)

Barker, C., 'The Ghosts of War: Stage Ghosts and Time Slips in Response to War', in C. Barker and M. Gale (eds.), *British Theatre between the Wars 1918–1939* (Cambridge: Cambridge University Press, 2000), pp. 215–43

Barker, C., 'Joan Littlewood', in A. Hodge (ed.), *Twentieth Century Actor Training* (London: Routledge, 2000), pp. 113–28

Behan, B., *Behan: The Complete Plays* (London: Methuen, 1978)

Behan, B., 'A Celebrated Interview', in E. H. Mikhail (ed.), *Brendan Behan: Interviews and Recollections*, 2 vols. (London: Macmillan, 1982), Vol. I, pp. 76–9

Bennett, S., *Performing Nostalgia: Shifting Shakespeare and the Contemporary Past* (London: Routledge, 1996)

Beynon, H, 'Images of Labour/Images of Class', in S. Rowbotham and H. Beynon (eds.), *Looking at Class: Film, Television and the Working Class in Britain* (London: Rivers Oram Press, 2001), pp. 25–40

Billington, M., *State of the Nation: British Theatre since 1945* (London: Faber, 2007)

Bolam, R., '*Richard II*: Shakespeare and the Languages of the Stage', in M. Hattaway (ed.), *The Cambridge Companion to Shakespeare's History Plays* (Cambridge: Cambridge University Press, 2002), pp. 141–57

Bourke, J., *An Intimate History of Killing* (London: Granta, 1999)

Bourke, J., *Working-Class Cultures in Britain 1890–1960* (London: Routledge, 1994)

Bourriaud, N., *Relational Aesthetics*, translated by S. Pleasance and F. Woods (Dijon: Les Presses du Réel, 2002)

Bramwell, M., 'A Cup of Tea with Joan Littlewood', in Joannne Tompkins and Julie Holledge (eds.), *Performing Women/Performing Feminisms: Interviews with International Women Playwrights* (Brisbane: Australasian Drama Studies Association, 1997), pp. 103–9

Brannigan, J., 'Form and Ethics in the Comedies of Brendan Behan', in Mary Luckhurst (ed.), *A Companion to Modern British and Irish Drama 1880–2005* (Oxford: Blackwell, 2006), pp. 247–57

Brunsdon, C., *London in Cinema: The Cinematic City since 1945* (London: BFI, 2007)

Brustein, R., 'Libido at Large', in E. H. Mikhail (ed.), *The Art of Brendan Behan* (London: Vision Press, 1979), pp. 128–30

Bulman, J. C., '*Henry IV, Parts 1 and 2*', in M. Hattaway (ed.), *Shakespeare's History Plays* (Cambridge: Cambridge University Press, 2002), pp. 158–76

Callaghan, D., 'Shakespeare at the Fun Palace: Joan Littlewood', in M. Novy (ed.), *Cross-cultural Performances: Differences in*

Women's Re-visions of Shakespeare (Urbana: University of Illinois Press, 1993), pp. 108–26

Callaghan, D., 'The Terms of Gender: "Gay" and "Feminist" Edward II', in A. Oz (ed.), *Marlowe: Contemporary Critical Essays* (Basingstoke: Palgrave Macmillan, 2003), pp. 182–99

Carey, J. (ed.), *The Faber Book of Utopias* (London: Faber, 1999)

Chambers, C., *Inside the Royal Shakespeare Company: Creativity and the Institution* (London: Routledge, 2004)

Chapman, H., *You Won't Always Be on Top* (London: Methuen, 1965)

Cole, T., and H. Krich Chinoy (eds.), *Directors on Directing: A Source Book of Modern Theatre*, 2nd edn (London: Peter Owen, 1964)

Cook, C., *The Play Way* (London: Heinemann, 1917)

Cooney, E. W., 'High Flats in Local Authority Housing in England and Wales since 1945', in A. Sutcliffe (ed.), *Multi-storey Living: The British Working-Class Experience* (London: Croom Helm, 1974), pp. 151–80

Corbett, J., 'Theatre Workshop: A British People's Theatre', *Meanjin*, Vol. 18 (September 1959), pp. 327–33

Croyden, M., 'Joan Littlewood', in Joseph McCrindle (ed.), *Behind the Scenes: Theatre and Film Interviews from the 'Transatlantic Review'* (London: Pitman, 1971), pp. 1–12

Curtis, B., 'Archigram: "A Necessary Irritant"', in D. Crompton (ed.), *Concerning Archigram*, 4th edn (London: Archigram Archives, 2002), pp. 25–79

Davies, A., and P. Saunders, 'Literature, Politics and Society', in A. Sinfield (ed.), *Society and Literature 1945–1970* (London: Methuen, 1983), pp. 13–50

Davies, A., and A. Sinfield (eds.), *British Culture of the Postwar: An Introduction to Literature and Society 1945–1999* (London: Routledge, 2000)

Davis, T. C., and T. Postlewait (eds.), *Theatricality* (Cambridge: Cambridge University Press, 2003)

Day, G., *Community and Everyday Life* (London: Routledge, 2006)

Day, G., 'Highs and Lows: The Problem of "Culture" in *The Ragged Trousered Philanthropists*', in H. G. Klaus and S. Knight (eds.), *British Industrial Fictions* (Cardiff: University of Wales Press, 2000), pp. 71–83

Delaney, S., *A Taste of Honey* (London: Methuen, 1959)

Delgado, M. M., *Federico García Lorca* (London: Routledge, 2008)

Dennis, N., F. Henriques and C. Slaughter, *Coal Is Our Life: An Analysis of a Yorkshire Mining Community*, 2nd edn (London: Tavistock Publications, 1976)

Derrida, J., *Archive Fever: A Freudian Impression*, translated by E. Prenowitz (Chicago: University of Chicago Press, 1996)

Derrida, J., *Specters of Marx*, translated by P. Kamuf (London: Routledge, 1994)

Dorris, G., '*The Projector, The Mock Mason* and Miss Littlewood', *Modern Drama*, Vol. 16, No. 3 (1973), pp. 265–8

Easthope, A., *What a Man's Gotta Do: The Masculine Myth in Popular Culture* (London: Routledge, 1990)

Eyre, R., and N. Wright, *Changing Stages: A View of British Theatre in the Twentieth Century* (London: Bloomsbury, 2001)

Fahmy, E., *Young Citizens: Young People's Involvement in Politics and Decision Making* (Aldershot: Ashgate, 2006)

Favre, J., 'Did Clive Barker Write *The Hostage*?', *New Theatre Quarterly*, Vol. 23, No. 4 (November 2007), pp. 326–30

Filewood, A., 'Coalitions of Resistance: Ground Zero's Community Mobilization', in S. C. Haedicke and T. Nellhaus (eds.), *Performing Democracy: International Perspectives on Urban Community-Based Performance* (Ann Arbor: University of Michigan Press, 2001), pp. 89–103

Foley, D., 'His London Appearances', in E. H. Mikhail (ed.), *Brendan Behan: Interviews and Recollections*, 2 vols. (London and Basingstoke: Macmillan, 1982), Vol. I, pp. 136–41

Foucault, M., *The Archaeology of Knowledge*, translated by A. Sheridan Smith (London: Routledge, 1989)

Foucault, M., *Discipline and Punish: The Birth of the Prison*, translated by A. Sheridan (London: Allen Lane, 1977)

Francis, M., and R. Lorenzo, 'Children and City Design: Proactive Process and the "Renewal" of Childhood', in C. Spencer and M. Blades (eds.), *Children and Their Environments: Learning, Using and Designing Spaces* (Cambridge: Cambridge University Press, 2006), pp. 217–37

Freire, P., *Pedagogy of the Oppressed*, translated by M. Bergman Ramos (New York: Continuum, 2006)

Fussell, P., *The Great War and Modern Memory* (London: Oxford University Press, 1975)

Fussell, P., and C. A. Carpenter, *Dramatists and the Bomb: American and British Playwrights Confront the Nuclear Age 1945–1964* (Westport, CT: Greenwood Press, 1999)

Glinert, E., *East End Chronicles* (London: Allen Lane, 2005)

Glover, J., *Humanity: A Moral History of the Twentieth Century* (London: Jonathan Cape, 1999)

Goodman, J. L., 'Joan Littlewood and Her Theatre Workshop', unpublished PhD thesis, New York University, 1975

Goodman, P., *Growing up Absurd* (London: Vintage, 1962)

Goodwin, C., and T. Milne, 'Working with Joan', *Encore*, Vol. 7, No. 4 (July–August 1960), pp. 9–20

Goorney, H., 'Littlewood in Rehearsal', *Tulane Drama Review*, Vol. 11, No. 2 (Winter 1966), pp. 102–3

Goorney, H., *The Theatre Workshop Story* (London: Methuen, 1981)

Goorney, H., and E. MacColl (eds.), *Agit-Prop to Theatre Workshop* (Manchester: Manchester University Press, 1986)

Green, D., 'Prologue', in D. Crompton (ed.), *Concerning Archigram*, 4th edn (London: Archigram Archives, 2002), pp. 1–6

Greenblatt, S., 'Invisible Bullets: Renaissance Authority and Its Subversion, *Henry IV* and *Henry V*', in J. Dollimore and A. Sinfield (eds.), *Political Shakespeare: New Essays in Cultural Materialism* (Manchester: Manchester University Press, 1985), pp. 18–47

Grene, H., 'Visions and Vicissitudes – the Story of Theatre Workshop', *The Stage and Television Today*, 31 January 1980, p. 103

Grene, N., *The Politics of Irish Drama* (Cambridge: Cambridge University Press, 1999)

Haedicke, S. C., and T. Nellhaus (eds.), *Performing Democracy: International Perspectives on Urban Community-Based Performance* (Ann Arbor: University of Michigan Press, 2001)

Hall, S., and P. Whannel, *The Popular Arts* (London: Hutchinson Educational, 1964)

Harker, B., *Class Act: The Cultural and Political Life of Ewan MacColl* (London: Pluto, 2007)

Harker, B., 'Mediating the 1930s: Documentary and Politics in Theatre Union's *Last Edition* (1940)', in A. Forsyth and C. Megson (eds.), *Get Real: Documentary Theatre Past and Present* (Basingstoke: Palgrave, 2009), pp. 24–37

Harker, B., '"Was There Another England?" Joan Littlewood in Manchester', *North West Labour History Journal*, No. 28 (2003), pp. 36–41

Harrop, J., 'The Last Laugh: Comedy as a Political Touchstone in Britain from "The Entertainer" to "Comedians"', *Theatre Journal*, Vol. 32, No. 1 (March 1980), pp. 5–16

Harvey, D., *Spaces of Hope* (Edinburgh: Edinburgh University Press, 2000)

Haywood, I., *Working-Class Fiction: From Chartism to Trainspotting* (Plymouth: Northcote, 1997)

Heddon, D., *Autobiography and Performance* (Basingstoke: Palgrave, 2008)

Hedley, P., 'Black Theatre Development at Theatre Royal, Stratford East', *Perfoming Arts International*, Vol. 1, No. 2 (1996), pp. 23–33

Heinemann, M., 'How Brecht Read Shakespeare', in J. Dollimore and A. Sinfield (eds.), *Political Shakespeare: New Essays in Cultural Materialism* (Manchester: Manchester University Press, 1985), pp. 226–54

Helve, H., and C. Wallace (eds.), *Youth, Citizenship and Empowerment* (Aldershot: Ashgate, 2001)

Henderson, H., 'The Edinburgh People's Festival, 1951–54', in A. Croft (ed.), *A Weapon in the Struggle: The Cultural History of the Communist Party of Great Britain* (London: Pluto Press, 1998), pp. 163–71

Hewison, R., *In Anger: Culture in the Cold War 1945–60* (London: Methuen, 1988)

Hewison, R., *Too Much: Art and Society in the Sixties 1960–1975* (London: Methuen, 1986)

Higson, A., 'Space, Place, Spectacle: Landscape and Townscape in the "Kitchen Sink" Film', in A. Higson (ed.), *Dissolving Views: Key Writings on British Cinema* (London: Cassell, 1996), pp. 133–56

Hill, J., *Sex, Class and Realism: British Cinema 1956–1963* (London: British Film Institute, 1986)
Hoffman, J., *Citizenship beyond the State* (London: Sage, 2004)
Hoggart, R., *The Uses of Literacy* (London: Chatto & Windus, 1957)
Holderness, G., *Shakespeare Recycled: The Making of Historical Drama* (Hemel Hempstead: Harvester Wheatsheaf, 1992)
Holdsworth, N., 'Joan Littlewood', in Shomit Mitter and Maria Shevtsova (eds.), *Fifty Key Theatre Directors* (London: Routledge, 2005), pp. 75–80
Holdsworth, N., *Joan Littlewood* (London: Routledge, 2006)
Holdsworth, N. '"They'd Have Pissed on My Grave": The Arts Council and Theatre Workshop', *New Theatre Quarterly*, Vol. 15, No. 1 (1999), pp. 3–16
Horelli, L., 'Young People's Participation in Local Development: Lip Service or Serious Business?', in H. Helve and C. Wallace (eds.), *Youth, Citizenship and Empowerment* (Aldershot: Ashgate, 2001), pp. 57–71
Huggett, R., *Binkie Beaumont: Eminence Grise of the West End Theatre 1933–1973* (London: Hodder and Stoughton, 1989)
Huizinga, J., *Homo Ludens: A Study of the Play Element in Culture* (London: Maurice Temple Smith, 1970)
Huxley, A., *An Encyclopaedia of Pacifism* (London: Chatto and Windus, 1937)
Hyde, L., *The Gift: How the Creative Spirit Transforms the World*, 2nd edn (Edinburgh: Canongate, 2006)
Jenkins, H., 'Towards the Civic Theatre', in E. Hillman (ed.), *Essays in Local Government Enterprise* (London: Merlin Press, 1964), pp. 15–26
Jenkins, R., *Pierre Bourdieu* (London, Routledge, 1992)
Karlin, M., *Some Sort of a Life* (London: Oberon, 2007)
Kennedy, D., *Looking at Shakespeare* (Cambridge: Cambridge University Press, 1993)
Kershaw, B., *The Politics of Performance: Radical Theatre as Cultural Intervention* (London: Routledge, 1992)
Key, J., 'The Atomic Drama', in T. Howard and J. Stokes (eds.), *Acts of War: The Representation of Military Conflict on the British Stage*

and Television since 1945 (Aldershot: Ashgate Publishing, 1996), pp. 110–26

Kirk, J., *Class, Culture and Social Change: On the Trail of the Working Class* (Basingstoke: Palgrave Macmillan, 2007)

Kirk, J., *Twentieth-Century Writing and the British Working Class* (Cardiff: University of Wales Press, 2003)

Kitchin, L., *Mid-century Drama* (London: Faber and Faber, 1960)

Kott, J., *Shakespeare, Our Contemporary*, translated by Boleslaw Taborski (London: Methuen, 1965)

Kuppers, P., and G. Robertson (eds.), *The Community Performance Reader* (London: Routledge, 2007)

Lacey, S., *British Realist Theatre: The New Wave and Its Context* (London: Routledge, 1995)

Laing, S., *Representations of Working-Class Life 1957–1964* (Basingstoke: Macmillan, 1986)

Landau, R., *New Directions in British Architecture* (New York: George Braziller, 1968)

Landau, R., 'A Philosophy of Enabling', in C. Price, *The Square Book* (Chichester: Wiley-Academy, 2003), pp. 9–15

Leach, R., *Theatre Workshop: Joan Littlewood and the Making of Modern British Theatre* (Exeter: University of Exeter Press, 2006)

Lefebvre, H., *The Production of Space*, translated by D. Nicholson-Smith (Oxford: Basil Blackwell, 1991)

Leighton, M., *Men at Work* (London: Jill Norman, 1981)

Lewis, B. N., 'Fun Palace: Counter-blast to Boredom', *New Society*, 15 April 1965, pp. 8–11

Lewis, S., *Sparrers Can't Sing* (London: Evans Brothers, 1961)

Littlewood, J., *Baron Philippe: The Very Candid Autobiography of Baron Philippe de Rothschild* (New York: Crown Publishers, 1984)

Littlewood, J., *Bubble City* (London: Fun Palace Trust, 1968), Theatre Royal Stratford East Archive

Littlewood, J., 'Home Fires Burning', *Guardian*, 28 December 1985, pp. 18–19

Littlewood, J., 'A Laboratory of Fun', *New Scientist*, Vol. 22, No. 391 (1964), pp. 432–3

Littlewood, J., *Joan's Book: Joan Littlewood's Peculiar History as She Tells It* (London: Methuen, 1994)

Littlewood, J., 'Non-Program: A Laboratory of Fun', *Drama Review*, Vol. 12, No. 3 (1968), pp. 130–4

Lobsinger, M. L., 'Cybernetic Theory and the Architecture of Performance: Cedric Price's Fun Palace', in S. Williams Goldhagen and R. Legault (eds.), *Anxious Modernisms: Experimentation in Post-war Architectural Culture* (Cambridge, MA: MIT Press, 2000), pp. 119–39

Lovell, T., 'Landscapes and Stories in 1960s British Realism', in A. Higson (ed.), *Dissolving Views: Key Writings on British Cinema* (London: Cassell, 1996), pp. 157–77

McCarthy, S., and H. Norris, 'Revenons à nos moutons', *Theatrephile*, Vol. 1, No. 4 (September 1984), pp. 57–61

MacColl, E., *Johnny Noble*, in H. Goorney and E. MacColl (eds.), *Agit-Prop to Theatre Workshop: Political Playscripts 1930–1950* (Manchester: Manchester University Press, 1986), pp. 35–72

MacColl, E., *Journeyman* (London: Sidgwick and Jackson, 1990)

McConachie, B., 'Approaching the "Structure of Feeling" in Grassroots Theater', in S.C. Haedicke and T. Nellhaus (eds.), *Performing Democracy: International Perspectives on Urban Community-Based Performance* (Ann Arbor: University of Michigan Press, 2001), pp. 29–57

McGrath, J., *A Good Night Out: Popular Theatre: Audience, Class and Form* (London: Methuen, 1981)

McGuigan, J., *Cultural Populism* (London: Routledge, 1992)

MacIntyre, T., 'This Dying Lark', in E.H. Mikhail (ed.), *The Art of Brendan Behan* (London: Vision Press, 1979), pp. 63–7

McKibbin, R., *The Ideologies of Class: Social Relations in Britain 1880–1950* (Oxford: Oxford University Press, 1991)

Marlowe, C., *The Complete Plays* (London: Penguin, 1969)

Marowitz, C., *Recycling Shakespeare* (Basingstoke: Macmillan, 1991)

Marshall, N., *The Producer and the Play*, 2nd edn (London: Davis-Poynter, 1975)

Marshall, T.H., *Citizenship and Social Class and Other Essays* (Cambridge: Cambridge University Press, 1950)

Mates, L. H., *The Spanish Civil War and the British Left: Political Activism and the Popular Front* (London: Tauris Academic Studies, 2007)

Matheson Cain, A., 'Death's Jest Book', in E. H. Mikhail (ed.), *The Art of Brendan Behan* (London: Vision Press, 1979), pp. 75–6

Mathews, S., *From Agit-Prop to Free Space: The Architecture of Cedric Price* (London: Black Dog, 2007)

Medhurst, A., 'If Anywhere: Class Identifications and Cultural Studies Academics', in S. R. Munt (ed.), *Cultural Studies and the Working Class: Subject to Change* (London: Cassell, 2000), pp. 19–35

Melvin, M., *The Art of the Theatre Workshop* (London: Oberon Books, 2006)

Milne, T., 'Art in Angel Lane', in C. Marowitz, T. Milne and O. Hale (eds.), *The Encore Reader: A Chronicle of the New Drama* (London: Methuen, 1965), pp. 80–6

Moreno, J. L., *The Theater of Spontaneity: An Introduction to Psychodrama* (Beacon, NY: Beacon House, 1947)

Morrison, S., *I Renounce War: The Story of the Peace Pledge Union* (London: Sheppard Press, 1962)

Mouffe, C. (ed.), *Dimensions of a Radical Democracy: Pluralism, Citizenship, Community* (London: Verso, 1992)

Moussinac, L. , *The New Movement in the Theatre* (Paris: Editions Albert-Lévy, 1931)

Murphy, R., *Sixties British Cinema* (London: British Film Institute, 1992)

Murray, C., *Twentieth-Century Irish Drama: Mirror Up to Nation* (Syracuse, NY: Syracuse University Press, 2000)

Nicholson, H., *Applied Drama: The Gift of Theatre* (Basingstoke: Palgrave Macmillan, 2005)

Norman, F., *Fings Ain't Wot They Used T'Be* (London: Samuel French, 1960)

Norman, F., *Why Fings Went West* (London: Lemon Tree Press, 1975)

Nuttall, J., *Bomb Culture* (London: Paladin, 1968)

Orwell, G., 'Down the Mine', in G. Orwell, *Inside the Whale and Other Essays* (London: Penguin, 1957), pp. 51–62

Osborne, J., *Look Back in Anger and Other Plays: Collected Plays*, Vol. I (London: Faber and Faber, 1993)

Ozbekhan, H., 'The Triumph of Technology: "Can" Implies "Ought"', in S. Anderson (ed.), *Planning for Diversity and Choice: Possible Futures and Their Relations to the Man-Controlled Environment* (Cambridge, MA: The MIT Press, 1968), pp. 204–33

Paget, D., 'Case Study: *Oh What a Lovely War*', in B. Kershaw (ed.), *The Cambridge History of British Theatre*, Vol. III (Cambridge: Cambridge University Press, 2004), pp. 397–411

Paget, D., 'Popularising Popular History: "Oh What a Lovely War" and the Sixties', *Critical Survey*, Vol. 2, No. 2 (1990), 117–27

Paget, D., 'Theatre Workshop, Moussinac, and the European Connection', *New Theatre Quarterly*, Vol. 11, No. 43 (August 1995), pp. 211–24

Paget, D., '"The War Game Is Continuous": Productions and Receptions of Theatre Workshop's *Oh What a Lovely War*', *Studies in Theatre and Performance*, Vol. 23, No. 2 (2003), pp. 71–85.

Pask, Gordon, 'Theatre Workshop and Systems Research: Proposals for a Cybernetic Theatre', unpublished manuscript, Michael Barker Collection, Harry Ransom Humanities Center, University of Texas at Austin

Patton, A., 'Jazz and Music-Hall Transgressions in Theatre Workshop's Production of *A Taste of Honey*', *New Theatre Quarterly*, Vol. 23, No. 4 (November 2007), pp. 331–6

Pick, D., *War Machine: The Rationalisation of Slaughter in the Modern Age* (New Haven: Yale University Press, 1993)

Price, C., *The Square Book* (Chichester: Wiley-Academy, 2003)

Priestley, J. B., 'Britain and the Nuclear Bombs', *New Statesman*, 2 November 1957, pp. 554–6

Raffles, G., 'Theatre Workshop: A British People's Theatre', in H. Hobson (ed.), *International Theatre Annual* (London: John Calder, 1958), Vol. III, pp. 167–79

Read, A., *Theatre and Everyday Life: An Ethics of Performance* (London: Routledge, 1993)

Reichberg, G. M., H. Syse and E. Begby, *The Ethics of War* (Oxford: Blackwell, 2006)

Richardson, A. (ed.), *The Spanish Civil War: The View from the Left* (Monmouth: Merlin Press, 2007)

Ridout, N., *Stage Fright, Animals and Other Theatrical Problems* (Cambridge: Cambridge University Press, 2006)
Roberts, K., *The Working Class* (London: Longman, 1978)
Robertson, G., 'An Art Encounter', in P. Kuppers and G. Robertson (eds.), *The Community Performance Reader* (London: Routledge, 2007), pp. 110–23
Russell Brown, J., 'Three Kinds of Shakespeare', *Shakespeare Survey*, Vol. 18 (1965), pp. 147–56
Russell Taylor, J., *Anger and After: A Survey of the New British Drama*, 2nd edn (London: Methuen, 1969)
Sassoon, S., *The War Poems* (London: Faber, 1983)
Schafer, E., 'Daughters of Ben', in R. Cave, E. Schafer and B. Wolland (eds.), *Ben Jonson and Theatre* (London: Routledge, 1999), pp. 154–78
Schafer, E., *MsDirecting Shakespeare: Women Direct Shakespeare* (London: The Women's Press, 1998)
Schechter, J. (ed.), *Popular Theatre: A Sourcebook* (London: Routledge, 2003)
Schneider, R., 'Archives: Performance Remains', *Performance Research*, Vol. 6, No. 2 (2001), pp. 100–8
Shepherd-Barr, K., *Science on Stage: From Doctor Faustus to Copenhagen* (Princeton, NJ: Princeton University Press, 2006)
Simpson, M., *Male Impersonators: Men Performing Masculinity* (New York: Routledge, 1994)
Sinfield, A., '*Macbeth*: History, Ideology, and Intellectuals', in A. Sinfield, *Faultlines: Cultural Materialism and the Politics of Dissident Reading* (Oxford: Clarendon Press, 1992), pp. 95–108
Sked, A., and C. Cook, *Post-war Britain: A Political History*, 2nd edn (London: Penguin, 1984)
Sontag, S., *Regarding the Pain of Others* (New York: Picador, 2003)
Spencer, C., and M. Blades (eds.), *Children and Their Environments: Learning, Using and Designing Spaces* (Cambridge: Cambridge University Press, 2006)
Spinetti, V., *up front . . .* (London: Portico, 2006)
Stead, P., *Film and the Working Class: The Feature Film in British and American Society* (London: Routledge, 1989)

Steedman, C., *Dust* (Manchester: Manchester University Press, 2001)

Storey, J., *An Introduction to Cultural Theory and Popular Culture* (Hemel Hempstead: Harvester Wheatsheaf, 1993)

Suleiman, S. R. (ed.), *Exile and Creativity: Signposts, Travellers, Outsiders, Backward Glances* (Durham, NC: Duke University Press, 1998)

Sutton, S. E., and S. P. Kemp, 'Young People's Participation in Constructing a Socially Just Public Sphere', in C. Spencer and M. Blades (eds.), *Children and Their Environments: Learning, Using and Designing Spaces* (Cambridge: Cambridge University Press: 2006), pp. 256–76

Taubman, H., 'The Theater: Joan Littlewood's "*Lovely War*"', *New York Times*, 1 October 1964, p. 30

Taylor, G., *Reinventing Shakespeare: A Cultural History from the Restoration to the Present* (London: Hogarth, 1990)

Taylor, R., and N. Young (eds.), *Campaigns for Peace: British Peace Movements in the Twentieth Century* (Manchester: Manchester University Press, 1987)

Taylor, W., 'The St. Pancras Festival', in E. Hillman (ed.), *Essays in Local Government Enterprise* (London: Merlin Press, 1964), pp. 37–42

Thompson, J., *Applied Theatre: Bewilderment and Beyond* (Oxford: Peter Lang, 2003)

Tillinghast, P. E., 'Leisure: Old Patterns and New Problems', in S. Anderson (ed.), *Planning for Diversity and Choice: Possible Futures and Their Relations to the Man-Controlled Environment* (Cambridge, MA: The MIT Press, 1968), pp. 143–54

Toffler, A., *Future Shock* (London: Bodley Head, 1970)

Topham, S., *Blow-up: Inflatable Art, Architecture and Design* (London: Prestel, 2002)

Topham, S., *Where's My Space Age? The Rise and Fall of Futuristic Design* (London: Prestel, 2003)

Turner, V., *From Ritual to Theatre: The Human Seriousness of Play* (New York: PAJ Publications, 1982)

Tynan, K., *Curtains: Selections from the Drama Criticism and Related Writing* (London: Longmans, 1961)

Tynan, K., *Profiles* (London: Nick Hern Books, 1989)

Tynan, K., *Tynan on Theatre* (London: Pelican, 1964)

Tynan, K., *Tynan Right and Left: Plays, Films, People, Places and Events* (London: Longmans, 1967)

Vaught, C., and D. L. Smith, 'Incorporation and Mechanical Solidarity in the Underground Coal Mine', in D. Harper and H. M. Lawson (eds.), *The Cultural Study of Work* (Oxford: Rowman and Littlefield, 2003), pp. 96–115

Weeks, J., *Coming Out: Homosexual Politics in Britain from the Nineteenth Century to the Present* (London: Quartet Books, 1977)

Weller, S., *Teenagers' Citizenship: Experiences and Education* (London: Routledge, 2007)

Wesker, A., *Fears of Fragmentation* (London: Jonathan Cape, 1970)

Wesker, A., 'Let Battle Commence!', in C. Marowitz, T. Milne and O. Hale (eds.), *The Encore Reader: A Chronicle of the New Drama* (London: Methuen, 1965), pp. 96–103

Witham, B. B., *The Federal Theatre Project: A Case Study* (Cambridge: Cambridge University Press, 2003)

Worthen, W. B., *Shakespeare and the Authority of Performance* (London: Routledge, 1997)

Young, M., and P. Willmott, *Family and Kinship in East London*, revised edn (Harmondsworth: Penguin, 1962)

Zarhy-Levo, Y., 'Joan Littlewood and Her Peculiar (Hi)Story as Others Tell It', *Theatre Survey*, Vol. 42, No. 2 (November 2001), pp. 165–76

Zinn, H., et al., *The Power of Non-violence: Writings by Advocates of Peace* (Boston: Beacon Press, 2002)

Index

Printed in Great Britain
by Amazon

57106504R00190